Diaspora Conversions

Diaspora Conversions

Black Carib Religion and the Recovery of Africa

Paul Christopher Johnson

UNIVERSITY OF CALIFORNIA PRESS

Berkeley / Los Angeles / London

University of California Press, one of the most distinguished university presses in the United States, enriches lives around the world by advancing scholarship in the humanities, social sciences, and natural sciences. Its activities are supported by the UC Press Foundation and by philanthropic contributions from individuals and institutions. For more information, visit www.ucpress.edu.

Parts of chapters 1 and 2 were previously published in different form as "On Leaving and Joining Africanness through Religion: The 'Black Caribs' across Multiple Diasporic Horizons," *Journal of Religion in Africa*, 2007. Chapter 4 was previously published in different form as "Joining the African Diaspora: Dynamics of Migration and Urban Religion" in R. Marie Griffith and Barbara Dianne Savage, eds., *Women and Religion in the African Diaspora: Knowledge, Power, and Performance.* © 2006 R. Marie Griffith and Barbara Dianne Savage. Reprinted with permission of The Johns Hopkins University Press.

University of California Press
Berkeley and Los Angeles, California

University of California Press, Ltd.
London, England

Library of Congress Cataloging-in-Publication Data

Johnson, Paul C. (Paul Christopher).
    Diaspora conversions : Black Carib religion and the recovery of Africa / Paul Christopher Johnson.
        p.   cm.
    Includes bibliographical references and index.
    ISBN 978-0-520-24969-1 (cloth : alk. paper)
    ISBN 978-0-520-24970-7 (pbk. : alk. paper)
    1. Garifuna (Caribbean people)—Honduras—Religion.   2. Garifuna (Caribbean people)—Honduras—Ethnic identity.   3. Garifuna (Caribbean people)—Honduras—Migrations.   4. Garifuna (Caribbean people)— New York (State)—New York Metropolitan Area—Religion.   5. Garifuna (Caribbean people)—New York (State)—New York Metropolitan Area— Ethnic identity.   I. Title.
F1505.2.C3J64   2007
299.7'892—dc22   2006032564

Manufactured in the United States of America

16 15 14 13 12 11 10 09 08 07
10 9 8 7 6 5 4 3 2 1

This book is printed on New Leaf EcoBook 50, a 100% recycled fiber of which 50% is de-inked post-consumer waste, processed chlorine-free. EcoBook 50 is acid-free and meets the minimum requirements of ANSI/ASTM D5634-01 *(Permanence of Paper).* ∞

For Anna Marie Andersson Almer (1905–2005)
and Anaïs Zubrzycki-Johnson (2006–).
Two beautiful lives; one already lived, the other just begun.

Contents

List of Illustrations ix

Acknowledgments xi

Introduction 1

1. What Is Diasporic Religion? 30

2. "These Sons of Freedom": Black Caribs across Three
Diasporic Horizons 60

3. Shamans at Work in the Villages 99

4. Shamans at Work in New York 125

5. Ritual in the Homeland; Or, Making the Land "Home"
in Ritual 146

6. Ritual in the Bronx 186

7. Finding Africa in New York 205

Conclusion 227

Appendix. Trajectory of a Moving Object, the Caldero 247

Notes 251

Glossary   287

Bibliography   291

Index   319

Illustrations

1. Area of Garifuna settlements and location of St. Vincent   4
2. Garifuna fishing village of Miami, Honduras   5
3. Watching the 1998 World Cup, San Juan village, Honduras   21
4. *A Family of Charaibes Drawn from the Life in the Island of St. Vincent*   61
5. *Chatoyer the Chief of the Black Charaibes in St. Vincent with His Five Wives*   68
6. New home built with funds from the United States   91
7. Crowd assembled for dügü ritual   97
8. Carlitos Amaya, buyei in villages of Corozal and Sambo Creek   109
9. Part of shaman's altar, Honduras   113
10. Central altar assembled in dügü temple before ritual   114
11. Buyei Tola Guerreiro consulting spirits on behalf of client, the Bronx   127
12. Palo Monte–style caldero on Garifuna shaman's altar, the Bronx   130
13. Objects dedicated to Yoruba and Afro-Cuban deities on New York Garifuna shaman's altar   138
14. Doll and baked apple set in honey: intervention to "sweeten" the heart of a client's runaway daughter   138
15. Construction of a temple building (dabuyaba)   151
16. Fishermen-ancestors arriving at dawn   162
17. Fisherman-ancestor in Carib-style palm-frond helmet   162

18. Wanaragua dancer performing at dügü   163
19. Singing women's songs in the temple   169
20. Ancestor arriving and possessing the body of her
    descendant   172
21. Group in the water at dügü, Trujillo   176
22. New York buyeis assembling altar for return
    of the ancestors ceremony   189
23. Buyeis' dance, return of the ancestors, Vamos a la Peña,
    the Bronx   190

Acknowledgments

To those who read parts or all of the manuscript, my heartfelt thanks: Elizabeth McAlister, Manuel Vasquéz, Matthew Hull, Erika Büky, and Geneviève Zubrzycki.

Important financial support for different stages of the project was provided by the National Endowment for the Humanities (2001, 2003), the Center for the Study of Religion at Princeton University (2004), the American Academy of Religion (2000), and the University of Missouri–Columbia (1998, 1999, 2001).

I am grateful for the friendship and direction of many Garifuna friends in Honduras and New York. Particularly supportive in Honduras were Herman and Mayha Amaya, Carlos Castillo, Marcelina Fernandez, the late Don Cornelio of Corozal, Carlitos Amaya, Nayo "Mala Polia," Salomon Anacleto Lino, Herman Alvarez, and Nicasio and Sandia Rivas. In New York, Bartolome Guerreiro was and remains a constant friend, adviser, and teacher. Thanks also to Francisco Yoba Ruiz, Felix Igemeri Miranda, Jorge Coqui Ruiz, Luz Soliz, Marleni Martinez, Mimi and Pa, Yolanda Guillen, Maria Elena Maximo, and Abraham Zumiga.

Geneviève Zubrzycki has been my beloved companion throughout. Finally, thank goodness for little Anaïs, who speaks wonders without words: *Ma plus belle tortue,* you always point the way.

Introduction

Toute séparation est un lien. [Every separation is a link.]
Simone Weil, *La pesanteur et la grâce*

The production of space, having attained the conceptual and
linguistic level, acts retroactively upon the past, disclosing
aspects and moments of it hitherto uncomprehended.
Henri Lefebvre, *The Production of Space*

Proust's masterpiece, *À la recherche du temps perdu* (*The Remembrance
of Things Past*), begins with the rush of memory erupting from a particular place and time. The narrator has returned to his old home. He
feels cold; his mother serves him tea and a small cake, a madeleine. As
he dips the cake into the tea and tastes it, his mind is flooded by places
and people of the past. They return from across a chasm, "like souls,"
crossing a great space (1: 49–50). The place of recollecting—his
mother's house—and the sensations of that place transport the narrator
to Sunday mornings of his childhood in Combray. In a sense all of the
colossal retrospection that follows is funneled through, and mediated
by, that one bite. Yet the arbitrariness of that moment and place that
were the prism of remembrance haunts the story. Suppose his remembering had begun not with a visit to the old house, but in a café, dunking a scone into coffee rather than a madeleine into tea; or near a wharf
with a whiff of fish. Suppose other places and objects had appeared, or
had been chosen, as the brokers of reminiscence. Might they have
opened different avenues of memory and forgetting? Might they have

I

called other souls, with different itineraries, to mind? I think so, and in the chapters that follow I will try to say why. Different positions and materials, or even the "same" objects positioned differently, evoke varying constellations of the past.

For the madeleine I substitute cassava bread; for tea, a strong *aguardiente;* and for Combray, a village in Honduras by the Caribbean Sea, recalled by ritual performers in the Bronx, New York.

. . .

This book is about "diasporic religion" (Tweed 1997). Diasporic religion is composed on the one hand of memories about space—about places of origins, about the distances traveled from them, and physical or ritual returns imagined, already undertaken, or aspired to. And on the other hand it is about how those memories arise *in* space, out of a given repertoire of the available and the thinkable. Memories are summoned from a position, a place of emigration, a destination. Diasporic religious agents recollect the past through particular territorial and temporal "ways of seeing" (J. Berger 1972: 8) and from particular places. Choices about ways of seeing are made and reproduced in ritual performances, which are assembled from the new site's materials and modes, its niches and needs, its plausible guiding ideas. In the ritual juxtapositions of objects and persons in space, horizons of memory are recalled to conscious reflection. In ritual performance, diasporic religious actors "make history" as they project present events, and their present selves, against the horizon of another territory and time, a horizon that is itself also in motion (Gadamer 1975: 271).

By becoming "diasporic," that is, by joining a diaspora through religion, emigrants do not just seek a past that waits to be discovered. "Seek? More than that: create" (Proust: 1: 49).

Joining a Diaspora

In this book, I try to push beyond the study of how diasporas conserve religious traditions in new spaces, and even beyond the study of how traditions are transformed in the process of their recreation. I make two analytical turns that are important to note. The first is to view diasporas as not simply determined by biological descent or by historical fiat, but rather as a possible subject position an individual moves in and out of, or a way of seeing adopted to varying degrees. This view doesn't deny the ways in which the range of available subject positions is constrained by the politics of recognition—most notoriously by race—but it does reframe the issue less as one of nature than one of culture—sentiments of affinity, gestural repertoires of ritual, discourses about identity, and choices made by individuals—all of which play roles in the privileging of some social affiliations among manifold possible ones.

Second, by joining a diaspora and becoming diasporic, a given religious group begins to view itself against new historical and territorial horizons that change the configuration and meaning of its religious, ethnic, and even racial identifications in the present. Take the example of the Garifuna, historically known as the "Black Caribs," whose religious practices I explore. The Garifuna are descendants of both Africans and "Island Carib" Amerindians who shared the island of St. Vincent in the eastern Antilles of the Caribbean beginning in the 1600s. *Garifuna* is actually the name of their language, which is affiliated with the Arawak linguistic family; the ethnonym proper is *Garinagu,* though *Garifuna* is more commonly used. According to at least one version, the earlier name, Black Caribs, was forwarded by the group itself, in negotiations with Europeans during the eighteenth century (Young 1971 [1795]: 8). Whatever its precise origin, Europeans readily adopted the descriptor *Black Caribs* to distinguish this troublesome, independent group from allegedly placid "Red" or "Yellow" Caribs who, already dying from European diseases, by the 1700s presented little sovereign threat.[1] *Garifuna* and *Black Carib,* then, refer to one and the same group. I use *Black Carib* to refer to the group's historical constitution and itinerary, and *Garifuna* to refer to representations drawn from the present.

Africans arrived on St. Vincent through Island Carib raids on Puerto Rico, as West and West-Central African survivors of slaver shipwrecks near the island of St. Vincent itself, and as maroons fleeing neighboring Barbados and elsewhere. Some of these Africans adopted the Indians' religion and language, and by the late 1600s they fought alongside the Island Caribs to defend the island against Europeans. By 1674, according to accounts from the Jesuit missions, they numbered as many as the Island Caribs on St. Vincent, and by 1700 they had already founded settlements separated from the Island Caribs. Soon after, these new, darker-skinned "Caribs" constituted the sovereign power of the island, though that power was increasingly challenged by

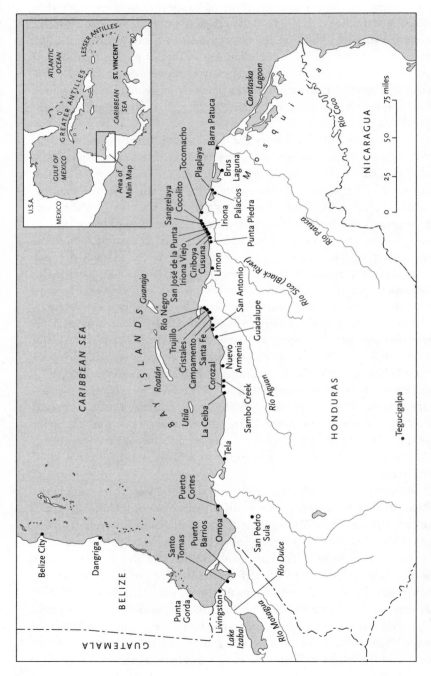

FIGURE 1. Area of Garifuna settlements. The inset shows the location of St. Vincent, the site of Garifuna ethnogenesis.
Source: Adapted from Gonzalez 1988.

FIGURE 2. The Garifuna fishing village of Miami, in Honduras.
Photo by author.

French and especially British colonists. It is appropriate to call them *Caribs* not only because they used that title themselves but also because, despite tensions between the groups, the Africans had intermarried with Island Caribs and had adopted the Amerindians' language and culture.

Long left alone by European powers as a Carib refuge, after 1783 St. Vincent became a permanent British colony and was slotted for the increasingly lucrative production of sugar. Sugar cultivation, however, required the expropriation of lands. Following a period of heroic military resistance by the Black Caribs in the Second Carib War (1795–96), beginning in February 1797 a British naval convoy deported them to Roatán, an island just off the coast of the Spanish town of Trujillo in what is now Honduras. Almost half of those deported died during a long internment en route, yet the survivors began to settle the Spanish Honduran coast by 1800. They spread along the Caribbean coast to found nearly sixty villages along the sea. This shore became the new homeland, the site of their reconstitution as a distinct ethnic group with its own specific set of religious practices.

As I describe in chapter 2, the Black Caribs quickly made themselves indispensable to the Spanish and British colonial economies in Central America. Later, beginning at the close of the nineteenth century, they provided much of the labor to the United States–dominated transnational fruit industry. With the regional decline of that production after the mid-twentieth century, the Black Caribs began to seek their fortunes in the North, a process dramatically accelerated in 1965 with the loosening of United States immigration quotas. Since 1965, about a third of the population of three hundred thousand has migrated abroad, especially to New York City (England 2006: 13). New York–based Garifuna are becoming attentive to the African components of their story of origin to a degree that has not occurred in homeland villages of Honduras. As they reframe ritual events within the physical environment and social networks of the city, the New York Garifuna are consciously joining the religious African Diaspora. This cultural transformation entails both agency and its constraints. Alongside the voluntary ethnogenetic and religious move of joining the African Diaspora lies the involuntary racial conversion of becoming "black," in part by being read into that category in the United States.[2] These two conversions suggest how the move to New York calibrates new subjectivities with new subjectifications (Ong 1999: 18), novel opportunities for social affiliation with sources of oppression that limit social mobility. Those subjectivities and subjectifications collude, however, in raising African historical horizons to prominence, as African Diasporic and black identifications, while far from the same, in practice often overlap and reinforce one another.

Migration's subordinations are not only losses, then; they are injustices that are also the conditions of new self-knowledge (Balibar and Wallerstein 1991: 4; J. Butler 1997: 2, 14–17). Just so, emigrants' religious practice is not merely stunted by being dislocated from its homeland or indigenous sites of performance, but also transformed and invigorated. Emigrants critically reevaluate, and revalue, the question of origins. Selectively remembering the past and the left-behind territory as an ideological problem ("having attained the conceptual and linguistic level," as Lefebvre puts it), opens new opportunities for social and political alliances as well as for cultural defense. The new religious identifications and affiliations fashioned by those "in diaspora," moreover, result in distinct homeland versus diasporic redactions of "the tradition." The two modes of religious performance, the "indigenous" and the "cosmopolitan," exert a mutual influence. In fact, the two are mutual stimulants and irritants, each pressing the other toward more strident assertions of power—the indigenous and territorial versus the diasporic and cosmopolitan—to justify their claims to religious authority. Ultimately, the two modes constitute a single diasporic religious system. The first mode is composed of tropes of depth, density, and authenticity (an "indigenous" articulation); the second is based in extensions toward new kinds of agency and affiliation (a "cosmopolitan" articulation). The two articulations signify in relation to, and over against, one another (Miller 2005: 27; Matory 2005: 109).

MULTIPLE DIASPORIC HORIZONS

Diasporic religions comprise members who share sacralized spatial horizons, against which the group projects its ritual acts to evaluate their "fit." *Diasporic horizon* is an apt phrase because it connotes both a spatial edge of longing and a temporal edge of, on the one hand, nostalgia, and, on the other, futurity and desire (Axel 2004: 27, 40). In the first sense, that of a spatial edge, remembered places are sacralized as the source of deep and abiding identity, and religious power is directly measured according to the perceived fidelity of actions done *here* to actions done *there*—in the direction endowed with "mythical feeling value" (Cassirer 1955: 85), an organic fusion of history, territory and emotional attachment conjoined and given tangible form in beliefs and practices surrounding the needs and desires of living ancestors. For the Black Caribs in Central America, the standard of authentic religious practice is that of the former homeland in St. Vincent. It is from St. Vincent that the ancestors return to take part in Honduran ritual events.

Many Garifuna who emigrated to New York, by contrast, have come to consciousness of themselves as African, to a greater degree than those in Honduras, and for them the former horizon of authenticity and roots now lies in the shadow of an additional diasporic horizon, that of Africa (cf. Zane 1999: 165). The importance of the ultimate authenticity of the diasporic horizon does not foreclose creative change, however, as it is the *representations* of that home place—whether Honduras, St. Vincent, or Africa—that are significant. Moreover, the Garifuna's three different diasporic horizons serve different roles and to some degree are in tension with one another as anchors of different identifications, creating dynamism that precludes stagnation or closure. The Central American diasporic horizon links them with Honduran Amerindians on specific occasions and for certain purposes, especially concerning contested land rights (England 1999, 2006).[3] And the St. Vincent horizon aids the Garifuna in processing their historical resistance to British colonialism, as well as in prosecuting current restitution claims against Great Britain for their forced deportation from St. Vincent in 1797 (recounted in chapter 2). Another key theoretical intervention of this book, then, is to consider how a single group can simultaneously view itself against multiple diasporic horizons, and how, within that multiplicity, a particular horizon may become dominant at a given moment in time. The Black Caribs were historically constituted by the tension between Amerindian and African identifications. Indeed, nearly all of the older informants with whom I was engaged in Honduras acknowledged that they possessed "dark" *(moreno)* skin compared to Honduran mestizos but asserted that their history, religion, and culture, like their language, were "Carib" and therefore "Indian." It is only in the past three decades that the idea of African origins has begun to eclipse the Carib, Amerindian horizon of origins and become central in Garifuna representations. This shift of diasporic horizon is to a large degree a function of cyclical migrations to, and returns from, the United States, as well as of the global transmission of the "African Diaspora" as a salient identification.

As a temporal edge, diasporic horizons point not only to the original past space, but also to a future in which a group imagines its possibilities: they are *transtemporal,* to take Thomas Tweed's term (1997: 95). Jacques Derrida writes, "As its Greek name suggests, a horizon is both the opening and the limit that defines either an infinite progress or a waiting and awaiting" (2002: 255; cf. Gadamer 1975: 269–74; Laclau 1990: 64; Keane 2003: 419). The notion of the diasporic horizon suggests not only the conservative element of continuities with a place of origin, but also a critical character, as "elements hitherto accepted as certain, as objective, are continuously rejected when it turns out that they do not fully accord with the unity of experience, or at least that, measured by this unity, they possess only a relative and limited and not an absolute significance" (Cassirer 1955: 31). For example, the Garifuna in the Bronx face a very different "unity of experience," including the reality of U.S. race structures and categories into which being Garifuna disappears: emigrants are read by many North Americans as simply "black." This reality points the weathercock of the "mythic feeling value" toward a new horizon, more fitting for the new terrain of the United States: the horizon of the African Diaspora. Emigrants enter a political context where race is the master key, a "metalanguage" that subsumes other sets of social relations into its referential domain of analogic relationships (Higginbotham 1992: 255). In such a context, Howard Winant notes, "The rise of diasporic models of blackness, the creation of pan-ethnic communities of Latinos and Asians, all seem to be hybridizing and racializing previously national politics, cultures and identities" (1994: 273).

DIASPROLIFERATION

Of course, *diaspora* is not the only term used by social scientists to gain traction in the study of culture unhinged from territory. Analytical puzzles created by the global transit of bodies, signs, money, pollution, rights, terror, and religion, to name only a few, have caused much ink to be spilled. We have been subjected to a massive *trans* lexicon, with *trans-* confusingly applied to connotations of both *across* and *beyond,* often without distinction: *transnational, transmigrants, transracial, transcoding, transculturation,* and more (Verdery 1994). Alongside these, the term *diaspora* is both older and au courant. Still, in what ways is it worthy of the prolonged attention I give it in this book?

Its distinction from the trans lexicon is nowhere absolute but rather one of degree. In tendency, perhaps, *diaspora* differs from the trans lexicon in that it points to sentiments of attachment, perhaps even a certain idealization of a homeland and its occupants as the foundational place and people "of origin."[4] This ability to summon strong feelings of attachment to an original foundational place is what yokes *diaspora* to use by religious actors themselves, as a widely used emic term. To announce a *diaspora* is not simply to express authentic origins but to actually press them into existence. Evoking distant origins by locating oneself "in diaspora" is itself a kind of founding act. Yet the act requires no actual physical encounter with the foundational site. The vocabulary of the trans lexicon, by contrast, is often used to connote institutional and infrastructural links between spaces, usually across nation-state boundaries, but is less often used by cultural actors themselves to make claims about territory and authentic pasts. Rare is the person who presents herself as being "transnational." To be "in diaspora," on the other hand, is an everyday colloquial identifier, a discursive marker of a person's conscious extension toward a given place or its imaginal representation. For example, by 1990 *dyaspora* had entered the everyday Creole parlance of Haitians to refer to those living abroad but retaining links with the homeland. The term is sometimes even applied to individuals, as in "She's a *dyas*" (Richman 2005: 28–29).

Diaspora is solidly lodged in the everyday discourse of religious actors, as the feeling of continuity and connections to one's origins are both highly prized within groups and persuasive to audiences outside them. Being diasporic is distinctive, then, not only in its strong emotional valence toward consciousness of place, which may be an imaginatively reconstituted one, but by presenting dual tracks of practical and analytical evaluation. That is, as a global culture of diaspora has emerged, it has been adopted by different diasporic cultures for their own purposes, even as the circulation and adoption of such terms has changed the very ways group identities are made and maintained.

Based on this confluence of practical and analytical uses and its uncanny ability to simultaneously connote ruptures and roots, *diaspora* has become, for better or worse, a key term and a lexical watershed. For the better, because the term's vogue catalyzes new questions about space and place,[5] memory, migration, culture, and so on. *Diaspora* calls attention to recollected golden ages and places, to territorial identifications perceived as having once been deeper and more vital than they are here and now. It links the social scientific study of migration to an engagement with memory and with the mythic. For the worse, because, as a term of both social practice and of social analysis, it remains slippery. As Rogers Brubaker recently observed (2005), we have seen in the last decades a veritable "diaspora of 'diaspora,'" an expansion of the term to refer to anyone who wants to claim it.[6] Yet, at the very least, analytical attempts to define diasporas refer to three issues: a group's dislocation, the incomplete assimilation of that group in a host society such that it retains a sense of its own separateness, and the ongoing relations of the group with a place and people left behind. Though the teguments of those relations vary widely, they may range from minimal ones such as sentiments or tastes to maximal ones that also include remittances of money and goods, or even frequent physical returns.

Despite this modest concord on analytical meaning, the term's implications for the study and practice of religion have barely been addressed (with rare significant interventions: see Williams 1988; Tweed 1997; Warner and Wittner 1998; Vertovec 2000). This book seeks to remedy the situation by providing both a theoretically rigorous treatment of diasporic religion and a study of its practical application in a history and ethnography of a unique and barely studied Caribbean religion, that of the Garifuna.

Horizons of Memory

It is all too easy to conceive of diasporic religions as products of deficiency, as invalid religions deformed by goiters and foreign growths. Benefiting neither from the cachet of long-term territorial stability and the sage spatial orientations of indigenous religions—however beleaguered they may be—nor from the streamlined packaging of mission religions that seem to make themselves at home wherever they travel, diasporic religions are caught betwixt and between. Unable either to fully assimilate to the hostland or to simply remain in the homeland, diasporic religions may appear everywhere oppressed and always in a state of malaise. That notion is often confirmed by diasporic religious agents, as the idealization of elsewhere is constitutive of the very character of being "in diaspora." Still, the view recapitulates the old fetishism of purity and bounded cultural units in the study of religion. New insights can be gained by viewing diasporic religions as products of superabundance rather than of deficiency. In fact, by giving attention to religions like that of the Garifuna and other African Diaspora religions that are overtly and proudly syncretic in their practice, drawing on the resources of multiple diasporic horizons, we can begin to see mélange as a condition of religious memory-making in general, rather than as deviant or derivative. And we will see that mélange is a continuing process rather than a characteristic of "primitive religions" later stabilized in "higher" religions, yet another specious teleology of religious evolution. Fixity is always in flux, always being negotiated. *Pace* Kant, even religious "rigorists" are inevitably also "latitudinarians of coalition, whom we may call *syncretists*" (Kant 1960: 18; emphasis in original).

DIASPORAS AS SPATIAL MEMORIES, SPACES OF MEMORY, AND REMEMBERED SPACES

Space and memory are the twin anchors of any discussion of diasporas, as diasporic sentiments of affinity for a distant place require spatial memories and their intentional evocation—the recognition of a present absence of a place that must be recalled, if not in physical then in symbolic forms. Diasporic religions are in this sense memory performances. The idea of performing memory by giving it material form in space means that diasporic memory performances are themselves "positional" (Ricoeur 2004: 48), in at least three senses: memories are carried by emigrants through space, they are reinscribed in space (at least if they are to be maintained over time), and they are about space. The first two of these senses are fairly obvious, and their relevance to the Garifuna is apparent in the descriptive chapters that follow. The third is less self-evident, yet it is constitutive of my own understanding of diasporic religions. The memory performances giving ritual form to horizons of the past are not only transported from a homeland to a new world but are also *about* the processes of exile, transport, and transmission. The most obvious example of this phenomenon is Judaism, which is not merely a religion that people carried with them into exile; it is a religion constituted by that exile. By contrast, though classical "mission religions" like Christianity, Buddhism, or Islam include sacred foundational sites toward which pilgrimages and even daily prayers are directed, the commemoration of those sites and the memory of the separation from them typically are not constitutive parts of ritual performance.[7] For contemporary Garifuna, ritual performances are diasporic not simply because they were indigenous and then were carried to New York, but also because the ritual content is *about* those crossings. As ancestral spirits travel to possess the bodies of ritual performers, the spirits repeat the epic migratory journeys undertaken by Garifuna ancestors themselves. To interpret the movements of ancestor spirits represented in ritual, we need to understand the actual historical emigrations of the Black Caribs. These are presented in chapter 2.

To be sure, the furnishings of a remembered space and past may be fantastically reconstructed, or even invented, both in the move to conscious recollection and in the additional move from individual to collective memory. Philosophers, social theorists, and ethnographers have pointed to the problem of the move from individual or spontaneous memories to the representations that stabilize, affix, and routinize them in forms of commemoration.[8] The representations of collective memory edit the past in ways that are sometimes intentional, often instrumental (Halbwachs 1992), and always transformative of the experience of the present. The editorial filtering performed by memory is not necessarily in the narrowly instrumental sense of the "past as used for present purposes," Halbwachs's idea usefully critiqued by Rosalind Shaw (2002: 12), but, more modestly, in how the memories of a distant site take shape in a material context that exerts "retroactive force" on the past, and in a context of specific ideas of future redemption (Benjamin 1968: 255, 254).

Listen to Proust on the beneficent retroactive possibilities of memory:

I had only the most rudimentary sense of existence. . . . I was more destitute than the cave-dweller; but then the memory—not yet of the place in which I was, but of various other places where I had lived and might now very possibly be—would come like a rope let down from heaven to draw me up out of the abyss of not-being, from which I could never have escaped by myself: in a flash I would traverse centuries of civilisation, and out of a blurred glimpse of oil-lamps, then of shirts with turned-down collars, would gradually piece together the original components of my ego. (1982, 1: 5–6)

Note the import of places in his description of remembering, and of the objects that secure it: the oil lamps and collars. Note the implication of redemptive force released by memories of the place of an earlier time. The passage is suggestive for thinking about how space and memory compose a dialectic. If diasporic religion constructs a ritual space out of memories of a homeland, that memory of the homeland is also shaped within the new space of the hostland and its constraints—by the mnemonic modes (Casey 1987), narrative schema (Bergson 1896), proxemic habits (Hall 1990), the relational judgments of distance (Cassirer 1955), and the sites, or spatial textures (Lefebvre 1991) and objects (Miller 2005), in relation to which remembrance takes place. Memory is always being reterritorialized, always "contaminated" by spatial categories (Bergson, quoted in Ricoeur 2004: 41). The rapture of memory that Proust describes occurs in a context that renders the memory salvific.

But for Black Caribs, that context was the constant threat of enslavement in a sugar-plantation economy that was devouring nearly every adjacent island. This plantation economy sought to instill its own homogeneous and brutal codes of behavior through its own mnemonic systems. Nietzsche described this sort of system in his *Genealogy of Morals:* "'something is burnt in so as to remain in his memory: only that which never stops hurting remains in his memory.' . . . When man thinks it necessary to make for himself a memory, he never accomplishes it without blood, tortures, and sacrifice; . . . the most cruel rituals of all the religious cults (for all religions are really at bottom systems of cruelty)— all these things originate from that instinct which found in pain its most potent mnemonic" (Nietzsche 2003 [1913]: 37). Whereas Proust describes memory as redemptive, Nietzsche construes it as cruel captivity and an imposed disciplinary regime. In his explanation a few pages later of how "negroes" do not feel pain to the degree that Europeans do (43), Nietzsche links their diminished physical sensitivity to the absence of memory, here echoing Hegel's denial to Africans of any consciousness of history whatsoever (Hegel 1956: 99). Whether memory is "a rope let down from heaven" or a pain "burnt in," diasporic memories are formed, erected, and galvanized as a reaction against a monstrous obliteration.

Yet there are less nightmarish forms of being possessed by memory. Gaston Bachelard describes in more neutral terms how childhood memory, and its spaces, structures all later memory, whether carved in consciousness or in bodily habits: "The house we were born in has engraved within us the hierarchy of the various functions of inhabiting. We are the diagram of the functions of inhabiting that particular house, and all the other houses are but variations on a fundamental theme. The word habit is too worn a word to express this passionate liaison of our bodies, which do not forget, with an unforgettable house" (1994: 15). Nor can it express the passionate liaison with an unforgettable *territory*. Spatial shifts like those caused by migration call up memory in response to a territorial crisis, and every new house or territory is "read" in some sense as a variation of the original oneiric place: the homeland now becomes the place of dreams. Yet the dream place begins to appear differently when it is remembered from different positions on an itinerary. In this sense Henri Lefebvre describes, in the passage I use as the epigraph for this introduction, how the production of space in the present acts retroactively on the past (1991: 65).

These considerations of memory and space return us to the thesis of this book: Diasporic religions are memory performances of place, staged in a space; rather than repeat "tradition," they create new identifications and social affiliations because the memory of the homeland is transformed as it is rebuilt, through bricolage, in the spaces of emigration.

FROM THEORY TO PRACTICE

By now it should be clear that diasporas do not simply exist naturally, nor simply as products of a historical juggernaut, even one as massive as the African slave trade. Consider the example of the Black Caribs in relation to the African Diaspora. At the end of the 1700s, they were despised by enslaved Africans who resided on St. Vincent, working the lands of British colonists. The Black Caribs, who themselves were never enslaved, were disparaged as "flatheads" for allegedly applying boards to children's foreheads to elongate them and thereby distinguish them from enslaved Africans, a practice adopted from Carib Indians (Young 1971 [1795]: 8; Anderson 1992: 229; Leblond 2000 [1813] 80, 110, 136). Several Black Caribs, including the leader Chatoyer's brother, Du Vallée, owned Africans themselves, employing them in the production of export crops like tobacco. In the Second Carib Wars leading to the Black Caribs' deportation in 1797, enslaved Africans and Black Caribs fought against each other rather than in alliance. Though we might imagine these rival groups as cells of a single diasporic organism, in some "biological" sense of originating from Africa, or even in the social sense of being collectively victims of the slave trade that landed them in the Americas, they did not conceive of or conduct themselves consistently as coactors faced with a common crisis. That is because there existed as yet no common framework of history, space, or destiny—in brief, no diasporic culture. This book attends to when, and how, such a culture arose and continues to develop.

Even with the establishment of a chronology of diaspora, it remains an open question how religious agents remake themselves by becoming diasporic as they engage the culture of diaspora. To take Stuart Hall's awkward neologism (1996b: 447), what shifts in consciousness does "diaspora-ization" entail? How does a "local" religion, like the ancestor religion of the Garifuna, change when it engages the broader nexus of a diaspora? How do diasporic productions of space—the narrowing of the gap between a lived place and a remembered place—act retroactively on the past to change the meaning of the present? And why does diaspora-ization guarantee so little consensus once the shared marker is adopted?

Moreover, what are the external conditions that call forth this particular kind of production—the making of the now and here using the tools of the then and there? The omnipresent contemporary discourses of "roots" might not have arisen at all without a set of conditions of inquiry: they were called forth by the modernity of the "antique" and its prestige (Tuan 1977: 193). The very interest in the concept of diaspora, in other words, must be seen as sating a contemporary hunger in relation to the "drive to discourse" (Foucault 1980) about roots in this particular historical moment. Cultural depth and specificity sell within a market of diversity, at least in cosmopolitan settings (Robertson 1995).

Finally, what are the specific cultural transmissions by which shifts in sentiment occur, such that we could begin to speak not only of theories about already existing diasporic cultures, but also of ethnographies of diaspora-ization as groups engage the culture of diaspora (Gordon and Anderson 1999; Palmié 2002)? To move closer to the case at hand, we need to examine how the African Diaspora signifies variously as it is joined by different ethnic groups, and how the pressures called forth by the attempt to discern sources of deep likeness produce not only new alliances but also social rifts and transformations in identity.

Introducing the Black Caribs, or Garifuna

The Black Caribs' story is a quintessentially Caribbean one, a story of enormous cultural exchange accomplished under conditions of constant threat. The Black Caribs emerged as a distinct society at roughly the same time as "the Caribbean" appeared in the European imagination, as a place and an idea; both were characterized as "mixed" and derivative, shallow in both history and memory. By giving attention to Black Carib religion, I aim to show why a region long shunted to the margins ought to take center stage in the comparative study of religion.

CENTER STAGE, CALIBAN!

Shortly after the figure of Caliban was born of Shakespeare's hand in *The Tempest*, the Black Caribs were being born as a new society on a small island in the eastern Antilles called St. Vincent. Caliban (a near anagram of *cannibal*), born to a North African witch on the island where he is found, is scorned by his master, Prospero, as a bastard and a "freckled whelp" (*The Tempest*, act 1, scene 2).[9] Pictures drawn of the Black Caribs were rendered in a similar palette. One British colonist wrote: "By the best accounts which I have been able to collect from the *Caribbs* themselves, the *Black Caribbs* originally sprung from the cargo of a *Guinea* ship which was wrecked on one of the *Grenadilloes*. They were brought over to this island by the *Yellow Caribbs*, who were the *Aborigines* or native inhabitants, with many whom they soon were connected, forming a motley mixture, such as we now see; but in which the negro-colour and features chiefly prevail" (G. Davidson 1787: 7; italics in original). Montaigne's "On Cannibals" of 1580, which influenced the creation of Shakespeare's Caliban (Parker 1999), celebrates the naïve purity of the Indians as a foil for European decay. Whereas Europe had the brutal Inquisition, these authentic people of nature had "perfect religion."

But the Island Caribs who, together with Africans en route to Caribbean enslavement, provided the two tributaries converging to form the Black Caribs, enjoyed little such descriptive benevolence. The Caribs often were accorded neither religion nor memory, with the two lacunae linked. The French Protestant Charles de Rochefort, for example, wrote of the Caribs in 1658: "They are not able to express what does not fall under the senses . . . they have no word to signifie [sic] spiritual things, as *understanding, memory, will*" (1992: 123; italics in original). The British historian Bryan Edwards described a similar lack of memory among enslaved Africans in the Caribbean, here presaging Nietzsche's characterization of the "negroe's" [sic] special tolerance for pain: They suffer less than European peasants since their pain is merely that of the passing present; whereas the European endures not only the perception of present suffering but also the remembrance of past suffering, and these two in turn "admonish him of the sufferings he has yet to undergo"

(Edwards 1799: 194). The layered deficiencies of racial impurity, religious impurity, and the lack of memory—three ciphers of inauthentic mixing and the absence of deep-rooted origins—cast Caliban as a predatory danger in *The Tempest*. The same alleged deficiencies kept the Caribbean and its peoples in general on the margins of the study of religion.[10]

But the Caribbean was no sleepy backwater. It was the very epicenter of modernity and religion's revaluation within it. In the Caribbean was orchestrated the first industrial manipulation of disposable human labor, of yoked hands forced to feed cane into endless presses and vats. From the product of this "repeating island" of plantations rushing to produce a lucrative and sweet, but also perishable, delight grew the first truly global economy (Benítez-Rojo 1996; Mintz 1985; Palmié 2002). In the plantation's shadow flourished a rich religious mélange. Because all religions are motley and mixed, impure, and resifted from multiple origins, because all religions offer possibilities of resisting aspects of modernity but also are made or remade within it rather than merely reacting to it (as though free-standing and ready-made somewhere outside history), the Caribbean and the Black Caribs are an auspicious place and people with whom to rethink general approaches to the study of religion. Just as the study of creole languages once played second fiddle to the study of so-called real languages but is now at the very center of attempts to understand language creation, so a focus on "creole religions" can invigorate the study of how religions form. Here, for example, is a society, and religion, that proudly and overtly syncretized African, European, and Amerindian influences, and that is correspondingly multisited, bursting the abstraction of "the closed horizon that is supposed to enclose a culture" (Gadamer 1975: 271). Here we encounter a saga of recurring territorial displacements and sacralizations, of exiles and the ways the places left behind were lit with the glow of the foundational and original, even in, and perhaps because of, their absence or distance. Here is a heroic tale that is unique and worth telling in its own right, yet which also inspires broad comparative reflection on religion, migration, diasporization, and memory.

In an eloquent formulation, Derrida described the modern "return of religion" as deeply cleft: on the one hand, religion is itself a form of globalization; on the other hand, it is a reaction of "declaring war against that which gives it this new power only at the cost of dislodging it from all its proper places, *in truth from place itself*, from the *taking place* of its truth" (Derrida 2002: 82, italics in original). When and how did this moment of religious modernity, this conflict of movements, this call and response between dislodging and the assertion of location begin? In one sense it began in the Caribbean, with the global trade in humans as machines and the heroic response of those people who indigenized and packed with meaning the very ground of their suffering.

GARIFUNA RELIGION:
A QUINTESSENTIAL CARIBBEAN STORY

The Garifuna can teach us about diasporic religion as the simultaneous negotiation of multiple horizons of memory. The Garifuna were first St. Vincentians and later people of the Central American coast. Many later became New Yorkers or Los Angelenos and then Africans by linking their ethnicity and religious practice to the meta-identity of the African Diaspora. Each new diasporic horizon appeared as another shore was left behind. Those horizons are recalled and reactivated in rituals that return the spirits of those places to the present through the bodies of priests possessed. As the spirits return from Honduras, St. Vincent, or Africa, the Garifuna carry with them memories that form a rich itinerary and repertoire of a multiply diasporic religion.

Yet their epic sojourns have been left on the margins not only in the literature on the Caribbean or religion but also in the literature on the African Diaspora (with scant exceptions, such as Gonzalez 1988 and Kerns 1997). They confound simplistic ethnic, racial, and religious classifications, having emerged as an ethnic group through a transculturative process (F. Ortiz 1995: 98) that marked them as anomalous and hybrid in colonists' and then scholars' gazes. Black Carib religion had incorporated West African traits, such as dances leading to possession by ancestor spirits, but it had also assimilated elements of Island Carib cosmology and ritual, such as the healing techniques of the shaman (buyei), who treated sickness by singing, blowing smoke over afflicted areas of the body, and removing disease-causing "penetrations" thrown by sorcerers or rivals.[11] The Black Caribs were also influenced by French Catholic missionaries, from whom they adopted rites of passage like baptism and techniques for invoking the benevolence of saints. The legacies of all these histories, and others, were conjoined into a distinct set of ritual practices. That distinct religious culture was maintained in a series of Central American villages that have remained relatively autonomous for more than two centuries. Most villages were spatially isolated enclaves near the beach, where residents could maintain an independent existence even while exploring labor opportunities in the

Spanish and British colonies. Men fished or took jobs in the colonial economy—soldiering for Spain or cutting mahogany for Britain—while women tended the home gardens and children and, over time, became the main transmitters of religious knowledge and practice. The Black Caribs were careful to guard and maintain their own land sites, language, and ritual traditions—most notably those associated with crises of death and the curing of illnesses inflicted by ancestors *(gubida)*—and this fidelity continued until recently.

MIGRATION TO THE UNITED STATES

In a second diaspora, beginning around the middle of the twentieth century, the Garifuna were drawn to U.S. shores through a combination of "push" and "pull" factors. They needed work to support their families: work in fruit companies was fast disappearing. And, during World War II, United States industries needed hands to replace those that were gripping rifles overseas. The first large migration, then, was in the 1940s, when Garifuna men flocked to the United States to fill jobs vacated by soldiers.

Subsequent migration can be broken into stages. The U.S. Labor Department actively recruited Caribbeans and Central Americans for manufacturing jobs and for sectors like the Merchant Marine (Miller-Matthei and Smith 1996: 137). A second wave began in the 1960s with the rise of a service-based economy and the increasing need for labor, coupled with the reform of U.S. immigration law under the 1965 Hart-Celler Act.[12] The act abolished overtly race-based prohibitions, opening the door to expanded Latin American and Afro-Caribbean influxes, including that of the Garifuna. The third stage coincided with the late 1980s and 1990s economic boom, again especially in the service economy. By this time, many Garifuna families already had migration "paths" in place: relatives already in the United States, roofs to sleep under at least temporarily, and potential job networks. These paths led especially to New York and Los Angeles, with New York especially drawing Honduran and Guatemalan Garifuna, and Los Angeles drawing those from Belize. What is more, a mythology had grown up around the idea of migration to the United States. The traditional model of a young man's adventuring to find a livelihood in lumberjacking or at sea, periodically returning home as a respected patron, now became a story of migration.

With so many outgoing migrants and incoming global signals, the villages faced difficult territorial and cultural transformations. All Honduran

Garifuna speak Spanish, and most also speak Garifuna. Yet many of those born after the arrival of electricity in many villages in the early 1980s, and the coming of television and radio, speak only Spanish. This is a cause for great concern, because language is the Garifuna's main distinguishing cultural mark. Moreover, since the 1980s, Protestant evangelicalism has gained a strong footing, initiating on one hand an increase in Garifuna language literacy—because of the value placed on being able to preach and read the Bible in their own vernacular—and on the other a vitriolic attack on traditional religious ceremonies. The burgeoning evangelical affiliations provide a specifically religious route of modernity. Through hi-tech sound systems, formal dress codes, and aggressive, charismatic preaching styles, the new churches emulate, and are often funded and seeded by, evangelical churches in the United States.

Even those who did not leave or convert to evangelical Protestantism began to dwell in a global imaginary of broadcasts from Miami, Mexico City, and Rio de Janeiro, because all households acquired televisions. Soap operas now provide the narrative frame for much of everyday chat among women in the villages, as televised soccer does for men. But the global imaginary also becomes flesh with the return visits of migrants from the United States, especially from the Bronx in New York. Loaded with goods like VCRs, NBA jerseys, and Nike shoes, those coming from the United States set standards of style and desirable livelihoods.

The counterweight to the status ascribed to those who have left for New York is the status now given by New Yorkers to those villages they left, which become a "homeland"—a symbol as well as a place—just as everyday homeland life becomes, when remembered from a distance, a "culture" or "tradition." As Garifuna society is remade by the juxtaposition of the partly real, partly imaginary entities of the "city" and the "village," and as these landscapes that are both lived in and imagined reflect one another, Garifuna religion takes a "second-diaspora" form. Second-diaspora religion balances and selects from ascriptions of special status and power to multiple possible homeland shores—in this case not only St. Vincent, the Garifuna's site of origins as a people, but also the left-behind villages of Honduras. But our story is even more complicated than that. This is because the consciousness of the Garifuna diaspora that is quickened in the Bronx—already a duplex form—takes shape alongside, and often as part of, joining the African Diaspora.

Migrants in U.S. cities are subjected to an unfamiliar racial system in which Garifuna identity is subsumed under the categories of "black" or "black Hispanic," and they return from the Bronx with a classifying

FIGURE 3. Watching the 1998 World Cup, San Juan village, Honduras.
Photo by author.

consciousness different from that of their relatives at home (Miller-Matthieu and Smith 1996; England 1999; Gordon and Anderson 2000). This difference is manifested both in the aesthetic realm, where hip-hop style, "African"-patterned clothing, and U.S.-produced "black" movies are valued in the village, and in discourses of self-representation. Ironically, such racial representations are the very terms that were strongly resisted until recently, and remain contested, because they confound Garifuna identity with that of other Afro-Caribbean communities. The territorial disjunctions of migration, the subjection to U.S. classifiers, and the symbolic appeal of black American culture come home to roost in the ethnic reclassification of Garifuna from "Carib" and Amerindian to more rigidly "black" and "African."

EFFECTS OF MIGRATION ON RELIGION

The phenomenon of frequent migration and returns, related to contemporary labor patterns, has had dramatic effects on the traditional religious practices of the Garifuna. One predictable effect is the assimilation and the abandonment of homeland rituals through either secularization or evangelical conversion. The second one, perhaps more

unexpected, is the revivalist growth of discourses and practices of traditional ritual events, whose meanings are transformed as the rituals are
revived. This book is focused especially on the latter effect. For the
Garifuna in New York, traditional ancestor rituals that were once considered indigenous and unique are increasingly understood as African
in origin. As emigrants to New York are exposed to the religions of
their neighbors, including Cuban Santería, Haitian Vodou, Trinidadian
Orisha, and Puerto Rican Santerismo, they have begun to view their
religion in relation to these others and to perceive themselves as members of the religious African Diaspora. The Honduran villages that were
once simply the landscape of everyday struggles are transformed into
sacred places of spiritual power and compacted identity, territories of
dense, ancestral Garifuna-ness, in comparison with U.S. cities and their
dynamics of diffusion, threatened dissipation, and revival. But that very
notion of ancestral Garifuna-ness is also being transformed by a new
diasporic way of seeing that locates it closer to Africa.

The two directions, one toward assimilation or Protestant conversion
and the other toward "African tradition," are not socially bifurcated but
rather work in tandem, though their signs signify against each other.
Both offer membership in global networks rather than local, village-
based ones. Even in the African revival paradigm, "tradition" is consciously forged through the culturally plural context of the big city and
relies on the most modern technologies of semiotic reproduction.
"Local" tradition is given global range—witnessed, recorded, publicized, and discursively defended and disseminated—to acquire exchange
value in a new identity market (Gilroy 1993: 193, 221; Palmié 2002;
Johnson 2002a). That is why the Garifuna have welcomed recent coverage from *National Geographic* and the *New York Times,* and recognition
from UNESCO and other international organs, in a mirroring process
of cultural performance and its recognition and reproduction, out of
which "tradition" is dialectically built. Thus the emerging forms of
Garifuna religion in New York are likely to be sedimented in relatively
permanent forms of rationalized memory, such as texts, photos, documented interviews, and videos. Because these are easily remitted to the
homeland, the cosmopolitan, African Diaspora form of Garifuna religion may soon become the dominant, "authentic" version.

Ethnography and Field Sites

The ethnography of the practice of diasporization required that my
own mobility match that of the Garifuna. Because my own horizons

and ways of seeing are contingent on the particular places and people that became my homes and my hosts, it is worth briefly describing the itinerary for my research.

I conducted fieldwork both in Honduras and in the Bronx, comparing shamans' work and ritual performances in each site as well as attending to the dynamics of exchange and circulation between the homeland and emigrant communities. By moving frequently between Honduran and Bronx sites over seven years of periodic fieldwork, I was able to document the effects of the religious changes in New York as they were remitted to the homeland, awakening conflicts between the homeland and cosmopolitan versions of Garifuna religious authority. I conducted extended fieldwork in two different villages in Honduras—Corozal and San Juan—and visited others, especially Triunfo de la Cruz and Trujillo, for specific ritual events. My focus was especially, though not solely, on three- to four-month periods of fieldwork during the summers from 1997 to 2003, though I also conducted fieldwork through the winter in 2000. Summer is the "ritual season" in Garifuna villages, as the presence of returning migrants is necessary both for full family assemblies and for the funding of rituals.

The advantages of fieldwork conducted over a fairly long duration included the ability to witness changes in the same villages over time and to compare different sites' ritual events. Over seven years of returns to the villages of Corozal and San Juan, for example, I saw communication networks between Honduras and New York evolve dramatically. When I began work in 1997, e-mail communications, through the nearby city of La Ceiba, were possible but almost never used. By 2000, Internet phone connections had been established, offering phone links at a fraction of normal international rates, and Corozaleños were constantly lining up at Internet providers in the city to phone their kin abroad. By 2002, many in the villages had acquired cell phones, a trend resulting in so-called cell-phone shamans who attached the devices to the sash that marks their office and could be interrupted for phone consultation even in the middle of ritual events. By the following year, land lines had been extended from La Ceiba to Corozal, and even those occupying "traditional" mud and wattle, grass-roofed *(manaca)* structures had not only televisions and VCRs but also telephones. The transformation of the word-of-mouth communications so essential to village life had begun.

Through television broadcasts from Miami, the increased circulation of U.S.-style "black" videos, and improved phone communications with New York, pan-Latino and African American cultural articulations of race, beauty, justice, political action, diaspora and "culture" itself began to be remitted not only by periodically returning migrants but also by mass communications.[13] My repeated visits made visible these transformations of the Garifuna communications network and the people's own responses to the transformations.

HONDURAS

I first arrived in Honduras in 1997 as a persistent tourist, spending time at the Garifuna museum and Garifuna restaurant in the coastal town of Tela and asking innumerable questions of the Garifuna who worked there. With their help, I began to visit nearby villages—San Juan, Tornabé, Triunfo de la Cruz, and Miami—and to interview religious leaders to whom they introduced me. I was informed of a *dügü,* the largest ritual event (see chapter 5), which was soon to be performed in the village of Corozal, a several-hour bus ride east of Tela. On arriving there, I quietly observed the construction of the dügü temple *(dabuyaba)* near the beach until, a few hours later, the young men working invited me to climb up on the roof and help in binding palm sheaves in place. Their offer, and my acceptance, transformed me from tourist into helper. Taking part in manual labor, I found, was the key to becoming a participant. My willingness to work demonstrated that I was not only curious about but also physically invested in the ritual. Once the ritual began, I arrived daily with goods that were important to the process: a few bottles of rum, or a sack of rice or beans. Over time, I developed friendships that facilitated future visits. Families took me in, legitimizing my local presence by making me someone "with people" in San Juan, Corozal, and Triunfo de la Cruz. I was fortunate to take part in three dügü performances in Honduras in 1998, 1999, and 2002, and I sat in on divination, planning, and preparatory sessions for many others.[14] Aside from these monumental ritual events, I took part in literally scores of smaller-scale rituals and daily attended the local shamans' consulting practices.

THE BRONX

Getting started in the Bronx, where I worked in one-month spurts from 2001 through 2004, was more arduous. Many Bronx Garifuna regarded me—with my habit of asking nosy questions and plenty of time to hang around—as an immigration or law-enforcement officer.

This small detail suggests how many of the Bronx Garifuna's main experiences with white people involve being policed, or the fear of it.

When one woman allowed me to tag along on her mission to sell coconut bread in the park, much as Honduran Garifuna women do when they go to town, I discovered niches in public space that the Garifuna had made their own: one at Tinton Park ("el Guatemalteco") and the other on the edge of Crotona Park (renamed the "Trujillano" by the Garifuna, after the Honduran town of Trujillo). Often I was interrogated as to my purposes and identity, and I explained that I was a professor interested in religion—as though that were a plausible or innocent occupation. Many interpreted this explanation as a euphemism for being an evangelical missionary. Eventually I was able to find common ground with Garifuna in the Bronx by going through the names of friends or acquaintances I had met in Honduras until my questioner recognized one. Many such former interrogators became great friends and took me on their rounds at work and into their homes.

On one warm fall evening in the park I was interviewed by a Garifuna man who called himself Shango, after the West African Yoruba deity of thunder. This choice was in itself intriguing, as it was my first cue as to the pervasiveness of the African Diaspora network the Garifuna had entered in the Bronx and the strong Yoruba influence within it. On discovering my interest in religion, Shango took me to meet his brother for an evening of drumming and songs. He in turn directed me to Bartolome ("Tola") Guerreiro, the religious leader of the World Garifuna Organization, and organizer of the network of Garifuna shamans working in the city. Her dual roles as civil and religious organizer suggested the importance of traditional religion in Garifuna culture more generally. Tola became a great friend and ally. By enthusiastically supporting this book (with the consent of her guiding spirits, *ahari*), she offered me an entrée into Garifuna religion as practiced in the Bronx diaspora, as well as to rituals in Honduras when the Bronx shamans led ritual events there. Felix Miranda, the vice president of the World Garifuna Organization and an initiated shaman in his own right, was equally supportive.

These leaders accepted me on the basis that the best prospects for protecting the Garifuna, gaining new rights, and pressing legal claims on issues like restitution from Great Britain for their 1797 deportation from St. Vincent lay in the production and public dissemination of knowledge of their history and contemporary lives. They reasoned that this book, in the context of the increasing output of their own books, documentaries, and music recordings, might aid the Garifuna in becoming publicly known as a culture, a tradition, and a religion—as an indigenous people, an African Diasporic people, or both—with corresponding rights and privileges (cf. Ramos 1998; England 1999; Povinelli 2002).

Both in Honduran villages and in the Bronx, my research relied on a combination of participant observation and informal interviews. Interviews were mostly conducted in Spanish, except with Garifuna of Belizean extraction or long residence in the United States, in which case English was used, and were typically tape-recorded and transcribed. In New York, structured interviews became more important, as the strictures of time and space demanded making specific appointments to meet rather than having the luxury of allowing prolonged conversations to emerge organically out of the day, as often occurred in Honduran villages. (This very transformation of social life in relation to space is, of course, precisely the issue this book addresses. Research methods were thus emblematic of, but also in a sense reproductive of, styles of interaction characteristic of life in the villages compared with those of the metropole.) Although the names of many of my interlocutors have been changed to protect their anonymity in my descriptions of tensions and social conflicts that sometimes emerged in ritual events or in discourses about such events, the real names of those who interacted with me in some "official" capacity, as representatives of specific organizations or as public cultural ambassadors, have been retained. I relied on the aid of native speakers to translate ritual song texts from Garifuna.

I hope that my effort does justice to the confidence that these leaders and their spirits entrusted to me. I have attempted to describe religious practice in terms most Garifuna themselves would recognize and approve of. Though this is a value judgment, as there is no consensus on what could constitute a complete or adequate theology, there exists at least a relative consensus on correct practice in large-scale ritual events. However, my work includes theoretical reflections that link the descriptions of ritual events to more general issues of religion and social theory. I take the ritual events seriously, as occasions for critical reflection, rather than only reproducing the discourses of religious actors themselves. Any refusal to accord Garifuna religious phenomena the same complexity of human motivations and conflicts accorded to all human action, or to present it in only cleaned-up, idealized visions, would constitute a condescending form of romantic primitivism.

To be sure, there exists a basic tension in the anthropological study of religion: scholars by and large treat religion as a human phenomenon, both an expression of and productive of human interests, needs, hopes, rules, and orientations in space. Religious actors, by contrast, view at least some of their actions as fulfillments of divine or ancestral mandates. There are no doubt clever resolutions of this basic epistemic impasse, but it seems best to resist attempting any. These modes can never be perfectly reconciled (cf. Chakrabarty 2000: 72–96), and the productive tension between them makes for interesting work. It would be naïve, of course, to think that description could ever stand free of analytical arguments. Because we selectively perceive the empirical world in accord with our own biases, or the theoretical foci that drive a given argument, we are always at risk of entanglement in a web of "synoptic illusions" that we ourselves conjure (Bourdieu 1977). But at least we can be clear about the theoretical issues that drive the parsing and arrangement of what we describe, and can hold the relative distinction of descriptive and analytical objectives as an ideal, marking each discursive arena, and the shifts from one to the other, in our rhetorical style (Proudfoot 1985).

Structure of the Book

The book follows a trajectory of theory (chapter 1), history (chapter 2), and ethnography (chapters 3 through 7), before returning to a theoretical frame (conclusion). Chapter 1 reviews theoretical approaches to the issue of diaspora and proposes a working definition of what I call diasporic religious culture. It makes an analytical point as well by showing the senses in which diasporas *make* religions. It also discusses the specificity of the African Diaspora, the issues faced by African diasporic religions in New York City generally, and the material processes of remembrance by which such religions are mapped into the cityscape. This discussion is important not only for describing processes of memory making and religious transmission but also because it is in this African diasporic religious context that arriving Garifuna migrants find niches for ritual performance.

Chapter 2 chronicles the ethnogenesis of the Black Caribs on St. Vincent and, after 1797, in Central America, focusing especially on their religion, insofar as it can be discerned from the records left by European observers. The chapter shows how Garifuna identity was forged, from its earliest days in the seventeenth century, out of defensive and reactive responses to the threats as well as the opportunities posed by European encroachment. I show how Garifuna "traditional" religion took shape as an itinerary of syncretizing events that produced multilayered diasporic horizons. Out of this itinerary, I present a snapshot, ideal-type description of homeland religious practice to which we can later compare diasporic religious practice.

Chapters 3 and 4 turn to the contemporary ethnography of Garifuna religion. Here I focus on the role of shamans as leaders who shape local understandings of Garifuna history through the ancestor spirits and spirit geographies they mediate in ritual. I compare the life stories, altars, and spirit geographies of shamans practicing in Honduran villages with those working in the Bronx to determine not only salient differences between homeland and diasporic shamanic practice, but also the tensions raised between competing versions of religious orthodoxy. I examine, first, the territorial, or indigenous, authority rooted in the sacrality of the homeland and a form of bodily knowledge embedded in ritual practice; and, second, the diasporic, cosmopolitan authority based on the comparative knowledge of analogous religions and the discursive savvy that articulates and sediments the religion's "meaning." While the former is devoted to the density of ancestral presence in specific locales, the latter emphasizes extension: it creates links to the broader social networks of larger and more established African Diaspora religions.

Chapters 5 and 6 present detailed descriptions of the largest ritual events in Honduras and in the Bronx, respectively: the dügü and the "return of the ancestors." I attend not only to the values of density and extension but also to the kinds of fissures and crises presented and resolved during rituals, which provide a way of assessing the distinctive types of social frames each ritual creates. In the homeland ritual, ethnic or racial identifications are unproblematic; ritual crises and resolutions are focused on intrafamilial tensions. In the diasporic ritual, the main problem addressed is the external boundary of the group in relation to the plural, public sphere. Intrafamilial crises are diminished, and ritual instead is devoted to the crises of maintaining Garifuna identity within the city.

Chapter 7 considers the specific version of African traditional religion that is dominant in the New York African Diaspora, namely Yoruba religion and its further redactions in Cuban Santería. Why did this particular religion become the face of African tradition that the Garifuna engage as they "return" to Africa? I consider the degree to which this ethnic conversion to Africanness also leads to shifts in racial identifications through which the Garifuna become "black."

The conclusion returns to an analytical comparison of homeland and diasporic religious practice in light of a key issue for diasporic religion, namely authenticity and the ways it is authorized. I return to the earlier themes of memory and religious transmission and take up the additional subject of the differing semiotics of religious transmission in homeland and diasporic ritual performance. Finally, I show how these disparate forms of authenticity and differing modes of transmission signify in relation to one another and mutually constitute one another as a single religious network.

CHAPTER I

What Is Diasporic Religion?

We can also say of every religion that it reproduces in more or
less symbolic forms the history of migrations and fusions of
race and tribes, of great events, wars, establishments,
discoveries, and reforms.

Maurice Halbwachs, *On Collective Memory*

We are not a diaspora, we are just trapped.

Emeline Michel, Haitian singer

This chapter lays out the parameters for the central theoretical issues of
the book, moving from the widest to the narrowest distinctions. I
examine, in turn, diaspora, diasporic religion, African Diaspora, and
African diasporic religions, the latter specifically in New York City. The
attempt to establish a solid theoretical footing for the starring phrase
among these, *diasporic religion,* may appear a fool's errand, since both
diaspora and *religion* are highly conflicted terms. How can we cheer-
fully head for the mountains with only these two frayed ropes in our
packs? I wager that the two ropes can be sufficiently rewoven, and
woven together, to hold the needed weight.

That Shared Something: Defining Diaspora Analytically

The notion of diaspora has been progressively widened over the last
century to include not only the dispersions of the Jewish, Greek, and
Armenian populations but also diasporas as disparate as those of

Calvinists (Weber 2002: 7), the Portuguese (Klimt and Lubkemann 2002), the Mormons (Smith and White 2004), and the New Orleans victims of Hurricane Katrina in 2005 (Gross 2006). The term has even been applied to the dispersion of individuals from a position of social valuation to one where little is accorded them, as in "the sexual diaspora of older women" (Merkin 2006: 18)—the experience of being sexually "in exile."[1] Suddenly, it appears, everyone is in diaspora. Well, why not? We all came from somewhere else and are at least dimly enough aware of it to be able to call up sentiments about our origins. Ethnic revivals are at least in part a reactive move, a standard means of vying for a fair share of the socioeconomic pie (Barth 1969; Comaroff and Comaroff 1992; Rumbaut and Portes 2001: 5; Baumann 2000; Berking 2003), and diaspora has become their reliable vehicle. The practical, colloquial use of the word suggests affiliations by virtue of biological descent, which allegedly transmit blood continuity across space: The Jewish diaspora, from this perspective, is the set of people whose families were from, but then were exiled or otherwise departed from, Israel during dispersions under Babylonia, Rome, or other conquerors. The Irish diaspora is built of the descendants of the families that left Ireland during the potato famines of the nineteenth century, and so on.

This concept inspires groups and galvanizes political mobilizations, but for analytical and comparative purposes it falls short on at least two counts. First, in this view, there exist natural groupings of humans who, through emigration, inevitably become diasporas. But there are no such natural groups and, it follows, no natural diasporas, either. The second obvious problem with the everyday uses of *diaspora* is that the category is overly broad. It is true that if we go back far enough, all human beings have their origins in East Africa (Palmer 1998); but the assertion that we are all members of an East African diaspora is not useful.[2] Although we all have ancestors from that region, that memory is not part of our conscious experience; nor is it constitutive, so far as we know, of our bodily habitus; nor is each of us seen by others as a member of that category. Folk invocations of diaspora fail to specify its cultural particularity: it depends not merely on having a family tree that sprouted in another place but also on having a double consciousness in relation to place. For members of a diaspora, that awareness is central, even actively conjured in their lived experience. They feel a gap between here and there, where they are "really from." They may even value that gap, seeing it not as a deficiency but as a resource or mark of distinction, and actively cultivate a sense of it (Malkki 1997: 62).

The prevalence of these confusing folk usages, not to mention the mixed approaches of analytical meanings—as social form, as type of consciousness, as mode of cultural production (Vertovec 2000: 142)—suggests that we need to spend some time giving boundaries to the notions of diaspora and diasporic religion.

DEFINITION BY ETYMOLOGY

The ascent of *diaspora* as an analytical term has taken several routes. One of these is the route of roots, the tracing of its etymology as a way to delimit its semantic range (e.g., Tölölyan 1996; R. Cohen 1997; Baumann 2000; Sheffer 2003).

Diaspora comes from the Greek verb *speirein* (to sow, or scatter, as in seed) and the preposition *dia* (over); thus, "to scatter over." The same Indo-European root, *sp-*, appears in words like "spore," "spread," and "sperm." Diaspora was first used by Greeks to describe the colonization of Asia Minor and the Mediterranean world, and it probably connoted a sacrificial loss of the homeland for the cause of Greek expansion; hence irretrievable separation though not necessarily forced migration or enslavement (Tölölyan 1996; Baumann 2000).

The word took on a different valence when applied to the Jewish experience, as a translation of the Hebrew term *galut* in the Greek version of Hebrew scripture, connoting severance and exile (Deuteronomy 28: 25, 58–68) and the Jewish dispersions (732 B.C.E., after conquest by Assyria; 586 B.C.E., after conquest by Babylonia; 70 C.E., after conquest by Rome).[3] Yet, at least in the later context of rabbinic teaching, the notion also carried the promise of ultimate return (Cohen 1997; Baumann 2000). In Jewish thought *diaspora* carries within it a soteriology, the promise of the future salvation of the people through a return to the place of origin. As Thomas Tweed (1997: 42) notes, other groups' religious diasporic practice may proffer analogous promises of geopiety projected into the future: "Next year in Jerusalem! Next year in Havana! Next year in Saigon, Palestine, and Llasa!" (cf. Wright 1947; Tuan 1976; Smith and White 2004). This common feature suggests how different diasporas draw on different imaginative and sentimental sensibilities: diasporas of hope, of terror, of despair, of desire (Appadurai 1996: 6).

DEFINITION BY LIST

A second route to definition has been the attempt to specify the empirical contents of a diaspora, so as to enable us to differentiate "diaspora societies" from other societies (Safran 1991; Tölölyan 1996; R. Cohen 1997; Van Hear 1998; Baumann 2000; K. Butler 2001). Scholars have reached a relative consensus on the traits constituting diasporas. Most obvious in these lists is the dispersion of a present group or of past ancestors from an original center to two or more new sites. Next is some retained collective memory about the homeland.

A third criterion is the maintenance of relations with the departed homeland, at least as an imagined community, which defines in significant ways the contemporary experience of the hostland. These relations may include economic as well as social and cultural remittances (Levitt 2001) in both directions, or it may entail ritual performances that call the homeland to mind in order to improve or transform the experience of the hostland.

Fourth, the best of these list-based definitions also call attention to institutional infrastructures that make and sustain diasporic sentiments in what I refer to as "stagings," or performatives (Axel 2004). This issue is important for the present study because, when a group of new arrivals in New York City claims identification with the religious African Diaspora, that group must enter the diaspora through institutional networks, material repertoires, and spaces already present in the city (David Brown 1999).[4] Emigrants rely on artifactual representations that recall the homeland to mind (Appadurai 1996; Tweed 1997: 97; P. Werbner 2000; Miller 2005).

A fifth defining feature often invoked is that a diaspora group remains at least partly separate, distinct, or alienated from the mainstream society in the host country. "Whoever passes from one [territory] to the other finds himself physically and magico-religiously in a special situation for a certain length of time: he wavers between two worlds," wrote Arnold Van Gennep at the beginning of the twentieth century (1960 [1901]: 18). By this criterion, full assimilation in the new place or the total severing of ties to the homeland renders a group no longer diasporic (Saint-Blancat, quoted in Baumann 2000: 326).

A sixth typical characteristic is the nostalgic idealization of the homeland and ancestral time, which may or may not be linked with the desire for actual permanent return (Appadurai 1996: 37–38; Tweed 1997: 94). Relatively few African Americans will actually return to live in Africa, though the ritual experience of momentary "return" both in space and in time is widely performed in African Diaspora religions of the Americas.

These rough criteria offer a fairly standard set of markers to use in analytical definitions of diaspora. These in turn should allow us to distinguish diasporic religious forms from nondiasporic ones.

DEFINING BY RELATION: WHO IS NOT IN A DIASPORA?

Diasporas differ from ethnic communities in themselves, Tölölyan writes, "by the extent to which the latter's commitment to maintain connections with its homeland and its kin communities in other states is absent, weak, at best intermittent, and manifested by individuals rather than the community as a whole" (1996: 16). Tölölyan's point about "extent" or degree of diasporization is important, but it may prove useful to confront an apparently simpler problem, at least as a thought experiment: Who is not in diaspora? To put this differently, if groups can undergo "de-diasporization" (Van Hear 1998: 48), what exactly does this process entail? One of Nicholas Van Hear's examples seems clear enough: when people return permanently to wherever they consider home, they cease to be in diaspora. Recent such groups include ethnic Germans and Greeks returning to homelands from the former USSR after 1989 and Palestinians who returned to the West Bank from Kuwait between 1990 and 1992 (Van Hear 1998: 6, 48, 195, 200). A second example is those always in transit, for example as nomads (Cohen 1997): the lack of any established homeland location precludes any sense of territorial dislocation. The Bedouins and the Romani ("Gypsies") represent this type.

Third, a community that is entirely uprooted to a new homeland is no longer dispersed; it remains "intact," merely in a new place, and the key spatial feature of diaspora, the engagement of hostland and homeland communities across a gap, is forfeit. Next, at least as a logical possibility, we can imagine a group that remains dislocated from a homeland community but which so fully assimilates in the hostland that it is no longer cognizant of the homeland and abandons the sort of "co-responsibility" that is constitutive of active diasporas (Saint-Blancat in Baumann 2000; P. Werbner 2000: 17). Eric Hobsbawm, for example, describes his childhood family life among the assimilated Jews in interwar Vienna. In his memory, Jews were simply part of the cosmopolitan cultural fabric of the city. Despite prevalent anti-Semitism, any specific meaning accorded to Jewishness was slight, as were his sentiments of loyalty: "I have no emotional obligation to the practices of an ancestral religion and even less to . . . the nation-state which asks for my solidarity on racial grounds" (Hobsbawm 2002: 10–12, 24).

Finally, a group lacking the resources, time, energy, and political clout to guard and fan the sparks of memory can cease to live in diaspora, as the exhausted-sounding epigraph from Emeline Michel suggests: "We are not a diaspora, we are just trapped." Diasporic affiliations and representations come into being under certain historical conditions and may be transformed or disappear under others (Clifford 1994: 315). Hence, writes Eddie Glaude of African Americans, "Most people don't live diasporic lives" (2000: 103).

In the most restrictive and precise definition, diasporic social formation is determined by consciousness and discourse about spatial dislocation, as in Martin Baumann's admirably concise definition: "The relational facts of a *perpetual recollecting identification with a fictitious or far away existent geographic territory and its cultural-religious traditions* are taken as diaspora constitutive" (2000: 327, italics in original).

To this review of definitions by etymology, list, and relation, I would like to add five further considerations to sharpen the meaning of *diaspora,* and by extension *diasporic religion,* to a more incisive point.

A diaspora is a specific kind of culture. Diasporas are cultural rather than biological forms.[5] For a diasporic culture to be maintained or transmitted, information like memories, tastes, and habits must be communicated from one individual mind to another. Each leap of "contagion"—to borrow an epidemiological metaphor (Sperber 1996)—entails a new reception, the adaptation of incoming information to a new psychosocial and material context. Change occurs as that memory is reconfigured within a semantic field of relevant schema or scripts by which an individual lives (Kertzer 1988; Shore 1996; Sperber 1996; Sewell 1999; Zerubavel 1999; Boyer 2001; Whitehouse 2000, 2004).

Individual minds must receive and reproduce the words, habits, and tendencies which, when assembled densely and consistently enough with those of a group of people located in another place, come to be called a "diaspora" in comparisons with other clusters of habits, memories, aesthetic preferences, or languages. Diasporic culture names a relative match among these clusters carried by individual minds, a sufficient though never complete similarity (Boyer 2001: 35–36). The reproduction of such a similarity requires communications between individuals. But diaspora culture is distinctive in that the transmissive gaps to be bridged are enormously widened.

Diasporas are cultures that cross wide transmissive gaps and are also about such gaps. Diasporic cultural transmissions entail not the reception and incorporation of words or ideas passed contiguously, through direct contact or immediate networks, but rather the exchange of signals and symbols through electronic media, the post, videotapes, or secondhand gossip networks. Cultural transmission is conducted not only through human copresence in known places, as in the homeland, but also across empty space dividing homeland from hostland. The wider the spaces those transmissions must cross, and the greater the number of rival signals in the cultural field of reception, the more variation may occur—even if, as is often the case in diasporic religions, strident discourses insist on fidelity to tradition and absolute continuity between the homeland and the diasporic group (Gupta and Ferguson 1997: 39).

Corollary to the spatial gap is the oft-perceived temporal gap, or "lag" (Brent Edwards 2003), where the homeland is made by those in diaspora to carry the symbolic weight of the "original" and the "inherent"; just as, for those remaining in the homeland, the diaspora often must bear the load of "modernity" (Gilroy 1993: 191, 197). Even messages exchanged in the here and now may be incorporated by individual persons according to schema derived from their memories of a place located in the past—depending on how long ago the emigration occurred—rather than the present. When a Garifuna person in New York receives a videotape of a ritual from a Honduran village and watches it in her high-rise apartment, she may view the videotaped actions as occurring not only in a different place but also in a different time, the time of her childhood (cf. Richman 2005: 25, 196, 213). The homeland is conceived both as a geographic backwater compared with the city, and as a hallowed place: hallowed because it mediates the past in some way that resists transience, even though the homeland village may be fully engaged with processes of modernity. Diasporic Garifuna often caricature the imaginary homeland and its dwellers, both to fortify their own superiority and to endow the homeland with the sacralizing power of ancestral authenticity.

A diaspora is a series of interventions, not a permanent state of being. The Irish Americans of Chicago may be sentimentally joined to the imagined homeland for a given occasion, like a Saint Patrick's Day parade or a Notre Dame football game, but the union requires substantial effort. For, after all, the Irish of Dublin and the Irish Americans of Chicago are not the same; or, rather, they are similar in certain respects and quite different in others. No doubt most members of both groups live through most days without giving the matter much thought, their minds preoccupied by other collectivities in relation to whom they reference themselves (Hefner 1993: 25) and that determine who they are: Catholic or Protestant; from Northern Ireland or Eire; conservative, liberal, or socialist; spouse or bachelor; punk rocker or traditional fiddler; and so on. Not only to be of Irish extraction but also to *feel* that identity and its spatial pull (Tölölyan 1996: 15)—which is of the essence in the restricted use of *diaspora* advocated here—is therefore a contingent and usually temporary state, as it is only one among a set of possible affiliations. Such emotions are evoked by some situations and not by others, which is why such diasporic conjunctions tend to require elaborate stagings.

These stagings include discursive acts, repeated performatives (Axel 2004: 38). But the manifestation of "the Irish diaspora" is also contingent on a long list of infrastructural supports: a special day on the calendar, the city's assent to closing streets for parades, the manufacture and sale of green hats and buttons, the green dye poured into the Chicago River, the massive surplus of beer. It entails a conjunction of commercial and civic interests that can be achieved only infrequently—or not at all, for diaspora groups that lack sufficient numbers, capital, and political clout. Without repeated commemorations, diasporas may disappear from the minds of potential members. When the homeland cannot be called to mind, or fails to evoke sentiments of affinity, a diaspora ceases to exist (though, to be sure, it may exist in another, archaeological sense, as a trail of bones or arrowheads [Mintz and Price 1992: 47]). There is no essence of diaspora external to the acts themselves (Gilroy 1993: 110).

Such commemorative labor is enjoined not only in large performances that are consciously and ideologically diasporic but also in small, habitual acts—a "quotidian diaspora" (P. Werbner 200)—often without any special awareness of it. Listening to merengue is more likely to evoke diaspora sentiments for Dominicans than listening to Brazilian bossa nova, and a Dominican in his car often sets his playlist accordingly. A Jamaican diasporan knows full well the colors her hat should bear to signal that identity to observers and to herself, though, again, it is not typically a matter given conscious deliberation. Diasporas are sentimental communities but also habit communities, and such emotions are quickened by forceful appeals to the senses in certain kinds of acts and events: religious rituals, musical performances, home-style meals. The homeland must be staged again and again. Even quotidian diasporas require work.

Why does anybody do this work? Diasporas are desirable because they are consequential actions. They are articulations across gaps that, like the articulations of hip or knee joints, allow for forward motility (Edwards 2003: 15). By naming a horizon of expectation, they provide solidarity, purpose, identity, and futurity. Against this horizon, diasporans not only perform rituals but also raise funds and mobilize campaigns. The Garifuna diaspora in New York, for example, generated the revenue that brought electricity to many Honduran Garifuna villages in the early 1980s. Moreover, their invocation helps to define borders within a competitive cultural market (Appadurai 1996; Zukin 1996; Berking 2003), which can lead to resources from city and state governments for social services or institution-building.

Diaspora culture is the elevating of one reference group over other possible ones. Because being diasporic *does* something, diasporas are interested interventions; they act as props or shims (Edwards 2003: 14) that temporarily level differences by demoting rival reference-group affiliations and elevating just one. The most common is the identification of ethnicity, especially among many Caribbeans in the United States for whom the racial reduction to "black" is viewed as a socioeconomic liability. As the sociologist Mary Waters showed, for example, Caribbean anglophone blacks in the United States often stress their West Indian–ness and may consciously maintain their distinctive accents so as not to be too easily conflated with African Americans, who are perceived as holding low social status (Waters 1999: 57, 103, 151, 332). Haitians in New York sometimes bank on the prestige of French to accomplish the same sort of distancing (McAlister 1998). A Haitian in New York may under certain circumstances feel, be identified as, or introduce herself as "African American," "African," "Caribbean," or "French"; but all of these identifications are likely to be suspended during a Vodou ceremony in Brooklyn in favor of an authentic "Haitian-ness," because that is the diasporic identifier befitting the occasion. Yet that same person might the next day attend a neighborhood watch group or a protest against police brutality, at which she identifies as black. Or she may visit a Cuban *botánica,* a store selling popular ritual tools like icons and candles, and, while chatting with a Cuban *santera,* enjoy the conviviality of a common African diasporic religious heritage.

Although diasporic affiliations emphasize one identification over others, the nomenclature of diaspora also connotes distance and the limits of complete identification. For example, to become a member of the African Diaspora both forges a link with Africa and guards a certain distance from it, allowing for its selective invocation. During the 1980s, African Americans were activists against South Africa's apartheid system in part by virtue of their African diasporic loyalties. The imagined community was broad enough to enable them to find common cause with South African victims of apartheid. Yet similar mobilizations have not occurred in relation to other African traumas, notably in Sudan and

Rwanda, because famines and massacres are not as easily related to familiar North American schema in the way that South Africa's racial segregation could be compared to the black experience in the United States. Diasporic sentiments, and interventions, may be limited by what is imaginable and salient within the cultural repertoire and material context of the hostland.

Diaspora culture is usually urban culture. In recent diasporas, the receiving social context of a hostland in which a diasporic group must be incorporated is not only pluralistic, it is usually also urban, because cities are where jobs, extended kin networks, and ethnic enclaves to receive newcomers are most likely to be found.[6] On the one hand, such urban contexts may appear quite homogeneous the world over, equally run by "money, the frightful leveler" that "hollows out the core of things" (Simmel 1950: 414; cf. Comaroff and Comaroff 1992: 54). The urban context transforms orientations in time and space, ideas of work and value, and even the experience of self-identity (see, for example, Simmel 1978; Soja 1989; Harvey 1990; Giddens 1990; Zukin 1996). Displacement can generate a sense of incoherence, anomie, and vulnerability, but that very incoherence opens possibilities and needs for new sodalities in the city (Weber 2002: 47; Sennett 1994: 371).

On the other hand, diasporic cultures are rerooted in and through what Robert Orsi (1999) calls "urban subjectivities," in which the marking of differences becomes valued as the shared expressive culture of the city. This kind of subjectivity is shaped in the context of frequent meetings with unexpected others, a cityscape of new and unfamiliar materials out of which meaning must be made, and a sort of self-awareness or mirroring quality of city people intensified by the observation of difference, as well as the possibilities for selective identity, which are more readily available in large cities than elsewhere (Orsi 1999: 44, 54–57). In the radical pluralism of the city, received signals may be regarded as precarious, contingent, and voluntarist rather than as cultural certainties or requirements. The city has a "contagion factor" that makes ethnic minorities privy to the styles and choices of others; thus diaspora societies may rub against each other to spark new, cross-diasporic fires (Zukin 1996; Sheffer 2003: 25).[7]

To be sure, the classifying processes to which most diasporic groups are subjected are far less flexible and far less graced by the privilege of self-selection. Instead, they are read into hostland scripts to play parts not of their own choosing, depending on their proximal hosts—the hostland groups in reference to which they are perceived by the mainstream majority (Mittelberg and Waters 1992). As Aihwa Ong (1999: 12–16) so well describes, the fluidity of terms like *globalization, diaspora,* and *transnationalism* have too often connoted notions of freewheeling mobility and cultural exchange without attending to the economic and political structures that radically delimit and constrain the lives of the vast majority. New subjectivities come wrapped in new forms of subjectification (Ong 1999; Asad 1993; Mahmood 2005). For example, the Garifuna in the United States tend to be read in relation to African Americans and, less commonly, in relation to Latinos, since many Garifuna are Spanish-speaking.

Yet even Garifuna immigrants to the United States, whose potential repertoire of identifications is far more circumscribed than that of most European immigrants, might on occasion forward Hispanic, Black, Caribbean, Honduran, Garifuna, or village-based identifications. In this pattern of code-switching that sometimes seeks to substitute ethnic or geographic identifications for racial ones, the Garifuna are similar to other Caribbean emigrant groups (McAlister 1998).[8] However, as chapter 6 shows, Garifuna shamans and devotees of traditional religion in the United States depart from this standard Caribbean model of using ethnicity to refute the racial reduction to blackness. Instead, traditional Garifuna religion becomes a vehicle of black identifications, through its links to the African Diaspora and an emerging African diasporic horizon.

The conditions of Garifuna subjection, then—being forced to emigrate to the United States to support families in Honduras, Guatemala, or Belize, and the marginal status immigrants occupy once arriving there—are also the conditions of a new subjectivity (J. Butler 1997), which includes the possibility of a greater engagement with other groups of the African Diaspora and with the diasporic subject position itself. The fact that diaspora identifications are usually maintained in urban contexts, where multiple identification options are juxtaposed, accelerates the problem of authenticity and origins as these are determined reactively. And this question of authenticity, among other things, draws diaspora into direct contiguity with religion.

Diasporic Religion

If diaspora is contested, religion is even more so.[9] To critically evaluate their relation, so as to justify the phrase *diasporic religion,* I begin by attempting to sketch a rough profile of diasporic religion.

Religious bases for identity are enhanced through exile (Herberg 1960; R. B. Williams 1988). Religious and national identifications may be fused in idealized representations of the departed land (Tweed 1997: 95; Orsi 1999: 56): to be Garifuna in the New York diaspora, for example, is a sentiment especially acquired in the practice of Garifuna *religion*. As migrants are forced to assimilate in the economic or productive sectors of life, they maintain a sense of continuity with the past primarily in cultural domains, such as religion, music, or style (Mintz and Price 1992; Gilroy 1993: 40, 57; Clifford 1994: 313).[10] Where Garifuna canoe building or cassava cultivation are impossible for migrants, religious performance becomes more important as a source of ethnic affiliation and for maintaining memories of home. Third, diasporic religion stresses "horizontal" over "vertical," social dimensions, as a shared exile status and a sense of equality take primacy over homeland hierarchies, opening spaces for the reworking of gender, class, ethnicity and religious authority (Tweed 1997: 97; Kasinitz, Battle, and Miyares 2001: 270). Membership in the religion becomes more important than status within it, inverting the valence that obtains in the homeland, where religious membership may not be a conscious issue. A fourth characteristic of this profile is that diasporic religion does not merely reproduce homeland religion but transforms it in response to constraints and opportunities posed by the host society (Warner 1998; Levitt 2001; McAlister 2002). Fifth, changes in diaspora religious communities transform the homeland through processes of social and financial remittances and actual physical returns (Foner 1978; Clifford 1994; Levitt 2001; Johnson 2002b). Through such transformations, both "locative" and "utopian" religious styles, religious acts and words based in geopiety and those detaching identity from territorial origins, take hold and exist simultaneously as distinct modes of religious action (Jonathan Smith 1978, 1987; Whitehouse 2000, 2004), so that diasporic religious identifications may begin to conflict with homeland religious practice (Hall 1996b; P. Werbner 2000). Sixth, diasporic religion, as a subculture stimulated by rival groups itself, is in part reactive, responding to comparison, boundary work, and defensive definition with and against religious neighbors who were in most cases absent or less numerous in homelands. A key part of such boundary work entails the discursive invocation and attempts at stabilization of what constitutes a group's authentic "tradition," leading to creative innovations and sometimes inventions (Hobsbawm and Ranger 1983; Handler 1988; Gilroy 1993; Clifford 1994; Palmié 1995: Zane 1999; Demerath 2001; Weber 2002: 47; Clarke 2004).

Finally, like diasporas in general, diasporic religion is not simply bestowed by imputed geographic, ethnic, or racial continuities, though such continuities may provide its tools. Diasporic religious identifications are created and maintained through the work of memory, transit, communication, consumption, political contest and, not least, of ritual.

While this profile is useful, and serves as a baseline for the case of the Garifuna, the relation between diaspora and religion can be developed further. Diasporas do not merely express or carry religions: in a certain sense, they make them.

If religions are sometimes the cause of diasporas, diasporas sometimes make religions. The classic case of diasporic religion, Judaism, proffers important leads for comparison. The etymological and discursive history of the term *diaspora* is strongly marked by Judaism. Indeed, when the phrase *African Diaspora* was first put in print by George Shepperson in the 1960s, he called it a metaphor drawn from the Jewish case (1968: 152). In one sense, of course, the Jewish diaspora can be said to have been "caused by" religion, by the resistance of Jews to the imperial religions of their conquerors. But it has also been argued that the diaspora caused Judaism.

For the ancient Greeks who gave us the word *diaspora,* the prospect of exile from one's land was a thoroughly religious problem: it was impossible to give up your land without also surrendering your religion, and vice versa (Tuan 1977: 154). But as Martin Baumann (2000) points out, *diaspora* was an ambivalent term for Jews. It described the move out of Palestine between the fifth and first centuries B.C.E., but it did not always imply forcible removal or exile, and it carried within it a soteriology of the anticipated return to the homeland. The Jewish dispersion therefore was not merely a loss but also a great source of vitality. "Babylon" was a cipher not only of exile and the loss of sovereignty, but also of a revitalized Judaism (R. Cohen 1997: 4–5). Out of the diaspora emerged an incipient scriptural canon, synagogues under the leadership of charismatic prophets, the exegetical style based in contact and communication with rival traditions, and the very notion, value, and ritualization of return. In other words, Cohen suggests, Babylon was the crucible that, in a sense, made Judaism into a fully articulated religion.

Jonathan Z. Smith articulated the matter somewhat differently (1987: 94–95). The destruction of the Temple brought forth of necessity a more portable, transmissible style of Judaism, one based not on temple ritual but rather on religious law and its interpretation, the Mishnah. Similarly, in Christianity, as the faith expanded, the ritual requirement of visiting the Jerusalem shrines of saints was replaced after the fourth century by the calendar of saints' days, changing a system of religious practice based in ritualizations of specific places into one that was utopian and mobile. In the context of the Americas, as Sabine MacCormack has shown, the Spanish destruction of Andean material religious representations forced Andeans to rethink and articulate theological concepts in newly systematic ways (1991: 408–11). And Harvey Whitehouse (2000, 2004) has theorized through Indonesian cases how a religion may shift from a primarily ritual, "imagistic" mode of transmission to a primarily "doctrinal" mode correlated with its capacity for spatial and social extension. It is this line of thought leads to the comparative proposition that diasporization makes religions.

How so? First, diasporas force the hand of practitioners using religious discourses and actions. Where once they were unmarked parts of the social environment and its quotidian routine, religious words and acts now become the objects of conscious selection. They must be planned for, allotted space, deliberated, and settled on. Which ideas and rituals must at all costs be recollected, retained and revived, and which can be left aside? By what criteria? Who decides? For groups in exile or emigration, religion is reified by being dislodged from its embedded, unspoken status to becoming a discrete object of contemplation and contest (P. Brown 1981; Jonathan Smith 1987; R. Cohen 1997; Levitt 2001). As John Thornton (1998: 235) noted with respect to the recreation of African religions in the Americas, "The merging of religions requires something more than simply mixing forms and ideas from one religion with those of another. It requires a reevaluation of the basic concepts and sources of knowledge of both religions in order to find common ground." This critical reevaluation can intensify religious sentiments, discourses and practices, as in the infamous Herberg hypothesis (1960: 27–28).

According to Herberg, although immigrants to the United States were expected to assimilate in most respects, they were also expected to retain their old religion; hence religion became the expression of ethnic specificity and heritage. Arguably this remains the case for immigrants to the United States who find religion to be conducive to collective action, and the thesis has been convincingly updated (Warner 1993). Yet it does not inevitably or universally hold true. Religious acceleration depends on the status of religion in the receiving country. It is not at all clear, for example, that Jamaicans emigrating to London become more religious by virtue of that transit in the same way that Koreans have

done in the United States, as "religion" is not a privileged and protected category for social organization in Great Britain as it is in the
United States That is why, rather than simply echo Herberg, I say that
religion is created as a discrete category of conscious reflection and
action and that its "hand is forced." As it becomes a problem for reflection, religion may be either forfeited or embraced more fervently than
before. What it will surely not do is remain the same.

Second, diasporas make religions in the sense that they demand public
recognition and summon new versions responding to that demand. The
most obviously public (and mobile) medium of transmission is that of
texts. Though once-indigenous religions becoming diasporic do not
inevitably become text-based religions, they must at least become to a
certain degree "public." Their relative security in the hostland—their
legitimacy as a recognized and protected "religion" whatsoever—
depends on a persuasive presentation (Vertovec 2000: 149). Going
public entails the articulation of cultural products so that they are perceived as both legible and relevant, or at least tolerable, to a broader
audience. When indigenous religions become diasporic, they must
become at least modestly more cosmopolitan in their appeal—available
and recognizable to audiences that did not produce them, and which
may be distant in time and space from the site of their origins. Newly
arrived religions may remain "under the radar" in a host society for a
certain period, but their long-term endurance requires the acquisition
of stable institutional niches; this in turn demands the rationalization of
their style in previously unknown ways. This was the case, for example,
with the Afro-Cuban religion of Santería. Once a secret religion of
immigrant communities in Miami and New York, in the last decade it
has acquired greater long-term security by surviving legal scrutiny of its
practice of animal sacrifice, by marshaling a thoroughgoing defensive
theology, and by reinventing itself as a church (do Campo 1995; Palmié
1996; Johnson 2005).

Third, diasporas make religions in the sense that they generate a spatial trail, an itinerary of sites which, by signifying golden ages of organic
integrity and autonomy, present multiple horizons of memory for
adherents. To be sure, emigrants spatially and ideologically replant rituals in new sites. Haitian devotees of Vodou found a new social niche in
New York at the Church of Our Lady of Mount Carmel in Brooklyn
(McAlister 1998). Cubans, including practitioners of Santería, reoriented
themselves to the shrine of Our Lady of Charity in Miami (Tweed 1997).
Cuban American *paleros* and *santeros* (devotees of the Afro-Cuban

religions of Palo Monte and Santería) rewrote city maps in accord with their own analogical logic of religious correspondences (David Brown 1999, 2003).When attached to new sites, religious objects and practices signify within a new system of relations, shifting the meanings they communicate (Sahlins 1976, 1985; Ortner 1984; Sewell 1999; Vásquez and Marquardt 2003).

But even as some features of diasporic religion are transferred to new sites, remembered spaces become sacralized as pivots of imagined communities (Laclau 1990; B. Anderson 1991; Appadurai 1996). And here religious and commercial links are strongly imbricated. Continuity with the homeland is brokered by merchants of material goods who sell the "authentic" to those in exile. In this commerce of memory making, the pure and original are rendered valuable commodities, so that diasporas and "purist" claims about origins are intimately associated (Matory 2005: 116). The anthropologist Karen Richman has even argued, with respect to Vodou, that the Haitian diaspora made religion in the sense that a whole new class of ritual specialists arose in the homeland to mediate absent migrants' suddenly problematic relation to the spirits left behind (2005: 119, 128).

Did the diaspora make Garifuna religion? By being exiled from the place of their ethnogenesis, St. Vincent in the eastern Antilles, the Black Caribs regained it as an idealized symbolic homeland. Two centuries later, when many Garifuna left Honduras, Belize, and Guatemala for New York City, the lands of their Central American home villages became idealized as perfect repositories of authentic, rooted identity. They became sacred as places set apart in memory; places to which Garifuna return with expectations of regaining traditional knowledge and experience; places religiously idealized, and materially bought and consumed, to save them from being defined by quotidian life in the United States. In the words of Tomoko Masuzawa (mediating the spirit of Walter Benjamin): "Once the reproductions proliferate and scatter about in the world, these countless simulacra do not leave the original alone in peace but . . . 'reactivate' the original" (1993: 18).

Moreover, the processes of migration, the reification (and sometimes intensification) of religion, the recoding of religion into transmissible forms, and its replanting in new sites of attachment can yield more surprising results than merely the idealization of the place left behind. New diasporic horizons may arise as historical memory is reworked (Appadurai and Breckenridge 1989: i). In such cases religion is not just a sacralizing process, surrounding previously banal ideas and personages with auras of infinite and unchanging authority, but rather a set of transformations in which ethnicity and even "race" are smelted down and remade. In the migration to New York, the Garifuna found Africa. They "became African," or reacquired a conscious Africanness, by virtue of joining the religious African Diaspora, through a series of complex processes of remembering and rerouting.

Diasporic religion is re-membered religion. Diasporic religions are assembled memories of the self in space that can be transmitted sufficiently well to attract a following, become a collective memory, and be sustained over time. Enduring over time is a problem for any religion, because between a symbol's production and its reception and reimplementation yawns not only the chasm of space but also that of culture. A symbol that had meaning in the homeland must be attached to new sites of meaning in the receiving land. How then can continuities of meaning be carried over from person to person, and from application to application, so that a religion maintains its distinguishing character?

Here I give close attention to a classic text on collective memory by Maurice Halbwachs (1992). Memory, in Halbwachs's assessment, is not primarily a matter of individual psychology but rather a social pattern into which the individual is born. It is a collective phenomenon in part because it is mediated by language: its precondition is words, each of which is embedded in its own history and conventions (173). It is also a collective phenomenon because the individual is socialized into a specific group comprising many individual members' recollections but relatively independent of any one of them (39). It is only to the degree that individual thought is placed in a social framework, and participates in its memory, that the act of recollection becomes possible (38; cf. Cassirer 1955).[11] Collective memory also exceeds and stands independent from individual memories because it is spatially defined in landmarks and territory (Halbwachs 1992: 183, 201, 204, 220, 222). This definition too composes a kind of dialectical process. Even as memory carries its own landmarks everywhere, it must be constantly reattached to the current space the group occupies, to objects that revivify remembrances (Halbwachs 1992: 95; cf. Massey 1993: 146; Durkheim 1995: 232–33). It is the materiality of religions, Halbwachs argues, their embeddedness in rites and "material operations," that provides their most stable component, as ritual action allows for multiple interpretations and is less subject than doctrine to splintering (116; cf. Turner 1967; Kertzer 1988). To the degree that it becomes impossible to renew religious memories through physical contact with their place of generation, therefore—say, under conditions of exile or relentless transit—memory suffers the dual processes of becoming "impoverished" and "congealed" (Halbwachs 1992: 106).

The two are directly related, as it is the risk of a religion's being forgotten that leads to the "congealing" of dogma and the transformation of sites and objects into second-order symbols that (metaphorically) represent the remembered territory rather than (metonymically) act as indices of it through contiguity (Halbwachs 1992: 117). Objects and sites that constituted the ritual apparatus of a religion's initial creation are transformed into "a teaching, a notion, or a symbol," each of which "takes on a meaning" (102). In the refrain "Next year in Jerusalem!" for example, the specificity of the ritual site and its "texture" (Lefebvre 1991: 42, 57, 235) are rendered smooth and seamless, and endowed with a previously absent coherence. This transformation can have spatial and social effects. Religions are transformed by immigration when their idiosyncratic textures are "smoothed" for adaptation to already legitimated religious sites. This process allows for the enlargement and transmission of a religion as a collective memory (Halbwachs 1992: 201), as previously "local" religion is joined to larger regional or transnational sodalities. But it also changes the religion into something new.

Several points from Halbwachs's work remain salient. The emigrant carriers of Caribbean religions arriving in U.S. cities must on the one hand discover, select, and stabilize agreed-upon new places of devotion, and on the other accomplish this task in relation to a cityscape already thoroughly parsed and designated by other religious and secular forces. The places selected must offer a "hook": they must seem familiar and relatively consonant with the objectives and practices of newly arriving African Diaspora devotees. For example, a mosque, a McDonald's restaurant, and a used-car dealership are unlikely (though not unthinkable) sites of religious implantation.

McAlister's (1998) study of the use of the church of Our Lady of Mount Carmel at 115th Street in East Harlem is illustrative on this score: Haitians' use of the site for pilgrimages in honor of the Vodou deity Ezili Danto depends, in part, on the Italian American community's assent and welcome. According to McAlister, the influx of Haitians is viewed positively by the site's older users because the Haitians have buoyed and revitalized what was once a dying ritual, precariously maintained by a waning Italian American constituency. Similarly, when the Garifuna began to establish a presence in the New York African Diaspora, they did so in part by calling on the resources of places like the African Diaspora and Caribbean Culture Center on West 58th Street. Though the center was established by an Afro–Puerto Rican santera, Marta Moreno Vega, and serves primarily as a Santería resource center, the Garifuna were welcomed as an expansion of the center's broad purpose. It offered both propitious and familiar hooks—the Spanish language, a broad-based clientele of people of color, and a religion based in material exchange leading to spirit possession—and space for newcomers who corroborated that broad religious profile. Yet, if this process generates new religious alliances by expanding the "African diasporic religions" identification, from the perspective of those operating the center, for the Garifuna the new threat posed by the possible absorption of Garifuna religion within a larger diasporic set provokes a reactive quest for determining specific, unique, and "authentic" Garifuna religious collective memories (Halbwachs 1992: 93, 98).

Spatial dislocation presents a religious crisis, but such crises call forth creative responses and religious innovations through the freedom from place (Tuan 1977: 152), and not only in religion. Migration provides previously unknown liberties for women, for example, offering means of independent wage earning and distance from family obligations (see, for example, Waters 1999: 92, 315). Migration also enables the formation of new and wider imagined religious communities and allows the Garifuna to rethink their practices as part and parcel of the African Diaspora. Their very subjection within a new hegemonic order generates new possibilities of memory making.[12]

The African Diaspora

To recapitulate: diasporas are social identifications based on shared memory bridges linking a lived space and a left-behind place. The remembered land must be sustained through periodic physical returns, imagined and ritualized returns, or both. If to be "in diaspora" is to reside in two or more spaces, at least imaginatively, it is also to occupy a memory space between them. At least two gaps are implied in diaspora religious "identity": between words or acts in a hostland and those in a homeland (a gap in space), and within those groups from one moment in time to the next, between a recollected past and a projected future (a gap in time and memory). Being "in diaspora" is best understood not as the final closure of those gaps, but rather as the active engagement with, and evocation of, such gaps as a source of meaning.

It follows that diasporic religions are never simply given, either in racial ciphers like blackness or ethnic ones like Garifuna-ness or Africanness. In cases of complete assimilation, or lack of access to the resources required to build and maintain the links, African Diaspora religions may be forgotten. And some individuals may simply choose never to join the African Diaspora, whether through religion or any other means.

The distinguishing analytical feature of the modern African Diaspora, associated with the Atlantic slave trade, is its emergence in relation to race (Palmer 1998: 64 n. 2). Membership in the African Diaspora is not usually a selective identity, because its racial correlation with blackness is imposed rather than chosen. Though it can be more or less embraced as an individual expression, that choice occurs in a larger context of imposed identity. In the United States, for example, pigmentocracy continues in force, as the Garifuna are read by outsiders in relation to African Americans and treated to the same rigidly racialist, and often also racist, classifications.[13] The racial bias against Caribbean migrants of color remains, albeit sometimes masked as an issue of class, in the segmentation of neighborhoods and job markets, the availability of loans, and access to good schools. It is not entirely by choice, for example, that the Garifuna, like so many other Caribbean immigrants, take up residence in Bronx or Brooklyn neighborhoods considered perilous by many whites, and that most typically work as live-in attendants for the sick or aged, to the detriment of their own households (cf. Zane 1999: 165).

Despite the force of this reception context, blackness and Africanness are not self-evidently linked: "becoming black" and "becoming African" are distinct, relatively autonomous processes. There is at best an elective affinity between black culture and African diasporic religious culture, just as there is only a loose overlapping between "race" and "ethnicity" (Hall 1996a, 1996b, 1996c). In fact, the two identifications are often at odds in the temporalities they signify. Black identity often stands for futurity, variously as a cipher of global cosmopolitan modernity or, conversely, inner-city postmodern decay. African diasporic religious identifications, by contrast, are often anchored to the past through ciphers of ancient origins and roots. "Black" and "African diasporic" identifications each have their mythologies, key symbolic tropes, and ritualizations that cannot be easily equated. My first analytical objective, therefore, is to complicate each and unlink them, to show how one could argue that the Garifuna, a "black" people, have only recently joined the African Diaspora through religion.

THE INCIPIENT AFRICAN DIASPORA:
THE IDEA OF A SHARED AFRICANNESS

The idea of an African Diaspora has been present for much longer than the phrase itself. It may be as old as plantation slavery, beginning with the fictive kin networks generated by the dislocation from Africa. For example, the historian Katia Mattoso writes of the existential indeterminacy confronted by slaves arrived in Brazil: "But try to imagine what it must have been like for a Muslim to find himself in a group of slaves practicing an animistic religion, or for a Bantu to join a community where Yoruban influence dominated, or, even more complicated, for a creole slave to confront black religions whose meaning he no longer understood. All these individuals must have been forced to find some compromise, to grope toward a modus vivendi in which unresolved contradictions must have produced constant tensions" (Mattoso 1989: 127).

Finding common ground required both conversion and convergence of subjectivities, and religion often provided an emergent, interethnic lingua franca, though which religion would play that role was far from a given. According to João Reis, describing nineteenth-century Bahia, Brazil, "Islam . . . was a heavyweight contender in a cultural free-for-all that also included the Yoruba orisha cult, Aja-Fon Vodum, the Angolan ancestor spirit cult, among other African religious manifestations. Add to this a creole Catholicism, and you will have an idea of the religious plurality in the African and Afro-Bahian communities of the time" (1993: 97).

Beyond this plurality, however, and allowing for the strategizing of shared projects like slave rebellions, lay some sense of an emergent Afro-Atlantic culture consisting of a loose association of aesthetic, religious, political, familial, and linguistic overlaps (Thornton 1998: 211). James Sweet, for this reason, even argued that "becoming 'African' was essentially an American phenomenon" (2003: 115–17), as diasporans created their homeland through a process of hybridization between ethnic groups formerly distinct in their self-understandings (cf. Palmer 1998; Matory 2005: 3, 10, 36).

The discursive notion of something like a diaspora, even if the term itself was not yet invoked, has been in play at least since the second half of the nineteenth century.[14] In the earlier stages of this incubation, at least, a putative relation to an actual, territorial Africa was often part of the consensus, whether in actual transport links and plans of return, as proposed by Marcus Garvey, or in discourses on continuities with the soil of Africa. When the Martinican Aimé Césaire first used the term *négritude* in 1939, for example, in his *Notebook of a Return to My Native*

Land (Cahier d'un retour au pays natal), it framed blackness in close relation to African territorial identity: "My blackness is not a tower or a cathedral, it plunges into the red flesh of the soil."[15]

THE NONTERRITORIAL AFRICAN DIASPORA

The African Diaspora did not exist by that name before the 1950s (Appiah 1992; Gilroy 1993) and was only definitively established in 1966 with a seminal article by George Shepperson in *African Forum*, titled "The African Abroad or the African Diaspora."[16] It was solidified as a discursive entity a decade later through the publication of a string of volumes that included the expression in their titles, edited by Joseph Harris (1971), Jacob Drachler (1975), Martin L. Kilson and Robert I. Rotberg (1976), and Graham W. Irwin (1977) (Alpers 2001: 7). This modest academic explosion pushed the term into academic currency and common usage.

The discursive arrival of *African Diaspora* was precisely contemporaneous with the post-1960 migrations from the Caribbean, which at once granted the new project a broader front and exposed its fissures. The Caribbean groups who arrived en masse in the United States and Europe had disparate ethnic, racial, and religious self-understandings, and the sudden copresence and confrontation between Portuguese-, Spanish-, French-, and English-speaking groups, all presenting claims on or resistance to the new nomenclature, strained the newly minted diaspora's links to even an imagined Africa. The putative organic bonds of territoriality were replaced by late-modern signifying chains, and, at least among intellectuals, the African Diaspora was redefined as a derivative of shared suffering under slavery and subsequent racialist regimes: the sublime slave (Gilroy 1993) on the repeating island (Bénitez-Rojo 1996). Here was a means of salvaging a common political project of resistance and partially shared structures of feeling. The new identification would be one not essentialized in race, ethnicity, or territory, but rather focused on history and the shared experiences of subjugation and racial terror (Mintz and Price 1992; Appiah 1992; Gilroy 1993; Clifford 1994; West 2001; but cf. Lovejoy 1997, Law and Lovejoy 1997, Thornton 1998, and Sweet 2003 for a somewhat different perspective). Africanness was rethought as a genealogy of claims and practices rather than a biological determination or territory (Matory 2005: 15).

Membership in the African Diaspora, it followed, was not an identification deriving from "hard" racial or ethnic essences. Rather, it was acquired through cultural processes—what Weber called "conscious monopolistic closure" around certain features—that entail a kind of "conversion" of consciousness (Sansone 2003: 10).[17] The disjuncture remains between the rigid racialist, and racist, classifications migrants were and are subjected to—but which had also provided the planks for the initial platform of the African Diaspora—and the newer idea of the African Diaspora as an imagined community variably adopted by agents in their own representational practices. So, for example, Césaire's *négritude* is still a point of reference, but it is now eclipsed by *migritude* as the buzzword of the new Franco-African literati, rendering the territorial consciousness of Africa increasingly abstract.

SEPARATING ETHNICITY FROM "RACE"

The uncoupling of ethnic from racial identifications has taken especially curious forms in the area of religion, as many Cuban and Brazilian practitioners of the religions of the African Diaspora are not black at all, either in their self-understandings or the perceptions of others (Pierucci and Prandi 2000). To take an extreme example, someone who identifies racially as "white" may under certain conditions of "soft racialization" (Sansone 2003: 53) mark herself as ethnically African when it is advantageous to do so. Such voluntary double consciousness may present double value (Gilroy 1993: 91), the ability to see and work with multiple audiences. White Cubans or Brazilians may become "African" by initiation into religions such as Santería, Candomblé, or Umbanda—though their willingness to do so depends on the ability to shift ethnic codes in other contexts.[18] Thus pan-African or African diasporic identifications must in at least some cases be distinguished from black modern identifications, the latter presenting a kind of "lateral diaspora" (Clifford 1994: 306) based on mutually recognized phenotype, style, music, musicality, and other tastes and habits. Multicentered and utopian, they have no reference to an idealized homeland or any aspiration of return.[19]

Given the fractures between African diasporic and black identifications, African diasporic religious culture may or may not be part of a person's repertoire. Some Caribbean emigrants become black through migration and in consequence of the globalized dissemination, and domination, of U.S.-produced "black culture" (Bourdieu and Wacquant 1998; England 1999). Others join the African Diaspora through associations with African diasporic religious affiliations. Some understand themselves as black but do not locate their ancestral homelands in or in relation to Africa (Gonzalez 1988; Torres and Whitten 1998: 21). Conversely, others locate the homeland there so naturally that they do not view such descent as worthy of the marked emphasis that diaspora consciousness often elicits (Appiah 1992: 6–7).[20] If joining the African Diaspora entails a conversion of subjectivity, the practical implications for collective identifications and representations remain thoroughly underdetermined (Gilroy 1991, 1993; Gordon and Anderson 1999; West 2001: 141; Sansone 2003). The distinctiveness of the African Diaspora perhaps lies in the confusion between the way its members read themselves in and through elective subjectivities related variously to blackness and Africanness, and the way they may be read by others as simply black within the suffocating monopolistic closure of U.S.-style pigmentocracy.

Still, even the race system faced by Caribbean migrants in the United States is not utterly determinate. The fact that ethnic and racial identifications are not the same, and that the conversions that bring them into being or transform them are not the same either, is apparent in the ways the Garifuna read themselves into racial strictures. Sarah England's survey of a sample of Garifuna declarations of their "race" on the U.S. census provides an example: 41 percent declared themselves "Afro-American/Black," 38 percent as "Hispanic," 16 percent as "other/Garifuna," and 5 percent as "other/Afro-Hispanic" (England 1999: 26). Whereas the first identifier indicates a race-based identification, the other three suggest one based at least partly in ethnicity or culture—in language, history, and geography.

The selection from among these identifications depends, presumably, on choices made about what to leave behind and on perceptions about already existing networks to which Garifuna social actors can attach themselves. Many such African diasporic networks available to arriving migrants, including the Garifuna, are religious ones. In the next sections I evaluate how the host city—New York City, in this case—is indigenized by incoming Caribbean migrants through African Diaspora religions.

African Diasporic Religions in New York: Making a World in the City

I define *African diasporic religions* as those sets of religious discourses and practices that invoke Africa as a horizon of memory, authenticity, and sacred authority—whether Africa is physically known, imagined, or ritually created—and which consider the distance from that idealized place as a problem that is remedied by rendering the place as present in ritual. Therefore African diasporic religions can be, and are, performed by those not of African descent. This view contrasts with the main sort of rival definition of African diasporic religion—that is, any religion performed by persons of African descent. African diasporic religions constitute a cultural category rather than a racially defined one. Still, the majority of its practitioners are, in fact, of African descent; in consequence, African diasporic religions in the United States are forged and maintained under strictures of racism similar to those endured by people of color. What is that constrained space like, and how do African diasporic religions occupy and reshape it?

Afro-Caribbeans in New York, including the Garifuna, tend to live in South Bronx or East-Central Brooklyn, an area Robert Orsi described as a "post-apocalyptic moonscape, part bombed-out Dresden, part Fort Apache" (Orsi 1999: 7). This landscape reflects the economic structure of the city: Manhattan is the showplace serviced by the Bronx and Brooklyn, replicating on a local scale Immanuel Wallerstein's description of a world economic structure consisting of a racially defined "core" and "periphery" (Balibar and Wallerstein 1991: 79; cf. McAlister 2002: 187). The workers come in under cover of darkness to sweep the downtown clean for each new day of Manhattan's dealing and dining. Then they return home across the rivers. The subway ride north offers a racial index of the shifting space: north of the 125th Street station, after the train passes under the Harlem River, the commuters are mostly black and brown, and English is far from the dominant language heard.

Yet the rationally planned cityscape is far from empty of religious life; nor does it necessarily produce, to take Max Weber's phrase, a "shell as hard as steel."[21] The pedestrian in the city engages in constant idiosyncratic enunciations of space. Her movements are in part directed by proper names, monuments, and lights, yet she makes the street her own by appropriating that space, selectively drawing to consciousness her own memories and associations that mark and sacralize certain spaces, passing over and forgetting others (Certeau 1984: 104). Michel de Certeau's (1984: 93–95) figuration of the World Trade Center as the city's panoptic eye and sacred center (now absented) serves as a prescient reminder of how rationally planned cities are bent by subversive appropriations and "symbolic hijackings" of space (Bourdieu 2000: 185), whether pedestrian or airborne. In the interstices of these enunciations occurs a "contagious intimacy" of immigrants and natives, constantly placing the boundaries of culture at risk (Robert Park, quoted in Orsi 1999: 30). The character of urban religion, at least of those religions not strategically built into the cityscape—consider Saint Paul's Church alongside the site of the World Trade Center, or the Cathedral of Saint John the Divine, powerfully paired with Columbia University—is one of disjuncture between territory and practice, or "ecological disso-nance" (K. Brown 1999: 86). That disjuncture is a religious crisis that calls forth creativity and innovation.

Religious memory and transmission first require representation within the limits and available repertoire of spaces and materials in the new territory. For "second diaspora" religions, already reconfigured from Africa to the Caribbean, and now again from the Caribbean to U.S. cities, the mapping of religions onto new territory occurs by three processes, which I simplify here for heuristic purposes. The first is one of metaphoric, metonymic, and synecdochic *hooking:* through the use of specific religious symbols and sites, immigrants attach homeland practices to the new landscape as they perceive similarities to other objects and sites already present in the new terrain. But these objects and sites in the hostland already carry their own semantic load. When homeland religious practices are carried in relation to this new material context, the set of references and therefore also the experience of ritual practice are shifted (Turner 1967: 45–47; Sahlins 1981: 46; Parkin 1991: 219; Sewell 1999: 58–60). The second process is *telescoping* (Bastide 1978a: 247–48), the condensation of objects and practices into ever-smaller spaces.[22] The third process is that of additivity (Mintz and Price 1976: 10, 45, 51), as African Diaspora religions begin to read themselves in relation to each other.

HOOKING

David Brown asked a Cuban priestess of Santería in New York how she continued her work without the territorial resources she had at home. She gave an example: "You have to find a mountain [to revere Obatala, the Santería sky god]. Where will I find a mountain in New York City? You have to find a similarity, Riverside Drive, you stand at the base of it [the rocks] and to you that's a mountain" (1999: 169). She hooked Obatala onto Riverside Drive in New York with a chain of associations. Yet the apparently simple substitution of urban rocks for mountain does not just allow the ritual action to occur; it opens possibilities for new significa-tions. Riverside Drive might itself be linked to Obatala; the signification *mountain* might be transferred to anything one stands at the base of; an advertisement for Busch beer admonishing viewers to "head for the mountains" might take on a different connotation from the one its producers intended; or a stone from the site might be placed on an altar to represent the mountain, and replace even the need to return to Riverside Drive.

The yearly Haitian pilgrimage to Sodo, with its shrine to Notre Dame du Mont Carmel—transcultured with the Vodou spirit *(lwa)* Ezili Danto—is now performed by a visit to the Church of Our Lady of Mount Carmel (McAlister 1998: 124; K. Brown 1999: 90). To preserve them, the rites were reinscribed on new maps. The same process occurs when *santeros* make the Statue of Liberty a site of the Afro-Cuban *ocha* (Yoruba: *orisha*) Olokun, god of the sea, or visit the East and Hudson Rivers as the domain of Ochun, goddess of fresh waters and femininity (David Brown 1999: 169).[23]

In another example, when Rastafarians rename North America as "the heart of Babylon," and thereby cast Jamaica and Africa as authentic centers (Hepner 1998: 209), or refer to Miami as "Kingston 21" and Brooklyn as "Little Jamaica," such valuations involve hooking. The spatial mapping of Jamaica onto U.S. cities entails the erection of dance halls, reggae clubs, smoking yards or "weed gates," select storefront vendors of Rasta apparel, ritual paraphernalia, and *ital* ("natural" and approved) foods (Hepner 1998: 206).

TELESCOPING

Telescoping is a common tactic in Santería and Vodou, which rely on distinctions between humanized and "wild" spaces. The everyday Vodou ritual practice of pouring libations of rum *(kleren)* on the earth for the ancestors of Ginen (Africa) may now be accomplished by in a high-rise apartment by pouring the libations into a pail of dirt. The pail becomes "the earth," which extends metonymically to represent "family roots" (K. Brown 1999: 85, 99). To reproduce the traditional Vodou agricultural rite of "cooking the yams," which lasts three days and is conducted on the family rural plot, the yam harvest is represented by a little pile of symbolic yams and the land by a few leafy branches, with Brooklyn's Prospect Park standing in for the *Gran Bwa* (Big Wood) against which cultivated land signifies (K. Brown 87, 91).

For santeros, the houses of the Yoruba-Cuban ochas are transposed and condensed to *canastilleros,* the shelved cupboard shrines of urban apartments (Murphy 1988; David Brown 1989, 1999: 161–62). Basements are the equivalent of the courtyards used as Cuban ritual sites, just as a park serves as "the forest" *(el monte)* and the backyard, for those lucky enough to have one, as "the bush" (David Brown 1989, 1999: 164–67; Murphy 1988: 57).

Telescoping and hooking do not simply mirror homeland religious practice in miniature by preserving memory. The process entails transformation and sometimes ritual reductions. As Roger Bastide's monumental *African Religions of Brazil* shows in great detail, the move from one social world to another entails loss, as collective representations lacking a place or function in the "modern world" fall away (1978a: 242). Religion is a set of memories that must be routinized and transmitted. Without the land, and landmarks, to which memory can be affixed, constitutive parts disappear, because they are forgotten. Much like Halbwachs, Bastide was mistaken, however, in viewing religious dislocation and reterritorialization as a zero-sum game in which preservation and forfeit were the only alternatives (Bastide 1978a: 253). The African diasporic religions are massively prolific.

ADDITIVITY

The reproduction of "traditional" religious structures in New York entails infusion and transformation. When the Vodou rite of cooking the yams is telescoped to symbolic yams, the chthonic dimension of performance is reduced, and the problem of social relations—exacerbated in the cityscape by the division of families, both biological and ritual—is accorded greater weight (K. Brown 1999: 89; 1991: 47). In New York, with the detachment of Vodou ritual sites from the actual earth where ancestors are buried, spirit possession by specific family ancestors is infrequent, while possession by the lwa Gede, the generalized spirit of the dead, grows (K. Brown 1991: 368). The "hot" Vodou Petwo deities, meanwhile, known for their fast work, attract greater numbers of devotees in New York than in Haiti, as they better reflect the needs of emigrants (McAlister 1992: 21).[24]

National and racial significations are also brought to the fore. As Haitians in New York make "pilgrimages" to the Church of Our Lady of Mount Carmel, this particular Virgin Mary and her associated lwa, Ezili Danto, become icons of national identity as well as of religious devotion, all the more so because the site, and festal day, must be shared and spatially contested with Italian pilgrims (Orsi 1985, 1992; McAlister 1998: 134).

Religions may also begin to be read against and combined with each other. Spiritual Baptists (or Converted) who have emigrated from St. Vincent are influenced by Trinidadian religious style in Brooklyn and may even adopt the Yoruba orishas in their practice (Zane 1999: 167–69, 175). In the Spanish Harlem barrio, Santería takes on a Puerto Rican style as Santerismo, combined with Espiritismo to reduce the wide range of ochas to "Seven African Powers" (Murphy 1988: 48; Brandon 1993: 107–8).[25] In this condensed form, the power of Africa is available for purchase in an aerosol spray can ("20% Gratis!") from any local botánica. For many New York practitioners of Afro-Cuban religions, the distinct homeland religious lineages of the ochas of Santería, the spirits of dead ancestors *(muertos)* of Palo Monte—an Afro-Cuban tradition with Kongo roots—and the spirit phalanxes of Espiritismo—a possession-based tradition originating in France and North America in the nineteenth century—are combined in ritual practice, remaking the religious grammar through code switching. The same ritual act or object can be discursively framed for different contexts and objectives (David Brown 1999, 2003; Olmos and Paravisini-Gebert 2003). The ochas may be especially invoked in relation to questions of "roots," tradition, and Africanness, compared with the Palo *ngangas* or muertos, often marshaled in support of missions involving money or lust (Palmié 2002). The ancestral spirits are discursively invoked for family concerns, while the discourse of Espiritismo may be viewed as effective in contexts calling for "scientific" debates or ecumenical religious comparisons on topics of evolution, spiritual cleansing, or reincarnation.

Stylistic crossovers in ritual practice are now also common. At one Garifuna ceremony I attended in the Bronx, a woman in possession trance behaved in a manner neither I nor any Garifuna present had ever witnessed. She picked up burning candles to pour hot wax on her chest and shoulders, perhaps to prove her trance or give evidence of the power of the possessing spirit. Because such demonstrations are nonexistent in Garifuna homeland possession trances but do occur in Vodou, she may have learned the new expression at a Haitian rite.

But such code switching between once-distinct religions especially occurs in relation to second-order verbalizations. Among the various groups who view and identify themselves collectively as African Diaspora religious practitioners, and therefore as members of a single supraethnic religious style, it is now common to hear comparisons of the various subreligions and their deities, and crediting them with distinct values. Santería is known for its attention to lineage and its divination specialists *(babalawos);* Vodou for its pageantry and the dramatic "heat" of its possession dances; Palo for its speed and ruthless efficiency; Garifuna religion for its rustic authenticity—the latter based on its vernacular and ceremonial use of an indigenous rather than European language, and the rough-hewn style of its drums and drumming.

What are the processes by which an emigrant group expands this religious superform in the city, joining the African Diaspora and thereby bringing into focus a new historical horizon of self-understanding? What are the consequences for practice in the homeland when it does so? With the conceptual apparatus of this chapter in hand, I examine these questions with respect to the Garifuna. The story begins with the historical formation of the Garifuna as a society with its own religious repertoire, beginning with its ethnogenesis on the isle of St. Vincent (Yurumein), the place that defined the first Garifuna diasporic horizon.

CHAPTER 2

"These Sons of Freedom"

Black Caribs across Three Diasporic Horizons

> The eastern part, which is chiefly in wood, is inhabited by
> about 2000 natives, who owe their origin (truly poetical) to
> a ship freighted with Negroes, from Africa to Barbadoes,
> and wrecked on these coasts. . . . Thus descended, and by
> Providence thus chartered, these Sons of Freedom are armed
> for their defence, and grown tenacious and jealous of their
> liberties.
>
> Sir William Young, *Some Observations*

Garifuna diasporic religion presupposes a distinction from something
else from which it departs, namely Garifuna religion as it developed at
home. But Garifuna homeland religion, too, emerged from a historical
and spatial journey, out of dislocations from Africa to St. Vincent to
Central America to the United States. It was formed across three diasporic horizons and out of the memories of three different homelands
left behind. Only one of these, the Central American Caribbean coast,
is today actually visited by New York Garifuna. The other two, St.
Vincent and Africa, are imagined places, in the sense that few contemporary Garifuna have visited their shores. Nevertheless, they are also
places that strongly influence even contemporary religious practice, and
a grasp of these layered pasts is needed to understand the ritual events
of the present. This chapter revisits the Garifuna passage through each
of these multiple homelands and the reasons for each of these spatial
dislocations.

FIGURE 4. *A Family of Charaibes Drawn from the Life in the Island of St. Vincent.* Engraving from a painting by Agostino Brunias (ca. 1770). *Source:* Edwards 1794.

An Afro-Amerindian "Colonial Tribe"

Black Carib religion provides a stunning example of the religious transculturation and syncretizing events that occurred throughout the Caribbean Basin during the centuries after Columbus's landing.[1] Seventeenth-century French accounts—from the Dominicans Jean-Baptiste du Tertre, Jean-Baptiste Labat, and Raymond Breton to the Protestant Charles de Rochefort and the Jesuit affiliate Sieur de la Borde—described Island Carib rites and beliefs on Dominica, Guadeloupe, and St. Vincent. Often the early reports described the residents as having no religion whatsoever (see, for example, Breton 1992: 110; G. Davidson 1787: 6). Carib religion was consistently read in relation to the religious polemics that divided Europe. La Borde accused them of being "not unlike the Calvinists" for want of priests, altars, or sacrifices (1704: 523), and British colonists in the eighteenth century found the Black Caribs' Catholicism, along with other "French" tastes, abhorrent.

In comparison with the urgency with which Europe devoured Hispaniola, Puerto Rico, Cuba, and Jamaica, many of the small, "lesser" Antilles in the southeast corner of the Caribbean archipelago remained relatively undisturbed until well into the eighteenth century. It was onto one of these islands, St. Vincent, and a world that was still largely the province of the Island Caribs, that Africans were propelled by the Atlantic slave trade. Out of this sudden copresence, an encounter not chosen by either group, a new synthetic ethnicity and religion— what Mary Helms (1969) called a "colonial tribe"—was born.

WHENCE THE AFRICANS?

Enslaved Africans destined for Caribbean labor were abruptly thrown onto the shores and mercy of the Island Caribs of St. Vincent, an island first named, and claimed, by the Spanish, then by the British, but thoroughly ignored by both. The rapprochements by which the Africans survived and, together with the Indians, founded the new ethnicity and religious culture of the Black Caribs remain something of a mystery. The presence of a large number of "negroes" on St. Vincent elicited explanations from various European observers. The British major John Scott ascribed it to two Spanish slavers intended for Barbados that were shipwrecked in 1635 off the coast of St. Vincent (Great Britain Calendar of State Papers 1661–68: 534), an account recapitulated often enough to become the standard account of the origins of the Black Caribs (La Borde 1992 [1674]: 150; W. Young 1764: 7; P. Gibbs 1786: 32–33; G. Davidson 1787: 7; Morris 1787; Edwards 1799: 104; Kerns 1997: 38; Gonzalez 1988: 26; Hulme and Whitehead 1992: 171; Leblond 2000 [1813]; Coelho 1995: 36). Sir William Young, Britain's future governor of Dominica, referred in 1764, and more specifically in papers published posthumously by his son in 1795, to a similar shipwreck of a Portuguese vessel in 1675 (W. Young 1764; 1971 [1795]: 6).

In the paradigmatic shipwreck narrative, surviving Africans were tolerated and assimilated by the Island Caribs for reasons that remain opaque. To be sure, the Africans augmented Carib military forces, which were facing expanding European encroachments. Island Caribs had already been displaced from many neighboring islands, and St. Vincent, along with St. Lucia and Dominica, remained relatively autonomous only as a result of a 1660 concord among European powers to allow it to remain a sort of early "Indian reserve," a compact renewed in the 1748 Treaty of Aix-la-Chapelle (W. Young 1971 [1795]: 3–5;

Conzemius 1928: 187; Gonzalez 1988: 15–16). The small island reserves were regarded as inauspicious for profitable agricultural development because of their rugged, mountainous landscapes and rocky shores, by contrast with their neighbor, "smooth polished Barbados" (W. Young 1764: 26). As a key British slave entrepôt from 1627 until the end of British slave trading in 1808, Barbados enjoyed no such calm.

Though the Island Caribs sometimes acquired large numbers of Africans in one fell swoop—such as the five hundred they captured from a shipwreck near Grenada (Vásquez de Espinosa, quoted in Thornton 1998: 284)—the shipwreck narrative of origins fails to account for the rapid growth of the Black Carib population on St. Vincent. There must have been additional influxes, such as earlier interethnic alliances between Africans and Indians. The historian John Thornton (1998: 272–303) collected descriptions of many Caribbean interactions between Africans and Amerindians. As early as 1546, for example, a letter from the governor of the island of Margarita to the city council of San Juan, Puerto Rico, advised the council to look out for Carib Indians and "blacks who go with them." Another report from Dominica, as early as 1574, noted that Island Caribs were integrating into their society both Spanish and African captives acquired in periodic raiding expeditions (cf. Gonzalez 1988: 26). An Afro–Puerto Rican named Luiza de Navarette, returned to her home island in 1576 after spending four years as a slave to the Caribs, reported the widespread distribution of Africans in Carib villages (in Hulme and Whitehead 1992: 40).

The Island Carib pattern of raiding European colonies and capturing enslaved Africans, already common by the early 1600s, was regarded as a serious problem by European powers. Thornton (1998: 290) notes that one Spanish official, Sancho de Alquiza, "estimated in 1612 that as many as two thousand Africans were in captivity in the Carib islands." In 1658, the Caribs on the island of Grenada accused the French of stealing *their* slaves, even as Jean-Baptiste du Tertre in the 1660s reported precisely the inverse complaint being lodged by the French on Martinique against the Caribs (in Gonzalez 1988: 26). In 1674, La Borde described the situation: "There are a great number of negroes who live with them, particularly on St. Vincent where their stronghold is. They have so multiplied that at present they are as powerful as them [the Caraïbes]. Some of them are fugitive maroons who were taken in war; these are slaves of the Caraïbes, whom they call Tamons; but the greater part came from some Flemish or Spanish ship which was wrecked close to their islands" (1704: 574; English translation Hulme and Whitehead 1992: 150).[2]

As La Borde made clear, the Island Caribs did not treat all Africans as slaves, but only those taken captive in military operations. Africans were at times enlisted as military allies, especially as many of those who found themselves in Carib hands as a result of shipwreck, capture, or marronage had already been seasoned by extensive military experience in Africa. Coastal Africans were likely to have been excellent builders of large canoes, moreover, and useful in the fashioning and manning of Island Carib canoes reported to carry fifty persons or more (La Borde 1704: 571; G. Davidson 1787: 18; Gonzalez 1988: 27). There were surely amorous reproductive exchanges, too. Father Raymond Breton reported from his sojourn on Dominica in the mid-seventeenth century the special terms applied to "les enfants engendrez des Sauvages & des Negresses" (Breton 1968 [1665]: 26; Leblond 2000 [1813]: 109).

The 1635 shipwreck date should therefore not be taken as a fixed moment of Africans' arrival, but rather as one of a series of syncretic events by which Africans came to St. Vincent. The ethnic group that by the second half of the 1700s came to be called the Black Caribs emerged between 1600 and 1796, not only from the notorious shipwrecks but also from Island Carib raids, from maroons fleeing the rising plantation economy on neighboring islands, and by intermarriage with Island Caribs on St. Vincent.[3]

But what about more-specific African origins? The sole specific reference to the African ethnicity of the Black Caribs that I have encountered is Sir William Young's report that the Africans shipwrecked in 1675 were "of a warlike Moco tribe," en route from the Bight of Benin to Barbados (W. Young 1971 [1795]: 6). This group is often identified with the ethnic group Efik of the Cross River delta and the slaving port of Old Calabar (in the Bight of Biafra, not the Bight of Benin). Yet Young's report provides at best a very small piece of the puzzle. Terms like *Karabali, Efik, Igbo,* and *Moko* often served as terminal-point ethnonyms for any number of interior groups joined under a single name at a port of embarkation (Kolapo 2004).

Moreover, the 1675 shipwreck is but one moment of a protracted ethnogenesis. Given the general demographic trends of the slave trade, the Spanish ships lost in 1635 would likely have carried cargo from Angola (Curtin 1969; Lovejoy 1983; Klein 1999). And these groups were augmented by Africans of other ethnic groups and languages arriving from nearby islands, especially Barbados, named as the primary source of runaway immigrants by the Dominican missionary Jean-Baptiste Labat, who lived on Dominica at the end of the seventeenth century:

Besides the savages, this island is also inhabited by a very great number of fugitive negroes, for the most part from Barbados, which, being to windward of Saint Vincent, gives the runaways every possible facility for escaping from their masters' plantations in boats or on piperis or rafts, and taking refuge among the savages. The Caribs formerly brought them back to their masters, when they were at peace with them, or took and sold them to the French or to the Spaniards. I don't know for what reason they have changed their method, nor what has induced them to receive these negroes amongst themselves and to regard them as belonging to one and the same nation. They regret it now very much and very unavailingly, for the number of negroes has increased to such an extent, either by those born in the country or by those come from Barbados to join them, that it much surpasses that of the Caribs, so that the negroes have forced them to share the island and to relinquish the windward side to them. But it is not even that which mortifies the savages most, but the frequent kidnapping of their wives and daughters, whom the negroes seize whenever they want. (Labat, quoted in Taylor 1951: 22; cf. Edwards 1799: 104)

Barbados was also identified as the main source of runaways by other colonial observers (including Commissariat Officer Roberts, in Hulme and Whitehead 1992: 173). Roberts cites the sympathetic ocean currents, but surely an equally important reason was that in the seventeenth century Barbados was the primary point for the redistribution of slaves through the Lesser Antilles. First practiced by the Dutch (until 1663) and then by the British, the trade in slaves was constant on Barbados. Many of these slaves were taken from the Gold Coast region of Africa, or from the area roughly comprising today's Ghana, so that the Asante, Ewe, Fon, and Fante peoples would have provided a large number of enslaved Africans after 1700. But, as the label *Moco* suggests, the Bight of Biafra also provided slaves for Barbados. In that region, slaves were captured from among the Yoruba, Efik, Igbo, and Ibibio peoples.[4] Between 1627 and 1807, almost four hundred thousand Africans were deported to Barbados, more than to any other destination in the English Caribbean, and Barbados became an early tinderbox of rebellions and desertion (Craton 1986; Bianchi 1988: 93). From Barbados, St. Vincent was on some days visible with the naked eye. It must have seemed close enough to reach out and touch its verdant peaks and to imagine a very different life there. The reputation of St. Vincent as a free island and destination for maroons grew in the 1700s, attracting new arrivals. As it did so, any specific anchors of ethnic African identity were complicated by a radical pluralism of cultures. The Africans adopted, and were adopted by, the Island Carib tongue and religion.

The Black Carib group identity was forged relatively quickly through the shared resistance to slavery. Though never laboring as slaves, they lived under the continual threat of enslavement and very much within the expanding sugar-plantation system.[5] Later in the eighteenth century, after living near the Black Caribs for two years, the British colonist George Davidson observed that they continued the Island Carib practice of flattening their infants' foreheads because they "perceived the necessity of a discrimination founded on more obvious marks than that of complexion" (1787: 10; W. Young 1971 [1795]: 8; cf. du Tertre 1992: 129). The young French doctor Jean-Baptiste Leblond observed the same around 1767 (2000 [1813]: 80, 110, 136).The reason they needed such "discrimination" was that they were at risk of being confused with runaway slaves, whom they often encouraged and provided with arms (Morris 1787).

The new ethnic group was a "colonial tribe," then, not only because it emerged in the 1600s Caribbean contact zone but also because it was born of the resistance to European colonization. In 1667, six hundred "African bowmen" were observed by the English governor William Stapleton alongside nine hundred Carib warriors (Bianchi 1988: 91; Kerns 1997: 17; Thornton 1998: 288). That the first recorded alliance joining Africans and Island Caribs was marshaled in resistance to European encroachment is not incidental.

YELLOW CARIB VERSUS BLACK CARIB TENSIONS

Despite the alliances that were formed, it would be a mistake to view the transculturation between Island Caribs and Africans as an always harmonious one. Initially the Africans were captives and servants of the Island Caribs. Armand de la Paix's *Relation* from 1646 reported that "some Negroes of St. Vincent of the isles, being in Saint Lucia, massacred some French people from Martinique by the order of their Carib master" (quoted in Taylor 1949: 382), implying that the Africans were at least initially perceived to be ruled by Island Caribs. Yet La Borde observed in 1674 that the Black Caribs were already as powerful as the Island Caribs (1704: 574), and in 1700 the governor of Martinique, who then held jurisdiction over St. Vincent, divided the island in two: the western "Red Carib" zone and the eastern "Black Carib" domain. By the 1720s, they were even reported to be masters of the island. The British Captain Braithwaite described being met by five hundred Black Caribs as he put ashore on St. Vincent, all of them armed and organized with martial discipline. After entertaining some of them on board his ship, he dignified them with the standard honorary cannon discharge "and received, in return, as regular vollies of small shot as I ever heard" (Uring 1726: 109). By the early eighteenth century the Black Caribs were already a semiautonomous, well-formed social and military organization. In reply to Braithwaite's attempts at negotiations, they said that "notwithstanding our specious Pretences, when had Power, we should inslave 'em; but declared, they would trust no Europeans" (Uring 1726: 109).[6]

A detailed letter dated September 3, 1705, written by Monsieur de Beaumont, a companion to the Dominican missionary Raymond Breton, suggests the spatial separation and the tensions that had already divided the Island Caribs from the Black Caribs. Beaumont interviewed a group of Carib Indians who passed his ship in pirogues en route to the windward (eastern), Black Carib side of the island to carry out a revenge killing. The Indians indicated their openness to European military aid against the Black Caribs, a prospect that left Beaumont salivating in his report: "That would be a good catch. It is claimed that there are about 3,000 negroes, all strong, fit to send to the Spanish mines. There is a war between them which can only be ended by a specific campaign, since it is based on the fact that these negroes kidnap the women of the savages, who are very jealous and never forgive" (Beaumont 1992 [1705]: 176). The spatial separation and rivalry between the two communities was suggested also in Braithwaite's report a few decades later of parleys with distinct chiefs, an "Indian Chief" and a "Chief of the Negroes" (Uring 1726: 108–10).

As depicted in British narratives, the Island Caribs were soon overshadowed and even eclipsed by the Black Caribs. In the official correspondence of Valentine Morris, the British governor in chief of St. Vincent in the late 1770s, for example, the "Charibs" he referred to were solely the Black Caribs, who caused him much trouble, dressing in "French colours" and inciting runaway Negroes to quit their masters (Morris 1787: 12, 16, 123, 126).[7] The shifting nomenclature, wherein "Carib" was often now applied to those of African descent, reflects the fact that the Island Caribs were by this point severely diminished as a group of political consequence in British eyes. Many of the "Yellow Caribs" had fled to the islands of Tobago and Trinidad, and those remaining had been driven to the leeward (west) side (G. Davidson 1787: 8; Leblond 2000 [1813]: 110). Many succumbed to the smallpox borne by Europeans, to which they had little immunity or resistance (Breton 1992: 110).[8]

FIGURE 5. *Chatoyer the Chief of the Black Charaibes in St. Vincent with His Five Wives.* Engraving from a painting by Agostino Brunias (ca. 1770). *Source:* Edwards 1801.

We must exercise caution here, however. As Peter Hulme proposes, the master narrative depicting St. Vincent as being wholly under the control of the troublesome Black Caribs, a distinctly African rather than Amerindian group, served Great Britain's colonial interests: "This Africanisation [of the Black Caribs] had a number of advantages for the planters. It emphasised the Black Carib role as usurpers. It helped avoid a repetition of the groundswell of British liberal opinion in defence of the indigenous Caribs during the war of the 1770s—which had forced the British to sue for peace. And it drew upon the traditional association of blackness with savagery and evil, exacerbated by the success of slave revolts in the Caribbean and, of course, especially in St.-Domingue after 1791" (2000b: section 2). Further evidence for this allegation can be found in the report of Jean-Baptiste Leblond, writing during the period of the first military clashes between Great Britain and the Black Caribs, from 1772 to 1773. He overhead colonists declaring that negotiating with the Caribs (instead of taking land by force) was unjust, "because the Black Caribs, far from being the indigenes of the land, were originally from Africa" (2000: 153, translation mine). Africanizing the Black Caribs by stressing their utter separation from the "Yellow" or "Red" Caribs had strategic value for British colonists: it rendered their own land appropriations equal in legal and ethical status to the Black Caribs' previous settling of St. Vincent. "Black," then, was as much a political classifier of groups especially resistant to colonial settlement on St. Vincent as it was a description of the Black Caribs' actual skin color, which must have varied widely among individuals.[9]

ETHNOGENETIC THRESHOLD

In 1763 St. Vincent was returned to British colonial jurisdiction under the Treaty of Paris, which ended the Seven Years' War between Great Britain and France, though the Caribs recognized no colonial authority. By this point, trade with Europeans dominated the Carib economy. A money economy had begun to take shape, as Black Caribs transported sugar to English ships anchored off St. Vincent's rocky coast, and stable communities were supported by trade not only in domestic animals like pigs and cattle but also in cash crops like tobacco and cotton. The director of St. Vincent's botanical gardens, Alexander Anderson, writing in the late 1790s, recounted that the Black Caribs conducted their business on a wide scale, transporting goods from Martinique to Trinidad in their great canoes. They had become players in the global market; Black Carib tobacco harvests were refined on Martinique as the "well-known Macuba snuff" for European consumers (A. Anderson 1992: 217; G. Davidson 1787: 18).[10] Meanwhile, the Black Carib named Du Vallée, like his brother, the famous chief Chatoyer, oversaw a small cotton plantation purchased with loans from "English gentlemen" on which he directed the labor of nine slaves (W. Young 1971 [1795]: 106–7; 1992: 203, 212; cf. Leblond 2000 [1813]: 111).

Around 1763, the island contained seven to eight hundred whites, two hundred free persons of color, three thousand slaves, and perhaps four thousand Black and Red Caribs (Leblond 2000 [1813]: 111; W. Young 1971 [1795]: 18). The economically savvy Black Caribs remained vehemently anticolonial but were now pragmatically so. They drew subtle distinctions between the European powers. French settlers, showing themselves relatively amenable to Black Carib territorial claims, were more tolerated than British ones. When French soldiers occupied the island from 1778 to 1783, while Great Britain was embroiled in the United States' War of Independence, they did so with the aid and assent of the Black Caribs. This cooperation had serious consequences. When France ceded the island to British control after 1783, this time for good, the Black Caribs were seen as suspiciously "French." After all, their names were mostly French; they spoke French along with Carib, preferred red wine to rum, and were completely unmoved by the zeal of English Protestant missionaries. The British authorities had feared as much: their treaty with the Caribs from 1773 had stressed, in article 7, "No undue intercourse with the French islands to be allowed" (W. Young 1971 [1975]: 92).

Black Carib Religion in the Eighteenth Century

We know little about what the Black Caribs' emergence as a distinct ethnic group meant for the practice of religion until well into the nineteenth century. We must, therefore, triangulate between seventeenth-century descriptions and nineteenth- and twentieth-century assessments to try to reconstruct a profile of early Black Carib religion. One could, of course, hazard a guess that St. Vincent religion comprised aspects associated with specific culture regions, like the "African" use of drums to induce possession trance by ancestors, the "Carib" practice of a shaman's blowing smoke on a patient's afflicted body to extract malevolent penetrations, and "Catholic" baptisms and images of saints. But such attempted religious morphologies remain speculative at best. The ability to discern the origins of distinct religious elements is long forfeit, and the move by contemporary scholars or Garifuna to plot that religious history as specifically Island Carib, Yoruba, or Bakongo must be viewed as in large part a contemporary effort to call up a religious genealogy from its absence. And yet we must begin tracing the sources of contemporary Garifuna religion somewhere, sometime.

THE ISLAND CARIB TRIBUTARY

St. Vincent had its own spirit geography for the Black Caribs: the Black Forest at the foot of the volcano had its spirits, as did the lake and the

Cavern of Death (Moreau de Jonnès 1920: 121). Those spirits of unique sites remained on St. Vincent when the Black Caribs were removed from the island. Yet the influence of this Island Carib culture on contemporary Garifuna material culture is everywhere, from the dependence on cassava bread as a staple food to the ubiquitous presence of hammocks; both are central to ritual performance. Many aspects of this legacy remain relevant for understanding Garifuna homeland religion today.

Ceremonies for the divination of illness and offering food to spirits were led by religious leaders known as *piaye* or *boyé*. Raymond Breton called these priest-doctors *boiyako* (1992: 113). These officials, now called buyeis, were shamans in the classic sense of that term (see Eliade 1964): Undergoing an initiation through a long period of seclusion, they learned to use tobacco and gourd rattles to achieve trances, and they traveled "on high" with the aid of their tutelary spirits to seek out and control malignant or neglected spirits who had caused illness. The buyeis mediated between the spirits and the living patient and onlookers, speaking in different voices to represent the spirits for the patient and other audience members; they "sucked" the illness from the afflicted body in the form of a small bone or piece of wood and appeased malignant spirits with food offerings (La Borde 1704: 539–44). The Black Caribs adopted this religious office and techniques from their St. Vincent hosts, the Island Caribs. De la Borde offered the best description of ritual on St. Vincent, which is notable because of his simultaneous observation of the presence there of "a large number of Negroes" living like the Island Caribs (574). His description thus offers a temporal reference point for the transculturation of Island Carib into Black Carib religion. He observed: "They sometimes put the hair or bones of their dead relatives in a calabash . . . and say that the spirit of the dead speaks within it, warning them of the plans of their enemies" (546, translation mine). This ritual practice suggests either the borrowing of West African religious practices, making the exchange a two-way street, or at the very least an Island Carib ritual grammar whose structure would have been strikingly familiar to the Africans.

Garifuna religion continues to rely on the leadership of such shamans. These buyeis orchestrate and direct sophisticated ritual performances that satisfy hungry ancestral spirits *(gubida)* with the influence of the helping spirits *(hiyuruha)*.[11] Contemporary buyeis use tobacco in trance and prepare tables generously laden with cassava bread and cassava beer to feed the spirits, as their Carib progenitors did.

AFRICAN TRIBUTARIES

The most elaborate ritual performances of contemporary homeland Garifuna religion, called *dügü,* use three drums to guide dances that culminate in spirit possession by returning ancestors. The ancestors are feted when, on possessing the bodies of their living descendants, they dance, consort, and consult with the living. The drummers' use of polyrhythmic meter for dances like the *punta,* once a funerary dance, and the *junkunnu,* a mask dance, punctuate and offset the use of monorhythms like the *amalihani.* Nowhere are such collective possession dances mentioned in descriptions of Island Carib religion (Gonzalez 1988: 29). The patterns do, however, recall West and West-Central African ritual music and dance.

Consider, for example, the report of Captain Nathaniel Uring from his 1701 visit to the port of Loango, Angola, before he sailed to St. Vincent. While in Loango, Uring by chance heard drums and, his curiosity quickened, sought their source. He found the drums in use in what he took to be a healing ritual. A sick woman lay on the ground surrounded by six to eight women singing to the rhythm of rattles they held in their hands and a man drumming on a hollow tree trunk covered with skin (1726: 43). Uring, like many before and after him, discerned "no religion" among these people, as their efforts appeared to be directed to the spirits of ancestors: "I could not perceive that they had any Religion among them: They have no Temples or Houses of Worship; nor did they pay Adoration to Any Thing that I could learn, tho' they built Hutts over the Graves of some particular Persons of Distinction among 'em; and in those Hutts I saw several Utensils, such as they make use of in Eating and Drinking. . . . I was informed that it was customary for the Relations of the Dead to carry victuals, and leave it in those Hutts in the Night in order to entertain their deceased Friends" (46). Parts of the ritual performed in Angola at roughly the time of Africans' arrival on St. Vincent resemble de la Borde's description of Island Carib practices a quarter century earlier, notably the preparation of foods left for the ancestral spirits.

Contemporary Garifuna rituals, like those of the Island Carib shamans, engage helping spirits to combat afflicting spirits, and all of these spirits are regarded as ancestors. It is tempting, if perhaps too convenient, to imagine today's rites as a confluence of African and Island Carib tributaries dating from the late seventeenth century. Yet this must remain a hypothesis in the face of the vague data available on

Black Carib religion in the eighteenth century. Davidson, for example, reported that the Black Caribs "have some faint ideas of a Supreme Cause which created all things, but they conceive that God commits the government of the world to subordinate Spirits. They make use of several incantations against Evil Spirits, to prevent their malignant influence" (G. Davidson 1787: 9–10). But the precise nature of those "subordinate spirits" can be only guessed at on the basis of triangulation with earlier views like La Borde's and later observations from Central America.

ROMAN CATHOLIC INFLUENCE

Catholicism also played a role in the formative stages of Garifuna religion. Today, all traditional Garifuna religious actors consider themselves to be Catholic, and Catholicism provides the overall mythic structure within which the ancestor religion is maintained. This influence certainly owes something to the visits of French missionaries. But it is also possible that some of the Africans who settled on St. Vincent were from the kingdom of Kongo that had converted in the fifteenth century, and that they therefore arrived on St. Vincent already Christians (Bianchi 1988: 98; Thornton 1998).

Catholicism provides the theological framework for much of contemporary Garifuna religion. Malignant *(mafia)* spirits, for example, typically associated with "the forest" *(el monte)*, are considered manifestations of the devil, while positive spirits are regarded as agents of God (Bungiu). Postmortem rites begin with "masses" *(lemesi)* adapted from official Roman Catholic liturgy and continue with *novenas* (ninth-night masses) and anniversary masses to remember and appease the dead. Catholic saints are prominent on Garifuna altars, and specific saints like Esquipula and San António are called on as ever-present sources of assistance.[12]

The Black Caribs of eighteenth-century St. Vincent were not fixedly Catholic or devoted to its orthodoxy, but it was within this nominal religious affiliation that their distinctive Afro-Amerindian beliefs and practices developed. Catholicism in Black Carib religion on St. Vincent was selective: some elements were elevated and given value, while other aspects were easily left aside or forgotten. Among the Black Caribs in Central America, for example, baptism was popular during the nineteenth century, while marriage was practically ignored, suggesting that syncretizing involves critical practice. Such selective appropriations motivated Davidson to complain about the lack of concern of French Catholic priests with any thorough religious instruction (1787: 9), leaving the Black Caribs, in his view, as yet in need of such religion as could make them "human beings" at all (6, 20). The British effort was a more activist one, and a Methodist mission was under way even as Davidson wrote. Yet the British Protestants made no headway, not least because the Black Caribs' allegiances already lay firmly with French republicans and French Catholics. The Methodist missionary to the "Black Caribb Division," a Mr. Baxter, registered his frustration on February 25, 1790: "The Black Caribbs still remain civil and kind, but will hear nothing of religion" (Coke 1790: 13).

In view of the Black Caribs' formation as a colonial tribe, the fact of the resistance to Protestants, and of Catholicism's influence, is not surprising. Catholic priests were essential players in the process of Black Carib ethnogenesis. In 1763, when the British took control of St. Vincent from France under the Treaty of Paris, the Black Caribs appointed as their political emissary the French priest they trusted more than any other European, Abbé Valladares (W. Young 1971 [1795]: 21; Kerns 1997: 31). And when the Black Caribs allied themselves with France against Great Britain during the same period, their relationships with the French priests helped fortify the alliance. William Young, not surprisingly, viewed this relationship in cynical terms, as French political strategy "under covert of religion," and "vamped up" as spiritual cosanguinity established through the institution of godparenthood (W. Young 1971 [1795]: 17–18). But the Black Caribs seem not to have perceived the French priests' efforts as merely instrumental. By the end of the eighteenth century, Black Caribs greeted Europeans with "Quelles nouvelles de la France? Quelles nouvelles de l'Anglaterre?" as William Young II was asked on Christmas Day 1791 (W. Young II 1992: 211). Though, by the time of their deportation in 1797, only about 10 percent of the Black Caribs were baptized (Gonzalez 1988: 82, 96), in their nineteenth-century Central American homeland, virtually all would become at least nominally Catholic.

The Deportation of the "French" Black Caribs

While both British and French colonists engaged in mutually profitable trade with the Black Caribs, only the British pressed for land concessions (G. Davidson 1787: 8). Only the British made plans to build roads and schools through Black Carib territory and sought to convert them not only religiously, but also culturally and materially.[13] "They live . . . without any established subordination, claiming large tracts of woodland intervening, of which they make no use," lamented the British commissioners of St. Vincent (W. Young 1971 [1975]: 27). The Black Caribs did not mark out plots of private property, plow the land into tillable acreage for sugar production, or otherwise maximize its profitability—at least not from the British perspective. Plans for the removal of the Black Caribs were aired as early as 1765, gained force following the Black Caribs' aid given to France during the French occupation of 1778–83, arose again when France declared war against Great Britain in 1793, and finally came to fruition in 1797.

The Black Caribs were bound closely to francophone networks long before news came of the French Revolution. Beginning after 1763, they frequently landed arms and supplies in St. Vincent after canoe journeys to Martinique, and at least one of their leaders referred to himself as "Monsieur le Général" (Morris 1787: 20; Leblond 2000 [1813]: 111). But this bond grew tighter as republican proclamations of "Liberté, egalité, fraternité" seemed to felicitously unite the Black Caribs' own desires with those of French "democratical whites" (Edwards 1819: 3) to be rid once and for all of British threats to their lands and rights. The Black Caribs likely perceived the percolating "French ideas" in local terms, as a rallying cry against British colonial power on St. Vincent and its neighbors, and began to maintain a state of constant preparedness for battle, the men always armed with both cutlasses and loaded muskets (G. Davidson 1787: 18).

On March 10, 1795, the Black Caribs, together with French settlers, erupted in insurrection against the British. When their chief, Chatoyer, was killed on March 14, in his pocket was allegedly discovered the following proclamation, as reported by William Young II:

Where is the Frenchman who will not join his brothers, at a moment when the voice of liberty is heard by them? Let us then unite, citizens and brothers, round the colours flying in this island; and let us hasten to co-operate to that great piece of work which has been already commenced so gloriously. But should any timorous men still exist, should any Frenchman be held back through fear, we do hereby declare to them, in the name of the law, that those who will not be assembled with us in the course of the day, shall be deemed traitors to the country, and treated as enemies. We do swear that both fire and sword shall be employed against them, that we are going to burn their estates, and that we will murder their wives and children, in order to annihilate their race. (1992: 206)

Though it is possible that the declaration in Chatoyer's pocket was a fabrication that retroactively justified the British deportation of the Black Caribs, the role of "French ideas" in the so-called Carib wars cannot be seriously doubted. The French mulatto revolutionary leader Victor Hugues, commissioned by the National Convention in Paris, gave direct aid to the Black Caribs from Santa Lucia and Martinique; and Alexander Anderson's account suggests that Hugues himself appointed a new military leader of the Black Caribs after the death of Chatoyer (A. Alexander 1992: 225). The proclamation, whether legitimate or not, suggests that the Black Carib war of 1795–96 should be seen in the broadest context, with roots dating at least to the Seven Years' War and decades of contest between France and Great Britain, and the shifting indigenous allies of each. This was a long-simmering global conflict fought in Europe, North America, and the Caribbean. It should be seen in light of the French Revolution and its ideals, the Haitian Revolution that began in 1791 and ended in 1804 with the transformation of Saint Domingue into a black and independent Haiti, and the very real threat to the colonists of slave emancipation not only on Guadeloupe, where Hugues indeed abolished slavery, but on Santa Lucia, Dominica, Martinique and possibly even Barbados, "little Britain" itself.[14]

A Black Carib and French victory on St. Vincent was in fact quite plausible. By the 1790s, St. Vincent already had more than sixty British sugar estates, worked by thousands of enslaved Africans (Gonzalez 1988: 17). Hugues and the Black Caribs hoped that these slaves would join the battle against their masters. As the British chronicler Bryan Edwards wrote, "Had the insurgents been joined by the negroes, all would, doubtless, have been lost. But it fortunately happened that between the slaves and the Charaibes there existed a deadly animosity, which prevented any junction; the former considering the latter as their enemies, because they were rivals in the sale of the produce of their gardens" (1818–19: 15).

Anderson explained the missed opportunity slightly differently, as a question of sheer jealousy: "The negroes bore them (the Black Caribs) a great antipathy. This no doubt originated from jealousy. The poor slaves, knowing them to be of the same extraction with themselves, yet being free and enjoying more liberty than the lower class of white men, going as gentlemen while they were laboring hard with sweat of their bodies. There was something natural to this dislike and was human nature only" (1992: 229). Still, even without the aid of the slaves of the British, the insurrection was by all accounts ferocious. The Black Caribs and their local French allies were supported by periodic reinforcements from Guadeloupe, St. Lucia, and Martinique during nine months of guerilla combat. But with the early death of Chatoyer, and confronted by seemingly endless British regiments with no major support from France forthcoming, the Black Caribs were overwhelmed.

By October 26, 1796, 5,080 Black Carib captives had surrendered, and most (4,195) were transported to the tiny nearby island of Baliceaux (Gonzalez 1988: 35).[15] There, half died from disease and lack of shelter.[16] The remainder, fewer than two thousand, were again herded into the holds of a British convoy chaperoned by the warship *Experiment*. After a short journey that included brief stops at Bequia, Grenada, and Jamaica, on April 11, 1797, they were deposited on Roatán, just off the coast of Spanish Honduras and the city of Trujillo (see figure 1, in the introduction).

Despite this abrupt and violent removal of the Black Caribs from their homeland of St. Vincent, the last decades of the eighteenth century are recalled in contemporary Garifuna oral histories as a golden age, a paradise lost (Coelho 1995: 42). They were prosperous, autonomous, proud, and beginning to face the Caribbean plantation economy on their own terms. Chatoyer is recalled today as the greatest Black Carib hero and in a sense the progenitor of all contemporary Garifuna.[17] With his demise, they were exiled from their homeland and forced to settle a new terrain. Yet the transition was not entirely a loss. In the move to Central America, St. Vincent (known as Yurumein in Garifuna) was reborn in memory, now as a sacred place and diasporic horizon.

Second Diasporic Horizon: The Black Caribs in Central America

Within a few months of their landing at Roatán, a single day's sail from Trujillo, the Black Caribs were visited by Spanish officials. By May 1797 their existence was already precarious, contrary to Edwards's giddy report to English readers that the deportees had been left in "a situation remarkably healthy, with excellent water and a fertile soil" (1818–19: 74). The British had indeed left some provisions, but many of the foodstuffs proved spoiled and unusable. One report suggested that the ship containing their resources was even allowed to sink at anchor, as the Black Caribs were so utterly "grieved at their banishment" from St. Vincent (Roberts 1827: 273). The situation was in any case dire, and the refugees were saved by being transported off the island. Surely their reputation as fierce fighters against the British in the Carib Wars of 1795–96 preceded them. They proved deserving of it not long after their arrival when, on May 14, 1799, one hundred Black Carib soldiers helped defend Trujillo against two British warships (Gonzalez 1988: 54).

A NEW TRANSCULTURATION

The Black Caribs arrived in a Central American mainland context of multiple African-descended, Amerindian, and mixed ethnic groups. As French speakers, their reception at Trujillo was facilitated by the presence of two to three hundred French-speaking exiles from Haiti and Guadeloupe (T. Young 1847: 140; Crawford 1984: 3; W. Davidson 1984a: 16; Gonzalez 1984: 53, 1988: 53), possibly including the Haitian revolutionary military leaders Jean-François and Biassou (Bianchi 1988: 104). There was also a black community of Kongolese origin in the vicinity of Trujillo as early as 1774: these were "Mondongo Negroes" who had fled from the Honduran interior, where slaves were used in gold and silver mines (Cavero, in Bianchi 1988: 106).[18] To the east of Trujillo were the Miskito Indians and the Afro-Indian "Sambos" (Miskito Africans) whose story of origin—of African survivors of wrecked slave ships being received and incorporated by Amerindians—echoed the Black Carib story on St. Vincent.[19] To the northwest, in and around the city of Belize in British Honduras, meanwhile, were Africans from Jamaica and other islands of the British colonial world. And there was also a quarter in Belize called "Eboe-town," named for the West African Igbo speakers who lived there (Gibbs 1883: 79). The presence of these communities points to a possible further process of transculturation for the Black Caribs on the Central American mainland.

In part as a result of the pressure for land created by the sudden influx into Trujillo, many Black Caribs pressed on to found other villages, especially in Mosquitia to the east, where they lived in close proximity with the Miskito (T. Young 1847: 130; Crawford 1984). Though the Black Caribs were considered to be rigorously endogamous in their reproductive patterns, including in their own ideal self-representations (Roberts 1827: 274; Froebel 1859: 184; Sanborn 1886; Conzemius 1928: 183; Gonzalez 1969: 27; Kerns 1984: 112), it seems likely that some interethnic sexual matches occurred, especially as men were typically away from their home villages much of the time. The new settlers soon lived too near for the Miskitos' taste, as the latter were displaced to settlements further east (Bard 1965: 316). Nevertheless, during the visit of the traveler Orlando Roberts to the Miskito king in the 1820s, two "Kharibee" also arrived to pay the king a visit, and Roberts observed that these men were "great favorites" of the Miskito leader (1827: 159–60).[20] This account is consistent with the record left by Thomas Young, a representative of the British Central American Land Company, which attests to Caribs, Miskito, and Creoles all being present at evening entertainments of drumming and dancing (1847: 32). Oral histories of 1960s Garifuna, meanwhile, report earlier generations' having intermarried in significant numbers with non-Carib blacks (Gonzalez 1969: 26).

The new process of transculturation in Central America may help to account for the surprising growth of the Black Carib population noted by outside observers (Roberts 1827: 154, 274). They were immediately the largest group on arrival in Trujillo, numbering at least 1,500, compared to an estimated total of 1,000 Spaniards, Ladinos, and French Creoles (T. Young 1847: 140). And that number grew at such a pace that the 1801 government census estimated 4,000 Garifuna in Trujillo, compared with 2,980 Spaniards, 300 English-speaking blacks, and 200 French-speaking blacks (Bianchi 1988: 104; cf. Gonzalez 1988: 53).

WORK AND THE TRANSNATION

The full range of the Carib dispersal across four hundred miles of coastline, from Stann Creek in Belize to the Black River in Mosquitia, was mostly accomplished by 1836 (W. Davidson 1984a: 15), though many sites within that span, especially those in western Honduras, seem to have been settled only during the second half of the nineteenth century and the rise of the banana trade (Gonzalez 1969; 1988).[21] Almost all of the nearly sixty villages between Belize and Mosquitia lie directly on the Caribbean coast. The new settlements were selected for their closeness to the beach, with its promise of fishing and trade, as well as for their access to fresh water. Horticulture was important if the new villages were to produce staple foods like cassava and plantains. Yet even at the outset it appears that village sites were also selected for their proximity to opportunities for wage labor: soldiering, mahogany cutting, agricultural work, and trading in markets (Cheek and Gonzalez 1986).

Travel was by canoe, dory, or pirogue, the last term referring to larger vessels with paneled sides that could carry both passengers and cargo. The Mississippian Charles Swett reported the size of one such vessel as thirty-six feet long by seven feet across, and "elegantly made" (Swett 1868: 27).[22] Such a vessel could carry several dozen passengers or several tons of goods and was apparently similar in its proportions to the famous Island Carib sea canoes. Black Carib males, especially, were incessant travelers in these vessels, laboring far from their home villages for months on end. This practice recapitulated the St. Vincent pattern, though the particular trajectory of these sojourns was new: the trade routes between Trujillo or Omoa in Spanish Honduras and Belize in British Honduras.

The best nineteenth-century description of Carib life in the new Central American homeland is Thomas Young's report of his reconnaissance of Trujillo and the Mosquito Coast in 1839–41. It depicts the men hiring themselves out as mahogany cutters for long periods before returning home "laden with useful articles, and invariably well dressed" (1847: 124). Young's near contemporary, the North American Samuel Bard (1965: 321), wrote that the men returned as "dandies" showing "fantastic taste"; they even pretended to have forgotten their own language and to speak only English, to show off their worldliness. These Caribbean rakes presaged the present-day phenomenon of the New York dandies' spectacular homeland returns.

Every nineteenth-century report of the Black Caribs corroborates their importance in the mahogany trade and the pattern of the men being absent on cutting crews for up to eight months at a time (Roberts 1827: 274; A. Gibbs 1883: 168; Bard 1965: 320; Froebel 1859: 184). But the timber trade also caused a striking scarcity of men in Carib villages (Stephens 1949 [1841]: 20). Douglas Taylor, doing fieldwork exactly a century later (1947–48), found the same phenomenon, with the caveat that now half the women traveled for work as well as nearly all the men (1951: 55).

Black Caribs labored in other occupations in the new territory, too. Women grew crops—rice, cassava, sugarcane, cotton, plantain, squash, oranges, and mangoes—and sold "Carib bread" (cassava bread) along with fish, mollusks, iguana meat, cassava, yams, plantains, and coconut, both in town markets around Omoa and Belize and for distant trade (Roberts 1827: 272; Bard 1965: 317; Froebel 1859: 185). They raised hogs, ducks, and turkeys both for sale and for local consumption. So productive were the Caribs that the German traveler Julius Froebel credited them with supplying much of the food available in the port town of Omoa: their canoes could be counted on to arrive every morning not only with food to bring to market but also with trade goods from the better-equipped British Belize, the one port through which all ships coming to the Bay of Honduras passed (1859: 164, 185). The new settlers on the Central American coast thus became indispensable both as skilled laborers and as suppliers.[23]

THE TRANS-STATAL BLACK CARIB

Soldiering was a major cause of the Black Caribs' dispersion from Trujillo during the first several decades after the deportation. In the territory surrounding the relatively autonomous Black Carib villages, Honduras stumbled toward becoming an independent state. Its steps included initial independence from Spain (1821), annexation to Mexico in 1822, the renewed revolt of 1823, and the subsequent formation of the Central American Federation (República Federal de Centroamérica [1824–38]), whose constitution notably included the emancipation of slaves. Far from remaining isolated in remote villages, Black Caribs fought on all sides. One leader, Walumugu (also called Juan Bulnes), is remembered as a near-mythic hero, having fought for the federation. Renowned for his immunity to being killed by mere humans, he is described in oral histories as having six digits on each hand and foot. Despite such exceptional cases, the Caribs appear to have typically taken the part of the Spanish royalist cause against the liberal federalist reformers.[24]

In 1829 the "liberal" Honduran leader Francisco Morazán overthrew Manuel José Arce to become president of the fledgling federation in 1830. Morazán advocated widespread reforms, including diminishing the Catholic Church's control over education, banishing monastic orders, encouraging religious freedom, abolishing the required tithes *(diezmo)* that supported the church, and opening Central America to international markets through an interoceanic canal (Becerra 1983: 110). But the Black Caribs, mobile citizens of their own trans-statal network, were unconcerned with macropolitical issues of state formation. Why then did they fight for the conservative, royalist movement? Nancie Gonzalez (1988: 57) has suggested that one possible reason was religion, especially after special missionaries were sent to Trujillo to attend to their communities in 1813. Because the emissaries of the church were largely conservative in their political sympathies, they may have influenced the group's actions. That religion was central in the conflict is revealed in counterrevolutionary slogans from 1834: "¡Viva la religión!" and "¡Mueran los herejes!" (Death to the heretics!) (Becerra 1983: 107).

Yet there are other possible explanations for the Black Carib alliance with conservatives. The liberals' nation-building project was also one of *ladinización,* the convergence of distinct ethnicities into a single national race (Barahona 1991: 278). The conservative loyalist vision of maintaining ethnic and racial differences (and hierarchies) may have held greater appeal, at least rhetorically, for the independent and autonomous group.

A key cause of the Black Caribs' dispersion out of the Trujillo region and into Belize was the 1832 loyalist insurrection that aimed to overthrow Morazán and reinstate the more conservative former president, Manuel José Arce. After its failure, the Black Caribs fled possible reprisals from Spain by hiding under Great Britain's wing, either deep in British-patrolled Miskito lands to the east or in British Honduras and the villages around Belize to the west. This exodus benefited villages like Stann Creek (Dangriga) and Punta Gorda, whose settlements grew enormously just after the failed insurrection (Stephens 1949 [1841]: 19; Taylor 1951: 27; W. Davidson 1984a: 18; Coelho 1995: 47).

Honduras could not afford to simply lose Carib manpower, and by 1836 a declared amnesty permitted their return to Trujillo. Many stopped en route, however, and settled in villages in western Honduras. These new settlements were often within trading distance of emergent towns like Puerto Cortes, Tela, and La Ceiba, all of which later became busy fruit-shipping ports. By the century's end, these burgeoning towns became new magnets for Black Carib labor. The ships leaving harbor carried not only fruit but also Black Caribs leaving for new destinations in North America.

In the meantime, however, the 1839 reassertion of nation-state boundaries after the political failure of the Federación Centroamericana presented additional opportunities for smuggling by ship, a niche the trans-statal, multilingual, seafaring Garifunas were uniquely positioned to fill. Their network of villages reached across the provisional and, from a nautical perspective, largely arbitrary nation-state boundaries that divided Central America.

Black Carib Religion in the Nineteenth Century

The Caribs arrived at Trujillo as nominal Catholics, the result of French missionary efforts during the colonial period on St. Vincent. The North American traveler and diplomat John Lloyd Stephens reported in 1841 that every Carib home in Belize included figures of the Virgin or other saints, and that he himself was in demand to act as a godparent for newly baptized children (Stephens 1949: 20). If his account shows that the Caribs were Catholic at least in name, it also indicates that their Catholicism was a selective version performed largely without priests, a matter noted not only by Stephens but also by the first U.S. consul in Honduras, E. G. Squier, in 1855 (Bard 1965: 317). On the rare occasions when a priest arrived in the village, noted Squier, women lined up en masse to have their children baptized. Thomas Young (1847: 128) described villagers' sending their children into Trujillo for baptism, presumably because priests rarely, if ever, circulated through the remote Black Carib outposts. Formal marriage, by contrast, was generally ignored (a pattern that persists), as men were frequently at work away from the village. Moreover, any special efforts by the church, such as the large-scale baptisms in Trujillo beginning in 1813, or the visits by the missionary Padre Manuel de Jesús Subirana (nicknamed "Apóstol de los Caribes") in the second half of the century (W. Davidson 1984b; Coelho 1995: 47), are noteworthy precisely because they cast into relief the general absence of priests.[25] Of this apparently unorthodox form of Catholicism among Black Caribs, one observer suggested: "He is a Christian where the Red Carib was an idolator, but he is, as his congener was, polygamous, superstitious, and migratory" (A. Gibbs 1883: 166).

To be sure, beyond noting its familiar Catholic features, most travelers were ill equipped to recognize, much less understand, this religious culture. For example, the early-twentieth-century North American adventurer Peter Keenagh echoed the eighteenth-century missionaries by finding "no religion" in Mosquitia at all, but rather only "a wild mixed ideology including Black Magic, Voodoo and all the extravagances of primitive superstition" (1938: 123; cf. Bard 1965: 245). Keenagh cast in particularly pejorative terms a religious mélange perceived by foreign witnesses as unsettling, but his caricature was by no means atypical. Reports of religious acts included tales about former slaves in Belize who "followed the African rites they had brought with them . . . keeping it up day and night," especially in the weeks around Christmas, which fell between mahogany-cutting sessions (A. Gibbs 1883: 76), as well as "duppy" belief, Obeah, and "soukeah" men among the so-called Sambos (Roberts 1827: 267; A. Gibbs 1883: 173; Conzemius 1928: 201; Keenagh 1938: 164–70). Even these caricatures are useful, however. For example, rituals against evil spirits called *mafia* were noted among the Paya Indians, as well as among the "Sambos" in Keenagh (1938: 141–42,

164), even though *mafia* was initially an Island Carib category of malicious spirits invoked on St. Vincent since at least the 1600s. That the same terms for spirits were in use among different ethnic groups hints at continual and ubiquitous processes of religious *métissage*.

That Black Carib religion of the nineteenth century was not Catholic, African, or Amerindian in any simple sense is best revealed in Thomas Young's travelogue. Young described two main occasions for large ritual feasts in the villages, one at Christmas, the other during "Devil feasts" (1847: 131). The description of the "Devil feast" is unmistakably the first detailed written account of what is today called the dügü, a massive ritual event that recalls, reveres, placates, and consults with ancestral spirits (gubida) and combats the feared mafia spirits. As described by Young, the feast lasted from three to seven days and entailed the arrival of numerous friends and relatives notified long in advance, who came to Mosquitia from as far away as Stann Creek in British Honduras. All the guests brought contributions of liquor and food, and the plates of prepared edibles were presented on tables decorated with "fancy tablecloths" and glass decanters. Foods that evoked memories of St. Vincent customs, like cassava bread, were held in special esteem. Large quantities of aguardiente were consumed, and women danced in a simple "to and fro" movement of the hands and feet, while singing in a "peculiar intonation of voice" (133). Young noted also that these were uniquely Black Carib ritual events, rather than merely borrowings from the Miskito or other nearby ethnic groups: he declared that Miskito (including "Sambos") rarely danced at all, though Miskito onlookers watched the spectacle of drumming and dancing with quiet curiosity (135).

Although Young's account is not comprehensive, we can infer fuller details of the ritual feasts from Eduard Conzemius's (1928) ethnography of a dügü observed in 1920. Conzemius wrote that the feast was referred to by Ladinos as a *baile mafya* (mafya dance). Conzemius described the *buyé,* or shaman, the specialist who led the event and manifested spirits of the ancestors (gubida) on behalf of an ill patient afflicted by a malevolent spirit (mafya), and the use of red annatto dye painted on participants' cheeks. This ritual structure is roughly similar to that described among the Island Caribs on St. Vincent. Though specific reports of nineteenth-century Black Carib religion are scarce, cursory, and biased by colonial and missionary objectives, by comparing Thomas Young's account to earlier ones from St. Vincent and even Hispaniola and the later account from Conzemius we can trace at least the outlines of continuities in religious practice. The preparation of food offerings for beneficial gubida spirits, who then expelled sickness-inducing "mafya" spirits by the third day of the dügü ritual, contains the elements of a centuries-old pattern. While Conzemius described the rituals as "immoral and shocking to a stranger" (1928: 204), a broader historical purchase renders the process anything but shocking, even familiar.

Were the Catholic baptisms and saints in Black Carib homes therefore a mere outward cover for the "authentic" practices that remained secret? Conzemius thought so (1928: 200). But in view of the longer itinerary of Carib religion, there is no need to ascribe authenticity to the dügü rites and the gubida ancestor spirits, and chicanery to Catholic ones. After all, the saints and rituals like baptism were obviously valued, and selectively used, on St. Vincent even when Catholicism was not enforced. And some features of Catholic practice may even have been brought to St. Vincent by African Catholics themselves.

Protestant missionaries also worked near and among the Black Caribs in the nineteenth century, especially in British territory, but, as on St. Vincent, they enjoyed little success (Kerns 1997: 34). Still, Charles Swett attended an evening service at a Methodist church in the city of Belize in 1868, where he encountered two hundred "colored" persons, some of whom may have been Caribs, compared with a scant three whites (Swett 1868: 79).[26] Conzemius noted many Protestant conversions of Black Caribs in British Honduras by the 1920s (1928: 200). It is possible that the presence of many black Protestants in the British territory swayed Carib settlers there in ways that the English missionaries could not. If so, this slight shift foreshadowed the last decades of the twentieth century, when fast-growing Protestant *evangélico* movements became influential in nearly all Garifuna villages.

In sum, we can characterize nineteenth-century Black Carib religion as composed of elements of folk Catholicism—the appeal to diverse saints in the form of miniature icons and the attention to godparenthood and baptism, but rarely to rituals of marriage or the Eucharist—embedded within and intertwined with indigenous practices focused on singing, dancing and feasting with ancestors who proffered powers of protection, cure, success, and fecundity. To these were assimilated possible new influences from the Haitians in Trujillo (Conzemius 1928: 192; Bianchi 1988: 114), and from anglophone blacks of the British Caribbean, like the practice of Obeah.[27] Garifuna religious culture was not only a transculturation of Island Carib, African, and French Catholic practices carried from St. Vincent, but also their implementation in new spaces. Yet this creative adaptive process was anchored to a unique Black Carib religious culture. St. Vincent acquired the prestige of a place of origin and was transformed from a lived to an imagined place, a diasporic horizon of mythic status, and a standard against which to gauge the religious identity performed on the Central American coast. St. Vincent was marked as the place from which the ancestral spirits come.

Black Caribs in the Banana Republic

In the last quarter of the nineteenth century, life on the Central American coast was thoroughly transformed. By 1870, schooners cruised the Honduran coast to purchase small amounts of fruit from natives (so-called *poquitero* buying), who transported it by canoe or dory to the ships anchored offshore (Gonzalez 1969: 31). This trade recapitulated the transport work performed by the Black Caribs' ancestors four generations earlier on St. Vincent, when they launched tobacco and other goods by canoe off a windward shore too rocky for a large-keeled ship to approach. Then, as in the later 1800s, the acceleration of a money economy dramatically changed village life.

During the 1880s multiple small fruit-transport companies cruised the Bay of Honduras as informal operations without developed infrastructures, buying locally grown produce and carrying it to other islands of the Caribbean or to New Orleans. By the 1890s, however, expanding fruit companies began buying up coastal lands to establish their own plantations.[28] Two of the largest of these—the Boston Fruit Company and United Fruit—were merged in 1899 to form the larger United Fruit Company under the direction of Minor C. Keith (Becerra 1983: 32; Raynolds 2003: 10). This was the organization that Central Americans would eventually call *el Pulpo* (the octopus). In 1889, the Italian-American Vaccaro brothers of New Orleans founded the company that carried their family name before becoming, in 1924, the Standard Fruit and Steamship Company.[29]

Whereas United Fruit initially focused its business elsewhere in Central America, Standard Fruit shipped bananas from Honduras to New Orleans. The companies both tapped and created the need for readily available fruit among U.S. grocers. Almost completely unknown in the United States before 1870, the banana quickly caught on and became a cultural icon with diverse significations: "the tropics," sensuality, health, fun, Carmen Miranda, phallic humor, and easy money (Acker 1988: 24; Soluri 2003: 62–64).[30] It was a cheap but nutritious food that easily fit into the lunchboxes of a growing mass of industrialized workers and enabled them to partake, in a modest way, of the exotic amusements south of the border (Soluri 2003: 57–64).

Honduran leaders were reciprocally seduced by the magic of the North, especially the idea of technological development that would both produce enormous wealth and build a nation (Becerra 1983: 131; Barahona 1991: 255, 270). They were particularly interested in the construction of a rail system that would link interior cities like Tegucigalpa and Comayagua with the coast and help transform insular regional identities into a genuinely national network. Fruit-company ships on the horizon seemed serendipitous. Mining interests, the traditional source of Honduras's meager wealth, were also encouraged.[31] The mostly North American–owned fruit and mining companies were lured by tempting incentives of low taxes, a dearth of restrictions, and wholesale land grants in exchange for the promise of railroads and ports. This quid pro quo was advantageous for the gringo fruit men. By controlling the ports, these companies avoided paying duties on their own exports and could charge duties on any rival imports and exports. This arrangement left the Honduran state utterly dependent on the foreign companies' benevolence (Euraque 1996: 4–8).

Rivalry among these companies escalated after 1910, when the United Fruit Company expanded from its bases in Guatemala and Costa Rica into Honduras. In 1913, United Fruit established the Tela Railroad Company and shortly thereafter a similar subsidiary, the Trujillo Railroad Company. These companies were given huge land subsidies by the Honduran government for each kilometer of new track they laid, in the expectation that they would build a national rail system. Instead, the companies built railroads that extended the reach of United Fruit and Standard Fruit reach along the northern coast and opened new territory for banana production. With new banana groves constantly required to replace lost revenues from those devoured by Panama disease, their need for territory was insatiable (Raynolds 2003: 12, 26; Euraque 2003: 239). And with no national rail system reaching into the interior, Honduran coastal towns like La Ceiba remained much closer, in terms of transport time, to New Orleans than to Tegucigalpa (Posas 1993: 18), opening an early trickle of Black Carib sailors to the United States.

Through decades of land subsidies, the companies came to control much of the most fertile coastal territory, and the port towns of La

Ceiba, Tela, and Trujillo became essentially company towns. The companies acted as mini-empires and controlled all the infrastructure in the towns they built and occupied.[32] Hospitals, schools, docks, the postal service, soccer fields, generators, and fueling facilities—even the police—were company-owned. And many Black Caribs who manned the company ships sailing from the northern coast began to feel just as much at home in New Orleans and New York as in Honduras.

At the zenith of United Fruit's power, after mergers with Samuel Zemurray's Cuyamel Fruit in 1919 and in 1937 with Minor Keith's International Railways of Central America, the "Octopus" controlled almost all Central American railways and about three million acres of land, most of it acquired for free. As late as 1952 it supplied more than 80 percent of the bananas in the United States Even today, under the brand name Chiquita, it is the world's largest supplier, rivaled only by Dole, the descendant of Standard Fruit, and Del Monte, a subsidiary of R. J. Reynolds.

BANANAS AND THE BLACK CARIB PARADOX

The very neocolonization of Honduras as a banana republic that proved so detrimental to nation building and to genuine national sovereignty was, at least temporarily, a boon for many Black Carib families whose huts adjoined the beaches near those ports. Company towns like Tela and La Ceiba provided nearby villages with steady, local labor opportunities. Picking, loading, and packing bananas close to home, many young men enjoyed a settled existence rather than voyaging for work as soldiers or woodcutters (Conzemius 1928: 198; Gonzalez 1969: 31). Indeed, some Caribs themselves became wealthy owners of banana lands around Tela and La Ceiba (Euraque 2003: 238–39). If the last decades of the eighteenth century on St. Vincent were recalled as a golden age of abundance fed by plentiful market opportunities alongside an incipient indigenous economy, many contemporary Garifuna recall the time when the fruit-company trains passed daily through the village as another golden age. Although more politicized Garifuna leaders recognize and call attention to the economic exploitation of that period (e.g., Centeno García 1997; Meléndez 2002), nevertheless many people subjectively recall it as a period of readily available employment, stable communities, and a thriving local social life, in comparison with the crises of the present.[33]

In interviews with me, for example, many Garifuna recalled the days when "you could pluck fruit right from the water." That specific phrase is repeated with surprising frequency. It seems to be less an individual memory than a stock trope of collective memory, a prop around which individuals' idiosyncratic narratives of the past are assembled. For example, the late Don Cornelio of Corozal, born in 1913, recited to me his grandfather's stories of how the Black Caribs would fill their canoes with fruit and paddle out to waiting ships. In the late nineteenth century, announcements that the companies would buy all fruit spurred memorable days of collective effort in the villages. Cornelio himself began working on the ships at age twenty-one. Despite a knife fight on the docks that led to two years in prison, Cornelio remembered the era with pride, as one of swashbuckling action folded easily into the common male life stories of "adventuring" for one's livelihood.[34] Best of all, said Cornelio, there was no great hardship at home: even if those at sea missed sending a paycheck home from time to time, their families "could get the fruit right out of the water."

Sandá, an elderly woman in San Juan, near Tela, recalled the mid-century period as one of abundance, when most local Garifuna worked for United Fruit. No one went hungry, she said, because plantains and bananas were freely available: poor families could get the surplus from ship loading at the Tela dock. When the extra was cast overboard, the fruit even drifted right onto the beaches, where "you could pluck it right from the water."

Nick Rivas, also of San Juan village, first embarked on the fruit ships in 1950, after having cleaned windows for Standard Fruit executives in Tela. One executive wrote a letter to help Nick secure a shipping job. Rivas sailed to New Orleans, New York, and other ports, and, though he was temporarily blackballed by the company for his role in a dock fight, he eventually became a cook on one of the ships. He remembered the fifties and sixties as good times. "I made $137 a month with the company. It wasn't much, but it went a long way when you could buy all your provisions for a dollar. Of course, I was young then."

Don Fausto of the village of Corozal was born in 1933. He remembered the Standard Fruit period positively, but qualified this observation as "only compared with the present." "There was six months of work for seventy-two men, just clearing woods to lay the rails. Later there were lots of jobs, stacking fruit in railcars, loading and unloading, and sailing with the ships. There were always Garifuna sailors shipping in and out from La Ceiba." To be sure, said Fausto, many of the bosses on the ships were cruel, "especially the Castilians. We spoke Spanish a little differently; I'd say *pana* and my boss *panaca*, and he would get

terribly angry about stuff like that and take it out on me." Fausto compared those days to the present. He pointed at each house in a row and
named the number of relatives living in the United States, muttering
about how lazy and dependent they had become. A typical house
receives $100 per month in remittances from abroad, already double
the local minimum that a Honduran postal worker could earn.[35] Fausto
also explained how the presence of Standard Fruit called forth the first
explicit organizations negotiating the terms of the Garifuna's relation
to the broader state and its economy. In Corozal, for example, the first
centralized village organization, called Repentina, was formed in 1930
to negotiate labor issues with the fruit companies. In Fausto's recollection, then, the fruit companies in a sense unintentionally brokered the
Garifuna's entrance into the local and national political sphere.[36]

In these idealized reminiscences, no one went hungry or fought with
their neighbor, in contrast with today's villages of empty houses, sporadic threats of gang violence, and heavy dependence on money sent by
family members in the United States. Younger, more politically active
Garifuna refute these nostalgic accounts as pollyannaish. For them, the
fruit-company period marks the beginning of the decline of traditional
culture caused by economic dependence. The current dependence on
remittances from the United States is but a new version of this earlier
scourge, in defense against which "the culture" must be revived and
made a source of pride.

These critics note the social consequences less often recalled in such
narratives. Many Garifuna moved into town, sent their children to public
schools, and adopted new styles and resources. Some of them eventually
abandoned their language, even passing as non-Garifuna *morenos*
("browns"; in this case, darker-complected mestizos) (Gonzalez 1969:
44; Centeno García 1997: 66–67, 77–78). At the same time, as the young
men who sailed with the fruit boats to New Orleans returned home with
the prestige of the world-wise (owing in part to the material objects they
brought back with them), a whole new set of "needs" was created that
threatened traditional authority. Class stratification opened new cleavages in the villages closest to company towns, as some residents started
to build homes from concrete blocks and floors rather than in the old
daub-and-wattle *(manaca)* style. This issue has become more prominent as migration has increased.

To be sure, a century earlier Samuel Bard had already described the
Black Carib dandies with the fantastic taste, who proudly bore articles
of European manufacture back to the village (Bard 1965: 320–21). The
process and structure were familiar, yet something was different. The

FIGURE 6. A new home built with funds remitted from the United States. Noteworthy here is the fence, now commonly used to set such properties apart from the rest of the village, in which houses are divided only by the footpaths between them. Photo by author.

new breed of voyagers were forging paths that would lead many to migrate north for the long term, sometimes permanently, rather than solely for temporary work.

DECLINE OF THE BANANA REPUBLIC

After peaking around 1930, the abundance created around the banana towns declined. Bananas as a percentage of Honduran exports dropped from a high of 88 percent in 1930 to 45 percent in 1960 (Ruhl 1984). One possible cause of the decline was crop diseases—Panama disease and Sigatoka—that decimated whole plantations and required costly chemical treatments to resist, all but shutting down local growers (Gonzalez 1969: 38). Organized labor and resistance to company dominance also contributed to the decline. These reached a peak in 1954 with the two-week-long strike of all workers in La Ceiba employed by the Tela Railroad Company and the Standard Fruit Company, many of them Black Caribs.[37] Although the strike was only modestly successful, for the first time the state of Honduras recognized the legality of labor unions and

drew a line between tolerating company towns in its territory and actually being a company state (Posas 1993: 56–63). The president installed
in 1957, Ramón Villeda Morales, instituted agrarian reform and social-
welfare legislation, and in 1960 linked Honduras to the new Central
American common market (Mercado Común Centroaméricano). For
the first time, the fruit companies had to negotiate with the government rather than unilaterally impose their own trade rules.[38]

Additional factors included destructive hurricanes (in 1954, 1974, and
1998) in Honduras that damaged docks and warehouses that were never
rebuilt, and the resulting dismissal of thousands of workers; antitrust law-
suits in the United States against the fruit companies; and perhaps most
important, the successful revolution and nationalization of Cuban banana
lands by Fidel Castro in 1959 that scared United and Standard into reducing their dependency on the Caribbean region. These factors led to a
greater diversification of fruit-company lands and interests, a practice of
subcontracting fruit production to local growers, and the geographic
move to new sites on the Pacific coasts of Colombia, Ecuador, and
Panama. Former fruit-company workers attribute the decline not only to
the 1954 strike but also to the mechanization of fruit packing and loading:
"By the late sixties, out of every two hundred workers, twenty-five were
left."[39] The companies and the trade ceased to dominate civic life, though
they are still present in the background. If this change was positive for
national development, allowing for the expansion of coffee, sugar, and
other export products, such issues were mere abstractions for most, and
the outcome was at best mixed. Exploitation on the macro level had
often meant job stability at the local level.

Fruit production in Honduras continued, and continues still, though
now on rusted rails and shaky piers. By the 1980s, Tela, La Ceiba, and
Trujillo were returning to their former quiet. The company sirens that for
decades had marked the passage of days fell silent. Many Black Caribs
now took work in the textile factories (maquiladoras) that sprang up
around Tegucigalpa and San Pedro Sula. Others applied for posts on the
cruise ships that began to slice through Caribbean waters more and more
frequently. Like the earlier occupations of woodcutter, fisherman, con-
trabandista, and soldier, the new jobs meant living away from home for
stretches of up to ten months at a time. But, as another golden age turned
to dust, the society was dependent on a cash economy, manufactured
goods, and the social and economic possibilities offered by nearby boom-
towns. With the old jobs now unable to fill bellies, much less the new
needs of the modern Carib village, the Garifuna again set their sights over

the horizon, this time to the United States. And, with another place left behind, another sacred homeland was born in diasporic memory.

Giving Boundaries to Homeland Garifuna Religion: A Pause in the Itinerary

As a basis for understanding diasporic Garifuna religion in New York, it is necessary to create a synthetic portrait of contemporary indigenous "Garifuna religion" in the homeland of Honduran villages. Such a portrait is problematic insofar as it is static, depicting an ethnographic present devoid of specific agents negotiating particular places, times, and challenges. It should serve as a heuristic marker for comparing homeland and diasporic cultural forms. The complex details of practice are restored to the portrait in subsequent chapters.

In Garifuna religion, ritual continuity is of greater significance than specific doctrinal tenets. The overall mythic and ethical structure is provided by Roman Catholic Christianity, and the distinguishing characteristics of Garifuna religion are found in its elaborate complex of ritual practices. Because specific beliefs and ethical postures vary widely in relation to popular adaptations of Catholicism, correct ritual practice is crucial to Garifuna religious identity. Myths and belief remain largely implicit, embedded in ritual performance, and discussions of them reveal wild variations. Maintaining the "tradition" is viewed as a question of ritual practice rather than dogma.

As a general rule, rituals focus on the problem of death and the change in status from living human being to exalted ancestor (gubida). Though the dead remain a source of power for the living, they need help from living family members to leave this world to become recently departed spirits (ahari) and eventually gubida in the otherworld. The otherworld is called Sairi, the home of the ancestors, and is often identified with St. Vincent. The postmortem journey is simultaneously one of spiritual advance and geographic traverse, or return, to the lost homeland. The ritualization of death is therefore in part an expression of diasporic consciousness: it is both a means of looking back and a performative return to a paradise lost.

Because ritual obligations to the dead are never completely fulfilled by the living, ancestors register their complaints through signs experienced by their living descendants as nightmares, bad luck, accidents, and unexplained illnesses. Garifuna religion is in this sense rigorously this-worldly.

It is concerned with alleviating concrete material problems by contemplating them as ruptures in the relations between the living and the ancestors. Such a crisis is addressed in a series of ritual interventions that demand progressively more substantial investments. The ability to prosper in the material world is therefore understood as directly related to and contingent on the attention devoted to the family ancestors' journey through the spirit world. Let's first look at some of the smaller-scale rituals.

VELURIA

When a member of the community dies, the corpse is placed in a coffin and laid out in the person's house for public viewing. Candles are lit and placed at each corner, and near the coffin a simple altar is erected on a low table, bearing holy water and statues of Catholic saints. Crepe-paper streamers are hung in a canopy over the body. Friends and relatives arrive at the wake and hold vigil through the night, drinking coffee and rum (aguardiente or guaro), playing cards, and talking. At dawn the corpse is interred in a graveyard that is near to, yet separate from, the village. The burial is accompanied by the wailing laments of female relatives and the pouring of rum into the grave by family members and friends.

AMUIDAHANI

Between six months and several years after the death, the family "bathes" the deceased. A small pit is dug immediately adjacent to the home, and a fresh change of clothes for the departed is suspended above it. Family members and intimate friends pour liquids into the pit, variously including fresh water, salt water, strained cassava water, herbal infusions, and favored beverages like coffee and rum. Tobacco and favorite foods may be offered as well. Following the bathing of the deceased, the pit is closed. The ritual is small, brief, and intimate and does not require the presence of a buyei (a shaman).

LEMESI

Around a year after the death, and again later if called for by the ancestor (through divination by the buyei), a "mass" is held for the spirit of the deceased (ahari), who is viewed as still present in the village. The occasion marks the end of a period of mourning for a surviving spouse

and, as an occasion marking the spouse's return to everyday life, is conspicuously festive. Food and beverages are served, and the celebrative
punta dance is drummed and danced in the yard. In the punta, dancers
typically form a circle into which a man and a woman enter in pairs. The
dance entails the rhythmic oscillation of the hips while keeping the
upper body perfectly still and the facial expression cool and calm. It celebrates both the life of the deceased and the ongoing force of the community despite the loss of one of its members.

Women gather to sing "women's songs" *(abeimahani)*, standing in
a line with little fingers linked and thrusting the arms forward in rhythmic concert, a gesture suggestive of shared labor. The song lyrics recall
the struggles of family life and loyalty and sometimes speak from the
perspective of the ancestors, pleading not to be forgotten. Men's songs
(arumahani) are presented in similar fashion. Their lyrics often recall
the necessity and dangers of travel for labor far from home and the
longing to return. In addition, traditional tales *(úruga)* may be told:
these are often humorous tricksterlike narratives. The festivities continue until dawn.

The foregoing rituals are required after every death. The most elaborate postmortem rituals, the *chugu* and the dügü, are called for only
when specifically requested by an ancestral spirit. An individual who
suffers unusual misfortune, recurring nightmares, or unexplained illnesses or pains consults a shaman. With the patient seated before the
buyei's altar *(gulei)*, the buyei lights a candle, smokes his or her pipe,
and summons his or her tutelary spirits *(hiyuruha)* by blowing rum
vapor over the altar to activate it. Blowing smoke over the head of the
patient, he or she consults with his or her spirits to discern the nature
of the problem from the movement of the smoke and the insights
granted by her helping spirits. This procedure is called *arairaguni,*
"bringing down the spirits." If the problem is one caused by the ancestors *(hasandigubida)*, the buyei negotiates with the afflicting spirit to
decipher what it requires. The intervention called for may be minor,
such as a lemesi, or major, such as a chugu or, in the most serious cases,
a dügü. Together with the patient, and taking account of the family's
financial resources, the shaman plots the course of action.

CHUGU

The chugu, literally the "feeding" of the dead, is a one- to two-day ceremony officiated by a buyei. In addition to all of the elements included

in a lemesi, it entails assembling a greater number of relatives and preparing large quantities of food offerings, including roosters *(gayu)* offered for sacrifice. Because a more intimate communication with the dead is required than in a "mass," the buyei erects his or her personal altar in the house where the chugu will take place. There he or she places the symbols of the key helping spirits as well as the implements of the shaman's vocation: the maracas *(sisiri)* used to call the spirit, the wand *(mureywa)* used to communicate with and control the spirit should possession trance occur, and bottles of rum and tobacco used to purify the room and to activate, or "heat," the altar. Traditional foods are prepared, including the sacrificed roosters and cassava bread *(ereba)*, to present an abundant table for the dead. Women's and men's songs are performed at length, and the spirit may also be celebrated with punta dancing. Much rum is consumed to create the atmosphere of exuberance and generous abundance favored by the ancestors.

At the conclusion of the day's events, the buyei concocts a punch *(furunsu)* of beaten eggs and hot rum. Each participant places his or her full cup on the altar while making requests of the ancestor, then exchanges the cup with another participant. The exchange unites the group. Finally, the buyei "burns the table," pouring rum over its surface and igniting it. A strong blue flame reveals the ancestor's approval of the offering and indicates that the precipitating symptoms of bad luck or illness that evoked the chugu will subside.

DÜGÜ

Just as the chugu contains all the elements of the "mass," the dügü contains all the elements of the chugu. Dügü is short for *adugurahani*, "mashing down the earth," perhaps referring to the long dances required. It is the fullest expression of Garifuna religion. It normally takes place many years after the death of a family member and only when mandated by a buyei. Announcements about the dügü circulate for at least a year to ensure that sufficient funds can be raised for the purchase of sacrificial roosters, pigs, and sometimes a cow that will feed not only the ancestors but also a crowd of up to several hundred participants for a week. All family members, even those residing in the United States, are obliged to attend. Indeed, the ritual's efficacy in resolving the perceived crisis depends on a complete demonstration of family unity. The emotional reunion of dispersed family members on village soil is part of the "cure."

FIGURE 7. A crowd assembled for a dügü ritual. On the left is the main temple structure, the dabuyaba; on the right is the dibasen, used for rest, socializing, and food preparation. Photo by author.

A ceremonial palm-thatched house (*gayunere* or *dabuyaba*) must be constructed in traditional style on the beach. Over several days a sequence of dances is performed both to honor the ancestors and create the conditions for their arrival through possession trance. Once they have arrived, the ancestors are fed and feted until they lift the sickness that first motivated the call for a dügü.

As the dügü summons and placates ancestors, it reinforces family bonds among the living. This aspect of the ritual has become more important with increasing emigration to the United States since the late twentieth century. In fact, performance of the dügü appears to be increasing in frequency. It is described more fully in chapter 5.

• • •

With this provisional portrait of Garifuna religion, we can begin to investigate how it is put into practice in the homeland and in New York. I examine not only how the two forms of the same religion differ but also how those differences come into being, and why. Whereas home-land Garifuna practitioners in Honduras regard St. Vincent as their place of origin, whence the spirits return, U.S.-based Garifuna view three places—Honduras, St. Vincent, and, increasingly, Africa itself—as territorial sites of religious power. How has migration led to the addition of not just one diasporic horizon, but two? Trying to answer this question will, I hope, provide clues for discerning how diasporic religion operates not just as a form of historical consciousness, but as a creative process directed toward the future, presenting chances for new identifications and social alliances by projecting present experience against previously unseen horizons.

CHAPTER 3

Shamans at Work in the Villages

They treat ritual like something you learn in school.
            Honduran shaman, on New York colleagues

They know what to do, but they don't know why they do
what they do.
                New York shaman, on Honduran colleagues

What does it mean to join a diaspora, to become diasporic, in practice?
The next four chapters try to answer this question. They are arranged
in two pairs: this chapter and the next compare shamans' work in homeland villages of Honduras and in the Bronx, respectively; chapters 5 and
6 compare large-scale ritual events as performed in Honduras and the
Bronx. I attempt to discern the distinctive qualities of diasporic religion
by comparing it with the homeland models it emulates, yet from which
it also departs and differs.

The Problem with "Homeland"
versus "Diasporic" Categories

There are several reasons why the opposition between New York and
Honduras is less clear-cut than one might wish. "Homeland" Garifuna
also act in relation to a diasporic horizon: St. Vincent, land of their ethnogenesis. It is from there that the ancestors return to possess the bodies of
their descendants during ritual events. Moreover, most households in the

99

homeland are financially dependent, and therefore in a sense also ritually dependent, on relatives working in the United States. Given the fluid exchanges within this transnational network, the United States diaspora is always embedded in what goes on in the homeland, and vice versa. Homeland rituals and New York rituals are both diasporic performances, though in different senses: the Honduran homeland version appeals especially to the horizon of St. Vincent, while the New York Garifuna version appeals to the horizon of Honduras, but also and especially to the continent of Africa itself. Only the latter, however, is overtly and consciously diasporic.

Whereas Garifuna in Honduran villages enact the return of the ancestors from St. Vincent, this journey is never discursively marked as a diaspora, or even usually as a "cultural" activity of remembrance. One meaning of "joining a diaspora" in the move to New York lies in the adoption of this practical nomenclature as an identity claim, a means of distinguishing previously unmarked acts and elevating them for special attention (Palmié 1995: 74). Next, the memory of St. Vincent has been carried with the Garifuna since their deportation in 1797. It is by now thoroughly indigenized, "traditional" and, in all villages, constitutive of Garifuna collective memory, but it serves primarily as a kind of placeholder for the idea of origins. Because there is almost no active relation with a population on St. Vincent or with its reimagining as a territory, it is what we might call a latent diasporic horizon—an available and viable, but mostly uncultivated, spatial memory. By contrast, emigrants to the United States undergo an active conversion of consciousness. Shamans not only rely on the spatial memory and sacralization of, and periodic returns to, Central American territory; they also engage the network of the African diaspora as a rival authentic horizon.

Finally, these strongly marked designations of homeland versus diasporic religion should be viewed as heuristic markers of degrees of difference. I am not following Durkheim in analytically comparing a single-celled, intact, and unified social system in the homeland with a complex, anomic city, nor Claude Lévi-Strauss in comparing ahistorical, unchanging, and "cold" societies with dynamic, "hot" ones. I am certainly interested in the ways homeland and New York Garifuna themselves read each other according to roughly these stereotyped terms. But my theoretical claim is much narrower in scope.

Arjun Appadurai argues that the phenomenological quality of "locality"—the sense of social immediacy, familiar spaces, and relatively stable patterns of social interaction—exists both in rural village and in big-city neighborhoods (1995: 205–15). Locality emerges only through cultural work, including ritual performance, that forms "local subjects" in tension with the homogenizing objectives of nation-states. But, as Appadurai himself notes, the inadequacy of the older sociological models does not mean that the challenges faced in producing locality are always and everywhere the same, as simplistic ideas of "globalization" sometimes suggest. Obstacles to locality may be more substantial in certain kinds of venues, such as spaces of radical cultural pluralism into which multiple emigrant groups arrive over relatively short periods. My argument is not that locality exists in one place and not in the other, or that rituals are "intact" and organic in the indigenous venue and "detached," mimetic, or artificial in the city. Nor is it the inverse, the fallacy of organicism as applied to cities as contained wholes (Lefebvre 2003: 1), perhaps most famously in Durkheim's characterization of "organic solidarity." Obviously, ritual is historically contingent, dynamic, and changing in both kinds of spaces and social networks.

But is this all that can be said? Surely ritual works differently in each place—places of varying material resources, performative spaces, daily habits, patterns of congregation, modes of transport and communication, and so on. To say that both a Garifuna village in Honduras and a neighborhood in the Bronx can produce social immediacy through religion does not mean that they produce it in just the same way, or that it has the same effects or even the same meaning in social actors' lives. It seems as empirically false and analytically lazy to say there are *no* significant differences between rituals performed in village and in urban contexts as it is to say that they are absolutely different. The trick is to avoid the primitivism of the latter claim and the naïve global ecumenism of the former. And, in keeping with the task of mounting an ethnography of diasporization rather than merely another theory of it, it is necessary to show *how* the two spaces of religious performance work differently, yet in relation with one another, on collective memory and the social process.

This chapter and the next focus on religious leadership: on shamans and their work. My point of departure is the framework of interpretation presented by Lévi-Strauss's *Structural Anthropology* (1963) in relation to a different set of Central American shamans, those of the Cuna of Panama. Shamans' cures are accomplished through the dual procedures of cognitively reframing a mysterious threat in a known and familiar set of terms and categories and of socially transforming an individual crisis into a collective one. This chapter begins with this familiar framework; chapter 4 goes beyond it, for the problems of a diasporic religion include determining just which categories are to be maintained as familiar and traditional as the religion is extended in space, and even precisely who the "we" of the collective should include. These questions are answered differently, and with different effects, for shamans working in homeland villages and those working in the Bronx.

For example, through the process of migration from Honduras to New York, Garifuna shamans are adopting Africa into their identifying practices, dramatically shifting the notion of the "tradition," and the definition of the collectivity. The particular history of the Garifuna offers several diasporic horizons: Africa, St. Vincent, and Central America. But their relative importance in cultural formulations of Garifuna origins or essence does not necessarily match the group's historical itinerary. In Honduras the "Black Caribs" became Caribs, and then, by the mid-twentieth century, just morenos. These characterizations were mestizo in origin, but they were incorporated into Garifuna discourse and remain in use today. Because Africa was associated with enslavement and linguistic assimilation, and because the absence of these were the exact two features by which Garifuna distinguished themselves from other groups of color, Africanness was an identification resisted as strongly by many Garifuna as it was by the nation-states in which they resided. In Honduras, *mestizaje* and *indigenismo,* not Africanness, provided the privileged terms of assimilation and nation-building. Until recent onomastic shifts led by Garifuna activists, *Afro-Honduran* was practically a non sequitur. But Africa is now being reinstated in the awareness of the Garifuna in Honduras. It has happened under the rubric of diaspora, largely through the agency of emigrants to New York. The move to New York has called forth ritual invention in the effort to make and maintain Garifuna locality in the new space. Locality is produced by emigrants to New York, paradoxically, through diasporism: resisting assimilation or the homogenizations called for by the nation-state—whether Honduras or the United States—through the appeal to distant origins and communities (Matory 2005: 108).

Favoring the "deep history" of Africanness over the immediate history of St. Vincent origins opens new opportunities for social affiliation, institutional networking, and religious performance. These developments have not occurred as a simple "recovery of the repressed." Even though that process is arguably a part of the story, we must also ask how and where such shifts in subjectivity and public expression are called forth, and what kinds of Africanness are produced in memory by shamans' work. To that end, I suggest, first, that joining the religious African diaspora implies a specific turn toward prescribed ethnic niches in the new religious field of U.S. cities. If the representation of deep Africa in the context of the Americas once favored Ethiopia or Egypt as synecdochic tropes, it now relies on the Yoruba of southwest Nigeria (Palmié 1995: 99; cf. Zane 1999: 156, 175; Matory 2005: 7, 50, 171). To join the African diaspora today follows a predictable pattern: Yorubize it!

Second, Garifuna religious and racial shifts are related not only to the difficulties of entering an already circumscribed religious field but also to new needs generated in the move from rural Honduras to the dense concrete battlements and iron crenellations of the Bronx. The terminology of the city as a battlefield is not imposed but emic; with the new space come perceived needs for protection against the threat of intrusion and harm, both physical and spiritual (cf. McAlister 1992; David Brown 1996). In the Bronx, these threats are addressed by assembling spirit "warriors" to secure and guard entryways of both apartments and bodies against a dangerous city, in a practice Garifuna migrants have adapted from Cuban redactions of Yoruba- and Kongo-influenced religions, Santería and Palo Monte.[1] Thus joining the diaspora involves selective identifications related to the needs of the present place.

Third, the Garifuna entered a foreign religious field that presented new social, practical, and religious needs, but also a new identity market. Joining the African diaspora is related to Garifuna adaptation to an identity marketplace where cultural authenticity, and its articulation in the public sphere, is fundamental to securing resources in the city: meeting places, offices, sponsorship for performances, seed money for social-service organizations, détente with police forces, and so on. "Being Garifuna," religiously and otherwise, has become a matter of conscious practical action rather than the fabric of lived experience as in homeland villages. This third factor entails the drive to discourse, the need to secure authenticity through speaking and writing rather than ritual practice; hence the "theologization" of Garifuna religion, or what I have called, in relation to Brazilian Candomblé, protestantization, the push toward verbal articulations of meaning for a religion once expressed and transmitted primarily through ritual (Johnson 2002a). Further, this chapter and the next describe how the transformations undergone in diaspora create friction between rival versions of authenticity and rival authorities seeking to affix authenticity.

The question remains, however, of how and where such religious and ethnic shifts occur, and where they can be documented—in short, where is diasporic religious culture in practice? I consider two empirical sites for interpretation, which are present in both Honduras and the Bronx: shamans' religious autobiographies, including their declared spirit geographies—the identities and locations of the ancestral spirit guides who serve as the source of their power; and shamans' altars, the objects through which religious power is constituted, located, and directed on behalf of their communities and clients. Shamans' stories, altars, and work act as local brokers of history, determining either through overt discourse or ritual leadership what exactly should be remembered, preserved, discarded, or revised as authentically Garifuna. As keepers of the ancestral spirits, shamans are, practically if implicitly, keepers of memory as it is mediated by the geographies and biographies of their spirits (cf. Shaw 2002: 46–69).

Shamans or Possession Priests?

One might ask in this context whether *shaman* is the best term for Garifuna specialists who present and broker relations with the ancestors, taken as it is from the Siberian (Tungus) word *saman*. The term classically denotes those specialists of spirit travel who, in the throes of ecstasy, send their spirits on journeys to recover the lost fragments of their patient's person. By contrast, specialists of spirit possession receive or are mounted by the spirits in the penetrating rites of *enstasy* (Eliade 1964). In spirit possession, the gods or ancestors descend to occupy human bodies; in shamanism, specialists ascend to track and intervene with the sources of affliction. The two modes—possession of spirits versus possession by spirits—have often been used to distinguish Amerindian from African use of altered states of consciousness. Another classic study, that of I. M. Lewis (1989 [1971]), contrasted shamans to possession priests in terms of their degree of control over the process. Whereas possession priests "mounted" by the spirits are understood to have little agency—with the authenticity and authority of the possession performance even depending on that lack of control—the shaman maintains control over her itinerary and the superhuman agents encountered along the way.

In relation to these classical oppositions, Garifuna buyeis exhibit features of both enstasy and ecstasy: they alternately are controlled by spirits who arrive to possess them (enstasy) and control spirits as they travel "out" to meet them (ecstasy). For example, in rituals connected with the return of the ancestors, they are "mounted" by the ancestors in dramatic dance performances. Yet in the next moment they slip away to their altar room (gulei) to consult with their superhuman aids *(hiyu-ruha)*. Then too, in their everyday work of consulting with patients and clients, they move easily in and out of modest trance states, consorting at will with one or another of their supernatural guides, who deciphers the causes of a patient's illness or pain. Finally, the Garifuna's own title for such persons, *buyei,* is an Amerindian designation. It is the same term that was used by the occupants of St. Vincent before the Africans' arrival. For these reasons we are justified in describing the vocation as shamanic, though the decision to do so is this scholar's conceit, as the buyei herself crosses between modes of spirit possession and spirit flight (cf. Zane 1999).

The following section presents the office and work of these shamans in Honduran homeland villages. Next, I consider the relation of shamans and Protestant pastors as co-constitutive authorities invoking competing conceptions of the past and future, respectively, in the larger religious field.

Shamans in the Villages

In Honduran villages, culture brokers are few. Each village typically has one or two local intellectuals who are authorized to speak about the past. While these figures are not exclusively religious actors, the shamans are distinct in that they link memory to the transcendent, inscrutable authority of the ancestors and therefore wield extraordinary influence. Their labor is divided between periodic and regular activities. Shamans lead intermittent large-scale rituals in the homeland (chugu, dügü), especially in the late summer. Their ongoing work, however, consists of consulting with individual clients who seek their services for physical cures, interventions in matters of luck, love, and finance, and for divining the future.

Shamans' ability to read patients' problems and divine ritual solutions derives from being selected by ancestral spirits (hiyuruha).[2] Ideally, they must undergo an initiation and apprenticeship under the direction of an established shaman to learn to mediate such spirits and intercede with them on behalf of clients—though, like all religious ideals, this one is negotiated rather than strictly adhered to. To see how this process of becoming a shaman works, I begin with shamans' own narratives about becoming aware of their differences from their peers. How do shamans themselves view their acquisition of the special talents required in this post?

BECOMING A SHAMAN

Salomon, who is over eighty years old, recounted his story of becoming a buyei:

It started when I was about thirteen. I was very sick with fever and had to be alone all the time. Then I couldn't even walk. I always had dreams of the dügü, and of the dead. I would sit on the floor under a table all the time. Sometimes when my legs were better I would go by myself to the forest, for days at a time. The hiyuruha were after me, and when they want you, you have to go. I told my family, though, and they didn't believe me. They really got on me! My father didn't accept it at all, even though my great-grandfather had been a buyei. My father, he was Rosicrucian, and could cure snakebite, any kind of snake. But he was scared of frogs. He finally accepted it when he saw that I was going to die. That I was getting worse and worse—fever, headaches, pain, not being able to walk. When he believed me, things got better.

But I still had bad luck. When I was seventeen, I saw the massacre of Garifuna in 1937. I fled to Stann Creek [Belize] for four months until things quieted down. Then I came back here to San Juan by canoe, and got a job working for a "Turk" [a generic term for someone of Middle Eastern heritage] as a watchman for his building. After five days they put me in jail—they said I left the doors open on purpose for thieves. I was in jail twenty-nine days. That was very bad. When I got out, some people tried to shoot me in the woods near Triunfo. I ran. I was in the woods a long time, hiding. When I got out I had little worms in my body. My mother took me to see a curandera to get them out.

Then I really started. I was nineteen. An old buyei from Aguan, Tino, came to see me and told my father that I had to work with the spirits. He wanted me to come with him to Aguan, but I stayed with my mother. Then I worked with Chichi, in Triunfo, and now I knew what I was going to do. I started to learn how to avoid the blows [como evitar un golpe], and what to do with this family in the big house, now I knew.[3] I did ceremonies with Chichi, six dügüs. When she was in the hospital I stayed with her all the time. Then I worked alone.

I had seven spirits. There's Maria, Yerme, Jenny, Luisa—she's a doctor, but this woman is wild. There's Dongal, he's mean, too; he was the nephew of my grandfather. Some I had were from my grandfather, who was a buyei. They're the old ones of the family. They change, though. One leaves and another arrives. You have to hear what they want. It's very hard. I sacrifice myself for these hiyuruha. If my friend says something I don't like, I get sick. I can't sleep in bed; I have to lie under the table. Then it calms down. Now I just suffer when I treat someone else. But now they [the hiyuruha] are looking for younger ones who have more time. If someone doesn't listen, they pick someone else. They come after me if I don't go the forest, go to the big house. Hiyuruhas are like doctors. The others, gubida, want something from you, some food, or to dance a little. You feel sick when they're asking, but not after. Hiyuruha aren't ancestors. Well, they are, but they don't bother you. They bother you, but it's because they're looking for someone to work with them. If you say no, they keep following you, causing trouble. After that, it's just the gubida that bother you. But if they don't need anything, they take care of you.

The narrative of the struggle to accept the spiritual vocation, and to persuade family members and others of its validity, is a recurrent one. Salomon's daughter Mina, a woman of forty-seven who is likewise a shaman, also recounted this sort of early conflict followed by resolution and resolve:

I was born with this, but I didn't want to accept it. When I was little, the spirits would take me, the gubida, and six men couldn't hold me down! They held me, but I ran away and would climb up in a tree. I ate fish without salt, like the gubida. I don't remember anything. Once I fell [entered trance] for a whole year! Even though I was little they had to hold me down, uncle!

I went from here to Bahamar, to Travessia, to Corozal, always running away. Now I have my job. There are eight spirits I'm working. Some things they say I don't understand, they use old words from Yurumein [St. Vincent], but I'm learning. When they arrive, they're tired—they fly like angels, they need guaro to be watered. Guaro waters the bodies of the spirits. They are the hiyuruha, the little ones. There's Theo, he's male, chief of the medicine, and easygoing [suave]. There's Justina, she's short and wide, a fat Indio. There's Ligiriugu, very bad, ferocious but strong. He doesn't have any hair. Another one hasn't given me his name yet.

Carlitos, a third homeland Garifuna shaman, is in his early thirties and something of a stylish local celebrity. He describes having felt a sense of his vocation since he was eight years old:

I dreamed a lot about medicines and plants, and what would happen in the future. I heard the spirits talking to me. When I told my parents, they were really worried. I got sick all the time—fevers, headaches. . . . I was different from other kids, very religious. I was an evangélico, but then became Catholic, and then was possessed for the first time during a dügü. I can't remember that, but that's what they say. My parents took me to see buyeis in Triunfo, in Belize, even in Orinoco, in Nicaragua. Older buyeis taught me, but mostly the spirits would tell me how to use the maracas, the different rhythms they like. For six years they taught me. They were always watching my behavior; they punish you when you don't act right. To serve the people with love, that's what they want. But I never really studied to be a buyei, I was born into this. I received seven spirits of my own, but I hear from other foreign spirits too—Africans, Haitians, Indonesian, doctors. . . . Dabwi is a Garifuna from Mosquitia, the chief of buyeis. He's Garifuna, but global *[mundial]*, he speaks French, orisha, all languages! His name is Latin. He's 116 years old and weighs 950 pounds, can't even fit in a house. He knows seven thousand herbs and their uses. Eventually he's going to teach me a cure for AIDS. Dada is another one, from Sambu, then there's Mama, and Baba from Belize. But Dabwi is going to die soon—just like me.[4]

All shamans describe an idealized initiation into the office of buyei, marked by the ritual of "climbing the pole" *(trepar el palo)*. This begins with a week-long period of seclusion in a hut (*dubai* [cf. Foster 1994: 33–34]), lying in a hammock and eating food "like what the spirits eat," without seasoning. Only the initiating buyei and one helper are allowed to visit, as the presence of others might distract the force of the spirits away from the novice. Seclusion is followed by a public demonstration of power, the climbing of a wooden pole. The pole, representing the herbal knowledge the shaman will eventually command, is cut and transported from the forest. Because it also represents the aspirant's desired moral character, it must be very straight. It is greased with cocoa oil or butter, red annatto-seed dye *(achiote)*, and rum. At the top of the pole sits a ceramic rooster (gayu), a symbol of the shamanic role, which the new shaman must reach and claim. As the candidate climbs the pole, the drums beat the rhythm of the dügü, and the audience sings three songs—roughly translated for me as "The spirit has the force, we wait for you, come down!" "When you come down we'll give you meat from the forest [*gibinadu*, raccoon]," and a song about the power of the shaman's main instruments, the maracas. The gayu then is given to the new buyei's mother or grandmother. Later it may be placed on the shaman's altar and "fed," along with the saints and the tools of the shaman's trade—the maracas, the small staff, and smoking utensils.

Strikingly, however, an initiation is rarely carried out in strict adherence to this ideal. Instead, as the above narratives suggest, many shamans progressively acquire the characteristics that fit them for the role of buyei. As children, they are distinctive, solitary, and sickly figures. They tend to be "feverish," reclusive kids, preoccupied by their dreams and by messages from the spirit world. Salomon, the oldest among those I consulted, described his frequent childhood lapses into

FIGURE 8. Carlitos Amaya, buyei in the villages of Corozal and Sambo Creek. The orange clothing, dyed with ground annatto seeds (achiote), and the sash that protects a shaman from malevolent attack show that work involving spirit possession is anticipated. Photo by author.

a dissociative state, staring into space or disappearing into the woods without warning. This wasn't just a condition of his past, though. He was frequently and unpredictably ill on many mornings when I stopped by his house. I often found him reclining on a cot by his altar, in various states of partial consciousness.

Yet the buyeis are neither social outcasts nor regarded as culturally strange, as an existing "script" and niche await them. After all, buyeis are *supposed* to act strangely, and they play an important part in village life.

Young women and men with at least some of the characteristics of the ideal buyei may be pushed by family members toward that role and attracted to it. At the same time, the self-conscious adoption of the role influences autobiographical narratives of their formative years. A good buyei, after all, does not simply elect that status, but must be recognized and accepted as such by the community. Their idiosyncratic characteristics mark them for their role, but that role in turn shapes the narratives that explain their unusual skills and childhood experiences. It is not surprising, then, that shamans' life stories feature a set of common tropes.

Becoming a buyei is therefore a question not only of completing a rite of initiation, but also of adjusting one's actions to the role in a convincing and persuasive manner. In many cases, comportment and demeanor compensate adequately for the lack or incompleteness of any consecrating ritual. Thus there exist multiple paths to the office of mediating the spirits: paths of family inheritance, initiation, or the expression of shamanic qualities recognized by an audience as "innate."

THE HOMELAND SHAMANS' SPIRIT REPERTOIRE

The buyeis' practice is similarly structured in all Honduran villages. Shamans work with their own spirit helpers, the hiyuruha, who are usually known by name, place of origin, and specialization. These spirits are regarded as beneficent, even if ill-tempered or demanding. In collective rituals, the shamans' work requires satisfying the demands of more ambivalent spirits, the gubida. These are the family ancestors of individual clients, ancestors who make themselves known only through afflictions they cast on the living as complaints against having being forgotten. To end these troubles, the gubida must be mollified and sated. Every shaman's altar is also filled with the images of Catholic saints. Many hiyuruha, a shaman called Tino told me, "never leave the church, they love the saints." The saints invite and initiate "deeper" work with the spirits. "Because the saints help the spirits," Mina confirmed.

A village's patron saint is an especially propitious ally. In Corozal (a large Garifuna village near the city of La Ceiba), Saint Esquipula, also called Cristo Negro (Black Christ), is the hero of countless miracle stories. Castillo, the political representative of the village of Corozal, provided an example: in the 1960s, there was a man who was a fine musician, and always played for Esquipula during festivals. One year, however, the musician refused to play his part in the traditional pageant of the Moors and the Christians, also a favorite of the saint. The next day the man was struck by lightning and badly burned on his arm. Despite his pain, he played music for the saint, and by the third day he was miraculously cured. During Hurricane Fifi, in 1974, many villagers remained in the church praying to Esquipula, and they remained unharmed.

The Virgin Mary is likewise revered. Mina told me that the Virgin's help is entreated for dealing with "light things," while the spirits are relied upon for "heavy issues." "I do a mass and ask protection of the saints, or when I go out to walk I ask their protection and light a candle on my return." But the saints, like the Garifuna spirits, can be volatile. Saint Simon, the popular but officially unrecognized peasant saint from Guatemala, said Salomon, "helps and kills too," as do San Antonio and San Cipriano. "San Antonio is very bad sometimes; if you put him out in the sun in the name of someone, that person will die, because Antonio gets angry." Miniatures of these auspicious saints are ubiquitous on shamans' altars.

In addition to these most familiar classes of spirits, there are the "people of the forest" (*yaguaraguna*, or *gente del monte*), viewed as maleficent agents who do only mischief. The saints and the buyei's helping spirits are mobilized against them. Every village, moreover, has a few select members, often social outliers like aged, poor women without family networks or resources, who acquire a reputation as sorcerers (*hechiceras*) or witches (*brujas*). Against these marginal figures and their malicious jealousy, clients seek protective actions and amulets from shamans.

One story circulating in Triunfo de la Cruz in 2001 told of a hechicero in the village of Aguan who had killed two twin girls a decade before. The twins had refused to dance with him. The next day they paddled their canoe to a nearby beach to load red mud for patching the floor of their home. Mysteriously, the canoe overturned and they died, leaving only their sandals floating in the water. Travelers in another canoe saw the shoes and rushed to tell the girls' mother. She already knew they were dead: she had seen two black butterflies enter the house after they left, a sign that a hechicero was on the attack.

Witchcraft is typically an accusation cast at other villages. In the village of San Juan, for example, it is reputed that the neighboring village of Tornabe is especially "dirty" (*sucio*), containing devotees of Haitian Vodou and Jamaican Obeah who retrieve cemetery dirt and leave it in the paths of their enemies. Tornabeans levy the same charge against their neighbors in San Juan. "Obeah-men" are hechiceros par excellence—they perform "black magic" (spirit work intended to do harm) and are doubly feared for practicing a foreign religion. These purveyors of wandering spirits are held to be especially dangerous because they live, like the spirits themselves, outside the bounds of trusted social relations. On several occasions I was invited to sit on the old, overgrown fruit-company railroad tracks to confirm fearsome sightings of "moving balls of light." These were explained as uncared-for dead, those ignored by irresponsible or inattentive families—notably the families of converted evangelicals, or the self-styled modernist Bahais and Rosicrucians—who no longer respect the old rites.[5]

SHAMANS' ALTARS IN HONDURAS

The altar or gulei is the key material representation of the buyei's work. In Honduras, altars that mediate the shaman's interactions with ancestral spirits are devoid of overtly African symbols. The shaman's tools are assembled, rather, from a repertoire of traditional Garifuna implements: maracas, pipes, candles, bottles of aguardiente, beach sand, wands, and images of the Virgin and the Sacred Heart of Jesus. While this collage is itself a hybrid, taken as a whole it presents a fairly coherent symbolic representation of a "Garifuna-ness" that dates at least to the 1800s and probably earlier (see, for example, T. Young 1847). The maracas and smoking implements like pipes were central to shamanic healing from the very earliest accounts of Island Carib religion.

Nineteenth-century accounts mention the selective quality of Carib appropriations of Catholicism. As shamans' own stories suggest, the saints are called on alongside the ancestors for curing and other interventions, whether for particular "light tasks" *(cosa leve)* or to share tasks with the other spirits.

Also prominent on Honduran buyeis' altars, especially during large-scale ritual events, are miniature hammocks, canoes, and sailing vessels. It is unclear when these began to appear on ritual altars; they are not mentioned in Europeans' nineteenth-century observations Today, they are universal and polysemic. One of their functions is to initiate the dügü. At the outset of that great ritual, two canoes go to sea for three days to gather seafood for the feast. Their return at dawn initiates the ritual performance proper, the feting and feasting of the ancestors who will return from the sea, just like the fishermen, albeit in possession trance. The miniature boats therefore link specific shamans' altars to the broader Garifuna religious process of remembering and bringing back the ancestors.

FIGURE 9. Part of a shaman's altar in Honduras. Note the central tools of the vocation: the maracas, the bottle of rum, the pipe, the cigar, and, standing upright on the left, the stick (mureywa) a shaman uses to moderate the possession trances of others by placing it on their heads. Photo by author.

During ritual celebrations the participants recapitulate and remember repose on St. Vincent by resting in hammocks.[6] The models of boats and hammocks call to mind the golden age on St. Vincent prior to the deportation as well as the journey itself. Through these objects, the Honduran beach is ritually remodeled to recall both the left-behind place of origins and the distance from it.

Virtually no objects on Honduran Garifuna shamans' altars refer to Africa as a place, or to the African diaspora as a collective memory. They index, rather, the specifically Garifuna memory of exile from St. Vincent, the distinctively Garifuna array of shamanic tools, and Catholicism.

FIGURE 10. The central altar assembled in a dügü temple before the ritual. The boat signifies, and effects, two kinds of return to the homeland: the return of emigrants and the return of the ancestors. Photo by author.

On the altars of New York Garifuna shamans, by contrast, Africa and its gods figure centrally.

DISCORDANT INDIVIDUALISM

Shamans work mostly independently of and in competition with one another. Although some villages have no currently practicing buyei, others, like Triunfo de la Cruz and Trujillo, boast several of repute. Reputation, indeed, is the crucial issue, as each buyei vies for a limited clientele and a limited number of rituals calling for their expertise. Some buyeis accrue large non-Garifuna followings of mestizos and anglophone blacks from the nearby Bay Islands, while others rely on a strictly local practice. Always, however, power is perceived to come from outside. Buyeis from distant villages are often considered to be more skilled and to have greater spirit resources than the all-too-familiar local figure. The local buyei, whose past and current actions are anything but secret, benefits less from the discursive massage that helps shape a buyei's legitimating past and current reputation. Hence I encountered many Trujillanos traveling half a day to seek out shamans in the villages of San Juan or Corozal, and many Corozalenos doing the same in Trujillo (cf. Kerns 1997: 143).

The ethnographer who travels and visits different practitioners cannot avoid becoming both a broker and a barometer of shamanic competition, as each buyei asks of the foreign go-between, "Tell me what you think of Franciso, whose work I hear so much about." The hope is, of course, that the rival's work will be reported as faulty, suspicious, or shallow; but the question itself is motivated by concern. Buyeis work mostly alone, yet they require validation by other shamans. The fear of rejection, one budding shaman told me, is constant. Every buyei looks over her or his shoulder to gauge the competition, especially in the larger villages like Triunfo de la Cruz or Trujillo. These centers of tradition are admired for their ranks of specialists, but they are also derided, even among Garifuna religious specialists themselves, as fraught with "buyei hype" *(buyeirazgo)*, a proliferation of people spuriously claiming special powers and authority. The individualist nature of the healer's labor leads to the constant elaboration of "tradition," as each must distinguish his or her knowledge with new revelations or discoveries of how things "ought to be done." Salomon lamented, "The new ones always want to do something different, to personalize what I taught them."

Yet the pressure to innovate in the name of tradition also has its limits. Too much charismatic innovation or showiness can undermine a buyei's authority. A relative, provisional concord is therefore maintained, even without written canons of orthopraxy. This practical consensus means that labor can sometimes be pooled. Several shamans often take part in the same dügü, so long as the hierarchy among them is well defined. Defining that hierarchy, however, depends on the goodwill of the patrons of the event and on their notoriously labile loyalties. Salomon, for example, told me of once being contracted to lead a dügü in a nearby village, only find on arrival that he had been replaced by Santos, a rival buyei from the larger, more distant town of Trujillo. This episode generated an antipathy between them that had not subsided even several decades later. Another leader reported the subtle but clear codes of mockery exchanged by buyeis. When one shaman arrives as a visitor at a ritual event, protocol requires the presiding buyei to invite the visitor into the gulei, the altar room, for a professional visit. The length of time a visitor is forced to wait—from an hour to a full day or more—is a measure of the visitor's status. Shamans are known to constantly test and contest each other's power, and every buyei can tell stories of attempts to "put them in their place"—attempts that, in the narratives, are always foiled.

At least one prominent shaman has proposed the construction of a permanent ritual structure, centrally accessible in Garifuna territory, to supersede rivalries and obviate the need to build another temple structure for every dügü. Yet such proposals are infrequent and resisted by most. The role of shaman is by its very nature composed for the soloist and for the religious virtuoso, not the ensemble. Thus buyeis closely guard their knowledge and clientele, even as they must reveal some proof of their knowledge to establish a reputation and attract a distant as well as local clientele (Johnson 2002a, 2006). Their reputation as guardians of traditional knowledge is built and maintained in part by the shamans' distinction of their role from the increasingly prominent role of evangelical pastors in Honduran villages.

A SHARED OFFICE NONETHELESS

The need for the Garifuna shaman to fit a cultural type creates relative stability and consistency among shamans' repertoires and methods, despite the fissiparous influences I address below. Shamans' personal qualities and life stories share much in common, and the tasks of the profession are also fairly well circumscribed. Shamans receive individuals as clients for consultation *(consultas)*, and they orchestrate and lead rituals as collective events. Their remuneration for this work is negotiated. The two tasks are closely related, as collective ritual events are initiated by individual consultations. Medical or psychological issues that are unresponsive to interventions, either shamanic cures of herbal baths and ointment or non-Garifuna medical treatments, fall into the category of gubida afflictions, manifestations of complaints from ancestral spirits that require communal attention.

On the morning of July 23, 2002, I witnessed an example of a call for collective ritual arising from a private consultation. A fifteen-year-old girl was brought from the city of La Ceiba by her parents to be seen by Carlitos in Corozal. The girl had been sick for two days. Her mouth was twisted, her tongue swollen, and her eyes rolled back in her head. Her hands were bent back to a contorted position, and she could not, or would not, speak. Laying her on the ground, the buyei began his work, blowing tobacco smoke over her body, spraying her with rum mist blown from his mouth, and shaking maracas over her afflicted parts. Local women were summoned to sing dügü songs *(amalahani)*. As she began to come to, her first words were a request for guaro. Staring fixedly at a lit candle on his altar, Carlitos discerned that she had been possessed by an ancestor, a great-grandmother from the village of Santa Fe who had died at the age of ninety-three. The family was told that they would need to mount a dügü ceremony during the next two years, or else the girl would die.

The consultations are always devoted to healing, broadly defined, in the sense that they seek remedies to immediate problems. Salomon named the most common ailments: pain *(dolor)*, chest pain, headaches or psychological issues *(cosa de cabeza)*, a perceived need for protective amulets, relationship problems, money troubles, and assorted everyday issues ("easy things"). Carlitos reports dealing with anemia, strokes, heart troubles, the need for work, sorcery *(hechicería)*, and protection against both black and white magic. Medicines in the form of baths, lotions, or swallowed liquids and pills are administered.[7] Carlitos said, "The spirits tell me what the person needs before they even arrive." Other clients come to try to recover lost or stolen objects. Shamans commonly prognosticate auspicious dates for travel and perform cleansings and protective rituals for newly built homes, the former by blowing smoke and rum from the mouth across doorways and windows, the latter by burying sharp stones and spiny sea urchins—"soldiers"— around the periphery of the courtyard. When the buyei is away, seekers leave request notes on the altar, and many are concerned with relationships: "Please 'tie up' Maria; she's taking all my brother's money"; "Please bring Marco back to me, lately always with that Flora."

Shamans also now minister to diasporic complaints. Mina of San Juan reports as her most commonly treated problem the fact that emigrant family members "don't send anything home." Carlitos frequently invokes the aid of his spirits in solving the visa complications of those hoping to emigrate or travel abroad. One regular client in San Juan complained to me that local women had learned from Dominicans in New York how to "zombify" their men, rendering them able to earn a paycheck but otherwise easily dominated.

The Shaman and the Pastor

As Protestantism, especially in the Pentecostal, evangelical style, has become a force in Honduras, it has influenced Garifuna practice and beliefs. In the villages, Protestant Garifuna are called *cristianos,* in contradistinction to *católicos.* Cristianos decry buyeis and their clients as devil worshippers, much in the style and terminology of early missionary accounts. The shamans increasingly are defined, and define themselves, as the guardians of tradition and culture in opposition to the cristianos. The cristianos provide an obvious foil for the shamans because they reject not only the spirits, the saints, and all the collective ritual events organized around them, but also the familiar recreational practices of informal punta dancing and the shared rum drinking and card games so crucial to men's friendship circles. Hence they are easily accused of abandoning the ancestors for the sake of imitating the U.S.-based denominations that often fund church construction. Conversely, as the "other" against which evangelical congregations are mobilized to action, the leaders of ancestor rituals are routinely demonized not only as diabolical but also as anachronistic. According to the pastor of the Baptist church in the village of San Juan (founded in 1982), "Buyeis are stuck in the past, leading a bunch of little old women *[viejitas]*." Evangelical Christianity, by contrast, for him represents dynamism and "the future." The fact that the cristianos' church is the largest and most modern structure in the village, equipped with a powerful sound system and filled with tie-wearing young men and carefully coiffed women, adds weight to the pastor's declaration.

To a degree, of course, the pastor's discourse calls equally on history and the past for purposes in the present. Jesus and the Holy Spirit act much like ancestors in the most general sense: they erect obstacles and then open paths for overcoming them, generating both needs and the techniques for their satisfaction. Among both evangelicals and traditionalist católicos, life crises are perceived as coded messages from the spirit world. Both groups occupy, moreover, a world perceived as a place of chronic spiritual combat. While the buyei's livelihood depends on her skills in protecting clients from bad spirits, Obeah-men, hechiceros, and displeased gubida, the pastor's bread and butter is the battle against traditional Garifuna religion. What is more, ritual events leading to revelatory states of consciousness—being "taken" by the spirits in one case, by the Holy Spirit in the other, but in both cases appealing to the authority of the past—are central to both groups' healing performances.

Despite these obvious similarities, we should draw a distinction between the expressed emphasis on continuity—"tradition" and "culture"—in one case, and on rupture, rebirth, and new beginnings in the other. Though both paradigms address the needs of everyday life, evangelicals focus their sermons and songs on radical transformation and systematic change. Significantly, conversion for cristianos must be manifested not only in personal piety but also in public, institutional shifts. This requirement is apparent in the life story of Pastor Nino of Corozal, who was converted from Catholicism in 1981 at a street mission in the large city of San Pedro Sula:

In 1982 I was saved, and my whole life changed. I started to follow the Word of God, and attended the Instituto Bíblica, in Tegucigalpa. I was frustrated with my work, and told God I didn't want to work for the church anymore. Then one night I woke up suddenly at 4 A.M. I felt a hand on my head, and heard a voice say, "Get up and go to Corozal." My wife and I got on a little 100cc motorcycle and rode to Corozal, pushing that bike up the hills sometimes, and going very slow, but always going. When we got there, a cristiano named Esteban told me they had been praying for a leader, and that I had been sent by God. But still we had no money and no place to meet. But now just look! We have a church, we've founded a nursery, and soon we'll be building our own primary school.

This narrative of personal transformation, leading to good works in the form of public institution-building, is quite different from those of buyeis. A shaman's life story typically emphasizes the discovery of the vocation during an unusual childhood or attributes it to a capacity inherited from a grandparent. The pastor's short narrative, by contrast, omits any genealogy or indeed the description of any life whatsoever "before Christ." Whereas shamans describe their work in terms of maintaining tradition and lament the changes of the present, the evangelical narrative reverses those values, ridiculing the "old" religion and celebrating futurity. This emphasis is evident not only in the pastor's narrative but also in worship services (cultos). In October and November 2000 I attended evangelical services in the village of Corozal. The speakers—both the pastor and the lay prayer leaders—consistently invoked biblical passages to justify looking ahead instead of to the past, the realm of the ancestors and their devotees.

In his sermon of October 17, 2000, Pastor Nino preached from the text of Joshua 1:1–10. In the passage, Moses is dead, and Joshua is called to lead. Despite his own doubts of his fitness to lead, Joshua will lead the people to the Promised Land of milk and honey. From the text, Pastor Nino leapt to the theme of facing obstacles in life, "crossing over them," and not giving up until change is achieved.

The next meeting built on the previous one. The story in the text, of the people crossing the River Jordan to reach the Promised Land, teaches us to "leave past failures behind" and move ahead toward a "week of victory." Repeated tropes of the sermon were those of "victory," "success," "achieving the objective," and, finally, "triumph over enemies" who seek to obstruct us (hacer frente) and "keep us in the past." At the third meeting, Pastor Nino preached about Joshua 5, a text dealing with circumcision. The sermon moved abruptly between the text and the argument that the people of God must "cut things from their old lives" in order to become new beings. The week after that (October 25), the congregation was directed to Psalms 18 and 28, in which King David calls on Jehovah to protect him against his enemies. Here Pastor Nino took the opportunity to inveigh against the enemies of Christ, foremost of whom are the "pagans" in the community who speak "words of evil." Jehovah is the "sword" who will cut them down in this ongoing war. The meeting closed with a song whose chorus was "You fight for me, I can feel it."

The focus on change and looking ahead is constant in evangelical Protestantism among the Garifuna. Just as Moses led the Israelites over the dried-up Red Sea, we too must "keep going forward." On November 5, the sermon discussed 2 Kings 22, a text in which Josiah rebuilds the Temple. The pastor used this is a platform to discuss "taking care of our bodies as temples." He lamented the behavior of his mother, who made sacrifices to the dead and was possessed by them instead of by the Bible. This situation would not continue for long, he proclaimed, for in her old body a new structure was being built. On November 8, Pastor Nino attacked the shamans explicitly: "When people see me on the street, they don't say, 'There's a buyei'; they say, 'There is a man who has the presence of God.'" He also attacked the católicos, often conflated with traditionalists who revere the ancestors. He pointed out that those who attend mass will likely be drinking afterward, and possibly even dancing in a discotheque later the same night. In coming months he planned a public outreach campaign that would place loudspeakers in the center of the village and broadcast worship services to disrupt the old habits.

On November 16, the twelfth anniversary of the church's founding, the text was Psalm 67 and the topic mercy, but the sermon highlighted those backsliders who "fall away into the past," and begin to again consult witches, prognosticators, and cartomancers or the false powers of the ancestors, the saints, and the Virgin.

The theme of radical transformation and futurity was further reinforced in the songs that play a key role in the evangelical culto, such as the following:

The chains that bound me have been broken,
You rescued me from enslavement
so that I won't die in sin.[8]

I'm so happy, He saved me,
I'm so happy, He saved me
Glory, hallelujah, He saved me,
Though I'm a sinner, He saved me.[9]

The church's aesthetics add yet another layer to the message. On the inside wall of the evangelical church, a bold sign reads: "God sent his word over Corozal and cleansed it and freed it from ruin" *(Envío Dios su palabra sobre Corozal y lo sanó y lo libró de la ruina)*. The sign captures precisely the evangelical view of the shamans, their cures, and the ancestor rituals they guide: they are debris and decaying ruins on which a new edifice must be built. The conflict between cristianos and católicos is in part, therefore, a battle over the temporal order that governs the village. Cristianos contest the traditional calendar, measured in intervals from one saint's festival to another and punctuated by large-scale ritual events, with the evangelical church week and the negation of the ritual and festal cycle. The same conflict is evident in the cristianos' discursive erection of a temporal order in which the shamans' work and the rituals of ancestors are dismissed as the culture "of the past."

Because the cristianos envision the future as both a time and a process involving the physical transformation of the village, their war against traditionalists is also one of space. Cristianos often attempt to occupy the public sphere, planting speakers and microphone stands on the main thoroughfare to transform not only the hearts of new converts but also the local sound- and streetscape. They build large, modern churches and schools. They offer chances for lay men and women to assume leadership as prayer leaders and musicians; these lay leaders convey economic prosperity through their careful grooming and dress. The evangelical cultos provide a new and exciting source of entertainment, with meetings at least four nights weekly, and so begin literally to beat out paths that lead away from the beach or the soccer field and toward these attractive, well-lit, loudly modern spaces. But the tensions between shaman and pastor are played out above all on the bodies of the sick.

WHAT IS A SICK BODY? CONFLICT IN THE RELIGIOUS FIELD

On October 30, 2000, in Corozal, an adolescent girl in a mud house suddenly broke out in anguished screams and howls. Neighbors rushed to investigate the disturbance and, peering in the windows, found the young woman rolling on the floor. Brooms were knocked over, and a pot crashed from a table to the ground. Family members tried to console her, finally pinning her down physically, patting her cheeks, and demanding to know what was the matter. A sister tried to force her to drink water. The girl continued to roll her head wildly from side to side, unresponsive to all questions. As curious onlookers gathered, her father closed the shutters. Her brother ran to seek out the local shaman, even as her grandmother screamed at him to stay put, that this was no place for a shaman to meddle. A loud argument ensued between the father and grandmother, the father defending the shaman's skills while the grandmother insisted that this was "devil's work." The grandmother began to pray loudly to Jesus, in the evangelical style, begging him to save her daughter from the evil spirits. The shaman arrived fifteen minutes later, by which time the girl was quiet, though she remained prone on the ground in a trancelike catalepsy.

The onlookers dispersed, debating among themselves the nature of the problem. One young man defended epilepsy as the most likely cause, while his friend declared that she was a known alcoholic who "lived for the bottle." It was widely reported, though, that the girl had been heard yelling that she wanted to visit the cemetery—a sure sign that the ancestors were responsible for the attacks.

After the buyei emerged, he explained that the girl had been stricken several times before. Through divination he had consulted his helping spirits and learned that the girl's deceased mother was making demands by causing her illness. In particular, the mother wanted a chugu to be performed on her behalf. The chugu is a costly ritual requiring a large amount of food and rum and the hiring of specialists like the shaman, drummers, and singers. It usually lasts one or two days, and it can cost anywhere from five to eight thousand lempira ($330 to $530), a sum well beyond the family's resources. The shaman spoke soothingly to the afflicting spirit and bargained her down to accepting an abundant "mass" (lemesi) in return for releasing the girl from the attacks. A mass is a cheaper half-day ritual that includes Catholic recitations in addition to food offerings but does not call for expensive sacrifices or musicians. The agreement was therefore a substantial concession from the spirit. But even this the family did not do. They took no action because the grandmother and the aunt of the household were cristianos who viewed both the attacks and the proposed ritual remedy as satanic.

By wiping the girl's head with rum, blowing pipe smoke on her, and shaking his maracas over her to pacify and control the attacking spirit, the buyei calmed the girl and then returned to his home to rest in his hammock. This was, he said, at best a temporary resolution. The family would have to make serious choices if she were to live.

The central question of the event was the role of spirits. Even a physical explanation offered by several observers did not resolve the larger question of why epilepsy or alcohol might wreak such terrible havoc on the poor girl's body. That spiritual forces were involved was not in serious doubt. The question was, were the attacks from spirits ultimately from Satan, or were they from a deceased relative insisting on respect in the form of a chugu ritual? In either case, the situation called for a concrete, material response. If the source of affliction were Satan, the solution would be a visit to Pastor Nino, who would counsel the girl to renounce her pagan past and come forward in church that night for special prayers and the "laying on of hands." The congregants would call on the Holy Spirit and Jesus to cast out her demons. If an ancestor spirit were responsible, the solution would be to attend more carefully to the obligations of the past. The family would arrive at an agreement with Carlitos the shaman and borrow money to hold the requested chugu. The ritual would satisfy the spirit of the victim's mother, at least temporarily, with food, drink, song, and dance. In a house united under either religious system, remedial action could have been taken. But in a house divided, with half of the family members calling themselves católicos and embracing the spirits and half calling themselves cristianos and rejecting the spirits for the Holy Spirit, no consensus could be reached.

The girl's twisting body provided a platform for each side to press their claims and accuse the other of misrecognition and blasphemy. In everyday life, the religiously divided household functioned normally, going out to work, preparing food, watching television, and gossiping. The grandmother and aunt attended nightly meetings at the church whose loudspeakers boomed from the other side of the village. The father and eldest son played dominoes and, when they had money, drank rum. The underlying tensions only emerged on the occasion of the girl's attack. Caught between two religious systems, her body was the symptom, sign, and site of the conflict. Ultimately the family offered the chugu, but this only partly remedied the girl's condition because the cristianos refused to take part. She continued to suffer sporadic attacks.

This house is representative of many houses in the village and the general social tension over rituals led by shamans. Because those rituals center on dancing and drinking, the cristianos proudly avoid any such gatherings. During a dügü, in which all extended family members are required to participate, the rituals are often said to fail and to have lost their power because the evangelical family members refuse to attend. The religious war is therefore also a culture war about what being Garifuna should mean. Such abstract questions were condensed, presented, and disputed in tangible form in the sick girl's body, rent between "the future" and "the past."

While the local religious field has been transformed by the widespread conversion of cristianos since about 1980, it is also being transformed through the influence of traditionals returning from New York. Some of these are Garifuna shamans who relocated to New York but who return periodically to recharge their forces through contact with a now-sacralized homeland. Some are not shamans but simply Garifuna emigrants who have discovered a previously unfelt need for, and interest in, the ancestor rites. When the traditionalist New Yorkers arrive with their cosmopolitan status—their stylish shoes and clothing, their DVDs and Courvoisier, and their knowledge of the broader African diaspora—they dramatically counter the cristianos' relegation of the buyeis to the past. Suddenly the "old" ritual is filled with English slang, video cameras, and elegant African couture. When the temple is possessed by the spirits, it signifies pastness but now also futurity, just like the temple of the cristianos' Holy Spirit across the village. The two modernities, the evangelical one and the neotraditional one, converge, compete with, and mutually constitute each other. I now turn to the source of this rejuvenation of tradition: the Garifuna shamans and their spirit world in the Bronx.

CHAPTER 4

Shamans at Work in New York

The traveler's past changes according to the route he has
followed: not the immediate past, that is, to which each day
that goes by adds a day, but the more remote past. Arriving
at each new city, the traveler finds again a past of his that he
did not know he had; the foreignness of what you no longer
are or no longer possess lies in wait for you in foreign,
unpossessed places.

Italo Calvino, Invisible Cities

The old buyeis didn't want to tell anyone anything, they all
wanted to be unique. But a culture can't keep itself closed.
For others to know you, you've got to talk about it.

New York shaman

In this chapter I consider Garifuna religious leaders in New York and
the processes through which a religion derived from African,
Amerindian, and European sources is being remade as an African
Diaspora religion—a set of practices consciously part of a specific religious family that includes Santería, Palo Monte, Vodou, Candomblé,
and Spiritism. I first present shamans' own stories of how they became
buyeis in a wider religious field and describe their altars as material
indices of practice. I then give special attention to spirit geographies,
examining the shifts in the places spirits are said to come from. I also
explore the degree to which the new version of Garifuna is "hardened"
into rational forms of texts and institutions and for that reason is likely

to endure. Finally, I describe attempts to remit such innovations to the homeland, and the fissures produced in contests between differing versions of orthodoxy: New York Garifuna religious leaders pit their cosmopolitan authority against homeland religious leaders' territorial or indigenous authority.

Religious Autobiographies

Many life stories of New York shamans begin by following the familiar account of becoming a buyei but go on to include striking departures from that predictable account. Here is the story of Tola Guerreiro, a senior buyei in New York:

At six or seven years of age I would "see" people in our house eating with us. I told my grandmother, who said that wasn't true, it couldn't be. She denied what I saw. I remember that at around twelve I wasn't normal—I wanted to hang around with the grandmothers *[las abuelas]*, and I loved religious things. By the time I was fifteen we were already in the U.S. I came with my grandmother. I was aware of the spirits, I could feel them, even though they never spoke to me. Once we went back to Honduras, to Triunfo, and I went to see the buyei named Tino; he said I would become a buyei too. My grandmother said no, that "those people suffer too much." My grandmother thought I would forget about all that in the U.S., that the spirits wouldn't follow me. I went to church a lot, and took herb baths to keep the spirits away.

At twenty-one, I got married and just wanted to have a normal life. But I still had nightmares of the spirits coming. I thought I was crazy! My family didn't accept what I had. There weren't any buyeis in the U.S. back then [ca. 1975]. I couldn't work, I was always hearing voices, or people singing. Finally I ran away from New York to New Orleans to stay with a relative. Things were quiet for a while, but then one day I came back from work and heard them: "We found you!" And the same thing started again. My relatives in New Orleans were Baptist, they didn't want me around at all, not like this, so I went to Miami to stay with an aunt. Same thing. In those days, I could hear people talking from a distance, and I overheard my aunt's husband saying things about me, that I had the devil, or that I was nuts. The next morning I left a note, and was gone. My husband and I loved each other, you know, but this thing was so big. We got together again in New Orleans for three years, and I got pregnant with my oldest son. Things quieted down a little.

Meanwhile, back in Honduras, in Triunfo, the buyei Tino had died, but Chichi, his successor, called for me to perform a dügü. The spirits really started calling for it now. One day I felt like I had to take a bath in guaro, or I would suddenly catch a trance. I saw the spirits speaking through the television: "Keimon, keimon Triunfo!" [Let's go to Triunfo!]. This was about 1981. I almost became a bag lady.

FIGURE 11. The buyei Tola Guerreiro consulting her spirits (ahari) on behalf of a client in the Bronx. Such consultations are part of the daily routine of established shamans. Photo by author.

Well, I went back to Triunfo, and I gave the dügü, and I had my initiations—two weeks closed up in the spirit house, then climbing the pole, and finally getting my maracas and setting up my altar back in New York. Then I felt fine. I didn't feel anything. Nothing! The old buyeis in Triunfo said it was because the spirits were content now, but they'd be back. When? No one knew. So I went dancing with my friends, had a good time. Until one day I was at a party and saw my uncle, but with someone standing behind him, like a shadow. I came home and dreamed about it, and then I caught a trance. When I woke up my mouth was funny and I couldn't move, and my sister called an ambulance. But at the hospital they couldn't find anything wrong. But I knew what I had! Later that uncle had to go the hospital with diabetes and glaucoma, that's what I had seen at the party. And so, little by little, I started gaining confidence.

Then I saw this woman on a bus, and I saw her body like an X-ray, her organs. I saw a black object behind her lungs. I knew it was cancer. She saw me staring at her. The spirits said I had to talk to her. But I was too timid. When I got home I caught a trance, but I just didn't have the confidence. Later I saw her again, and she asked me, "You were looking at me before. What did you see in me?" I was sweating! I asked her if she ever felt pain in her lungs. She said she did, and I told her she needed to see a doctor. I didn't tell her it was cancer. But sure enough, she saw the doctor and had surgery for lung cancer to get that out. That's how I started.

Tola's story up to this point contains many familiar themes from the life stories of homeland shamans: the sensation of being different as a young person, experiences of visions and dreams, the attempt to flee her destiny by moving from place to place, the resistance and denial from family members, recognition at some point by a respected older buyei, and the gradual replacement of uncontrolled torment by the spirits with the assistance of spirits now won over as allies. The buyei accomplishes in her own body and in a permanent way the transition through which she will later guide others in ritual: the transformation of spirit afflictions into spirit benefits. This unfolds according to the same basic pattern as in the homeland, by changing the status of the spirits from that of fearsome outsiders to that of family members with responsibilities toward the living. In emic terms, this transition occurs by submitting the power of gubida (demands and afflictions) to that of hiyuruha (powers and benefits).

At this point, however, new elements enter Tola's narrative, as she begins to reread her religious tradition in light of other religions of the African Diaspora.

There was this event in Brooklyn in June one year. It was about Afro cultures. Someone saw it on the Internet and sent it to me, and I just applied. I explained on the forms who we were, and we got in! Six buyeis with drummers went. There were groups from everywhere there, Cubans, Brazilians, Africans. We got to know each other and talked. Some of these people started coming to my January 15 ritual, the return of the ancestors. Their religion is the same as ours. The Cubans use conga drums, and we use more traditional ones, but it's the same.

I went to Cuban *toques* [Santería ceremonies with drums], and I have some Cuban friends I learned things from. I taught them how to use sand on their altars. Now I wear Cuban *collares* [necklaces marking orisha affiliation]. Buyeis always wore something like that, so why not? All this is from Africa, just in different words. They have Yemoja, the goddess of the sea; we have a mermaid too, Mowumed. They have the river goddess, Ochun; we have the same thing, Agayuma. They have Eleggua, who opens doors and guards crossroads; we have the *iyayawa*. Some say, "I'm not going to Santería, I'm no santera." I say, why not? We've got mermaids, like Yemoja, we dance by the sea. So what are you fighting me for?! Then the people say, "Yeah!" I see it, and then I write it down and tell people about it.

Tola also mastered techniques learned from Cuban *paleros,* practitioners of Palo Monte, whose tradition she viewed as similar to her own. Tola notes the common use of *palos* (staffs or sticks). Moreover, both the Garifuna tradition and Palo Monte include "soldiers," ritual objects enlisted to protect the shaman from evil spirits. Influenced by Palo Monte, Tola maintains a *caldero* (also Spanish *prenda,* Bakongo *nganga;* see the appendix)—an iron pot that contains material objects symbolic of a contract between the caldero's owner and a spirit of the dead—as part of her extended altar, and refers to it as her "soldier": "Any bad spirits chasing me, it will chase away."

Tola calls such spirits *my gang.* Lydia Cabrera wrote in the mid-twentieth-century Cuban context that "all these animals [contained in the Afro-Cuban nganga], each one according to its character, are the *slave gangs*" (Cabrera, quoted in Palmié 2002: 176, italics mine). When a Garifuna shaman in New York refers to the spirits of the dead contained in her caldero as "my gang," however, she invokes a new meaning, namely the dangers of the city streets, and a perceived threat to her safety countered by her own defenders (cf. K. Brown 1991: 302; McAlister 1992).

Moreover, the toy car that rests atop her caldero, one of the material aspirations for which she enlists the aid of the captive *muerto* (spirit of the dead), provides an index of her relationship to space in the city, the need for greater mobility and speed, and her desire to open up her territory.[1] The demands of the new space, where "time is money," create a drift toward the spirits who work fast. Elizabeth McAlister documented such a drift among Haitians in New York toward the fast-working Petwo spirits, the spirits that can be bought, and away from the "pure" Ginen (West African) spirits (1992: 20). The same phenomenon occurs among the Garifuna in New York. As their religious practice draws selectively from extant African Diaspora religions, especially from the pervasive Cuban repertoire of Santería and Palo Monte, they have adopted not only the orishas but also the muertos and the calderos that contain them. As one Garifuna shaman told me, "The Garifuna ancestors, they're family, but they can be slow; the muertos [of Palo], you have to watch out, because they eat *everything,* but they work fast." Working fast, covering ground, allying with a gang that watches your back—this is the semantic context of the caldero in New York.

I asked Tola why she now uses the terms of Cuban Santería and Palo Monte instead of the names for the similar Garifuna entities—why she now speaks of Eleggua and Yemoja, or the muerto contained in her caldero, in place of the equally "fast" and "hungry" Garifuna spirits of the forest. She replied, "Because it's more common here. I'm trying to help our people get educated a little, and they're accepting it little by little." This last phrase is important because it points in her own terms to the

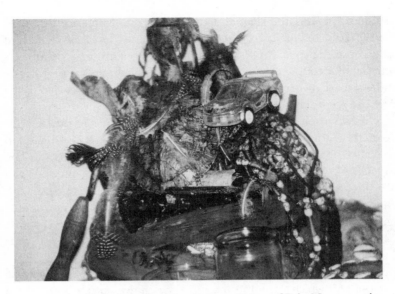

FIGURE 12. A caldero from the Afro-Cuban religion of Palo Monte on the altar of a Garifuna shaman in the Bronx. Turtle shells remain from a sacrificial offering, and the toy car models the transportation this spirit is expected to provide. Photo by author.

transformations I am trying to describe. As Garifuna religious culture is articulated in the new space, both by insiders and by outsiders, it is fitted to existing categories, semiotic niches, and social groups. Garifuna religious actors adopt this new language and worldview partly to translate themselves into terms familiar to the host communities. At the same time, they begin to adopt those terms into their own practice and self-understanding.

On another occasion when I asked Tola why she was adopting non-Garifuna spirits, she told me they added flexibility to her work: "What if I need work done when the hiyuhura leave for Sairi [from mid-December to mid-January]?" At other times she presented the caldero and its muerto as "the same" as spirits of the forest in the Garifuna pantheon: both are characterized by their capacity for violence, speed, efficiency, and a mercenary focus on "getting the job done," regardless of motive. Yet she sometimes also deferred to the specific rules of the adopted spirits and acknowledged the need for outside help in negotiating the demands they made on her. "Sometimes I call my Cuban *madrina* ["godmother," the guide of her Palo initiation] to help, because I have the caldero and it needs to be fed; like if I'm menstruating, she has to take care of it." Once adopted, the new religious needs are self-perpet-uating: the contract between a priest and a muerto can never be abandoned or renounced without drastic consequences.

The adoption of and interaction with non-Garifuna spirits might be said to mirror, model, and present to consciousness the tension between homeland and diaspora. The Garifuna spirits are familiar but, like family members, demand constant attention, negotiation, emotional invest-ment, and faith. The foreign spirits, by contrast—the muertos and orisha warriors—are absolutely rational. Models of efficiency, they work for pay, and although they may be demanding in financial terms, requir-ing repeated costly offerings, they present few of the emotional com-plications of spirits, or family members, from the homeland. The new spirits work on the terms of the United States: they are contracted as wage labor (cf. Palmié 2002; Richman 2005).

Working with multiple spirit groups, the familial and the foreign, and negotiating the distinct social relations of each constructs a micro-cosm of the diasporic experience in general, with its alternating attrac-tions and resistances to new sources of power in the host land. Like the host society itself, the Cuban and Puerto Rican specialists and their spirits are sometimes viewed ambivalently. On October 23, 2004, I attended a Palo ceremony with a group of Garifuna shamans. Riding in the van en route, one of them spread white eggshell powder into all the passengers' open hands, and we rubbed it over heads and necks for "protection." "You never know what you're going to face when you go to one of these things," she said. On another occasion she recounted how one *padrino,* a leader in Cuban Santería, had tried to control her and her ancestors. Her Garifuna spirits fought back: "I heard a voice in my head in Garifuna, 'This son of a bitch isn't going to tell us what to do,' and they [her spirits] lifted these plants into the air and smashed them onto the table. It was like a movie or something! And this Cuban padrino fell over backward in his chair, saying, 'Those [spirits] are bad!'"

The new families of spirits hold out both an attraction and a per-ceived threat to the distinctiveness and autonomy of the Garifuna spir-its. The adoption of the new spirits, however ambivalently undertaken, represents a striking shift. For Garifuna buyeis born and raised in the United States, or those newer to their religious vocation, that shift is far more pronounced and is now an integral part of becoming a Garifuna specialist of spirit work. Unlike most homeland shamans, most of the ten New York shamans I interviewed and whose rituals I visited reported having only a slight religious interest during their childhood.

Moreover, in most cases they underwent conversions to traditional Garifuna practice based on experiences specific to New York. One female shaman declared: "There [in Honduras] the culture is just the air you breathe. When you come here [to New York], you realize what you are." That is, they arrived at their heightened consciousness *as* Garifuna precisely through a reactive process of an assertion and defense of their identity. But this reactive Garifuna identification is also forged in the context of the religious network of New York, and particularly of the African Diaspora. As an elderly female shaman affirmed, "When I was a girl, we didn't know we were African, that we had a long, ancient history. Nobody talked about that. Just that we came from St. Vincent."

How did they embark on their occupations as Garifuna traditional religious specialists? Consider the life story of another shaman, Felix Miranda, who was raised in the Belizean village of Hopkins:

As a boy growing up in Hopkins, I used to "get in the spirit." Coming from school or playing, I would see these people coming toward me, and then not remember anything. I was about nine or ten years old. My grandmother was the only person who could help. She would bathe me in certain herbs, and I would sleep, and then wake up not in trance. She was a medicine woman. By the age of thirteen to fourteen it no longer happened. I always wondered what it was.

I came to this country in 1971, on my twenty-fifth birthday. I did a bachelor's degree in business administration and a master's in finance. In 1985, just after I finished graduate school, I remembering going to work and hearing my grandmother's voice saying, "Let's go home." I would feel like I was floating.

Since 1991 I was the host of the first Garifuna radio show in the U.S., Lumalali Garifuna [Voice of the Garifuna], broadcast from Medgar Evers College. One day, it was February 1992, I heard this radio show on WLIB. It was a show on "ancestors and ancestor worship," and I called in to participate on the program. The woman hosting it asked me to call her off the air, after the show. She was a professor of sociology at Medgar Evers, and she was a Yoruba priestess. She did divination for me, but instead of the orishas, it was more my ancestors manifesting. She told me I have ancestors around me and that I have to do something for them. In 1996 I was initiated as a Yoruba ancestor priest [egungun egbe], at Oyotunji in South Carolina. That's where this priestess was from. In fact, her husband was a Yoruba priest and became my godfather during my initiation—since men can't be initiated by women into the egungun [a Yoruba ancestor-devotion and masquerade society]. But then I was told by the king at Oyotunji that "we can't do more for you until you become a Garifuna priest. That's what the ancestors want you to do."

My dreams got more intense. Now they were of family members telling me exactly what they want done. This Garifuna lady in New York, from Livingston [Guatemala], who was just an acquaintance, called me and said she'd had dreams about me, that I had to be initiated. So after that, I got closer to Nitu [another Garifuna shaman in New York], and we started talking more about organizing a group of buyeis. And again it came up that I had to be initiated. But still it took a long time—till last year [2000], then I went to Belize to be initiated, to climb the pole. I wasn't in trance all the way during that. I remember I felt light-headed. Something envelops me until I want to shed tears. Then I know they're around.

For Felix, these transforming experiences were specific to New York City.

There was a reason why I came here [to New York]. Much of what I know today, and much of the pride I take in being Garifuna, would not have happened had I not come to the U.S. There's so much in books, so much resources [sic], of symbols, even in people that you interact with, and you begin to see similarities [between groups of African descent]. Coming here has really opened my eyes, a millionfold. Particularly about who we really are. Because I had to find out who I was. One of the things I dreaded was, what if somebody asks me who I am, I would say I am a Garifuna, and they went, "What is that?" Today I don't have to panic, because I know our African roots. But growing up in school I thought this whole thing was Indian!

Felix's story suggests that his arrival to consciousness as Garifuna in New York had important effects on how the tradition is remembered and reconstituted. For him, the pan-African network in general, and the Yoruba tradition in particular, were and are the prism through which he began to see and appreciate Garifuna religion anew. This way of seeing has both the general effect of giving value to an African genealogy that was forgotten, neglected, or suppressed and specific effects on the way given symbols are viewed. In regard to the Catholic crucifix, a symbol typically present on buyeis' altars, for example, he commented, "When I studied Yoruba religion, and the symbol of Elegba being the crossroads, I realized the cross has been used even a long time before the time of Christ. So to me, the cross represents a pathway, a crossroads." For Felix, the present is a purifying and desyncretizing moment: "We do not need the symbol of the force, the saints, anymore to call upon the force. We don't need that symbol anymore, because we now know and understand that force."

There are other examples of the conversion to a conscious Garifuna identity occurring through the prism of the African Diaspora religious networks of New York. Another Bronx-based Garifuna shaman was a professional dancer and studied Yoruba orisha dance moves in dance classes before she began her initiation as a Garifuna shaman. Based on such experiences and reading on the Yoruba orishas that followed, she had already equated the traditions as "the same" before beginning her specifically Garifuna practice.

A fourth Garifuna shaman in the Bronx, Marilene, was rescued from a psychic crisis by her building superintendent, who found her on the floor staring fixedly at an overhead light bulb. The super was a Cuban santera. Regarding her helper as "spiritually more advanced," Marilene underwent preliminary initiations in Cuban Santería. Only when she was possessed by spirits speaking in Garifuna did she elect to pursue her own religious tradition. Thomas, a young shaman in the Bronx who also leads rituals during yearly returns to his Honduran village, Triunfo de la Cruz, has been advised by his Garifuna ancestors that he needs to "seat" (be initiated to) Santería deities, the ochas, and is seeking the extensive funds required.

Tola, meanwhile, the longest-practicing Bronx Garifuna religious leader, enjoys visits to Palo and Santería ceremonies and has attended Vodou rituals as well.[2] She has invited leaders of these other religions to visit Garifuna villages with her and has shown and discussed with them videotapes of Garifuna homeland rituals.

All the Bronx shamans I interviewed read popular books about the Yoruba pantheon. In addition, they shop for their ritual herbs and implements where they are most readily available, namely at the botánicas owned by Puerto Ricans, Cubans, and Dominicans that dot the streets of the Bronx and Harlem, and which commingle Spiritist and Afro-Latin products among their wares. Many shamans ride the subway to shop at El Congo Real, a large botánica located near 110th and Lexington, in Manhattan. From the shopkeepers there, Garifuna leaders acquire advice on the "correct" use of the herbs and implements.

Garifuna religious leaders in New York are articulating their notion of ancestry and orthodoxy in a dramatically different religious field from that of the homeland. As a result, and in taking advantage of its established economic and social niches—its botánicas, popular literature, meeting places, and already-developed clientele—Bronx Garifuna religious leaders now view the Garifuna tradition as one spoke in the wheel of the African Diaspora—a diaspora which is, however, strongly circumscribed by longer-established groups in major U.S. cities like New York. One leader, Francisco, reflecting a sentiment widely reported by Bronx Garifuna, declared: "We didn't know exactly who we were or where our roots were. To survive here [in New York], Garifunas made themselves pass for blacks of other nationalities [i.e., Cubans, Haitians,

Dominicans, Puerto Ricans, and Jamaicans]." The nature of that available black and pan-African identity was primarily Yoruba and to a lesser degree Kongo and Spiritist, as mediated by those "blacks of other nationalities." The Garifuna, relative newcomers to the religious marketplace of the Bronx, had to find a place in an urban religious territory already parsed and marked.

Spirit Geographies

The niches to which Garifuna religion is adapted in New York shape its practice. The urban geography and social terrain influence the spirit geography, the places of origin of the spirits who aid and instruct buyeis. Since these spirit guides act as both individual alter egos of the shaman and as ancestors, as an implicit collective memory, those spirits' places of origin offer a way of interpreting subjective views about ethnicity. They indirectly suggest emic answers to the question, Where are you authentically from?

Never in my extensive work with five homeland shamans in three Honduran communities (Corozal, San Juan, and Triunfo de la Cruz) were the tutelary spirits said to originate from Africa. For example, Salomon, the shaman of the village of San Juan, named seven helping spirits, each with particular characteristics and skills, and described them all as "little people" from St. Vincent. Carlitos, in the village of Corozal, had four tutelary spirits. Of these, one was from Sambu (Sambo Creek, a neighboring village), another from Corozal, and two others from Belize, all Garifuna villages. Though one of these spirits, Dabwi, was introduced as "global" and said to speak "French, orisha, all languages," his origins are local. Mina, from San Juan, spoke of several hiyuruha, all from Honduran villages. Mina's spirits cannot derive from elsewhere because, unlike some leaders in Honduras and all those interviewed in New York, she has never attended a conference, traveled abroad, or read books about other places—never, in other words, developed a wider sense of imagined community that her spirits might begin to represent and express. Even the story of St. Vincent is hazy to her. Her spirits' local geography refracts her own known world and its boundaries.

Among Bronx-based shamans, by contrast, at least one tutelary spirit is nearly always African, either *nkisi* (Kongo) or orisha (West African Yoruba). Marilene, for example, works with three spirits. Matuco is an indigenous Indian from Honduras. Cresencia is one of Marilene's own ancestors, a great-grandmother who acted as a midwife. The third, Hermanito, also called *el negro,* was the "chief of an African tribe." Tola used to work with many spirits, but now the two most influential are Lulu (Mary Louise), from Dangriga, in Belize, and Oyendi, an African male "from Kongo." Oyendi reflects Tola's growing experience with other, especially Cuban African, diaspora religions. She has undergone a Cuban Palo Monte initiation, a religious complex explicitly invoking African (Kongo) origins.

Felix also has two main spirit helpers. Travil David is a spirit from St. Vincent. "He takes me from present to past and into the future," explained Felix. "I can see what happened even during slavery; he showed that to me." His second hiyuruha is an African American spirit who reveals himself only as Prodigy. This spirit told Felix about the location of the bodies of former African slaves interred underneath 26 Federal Plaza, declaring that the ancestors located in this burial ground were being expelled by the city. In this case, the spirit's intervention was related to a specific political crisis, a controversy surrounding a burial ground near City Hall.[3] "We did a ritual for those ancestors, but not much. There were a variety of leaders with different opinions about what should be done, and you know, who am I?" While Felix's spirit geography departs slightly from the pattern I am describing, it embraces a broadly pan-African perspective that differs from the spirit geographies of most Central American buyeis.

The influence of the broader African Diaspora religious network is expressed in material ways as well. Many Bronx shamans wear plastic bead necklaces, *collares,* that mark their orisha affiliations. one young woman named Belgium, for example, wears five such necklaces; Felix wears a bracelet *(ide)* linking him to the patron of Yoruba divination, Ifa. Others are presently considering performing Santería or Palo Monte initiations, having been informed by their Bronx neighbors that they "need" to undergo them. In the homes of many Bronx-based Garifuna shamans, altars to Eleggua or his palero counterpart, Lucero, guard corners and doorways. These spirit warriors and guardians do not exist in the repertoire of traditional homeland Garifuna practices.

ALTAR SYMBOLS

Bronx shamans' representations of their sources of power at their physical altars, unlike those displayed on homeland altars, are replete with objects familiar to students of West African–influenced religions in the Americas. These often include the trickster, messenger, and keeper of doorways and crossroads, Eshu-Eleggua (or Lucero); the goddess of oceans, Yemaya (or the palero Madre de Aguas, or Tiembla Tierra); the forest hunter, Oshossi (or, in Cuban and Brazilian representation, an Amerindian *caboclo*); the god of iron and war, Ogun (or Zarabanda); and Shango, god of fire and lightning (or Siete Rayos). The use of dolls, scissors, and other physical objects metaphorically and metonymically communicates the desired ritual effects of "binding," "reversing," or "sweetening" a given person or situation. These latter objects suggest influences that may include Vodou practices derived from West and Central African (Dahomean and Kongo) ritual.[4] In addition, the altars of Bronx Garifuna shamans have incorporated the iron calderos from Cuban Palo, La Madama from Puerto Rican popular practice, and the entire orisha complex from the semiotically hegemonic pan-African religious system of representations, a condensed and standardized canon of the Yoruba pantheon.

They have also incorporated new forms of ritualization, the most striking of which is the practice of securing and protecting the doorways and crossroads of apartments and communal ritual sites through sacrifices and offerings to "pay," "feed," and replenish the spirit gang. This practice also echoes Cuban-redacted Kongo and Yoruba ritual practice, with its focus on mediators and protectors against unwanted intrusions, on "soldiers" who patrol the periphery. The ritualizations indicate not only a new religious field but also the Garifuna encounter with new social needs that no traditional Garifuna entities are seen as equipped or trained to serve.

All of these trends suggest an emergent pattern of transculturation: not the ballyhooed merger of African gods with the Catholic saints, but the "compartmental syncretism" (Bastide 1978a: 260–84) of Garifuna spirits' material representations and those of Cuban Santería and West African Yoruba spirits. This pattern justifies a view of Garifuna as a dramatically innovative and additive religion (Mintz and Price 1992: 10, 45, 51; cf. Bastide 1978a, 1978b). However, Garifuna religion not only adds to its pantheon and repertoire but also is changed. Its leaders become purveyors of a new religious system that is both ethnically narrowed and semantically expanded. Adopting signs and symbols clearly defined as "African" lends the practice authenticity and depth, yet also distinction from simple U.S.-style blackness; it also becomes, de facto, Yoruba focused. But it is semantically expansive as well: Garifuna ritual practice now not only signifies the reverence of family ancestors but also incorporates Africa, Africanness, and the multiple neighboring Bronx religions that represent and construct them.

FIGURE 13. Part of a New York Garifuna shaman's altar, with objects devoted to Yoruba (and Afro-Cuban) deities. The iron cogs and tools on the left represent Ogun, orisha of iron, stubborn strength, and technology. The figure with the face of shells is Eleggua. On the right are the legs of a folkloric Amerindian representing Oshossi, the Yoruba deity of the forest and the hunt. The opened scissors set on an overturned glass, I was told, signify and materialize the intent to cut and reverse a particular set of difficult circumstances. Photo by author.

FIGURE 14. A doll and a baked apple set in honey on a New York Garifuna shaman's altar. This intervention was intended to "sweeten" the heart of a client's runaway daughter to induce her to return. Photo by author.

MAKING THE HOMELAND FROM AFAR

As new elements are added to the Garifuna religion through association with a broader religious network, old elements are resignified. One example is the relative valuations of the homeland and New York by the diasporic shamans. According to Tola:

In Honduras, I have much more spiritual power, because of the nature. Here in this concrete, these walls, this takes everything out of you. The spirits don't like the cold weather. They always go back to St. Vincent, that's the homeland, they always go, always. In Honduras they stay around more than here. Everything is there, in the nature, but not here. So I go there every year to refresh my energy. . . . I tell the buyeis here [in New York], you have to go to Honduras to learn more, because they have more experience there. Here they just know what I tell them, but it's not the same, hearing and doing.

Yet even as Honduras becomes a diasporically imagined homeland, an idealized and sacralized place endowed with special force, it is also a place where New Yorkers feel a degree of social alienation as expatriates. Here is Tola speaking again:

What I notice when I go is that I don't know many people anymore! Some of the people I grew up with are in New York; others are in Belize, or got married and went to another village. The new generation, they don't know you, they look at you like an outsider. My kids, the U.S. is their country. For me, too, after being in Honduras a while, I like to come back. But the kids have more trouble. When we're there, they would always ask, "Ay, Mami, you don't miss the sirens, the firetrucks? Eating 'Kentucky' [fried chicken]?"

For those born in New York, second-generation migrants, the cityscape is home, and Honduras is the exotic place. Traveling to the homeland villages, for these children of emigrants, evokes mixed sentiments. They enjoy special status there, and elicit attention with their clothes, music, and electronic toys, all of which communicate superior socioeconomic status. The perception of those differences begins a socialization process by which homeland children very early realize that the successful people are those who emigrate abroad. Yet for children born in New York, their special status in the village wears thin after a few weeks. They find far less stimulation there than at home in the city; the attractions of the "tradition" consumed so eagerly by their elders miss their mark with the returning youths, who report missing the speed and sound of busy streets.

SEDIMENTING "GARIFUNA CULTURE"

Let us distinguish two distinct processes with regard to sedimentation. The first is the concern to mark out a given discursive terrain as "Garifuna culture." The second is to transform that bounded category into forms that can be taught, transmitted, and institutionalized.

Tola's words illustrate the move toward creating "Garifuna culture" as a discursive, public entity: "The buyeis are the people who maintain the culture, the faith." In Honduras this mission opposes the efforts of the evangelicos, but in the United States buyeis must work against not only evangelicals but also the risk of assimilation.

Here I don't have as much time for consultas because there is so much organizational work, plus the need to talk to kids about our culture. . . . Here in New York, there's the good and the bad parts: we learn about other cultures, but some people leave their culture. But one thing that makes me happy is that in the old days the Garifuna culture was a culture of whispering [*susurrava mucho*], it was like a taboo, you couldn't talk about the spirituality. But we've started to change, and even the professional people have started opening their eyes to our spirituality—the Ph.D.s, the lawyers, now they lower themselves to learn their culture. That never happened before.

Tola notes how "the culture" and "spirituality" have become important even to those usually perceived as the most recalcitrant to the spirits and the most assimilationist: the college-educated professionals in the diaspora whom she perceives as now returning to their roots and adding cachet to ritual events. At the same time, this choice reflects a transformed idea of ritual in relation to other spheres of action: not an obligation, as in the homeland, but rather a selected form of leisure and recreation, albeit one expressing and generating diasporic solidarity. Another buyei in the group described how the pluralist context of New York engenders a new ethnic pride: "In Honduras, if you go to the cities like Tegucigalpa speaking Garifuna, you don't get a job, so people always blended in as *hispanos*. But here, on the subway you hear every language. Now we're proud of it. Sometimes people hear us speaking and ask, 'What's that language you're speaking?' and they're jealous of what we have."

The interest in Garifuna "culture" extends beyond encounters on the subway. Several of the New York–based buyeis now regularly give lectures, grant interviews to newspapers, and welcome opportunities to publicize the religion. The possession and practice of a distinctive religion is what most legitimates a culture or tradition; and *culture* and *tradition*, in turn, are the key terms of political practice, whether the issue is land rights or city sponsorship for a festival. Giving a previously hidden group a public face as a recognized, distinct "culture," "tradition," or "religion" can generate real political effects. At least, this is the view of nearly all the New York–based Garifuna shamans and of many (though fewer) Central American religious leaders. As Felix told me:

In 1991, the Garifuna language was recognized by the State of New York as an official language category for students entering the public school system. By giving it a proper code, in essence you are recognizing a people. In the same year, we got November 19 recognized by New York as Garifuna Settlement Day. So the entire cosmopolitan area began to know more about the Garifuna people. Then we were recognized at the United Nations in 1992, as part of the Year of Indigenous Peoples, and also by the Caribbean Organization of Indigenous Peoples (COIP). So things began to happen! From that point on, we begin to be recognized as a people. So I guess, we are "African Americans" when it benefits us, but we are Garifuna all the time. We have options, and we become a part of it. Now you have a role to play as a people.

Now, with the World Garifuna Organization—that was registered a year ago—its purpose is to seek restitution and reparations and economic development from England.[5] We learned that given our condition and given our history and what happened, we meet the legal requirements for restitution. Yeah! It's the first world Garifuna organization. We were always Garifuna, but because of information, we become more proud of it.

Felix's narrative indicates that institutional recognition is central to the experience of existing as "a people," in this case under the indigenous identification, which is distinct from the African-American rubric. This code switching opens new horizons, giving the Garifuna "options" and "a role." He then described how these recognition battles in the host society migrate back to Central America: "When New York State recognized the Garifuna as a people and a language, I wrote the bishop in Belize, who is Garifuna, I wrote the board of education in Belize, I wrote the National Garifuna Council there. And it was the National Garifuna Council that took up the task of advocating the recognition of Garifuna and its history in Belize, and eventually came up with a language policy."

Similar attempts at recognition for Garifuna religion are under way, and, like the definition of language and culture, or the establishment of official existence as a people, such attempts begin by consolidating and rationalizing to establish clear boundaries. Felix reported:

We are trying to duplicate our buyeis' council here in Central America, to establish orthodoxy and reduce individual differences. Our spirituality can be standardized because you're always calling on the same forces. But what will happen with our council is to expound on those forces, to *identify* those forces, and identify those forces by *name,* which some of our buyeis in Central America might not know by name even though they are familiar with that force. Now we can talk about the particularities of the force. It is that kind of influence that I think the council can have on the buyeis at home, and thereby help to standardize. . . . But just because we are standardizing doesn't mean their opinions don't count. You see, but then, one of the things that humans must understand, opinion is not truth. Opinion is a vehicle to arrive at the truth.

Asked if this effort was being met with resistance from buyeis in the homeland, Felix responded: "There are individuals. It's from lack of knowing, not so much from buyeis, but from the practitioners, they resist it. We want to show them that it shouldn't be a threat, and that it is not. We want to quell that fear."

As Felix makes clear, the incipient institutions in New York have a clear philosophy and strategy. Political recognition of a people includes the recognition of its religion. That recognition can be accomplished only by systematizing the group's beliefs, practices, and distinguishing features. Further, that consensus of orthodoxy and orthopraxy must be given tangible, transmissible form; it must be written, publicly spoken, and taught. In short, it must take on harder, more sedimented forms to constitute a foundation on which to build. Not surprisingly, given the individualist nature of Garifuna religious leadership, and the occasionally elitist tenor of diaspora leaders' attitudes toward the opinions of those in the homeland, such attempts meet with resistance in the villages.

Cosmopolitans in the Country

There are at least two primary avenues of religious remittance from the Bronx to the homeland. The first is the periodic return of Bronx Garifuna shamans to lead rituals in Honduras. The second is the literature produced by homeland Garifuna with international travel experience, acquired through conferences and touring performance groups, written for audiences in Honduras, Guatemala, and Belize. I deal with the first of these avenues of remittance here; the second is addressed in chapter 7.

To claim that returning New York shamans are agents of change in Honduras is not to say that the transformation of homeland religious practice depends wholly on trans-statal networks; that perspective would reproduce the mid-twentieth-century structuralist divide between "hot" and historied and "cold," static societies. It is, rather, to observe that the culture brokers motivated to assign discursive meaning to homeland practices are those who have negotiated the religiously plural contexts abroad and who have articulated defenses of what is distinctively Garifuna in contexts where such definitions were at risk of becoming blurred.[6] These spokespersons are modern traditionals because they write, grant interviews to newspapers and magazines, and consolidate the locations of histories and origins from the posture of the drive to discourse (Foucault 1978; Appiah 1992). Such articulations do not, however, go uncontested. Remaking religious identity in the diaspora creates the prospect of change in the homeland, and the result is a religious turf war between those claiming the authority of place—the enduring occupation of the homeland—and those claiming the cosmopolitan authority of the city.

TWO KINDS OF RELIGIOUS AUTHORITY

African diaspora religious identity arrives in the homeland with the returns of Bronx-based religious leaders to Honduras to visit and to guide ritual events. Such returns are frequent because Bronx families are often the instigators and patrons of homeland rituals. They are motivated to accelerate homeland ritual performance by nostalgia for "home" and also disproportionately able to fund and influence such expensive ventures because of their earnings in the United States (Johnson 2002b; Richman 2005). Because the shamans they know best are located in the Bronx, and because these are the shamans whose divination has called for such rituals, Bronx-based shamans are now central actors in homeland rites.

In the summer of 2001, I accompanied a group of Bronx shamans to the homeland, and documented the tensions between homelanders and emigrants reported by both sides. Homeland shamans perceived the visiting New York–based shamans as threatening: first, because they arrived as an ideological bloc with a preconceived consensus on the meanings of Garifuna religion, meanings formed by locating the tradition in the framework of the African Diaspora; and second, because they presented an institutional anomaly, officiating in rituals not necessarily related to their family lineage. There were more basic concerns as well, including material wealth and the uses of it. One homeland shaman complained, "They arrive with suitcases full of clothing changes instead of food [for ritual offerings]," levying a criticism of the materialism of those in the diaspora as well as their ignorance of ritual protocol. Such criticisms

were put into practice by excluding Bronx shamans from gossip networks and practical tasks demanding overt instruction.

The need for "instruction" was itself one source of tension.
Homeland shamans disparaged those from the Bronx by declaring that
they lacked the practical knowledge acquired through years of routine
ritual work, and that, moreover, they do not treat the ritual with the
respectful secrecy it mandates, instead regarding it as knowledge learned
"like in school." When one of the New Yorkers carried a tape recorder
to document ritual songs she didn't know for later rehearsal, Honduran
shamans reacted with disdain. One local woman tersely dismissed her
by exclaiming, "Why don't you just go play your maracas?"

Bronx-based shamans acknowledged the justice of some of these
criticisms but countered with comments such as this one from Lucia:
"They [homeland ritualists] can't compare, all they know is the
Garifuna way. They know what to do, but they don't *why* they do what
they do." Or from Maxima: "They don't know any better, they've been
doing the same thing forever." Bronx-based shamans' romantic notions
of a pilgrimage to the simplicity, beauty, and purity of the village was
tempered after several weeks by a growing sense of being among country cousins. The New York diasporans' public reverence for the homelanders' depth of practical ritual knowledge is imbricated with an elitist
view of the village as rooted in the dusty past rather than the dynamism
of the African diaspora, whose space in New York city aesthetically conveys sound, action, even "the future." That subtle elitism was not lost
on many villagers. For them, the "city knowledge" of other religions of
the African diaspora was unwelcome, even problematic. The permanent
homeland Garifuna saw their U.S. counterparts as "materialistic,"
"lost," "lacking in generosity," and "know-it-alls."

Finally, homeland Garifuna perceived Bronx shamans' children as dis-
turbingly "like American blacks." The new spirit geography of the African
Diaspora was seen as arriving hand in hand with the material signs of
black modernity and U.S.-style blackness. The emigrants' children
brought codes of style, music, movies, culinary preferences, jewelry, and
"lack of respect for elders" that were taken as disruptive to village life,
even more so because the city cousins quickly became socially pivotal, the
talk of the town. The gifts and money they brought rendered them more
powerful social players than those who had remained in the village.

The tension between the homeland and diaspora groups was fueled
by corrosive gossip. This gossip can be seen as an ongoing debate
between two kinds of authority: on one hand, that of remaining "on

the land," an authority constructed through the spatial metaphor of the density of sacred power, and conveyed by the homelander habitus of corporeal, and largely unspoken, practical knowledge; and on the other hand, that of the city, a form of authority constructed through the spatial metaphor of extension, conveyed through the interreligious perspective and discursive skills of the New Yorkers. I think of these as competing indigenous and cosmopolitan bids for authority.

The new knowledge claimed by Bronx-based shamans, the knowledge they seek to remit to and instill in Honduran villages, is based on and valued in relation to deep Africanness. The New York Garifuna read their tradition in terms of similarities between it and other religions of the African Diaspora and have adopted the phrase *African Diaspora* as central in their practical lexicon. As Garifuna religion is clearly located in a network of Africanness, previous ethnic and racial designations that were ambiguous, unspoken, or irrelevant become crucial. The relation of Garifuna to African religious practice (that is, Yoruba or Kongo mediated through Cuban Santería and Palo Monte) is now tendered as vital to orthopraxy. In Honduran villages, such semantic accretions are viewed as aggressive foreign incursions on "our tradition." The diaspora shamans' presence is welcome but also disruptive to the village, as is the new repertoire of styles and tastes of Bronx-based returnees. In sum, while New York Garifuna religious leaders have thoroughly joined the African Diaspora, this identification remains as yet unformed in the homeland. It appears to be under construction.

The growing consciousness among New York shamans of sharing in the religious entity of the African Diaspora has clarified the answers to some identity questions and opened others. Both homeland and diasporic religious leaders, however, demonstrate their authority—based on spatial principles of density and extension, respectively—in the richly complex ritual performances they prepare and direct. The next two chapters compare the main ritual events in Honduras and in New York.

CHAPTER 5

Ritual in the Homeland; Or, Making the Land "Home" in Ritual

Our journey has been sad, my grandchild,
We have been searching for our grandchildren.
We have been crossing the deep ocean,
For our descendants are far away.

Dügü song

This chapter and the next juxtapose readings of ritual performance in the homeland and in the diaspora. In the homeland, the central ritual event brings into being, through performance, the momentary fusion of kin, ancestors, and territory. With the external boundary of the ethnic group rarely in question in Garifuna villages, the ritual primarily works on social relations at the level of the extended family. In the diaspora, the central ritual event defines and defends the social boundary of the ethnic group as a whole in relation to the plural urban context. This difference of emphasis transforms the ritual process. It becomes more verbally elaborated, more symbolic (in a Peircean sense), and more ideological, in that authenticity becomes a conscious problem. The ritual adapts to neighboring religious paradigms and seeks points of common ground. To make this distinction is not to call the homeland version original and the diasporic version mimetic. Both require representations of the homeland: even in rituals occurring "on the land," physical space still must be transformed into a religious grammar and be made digestible in the form of power or cures conferred. The ritual "cures" by intensifying the experience of the land; it builds layers of consciousness of that space in physical structures, songs, and boundary purifications that bodily inscribe the notion of return. The return is to the ancestral territorial center in a given Honduran village, and its message of return is doubled in the mirrored images of traveling family members and journeying ancestral spirits.

Among New York Garifuna, not surprisingly, the natal land is represented primarily through memory and its technological extensions (photos, videos, and music recordings), and out of different material artifacts. The semiotics of territory and territorial belonging here, too, entail acts of representation, but diasporic ritual has a material and sensory character distinct from that of the homeland. Moreover, the territory that is remembered and ritualized is less self-evident in New York than in Honduran villages. Africa begins to occupy a place as important as that of Honduras and St. Vincent: it becomes a third diasporic horizon.

I first describe the ritual sequence itself in detail, followed by accounts of crises that necessitated adaptation and improvisation and created opportunities for revision. I take these disruptions as windows of opportunity for analysis, as otherwise-hidden aspects of the ritual structures become conscious, visible problems in need of practical resolutions.

I describe how homeland ritualizations exert centripetal pull and territorial authority over the New York–based emigrants but also construct their own indigenous authority in relation to those emigrants, by casting them as being in need of periodic territorial redemption. The diasporic and homeland modes of religion constitute a single system, each part of which constructs its authority in relation to the other.

The Dügü

The most elaborate of Garifuna rituals, the dügü, contains within it all the lesser interventions with the ancestors, like the chugu and the mass, and so is the fullest realization of the abstraction *Garifuna religion*. Yet although there is a general sense that dügüs must occur every year somewhere in Garifuna territory, there is no prescribed rhythm or cycle that affixes the frequency or location of the ritual. It must be called for by the spirits themselves.

THE CALL FOR A DÜGÜ

The high god, the God of Roman Catholicism, is called Bungiu, and *lumu Bungiu*, "praise God," is an everyday expression in Garifuna villages.

Rituals are not devoted to Bungiu, however, but are reserved for more fickle and proximate powers, the ancestors. This generic category is broken into smaller categories whose precise order and rank depends on the speaker. In practice, the ancestors are divided into two groups: the ahari (or hiyuruha), "higher" spirits or "people," who are the aides and guides to shamans, and the gubida. The latter are ancestors who have material needs and demands and who may afflict their descendants if not commemorated. The shamans' subtle gradations are lost on most laypeople, and the various agents constituting "the ancestors" are lumped together as beneficial but potentially dangerous (see chapter 3 n. 2). They rely on living family members for periodic ritual offerings to remember, honor, and fortify them and to furnish them with the lost pleasures of earthly life. In the chugu, or even the lesser mass, an ancestor returns by taking possession of a human body, taking up a cigar (puro), swigging guaro, eating favorite earthly dishes like fish, coconut soup *(hudutu),* and cassava bread (ereba), lying in a hammock, and even joining in simulated sexual relations. But when these periodic offerings are not forthcoming—a common plight in view of the expenses involved—the ancestor communicates her need to a descendant through dreams, headaches, sickness, misfortune, or mental illness (Bianchi 1988: 252; Foster 1994: 16–34).[1]

The buyei, seated by her altar, blows cigar smoke or rum mist from her mouth over a candle and watches the reaction fixedly. She moves into a mild trance state, and one of her helping spirits helps her to determine the identity of the complaining ancestor, if indeed that is the cause of the trouble. Now the negotiations between the ancestor and the family over demands and resources can begin.[2] The demand for a dügü tends to arise in response to a situation that has already spun out of control and led to a life-threatening crisis for a family member. Still, given the cost of a dügü, the family tries to bargain with the gubida through the shaman and persuade the ancestor to settle for a lesser offering, or at least to postpone the demand for a few years until the family's fortunes improve.

Other situations may also warrant a dügü. Shamans' vocations are legitimized by performing at least four dügüs, one for each grandparent. For this reason, a dügü may be initiated by a buyei himself in honor of one of his ancestors. Then too, many families consider it obligatory to offer a dügü at least once in a lifetime and to use the rite as a kind of family reunion that extends to include the dead. Given the expense of a dügü, several extended families may join forces to hold the event.

Part of the healing that the ritual is supposed to achieve is restoring family harmony. Such harmony is often precarious as things get under way. The dügü assembles a large group descended from a common afflicting ancestor—a grandparent, say. Though all might consider one another "family" during the event, and use kinship terms when addressing one another, the group exists nowhere else but in this precise ritual context (Foster 1994: 37). While for some the ritual is an occasion of joyous reunion, others must create "family harmony" with relatives whom they barely know. Moreover, because familial relations of mutual dependency are strongly focused on women, with men often having progeny in multiple families and in far-flung communities (Kerns 1997), affinal relations are often tense. Under these circumstances, the generation of a genuine sense of family among the extended kin network may be something of a ritual miracle in itself.

In its simplest schematization, the ritual entails a sequence of dances that honor the ancestors and create the conditions for their arrival in possession. When the afflicting ancestors (gubida) arrive, they are feted, fed, praised in song and dance, and consulted. Finally, after the offerings have been accepted by the ancestors—and there are repeated empirical tests within the ritual to confirm that they are—kin groups run into the sea together, sometimes gripping a single long cloth, in a moment of apparent communitas, thus reaffirming their bonds and the momentary transcendence of bitter conflicts. Yet if by its conclusion the dügü conveys harmonious unanimity, and indeed demands its dramatization, achieving it is no easy process. The ritual demand for unity means that the dügü also is an arena for presenting and pressing conflicting claims, each of which must be at least temporarily superseded.

PREPARATION

Talk of a dügü began when a twenty-year-old man in New York suddenly lost the ability to walk. Doctors were unable to help him, and he testified to recurring dreams declaring his need to return home to the village of Corozal. His dreams, which depicted him there with a crowd of people gathered around him, were interpreted as an ancestor's request for the great rite.

His family contributed most of the necessary funds, around L80,000 (then approximately $5,333), a relatively modest outlay for a dügü today.[3] The ritual was also supported by two additional extended families in Honduras who shared common great-grandparents with the patient's family, for reasons one family member described as a sense of the families' "losing touch." These families engaged the ritual process not out of immediate obligation but as a prophylactic against future troubles and as a means of reconnecting with each other and with their "roots."

The sick patient played almost no role in the ritual performance. After arriving from New York, he lay in a hammock strung for him in the temple, leaving it only to eat or go to the toilet. The families' unity and the relation to ancestors took center stage. Indeed, that inversion— minimizing the individual malady by "absorbing" it into the network of relations between family members living and dead—in part constituted the cure.

The Honduras-based family of the sufferer in New York consulted the local shaman, who consulted his spirit helpers at his altar, and a course of action was plotted. Because the local buyei was a member of one of the participating families, it was assumed that he should lead the affair. But in the dreams of one of the patrons, the ancestors announced their preference that a specific buyei from a more distant area should lead the event. In the end two leaders were contracted for the event, one local and related to one of the patron families, and one from Trujillo, a few hundred kilometers distant. Seeds of trouble were present right from the outset, but preparations were set in motion as usual. Announcements about the dügü were circulated throughout Honduras and to New York a full year in advance to ensure that sufficient funds would be raised and that all family members, especially those in the United States, would have time to make travel plans.

A ceremonial temple (dabuyaba, or gayunere) was constructed in traditional style on the beach. While most buildings today are constructed with cinder blocks and tin roofs, the temple must adhere to the old style, using saplings and palm thatch bound with twine for the roof and walls. A house must be constructed anew for every dügü, despite occasional proposals for the construction of a permanent ritual structure. This temple was large and cost L18,000 ($1,200) to build, a bargain compared those in other communities that reportedly cost up to L45,000 ($3,000). Despite the high fee paid to a group of young Garifuna men who were supposedly conscientious about their work, the roof leaked when it was finished, and the men refused to fix it. Under pressure from their own family members, they were finally

FIGURE 15. Construction of a dabuyaba, the "big house" or temple for hosting a dügü. Photo by author.

coerced into inspecting the job, but their repair consisted of jury-rigging a blue plastic sheet across one side of the roof. A long debate among a group of elder women ensued as to whether the ancestors would find this functional but aesthetically dubious solution acceptable, as it would not be familiar to them. The local buyei, however, decreed the bright blue sheet tolerable even to the eyes of the gubida.

Several weeks before the formal beginning of the ceremony, cardboard boxes filled with loose pants and shirts, all newly dyed orange-red, had been stored in the rafters. The posts of the temple had been painted with crosses. Loose-woven baskets of palm sheaves (*guagai*), of which each nuclear family was expected to supply four, were being suspended from the walls and stacked around the miniature sailboats placed at the center of the temple—the latter reminders of the travel being undertaken by both participants and the ancestor spirits. Large bags of rice and beans had been piled high on one side. With each arrival of a consignment of goods or money, informal gatherings were called by the local buyei, the message spreading by word of mouth. All available members of the families, mostly older women, arrived to comment on the amount and quality of goods and note from whom they had been sent.

An adolescent girl abruptly announced the arrival of a donation from relatives in the village of Santo Antonio, a half-day bus journey distant. Two auspicious-looking envelopes were placed on the incipient altar, a wooden stool accompanied by a candle and a rum bottle, at the temple's center. With all eyes on him, the buyei opened them. The first contained L1,050 ($70), an auspicious beginning. The second held a friendly letter and a measly L100 (about $7). The buyei winced. "Dollars," he muttered, rubbing his thumb against his fingers, "are what we need."

Among Honduran relatives, about L500 is considered a respectable contribution to the collective fund. This is no small amount for many, especially in addition to the roosters, rum, baskets, and special clothing they are expected to supply.

Stories were exchanged about the uncanny power of the spirits. Dona Pupa recounted a chugu given for her deceased mother: the mother was so happy she wouldn't leave, and nobody could get Pupa out of her trance! Adolfo told of the time his brother was supposed to send a cow for a dügü even though he couldn't be present. The brother reneged, but the cow showed up voluntarily, wandering into the village right on time. Then Francisa spoke: Did you hear about the cristiano girl in the Chaves family who said she wouldn't attend the dügü? She got very sick, vomiting and retching. But when they brought her to the temple, she danced to the drums and improved. She'll be attending now, yes sir! There were comments on materials still missing: *hiu*, cassava beer, for example. I nearly fell asleep lying in a hammock in the temple, provoking approving comments that this is truly a place of repose, *descanso*. The new arriving goods were consecrated to the ancestors by the singing of dügü songs *(adugurahani)*, guided by the heavy, ponderous beats of the three drums.

The mostly elderly women in the hastily assembled chorus sang the refrains with as much enthusiasm as could be mustered on a hot afternoon in July, still weeks before the event proper. They sang, "We're painting the boats"; "The children are all here lined up, one is still on the way"; "The roosters have come to dance"; and "They come from Sairi bringing peace."[4] Many songs took the perspective of disgruntled ancestors: "The roosters are calling us"; "Two grandchildren are missing, why don't they arrive?"; or "My gulei [altar] is empty, no one is there. Put on your *sundara* [shaman's sash], grandchild, and go take care of it!" Byron Foster recorded another dügü song in the village of Hopkins, Belize:

Our journey has been sad, my grandchild,
We have been searching for our grandchildren.
We have been crossing the deep ocean,
For our descendants are far away.
We have been standing on the shore of the Aurayuna,
On the resplendent shore of the Aurayuna, shedding tears.[5]

The song, like many, describes travel from St. Vincent, where the ancestors dwell, and of the need to regather the family over great distances. Aurayuna was a local group of the St. Vincentian Black Caribs.

After forty-five minutes of singing, Adolfo, the buyei, planted his chair in the center of the temple to address the group and the changing needs of the imminent event. He addressed the first problem: "The temple is sad, there's no joy. A dügü is supposed to be about happiness! Those who are in mourning have to change by the beginning of the ritual, when the ancestors return." Second, Adolfo pointed out that some in the group were lamenting the fact that the New York relatives would arrive wearing nice matching uniforms, whereas the villagers had no money for such things. "The dügü doesn't require 'uniforms,'" he assured them. "Our poor *achiote*-dyed shirts will be just fine." (Some women interjected that though uniforms may not always be necessary, in this case the ancestors had specifically requested them.) Third, Adolfo suggested that a handful of people were doing all the preparatory work, while most of the people were "lazy." Loud protests followed. One speaker jumped to her feet and shook her fist, her voice trembling: "Some women just come and leave their roosters here, but I have to clean up all their shit!" Finally, Adolfo wanted to know why it was that when the rival buyei from Trujillo came to town the temple was jammed, but when he was there almost daily it remained only half full. "You've got to give me your confidence, I represent our community! The woman from Trujillo may stop in once in a while, but I'm the one here all the time." The temple was quiet; clearly he had touched on a difficult issue. Eventually the patrons sutured the potential split by retaining only the local buyei to direct the affair.

Before leaving, many of the women massaged rum into their heads, the back of their necks, and their legs. The rum would "heat" and loosen old muscles for the walk home, but it would also protect and purify. Those spending time in the temple were engaged in spirit work and more vulnerable to attack than usual. The rum helped extend the protection of the temple. Meanwhile, the buyei retreated to his own quarters, still muttering about the lack of preparations: "This dügü won't be any good. They're not prepared, not unified enough." Nayna, who prepared his meals, leaned on her broom and agreed.

DAY ONE, TUESDAY: THE MASS

In the middle of the temple, the mountain of food grew. There were stacks of hard cassava bread; cases of Tatascan rum (the brand preferred by the ancestors); burlap sacks of cassava, beans, and rice; cases of canned tomato paste; and wads of envelopes of chicken bouillon and soup mix. Though in an ideal world the ritual would include only the traditionally produced goods beloved by the ancestors, such purity is not easy to maintain. As one old-timer observed, "Most buyeis around here are completely modernized." Before the day of the mass, the food was moved into the attached enclave reserved for the shaman and his approved helpers, a space referred to, like his personal altar assembled there, as the gulei.

Six days before the dügü was to begin, a mass was celebrated in the village's Catholic church. It began at 7 A.M., led by a Panamanian priest. Though the priest knew little about Garifuna religion, he presided over an "inculturated mass," complete with Garifuna drummers and dancers. His homily observed the schedule of the official church calendar, Transfiguration Day, but he also spoke of indigenous peoples, the diverse forms of communication with God, and the need for the ancestors' help in the fight against AIDS. Many nodded as he spoke. We exchanged the sign of peace, greeting each other across the aisles. After the mass, the priest was driven in a pickup truck to the temple, where he danced with the people during two songs, accompanied by the drums. He flung holy water over the interior and called out, "Bless this dügü, bless the ancestors, bless your people, the Garifuna!" Then he disappeared back to town.

In a huge iron tub, the buyei's assistants concocted a brew that included cassava beer, seawater, rum, lemons, holy water, and the leafy vines of a local plant that were combined to make *medicina*.[6] Abruptly, the initiated buyeis present, three men and five women, cleared the temple of other people, hurling the solution everywhere. Scooping half-shells of gourds into the tub, they soaked the sand floor, the ceiling, and the walls, and then the outside walls. Urged on by the drummers who played just outside the temple, this "cleansing" was followed with further immolations of rum and cigar smoke aspirated into every corner and around every doorway. The buyeis shook their maracas in nooks where malicious shamans might have concealed evil objects after the structure was built. They also treated vulnerable parts of each others' bodies by blowing rum across them, especially across the back of the neck. This gesture is commonly used to help prepare the body for spirit possession by "heating it up." (By contrast, the same move done with cool water, or "holy water," removes the trance by "cooling" [cf. Foster 1994: 46].) Following the temple's purification, they encircled it with a line drawn in white powder (variously made of talc, eggshell, chalk, or flour). This line marked the barrier between the temple and outer, profane space.[7]

With the temple now secured, the food was returned to the center to be presented to the ancestors for approval. Dügü songs followed, played on the drums and danced in twenty- to twenty-five-minute intervals, alternating with breaks of about the same duration until sundown. Toward dusk the drums' sound competed with a pastor's voice amplified by loudspeakers from the Pentecostal church a few blocks away. The voice thundered, "Tonight the devil will be beaten!"—a less than subtle reference to the dügü getting under way.

DAY TWO, WEDNESDAY: MAKING THE HEART OF THE DÜGÜ

The work of the day began at a lazy 8 A.M., with the sun already high in the sky. As the drumming, singing, and dancing of dügü songs continued in half-hour cycles as on the day prior, two other tasks were pursued: dyeing clothing in orange-hued achiote and building the *mua*, tablets of earth to be laid at the center of the temple. The dye was made in a large washtub from seawater, lemons, detergent, and achiote. Contributions of the dyestuff had arrived in various forms, ranging from premixed paste or pellets sold in plastic bottles to the seeds themselves wrapped in newspaper. The seeds were grated and sifted before use. Head wraps, buyeis' protective sashes (sunduru), skirt wraps, and blouses were dipped and then hung in the sun. These garments were now *galati,* "having meaning or significance in it" (Wells 1982b: 45). The use of achiote recalls the Caribs from St. Vincent, called "Red" or "Yellow" Caribs by Europeans because their skin was always painted with the dye (Conzemius 1928). The Garifuna use the dyed clothes to signify the ancestors, and attempts to make contact with them. The dye is never used outside that context (Wells 1982b: 49).

The second task, of building the earthen tablets, was even more important, so much so that no photo or video record of its making was permitted, either by Garifuna themselves or by me: it was one of only two such moments in the entire week-long ritual. The making of the tablets began with two large wooden trays placed on either side of the center altar. The trays were covered with white, chalky dirt, earth from the birth city of the gubida spirit who caused the New York boy's sickness that had motivated the ritual in the first place. Two assistants worked the dirt with their hands as the local buyei added liquids: Salva Vida beer (a well-known Honduran brand), Absolut vodka, orange juice, Bacardi Gold rum, Golasu rum, and Canadian Club soda water. The substance began to take on a claylike texture, and the lead buyei took over its manipulation, singing in a low voice a simple song that repeated the word *mua* over and over. When the two slabs were complete, they were placed carefully on large palm branches to harden. The two ovals were about two feet long by one foot wide, with a texture like clay or flattened dough. One was slightly larger than the other and called the male; its companion was female.

Individuals approached to make small contributions of money into a half-gourd placed alongside the tablets, offering their petitions to the ancestors as they did so. Once the slabs had hardened, a woman painted orange and blue crosses on them. Another woman guarded them all day long. An aged man was also needed to stand guard, but no one suitably respectable for the post offered his services until later in the week. In the meantime, the old woman watched over the tablets alone.

What are these earth tablets? One buyei's assistant confessed that she didn't know. Another suggested that they represented "ancestors of two families." The lead buyei clarified that the dirt for the tablets must come from where the patron ancestor's umbilical cord was buried: it represents the patron him- or herself. The second tablet is for the patron's spouse. This natal earth must be animated or "heated up" by liquor of at least five different kinds, "balancing the male and female forces." In Conzemius's description of a 1920s dügü, a mound of earth was placed at the center of the temple and called its "heart" *(lanigi)* (1928: 203, 205). Foster (1994: 45) reports that in oral histories in Belize the earth mound is described as coffin shaped, an analogue of the grave whence derived the voices of the ancestors. It is possible, then, that the contemporary earth tablets are an elaboration of what was previously a single mound.

Garifuna informants' comments suggest that there are no consensual meanings other than those embedded in the practice itself. The tablets were bathed daily in rum, just as the arriving ancestors were offered abundant liquor both to consume and to soothe their skin. And the tablets were also used to measure the success of the dügü in toto. At the conclusion of the event, each was carefully overturned. If either one broke in the maneuver, the associated ancestor-patron was considered dissatisfied. If only a little piece broke, then "only a little part" of the ritual wasn't right. Because the slabs incorporate the very soil of an given ancestor's territorial home, they have great significance. They must be kept intact and cared for, and bathed. Any sundering of their substance serves as dire warning of the ancestors' dissatisfaction.

The social sanctions against filming the formation of the tablets were buttressed by the vigilance of the ancestors. According to a story I heard repeated in multiple villages, once there was a *chino* (a person of Asian origin) filming a dügü. When he filmed the mua, the spirits took him and his camera and ran him into the sea.

DAY THREE, THURSDAY: MAKING BREAD

The third day of the dügü was more leisurely than the previous ones, occupied with bread making for the "departure of the fishermen" *(idugahatiñu)* on the following day. The fishermen's role involves not only gathering seafood in traditional style but also dramatizing the return of the ancestors as the most intense part of the ritual begins. Just as the ancestors must be feted and made as comfortable as possible, so must the fishermen who play their roles. In the temple, women shaped dough of various kinds—*pan de coco* (coconut bread), *keke* (johnny-cakes), and *pan dulce* (sweet bread). They sang songs that announced the activity to the ancestors: "Now we've made the bread." For the fishermen's journey, large grain sacks were stuffed full of bread, along with ample cigars and rum. Aside from being paid for their services, about L1,000 ($66) each, the fishermen were well supplied with worldly comforts.

Around dusk, two large canoes *(cayucos)* were steered onto the beach to prepare them for the next day. Six buyeis went to work on the boats, pouring and blowing rum inside and outside the hulls, passing incense under the seats, and dousing the boats with the same infusion used to sacralize the temple walls. The outboard motors and gas cans were carried into the temple to be specially treated overnight. Modern innovations like motors are frowned on by some as betrayals of tradition, but they are tolerated by most as a technology that facilitates the ritual.

Even outboard motors could be rendered fit for the ancestors' use by treatment with smoke, rum, maracas, and songs, and by being contained overnight within the temple walls.

With the arrival of the canoes came another crisis, however. One of the boats was being lent as a favor by a relative, but the other had had to be rented in another town. The owner demanded the right to captain his vessel throughout the ritual. What was worse, at the last minute his price came in much higher than expected, at L5,500 ($367). "For some people it's all business, a dügü industry," spat one assisting shaman in disgust. "They think it's all New Yorkers paying for everything, even when it isn't." Adolfo called a hasty emergency meeting with all nearby participants to offer a plea for last-minute contributions to meet the owner's demand.[8] Loans were secured, donations made, and another crisis was averted, though not without bad blood between the rituals' patrons and the canoe owner.

DAY FOUR, FRIDAY: DEPARTURE OF THE FISHERMEN

Now arrived a momentous day. We gathered at 5 A.M. Those newly arriving at the temple bathed themselves in "medicine" before changing into the red and white uniforms marking their membership in one of the patron families. The drums began to "heat up" the room by 5:45, and by 6 the assembled hundreds left the temple, circled it once, and proceeded, singing, toward the beach, led by the buyeis and drummers. Adolfo, the lead buyei, pushed forward to the boats, already refitted with their motors, to "send them out," throwing his arms forward toward the sea with his maracas in one hand and a bottle of rum in the other. As the boats were loaded, a cry of surprise and then laughter arose. A woman had been "kidnapped" by the fishermen at the last second and carried off to the boats. She would serve as their cook during the three days' absence from home. This kidnapping was prearranged, but it was said that in the old days the choice was genuinely spontaneous.

As the boats pushed off, the crowd waved red handkerchiefs toward the sea. The drumming increased in volume and speed. An assistant buyei fell into trance and lay in the sand twitching to the beat of the drums. Just offshore, the boats paused and cast their nets once, a gesture signaling their role and the work that was to come, then motored off rapidly. The drumming and singing continued, urging them on until they disappeared from sight. In procession, we returned to the temple, circled it again, and continued the singing inside for fifteen minutes until a simple breakfast was served.

The second great task began in the late morning: hanging the baskets. As the drums swung into their slow, steady rhythm, a woman "caught a trance," falling backward until she was caught and held up from behind. She spoke softly with one of her helpers, who repeated what she said with great excitement: "Marisco Amaya!" the person holding her yelled. "It's Marisco!" Elder women from the Amaya family ran to touch the relative returned from the dead. They both cajoled and comforted him: the first because they revered him as a transmitter of special knowledge, the second because he was unaccustomed to the contemporary world and needed help. The ancestor guides, but is also guided; he is both sage and child. At one moment Marisco offered solemn counsel; in the next he careened about the temple like a tipsy teenager, plopping himself into the laps of women and demanding rum. Mostly Marisco did what the ancestors most often do when they arrive: he inquired about missing descendants, offering thinly veiled threats of the ills that might befall those who didn't bother to attend (cf. Foster 1994: 39). The main message from the ancestral world (Sairi) is straightforward and twofold: the whole family must be here together, and it must remember and commemorate us in ritual.

Several shamans also entered trance, but their possession was by their hiyuruha (or ahari) rather than gubida spirits. These possessions had "tactical" effects (Foster 1994: 56): they shifted the ritual to a more intense, attentive, and focused mode. The hiyuruha, when they descended, did not speak but rather danced with fierce concentration, tracing the path of a large cross between the four doorways of the temple. Manifest in the bodies of the buyeis, they shook their maracas intently at each potentially dangerous point of entry to the temple. One buyei named Solya irritated her fellows by spewing rum not on their heads or over the backs of their necks, as was expected, but directly in their faces. Gingerly wiping her eyes, one colleague exclaimed, "She wasn't in trance, she just felt like doing that!" In gubida and hiyuruha possessions there is room for controversy and accusations of faked trance. Town drunks are often suspected of playing the part of ancestors in order to obtain their daily dose under ancestral auspices. Even shamans are not immune from such speculations.

Meanwhile, the clusters of handwoven baskets (guagai), about one hundred in all, were unstrung from the walls where they had been stored.[9] Each contained several half gourds. The baskets were carried in a short circle dance and then taken out of the temple into the adjacent shelter *(dibasen)*. The gourd shells were removed and scrubbed with "medicine," then painted in a cross pattern of orange and blue by the shamans and their assistants. This task took about two hours. The gourds were then placed back into the baskets, and women carried them in another circle dance, shaking the baskets to make the gourds rattle in time with the drums.

At this point four idle drummers climbed into the temple's rafters, and baskets were passed up to them. As three other drummers accelerated their rhythm, the young men worked in pairs on either side of the temple to attach the baskets to the rafters. Those in the watching assembly craned their necks upward and sang:

> Let me hang the baskets
> In the temple of Wasana.
> I am for you, you are for me,
> I see you clearly from Sairi.[10]

First tying the baskets to the lowest rafters, they next untied them and passed them down again; they climbed higher and reattached them at a higher level, and then carried out the process a third time. The two teams worked at a furious pace and with astonishing strength and dexterity, much to the delight of the onlookers below, competing to finish hanging their complement of baskets first. Finally they descended to hearty congratulations, applause, and offerings of rum and cigarettes.

Though singing and dancing of dügü songs continued until 9:30 that evening, the rest of the day moved at a pace of well-earned relaxation. Many people slept in hammocks suspended in the temple or under the shelter just alongside.

When I asked the lead shaman about the hanging of the baskets, he rejected out of hand my attempts to decipher the symbolism or meaning of the action. "It's a joke *[chispa]*," he said. "It's entertaining for the ancestors to see the hustle and commotion. And it also keeps the drums going for a long time without a break, which is important for the fishermen. For *them* to keep going, *we* have to keep going. But mostly it's just fun, entertainment to please the ancestors." Though Adolfo's response closed one line of interpretation, it opened another that became clearer during the week. The ritual actions performed in the temple have direct effects on events elsewhere. Like a beating heart, ritual action in the center sustains the extremities—whether the fishermen gathering seafood or migrants living in New York.

After the departure of the fishermen and the hanging of the baskets, there followed a three-day interlude during which many participants paid visits in town, attended wakes in neighboring villages, or took care of everyday business. Most important, many more out-of-towners from the United States, Belize, and Honduran cities finally arrived as we approached the core of the ritual, the four days of the dügü proper.

By Monday morning the temple came to life again. The sacrificial animals were brought over: new offerings of roosters were tethered inside the temple, and four pigs and a cow were tethered outside. Every person participating was required to bring two roosters, as these would be the key offering to the gubida and the symbol of their communion. A number of select families were commanded by the gubida to each contribute a pig. One of the patron families provided a cow, which had no sacrificial purpose but served to feed the hungry crowd.

DAY FIVE, SECOND TUESDAY: RETURN OF THE FISHERMEN

The dügü rolled into motion again with the return of the fishermen at dawn. Attired in traditional palm helmets, they were greeted with exuberant songs by family members wearing orange-red uniforms. The uniforms, used only in making contact with the ancestors, marked the return of the fishermen as also a return of the spirits, and they were treated as such. One of the songs took the perspective of the ancestors-fishermen: "We've arrived, the providers, to embrace our children." As personifications of the ancestors, but also their indexes—representations not merely depicting but also precipitating and inaugurating greater visitations from the ancestors, a parade which they now began—the fishermen were honored with rum, cigarettes, and hearty welcomes, and led away to rest in hammocks.

Dance of the Masks.   As the fishermen returned, two children who had sat in the bows of the canoes for the final approach presented the *wanaragua* (also called *máscaro,* or *junkunnu*) dance in distinctive pink-white, or "European," masks decorated with pencil mustaches and long, feminine gowns.[11] The dance is performed by young males to the accompaniment of rapid-fire drumming; its leaps and low crouches call for enormous athleticism. It is described as a Garifuna warriors' dance, with the masks and gowns representing subterfuge from the St. Vincent wars. There, according to oral tradition, Garifuna warriors disguised themselves as whites in order to approach close to

FIGURE 16. The fishermen-ancestors arrive at dawn and inaugurate the arrival of the ancestors in spirit possession. Photo by author.

FIGURE 17. A fisherman-ancestor in a Carib-style palm-frond helmet, receiving cigarettes from an assisting shaman. Photo by author.

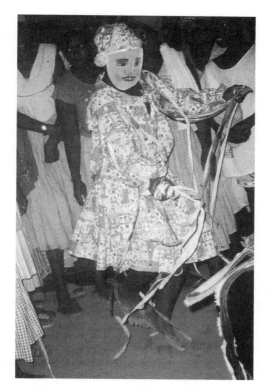

FIGURE 18. Wanaragua dancer performing at the beginning of the dügü.
Photo by author.

the enemy before attacking.[12] But the dance can also be viewed as an
appropriation of European power by its imitation and criticism.
Meléndez (2002: 102) offers a transcription of one wanaragua song
implying as much:

> Three years I've had to work
> And the white man hasn't paid my salary
> What will happen to him?
> I feel pity for him.
> My heart gives me no more space, Grandmother,
> for my ability to wait is past.[13]

Here is a warriors' song indeed, but one applied to present-day battles of race and class. Other wanaragua songs I transcribed treat more
familiar themes. For example, shortly before his death, the beloved

Don Cornelio of Corozal recalled the following song from his boyhood eighty years earlier:

> They keep questioning my older brother,
> To forget their own problems.
> We all have defects, one is just like the other.
> They keep questioning my older brother.
> Pack your bag and come to the city,
> This will pass, and will be forgotten.

Here is yet another example of a wanaragua song narrated from the perspective of a compromised woman, who uses the term *brother* to refer to her lover:

> Give me a ring of commitment, brother,
> So I can answer when my father asks.
> When I get to my house, brother, I'll tell my mama.
> If I'm already lost because of men, I'll ask for my fare from Jobita's papa.
> I hope there's a trip today.
> This year, brother, I'll make my home with you.

Wanaragua songs, like many Garifuna lyrics, reflect the troubles of everyday life: hopeful or failing relationships, the loneliness of traveling long distances for work, the trauma of village gossip, and tensions between family loyalty and love. Yet when these songs are performed in the context of the dügü, such concerns are also made the province of the ancestors and their power.

Presenting the "Catch."   The fishermen arrived at around 6 A.M., and the wanaragua dance outside the temple was completed by 7. From about 8 to 9 came the *abelaguduni,* the dance and song celebrating the arrival of the fishermen's catch in the temple. With the new provisions came also the repurification and fortification of the boundaries of sacred space by the buyeis. They patrolled the doorways and periphery of the temple armed with cigars, rum bottles, and incense, fumigating the sites where chinks in the protective armor were perceived to remain.

Appeasing the Ancestors.   If the spatial heart of the dügü lay in the mua tablets, made of natal dirt and representing the original progenitors, the temporal heart of the event lay in the amalahani (or *mali* for short), the "placation" songs presented to the ancestors exactly eight times.[14] On this day, for example, the mali were performed at around 10 A.M., 4:30 P.M., 9:30 P.M., and 3 A.M. The next day followed a similar schedule, with four mali dances. On these occasions recording devices were prohibited. When a mali dance was announced, ritual action accelerated to a rush of coordinated movement. No one remained in a hammock or working outside. Loud voices cried the summons: "Mali! Everyone, come on . . . *mali!!*" Women scrambled to drape the orange skirts over their work clothes, marking the shift to direct exchange with the ancestors, and to snatch up their roosters from where they had been tethered behind the benches along the walls.

Then began the dance itself, which was conspicuously festive. Instead of remaining seated as usual, the three drummers stood, carrying the weight of the big wooden drums on shoulder straps. The chief buyei and two assistants faced the drummers, maracas in hand. The drummers and the crowd followed the buyei's lead as he signaled quarter turns counterclockwise, until the drummers' backs were in one of the doorways. During each rotation, the drummers danced out of the door and back in the next in a three-man weave and twirl, pounding the rhythm throughout in a dazzling display that left the congregation laughing and high. At each pause, the buyei directed the group to dance lower and lower until, crouched near the ground for a prolonged, pregnant second, all sprang into the air, thrusting their roosters into the air with a joyful whoop. "Shake your rooster to make him crow, the ancestors will see it better!" someone yelled. The roosters were offered up in song: "Here is your rooster, look! This is for you; sing, gayu!"

Amalahani songs played on the theme of travel, referring at once both to the travel of distant relatives to the temple and the travel of ancestors to rejoin the living:

> Hey, hey, hey, we're traveling by boat,
> We're sailing, little granddaughter.
> I've broken the pole on my canoe,
> I've broken the pole on my canoe.
> Women are my companions in the canoe,
> Till we get to the temple.
> I'll gather what we need for the dügü.

Still other amalahani are narrated from the perspective of the buyei, allowing all the communicants to share, at least imaginatively, in the role of shaman:

> It will be me, I will take them [the fishermen] to find it [the catch].
> I will guide those looking for shellfish, supported by my staff.
> I've already prepared my canoe, there in the house of the ancestors,
> There is my canoe behind me.

Still others directly narrate the ritual process of placating and soothing the ancestors and calling on their reciprocal generosity. One such song, recorded in Belize, goes as follows:

> My grandmother, we are quieting you down.
> Great-grandmother, we are quieting you down, great-grandmother.
> [Unknown text fragment] . . . We are quieting you down.
> My grandmother, the cock is crowing, great-grandmother.
> The cock is crowing, great-grandmother.
> Great-grandmother, it is silent now (everyone should be quiet now, great-grandmother).
> I am for you, you are for me.
> Grandmother, water, great-grandmother.
>
> (Mariano and Castillo in Greene 1998: 176)

The songs chosen depend on the buyei and, to a lesser degree, the song leader of the chorus (*gayusu*). The lyrics, however, were in this case less important than the dance. Some danced with a rooster's neck clenched in each fist, one for themselves and one on behalf of an absent family member. The exuberant stomp lasted a half hour, which seemed an eternity to keep up such a performance. At the conclusion of the last mali dance of each of the two days, in the middle of the night, each dancer presented a rooster to one of the drummers, now released from their musical duties. Taking the roosters by the neck, one by one, the men swung them in a long arc ending with a resonant smack on the sandy floor that instantly snapped the birds' necks. By the next morning the fowl reappeared, plucked and boiled, in a buffet of food piled to an impossible abundance, to welcome, honor, and feed the spirits.

Throughout the structured mêlée of the mali, at the center of the temple sat two elders, a man and a woman, impassive in the midst of the sound and fury. They kept watch over the mua tablets, the spatial center of the dügü.

Minor Hitches.   All agreed that the day had gone well and that things were off to an auspicious start. There were hitches nevertheless. The butchering of several pigs between dancing sessions, for example, presented a real problem. The men killing the pigs outside the temple weren't skilled at the job, and the squeals of the beasts reverberated through the temple. Adolfo demanded a change in method and personnel. Although sacrifice is a key part of the ritual process, its enactment should not disturb the gaiety, plenty, and vitality of the reunion with the ancestors, whose very purpose is the elision of death, not its terrible recapitulation. Similarly, when a funeral procession passed by in the solid heat of midafternoon, we rushed to close the doors of the temple and to dissuade the funeral marchers from passing any closer. Death must not pollute the dügü. If Adolfo's earlier comments suggested how the actions in the temple bear on events unfolding elsewhere, here was evidence for the converse. The sounds and sights of the outside world can pollute the sacred center, ruining the ancestors' returns, if it they are not filtered and controlled.

Another issue was that the leader of the chorus kept falling into trance, at times inappropriately. "What's wrong with you, falling like that all the time?" her friend asked. She replied, "I don't know! I gave everything I was supposed to to my [late] grandmother. I don't know why they're bothering me." Other women gossiped that she was being punished for her drinking.

Facing Down the Devil.   From the perspective of the chief buyei, the crucial point of the dügü was not the amalahani as much as what followed it that night. On the first night after the return of the fishermen, the shaman must retreat to the forest *(el monte)* around midnight to bind the evil spirits that might otherwise interfere with the dügü. Every buyei calls this the most fearsome struggle, the moment that divides real shamans from impostors. Salomon of San Juan explained: "You find a big tree in the forest, set out your food plates and a candle, and then wait. Sometimes you might feel objects thrown at you from the forest, or you might see the eyes glowing, or shadows by the candle that suddenly gives no light. Then you back away very, very slowly." Other buyeis use their standard tools—rum, cigars, holy water, and white powder—to erect a barrier around the tree where the evil power is located. Another trick is to leave sweets by the tree as a temporary diversion for the bad spirits. After securing the tree, en route back to the temple the buyei may sing, "Evil was here, now it's gone; the earth is calm and quiet."

This process doesn't always go smoothly. Tola Guerreiro recalled an occasion from 1993 in the village of Másca when she went to confront the spirits at the appointed meeting place, but her invited apprentice did not show:

When she didn't come, I knew she had turned back from being scared, and that the spirit had followed her. So I ran back. And all hell was breaking loose! The power was out, and they had put a gas generator in place. But the gas had leaked, and a flame was moving across the ground toward the gas cans by the temple.

I threw the gas cans away, but a fire started anyhow. One of the drummers then saw a vision of his aunt in the flames and wanted to save her, running in the flames, but no one was there! I tackled him and threw him on the ground and slapped him until he came around. It was a commotion for an hour and a half. My children were clinging to me, everyone was afraid. And I wanted to cry, or quit, but you can't cry during work, because it interrupts the flow of the ahari. So we started again, the drummers playing like never before! And me playing maracas like there was no tomorrow, my arms out, calling power! Everyone remembers that night. And I am respected for that night.

With Adolfo confronting the evil spirits, almost everything went as planned. The sole hitch was that one assistant who was scheduled to meet the party en route got scared and showed up late. This delay changed the plan slightly but had no apparent consequences other than damaging the reputation of the newly initiated shaman. As the drums played in the temple to sustain them, the buyei and two assistants entered the forest and secured the tree, binding the malevolent spirits (mafia). One of those present recounted the mission to me:

One woman was scared and showed up late. So we went together, in a group, not singly like we were supposed to. We walked to the forest near Puente Diablo, by that curve in the road. You could feel there was something there. We worked on it with guaro, with agua bendita, we smoked our puros and kept our sashes tight. Adolfo spoke to "him" quietly, playing his maracas. Then we backed away, real slow, and then turned and walked quickly away without looking back, no looking back no matter what!

With the potentially intruding spirits bound, this dügü would, it appeared, run smoothly. The ritual day ended at around 4 A.M. with the sound of roosters slapping against the ground, concluding the last mali.

DAY SIX, SECOND WEDNESDAY: THE BANQUET

With the exception of the cooks, who worked through the night, everyone had a slow start the next day. At midmorning many were still asleep in their hammocks in the temple. At the buyei's behest we began carrying in wooden tables, placing them end to end to form a single, very long table over the earth tablets. The tables were covered with palm leaves, then by half circles of flat, hard cassava bread.[15] Others arrived laden with plates and bottles of different beverages.

With the noise of this activity, the sleepers awoke. The temple began to creak to life again. Under the table, the bottles were placed, uncapped or capped only lightly with cotton balls, along with lit candles. Washtubs

FIGURE 19. Singing women's songs in the temple for the ancestors while they eat. Photo by author.

filled with food were carried to a corner, and plates brought were heaped with food: chicken and pork, rice and beans, ereba, coconut bread, avocado, mango, papaya, watermelon, and sweet bread. The meal offered a bounty far beyond any family's everyday fare. Finally the table of offerings was consecrated to the ancestors with blown rum, incense, cigar smoke, and the sound of maracas, with one maraca left resting atop the mountain of food.

Though we all ate heartily, the bulk of the feast was left for the ancestors' consumption. Admiring the quantity, several people discussed the nature of the spirits' "eating." A visiting New Yorker offered a comparative consideration of the feeding of the ancestors: "The Bible talks about offerings, you know, like the Passover lamb offered so the firstborn wouldn't die. It's the same for us. In the dügü we give food to the ancestors so we won't die." Another suggested that the ancestors consume the spiritual essence: "Just like us, we get rid of most of what we eat in the bathroom, keeping only the essences." A buyei explained that the food on the banquet table was for the gubida. The hiyuruhas' food, by contrast, remained in the gulei. He said, "You can see the gubida spirits in the flies hovering over the table. See how the flies disappeared when the food was taken away? The ancestors were done eating." He offered a story: "Once this woman wouldn't eat any of the food, saying it had too many flies on it. The ancestors didn't like that; later she caught a trance and was stuffing herself with that same food." An elder singer jumped in to offer another story of the dangers of offending the ancestors. A woman had her hair nicely coiffed for a dügü and told the buyeis not to blow rum on her, which might ruin her hairdo. Later they possessed her and caused her to pour a whole bottle of rum over her own head. The gubida won't stand for vanity!

Women's Songs, Men's Songs.   As the gubida "ate," their descendants entertained them, and each other, in song. A women's chorus lined up on each side of the long table to sing *abeimahani,* women's songs. They had already been singing abeimahani during breaks in drumming and dancing over the last several days, with members of the choir trying to outdo one another in a good-natured competition of remembering lyrics, but now the singing was protracted and in earnest. The most knowledgeable women diligently tried to teach others songs they had learned, either old, nearly forgotten ones or new ones they found appealing. The women also sang a set of men's songs, *arumahani,* as few men still remember them.[16] The women hiked up their skirts to the knees to simulate men. One ribald jester kept the crowd in gales of laughter as she added to the impression by moving a stick of wood like an erect penis below her garments.

Women's songs are often about the fear of dying alone; men's songs frequently treat themes of being forced to travel, or being betrayed. Here is an example of an abeimahani:

> In the house of my relatives in Chalacha, that's where I'll be.
> In the house my relatives in Chalacha, that's where I grew *zacate*
>   [algae sprouts].
> I always see them.
> Who will bathe me, really?
> O, who will bathe me on the day that I lay down to die, my children?
> It will be sad around me, perhaps.
> It will be sad all around me on the day that I die, perhaps.
> Sad around me, it will be sad around me;
> Ende's mother came back home.
> But my relatives are gone, and it will be sad around me.
> Ende's mother came back home, but my relatives are gone.
> It will be sad around me.
> Ende's mother came back, but my relatives are gone.[17]

Here is an arumahani:

> Yunisi, come see me. Yunisi, come see me.
> Sister of my brother, come, my relative.
> The sun burns hot on me, woman. The sun is truly too hot.
> I'm packing my bag.
> Did I kill his mother or something?
> Why is he clawing at me all year long?
> The sun burns hot on me, woman. The sun is truly too hot.
> I'm packing my bag.
> Those are the orders of my uncle.
> I knew he would force me.
> Man, the sun burns hot on me. The sun is truly too hot.
> I'm packing my bag.

To sing, the women formed a line, little fingers linked. They thrust their arms forward in time with the songs, in motions similar to those used in the work of grating cassava.

The Ancestors Regain Their Youth.   In the early afternoon, elders began preparing for a ritual enabling the ancestors to enjoy the vigor of youth. Young people ranging from about six to twenty years of age were dressed with sacred sashes across their chests, like the buyeis; their heads were covered with scarves and their cheeks marked with orange achiote-dye crosses. Their heads were caressed with rum and they were seated before a lit candle and a bottle of rum. The ancestors were invited to visit them. A choir of women sang abeimahani to the prepared girls under the dibasen just outside the temple. Inside the temple, a few old men sang arumahani to the boys. The old men often lost their way in the songs and needed prompts from a woman who ridiculed them but nevertheless helped complete the songs. Despite these complications, several of the boys succeeded at falling into trance. They were laid in hammocks with rum bottles and candles placed in the sand underneath. The girls in trance were supported on the arms of sturdy female guardians in a line of women who sang abeimahani. The girls bobbed in the rhythm, their heads rolling from side to side. The dead and the living were aligned in a single arc of song.

Crisis.   One of the buyei Adolfo's most valued assistants was his younger brother, Davíd, a young man of about twenty. Davíd was one of the youths assigned to receive the ancestors. After singing the men's songs and being laid in a hammock for gentle repose, all without incident, he

FIGURE 20. An ancestor arrives and possesses the body of her descendant. Photo by author.

abruptly spun out of his hammock and writhed on the sand. Assistants retrieved him, and, holding him fast, tried to calm him with guaro and cigar smoke; finally they even waved camphor under his nose. Nothing soothed Davíd's agony. Even after being carried forcibly back into the temple, he gripped the sapling beams crisscrossed overhead, screaming "Mommy!" over and over, and sobbing intensely. He pushed off his holders and pulled himself up toward the rafters despite being held by several large adults. More people rushed to the scene, and many hands held him down on his hammock as senior shamans blew smoke and cold water on his head and the back of his neck to try to "cool" his possession, all to no avail. Finally, Adolfo, himself a big man, threw Davíd over his shoulder like a sack of potatoes and carried him into the inner altar room to conduct a private interview with this agitated ancestor. When the younger brother emerged an hour later, still in trance, he retired peaceably to his hammock. Later he even danced joyfully with other members of his family, thereby also fulfilling the expectations of ritual protocol.

Even after the episode had passed, it caused a public tremor that set off waves of gossip. It was rumored that Davíd had for years wanted to complete his initiation as a shaman, a confirmation that would allow him to lead dügü rites. Adolfo had always resisted, under the guise of "protecting" his brother, by publicly declaring that the shaman's path is a hard one of sacrifice, one he would not wish on anyone, least of all his own kin. But the gossip told another story. Davíd is a charismatic and much-beloved young man in the community. Adolfo, by contrast, lives part of the year in New York and does not enjoy the same everyday intimacy with the villagers. Because dügüs are infrequent, occurring perhaps only once every few years in a village, competition to lead them is fierce. Did Adolfo corner the ritual market by refusing to sanction his brother and rival? As Davíd attempted to pull free from his restrainers and lift himself upward, didn't he advance his right to ascend, not merely into the rafters but also as a shaman? Yet the claim could not be dismissed as Davíd's personal ambition: this was the ancestors' demand.

In the face of that demand, Adolfo could not simply rebuff Davíd or ignore the issue. But he also did not have to lose face. A problem of status between brothers, recast as a shaman conversing with an ancestor, allowed a compromise of sorts to be reached. The promotion and full initiation of Davíd as a buyei could take place two years later.

Mali Dances Again.   After the disruption, the rest of the day went off without further complications. The banquet tables were disassembled, the ancestors having taken their fill. The remains of the food were swept into washtubs, to be returned to the earth and the sea at the dügü's end. The mali dances began later than on the previous day, in the early evening, but still the requisite four of them were done by 4 A.M., when the tired group disbanded.

DAY SEVEN, SECOND THURSDAY: REPRISE

Thursday proceeded very much like the preceding day, with the assembly of the banquet, the preparation of the young, and the singing of women's and men's songs. But there were several differences. On this day, no mali were performed, the roosters (gayu) having all been offered by the end of the previous night. Along with the banquet set out for the ancestors, large slabs of pork and beef were cut for distribution to drummers and chorus members—part of their compensation for services rendered. The day's ritual was concluded by early evening, when the tables were carried out. At the center of the temple, the baroque variety of foods and symbols present at the outset of the dügü was now replaced with austere simplicity: the earthen tablets, a single candle, and a basket holding a few raw cassavas.

A mood of lighthearted festiveness took hold. Many participants were by now half-giddy from hard work and insufficient sleep. The heaviest labor of the dügü had been accomplished: the fishermen-ancestors had arrived and been welcomed, threatening evil spirits had been bound or staved off, the eight mali dances presenting the roosters were all done, the banquet had been presented to the gubida, and the ancestors had regained their youth. There was another day of ritual yet to come, but it would be a festive day. Why not start the fun a bit early? The buyei brought bottles of beer out of the gulei room. Prodded by insistent women, the drummers launched into fast punta rhythms.

Though the punta has associations with funeral wakes, it has by now become a mostly secular diversion. The dance is an individual or paired one of restrained sensuality, marked by a very still upper body, an impassive facial expression (at least for women), and the supple side-to-side movement of the hips. If the dügü dances call for an absorption in collective movements, the punta gives room for personal display and demands attention. The lyrics, which are about everyday concerns, are sometimes bawdy but often contain gentle moral cues as well. Here are two examples composed by Beatrice Meléndez, a well-known singer in Corozal.[18]

> I'll be watching you, little sister.
> The dead don't come back, like the migrant comes back.
> If you want to feel at home, quit saying bad things.
> The world has changed, quit saying bad things.
> And follow your path, little sister.

> My hands are my only machetes,
> My hands are my only axes.
> I've got no money left for fun.
> Don't be annoyed with me, and don't be sad,
> That's the destiny God gave me.

Tired people slowly drifted away, but the diehards kept up the dance until late in the night.

DAY EIGHT, SECOND FRIDAY: DIVINING SUCCESS

The drums began to thrum quietly at a little past 7 A.M., gradually becoming insistent. The baskets were lowered from the crossbeams above, each family gathering their own and leaving them alongside the earth tablets at the center. The raw cassava tubers of the previous day had been ground to a paste; wrapped in banana leaves, they were placed in the baskets along with packets of meat. The food was being packed for the ancestors' return journey to Sairi or St. Vincent.

Turning the Tablets.   Once the food was packed up, the lead buyei began to turn the tablets. The congregation pressed in around him to watch, in silent, rapt attention. After all, here was the first sign as to whether all the work of the dügü had paid off. Adolfo worked slowly and cautiously, ensuring that no edges were sticking, gingerly raising one corner and then another. Finally he hefted an entire tablet, cradled it, reversed its face and returned it to the ground. There were broad grins and sighs of approval all around. When the second tablet was turned, with equal success, the relief was loud and immediate: applause, shouts, thumbs-up signs, claps on Adolfo's back. The tablets were wrapped in orange-dyed cloth and placed in the baskets.

We marched in procession to the sea, everyone carrying a basket, and loaded them into canoes. Washtubs of food were likewise stowed aboard. On top of the cargo were placed two little model sailboats that had hung from the rafters in the temple since the raising of the baskets. These were to be set adrift on the swells. Wherever they washed ashore, they would indicate the need to perform a dügü.[19]

Revels in the Sea.   The canoe departed, manned by two paddlers, over the breakers. When it was nearly out of sight, a giant bathing party erupted without warning, though everyone was fully dressed. One friend tackled another and dragged her into the sea, and others launched themselves headlong into the waves. Still others ganged up on shy or reluctant relatives, throwing them into the water and emerging again for other victims, splashing and dunking, making sure no one stayed dry. At some dügüs, family groups among the kin of the afflicted run to enter the sea together, gripping a single long cloth, or bobbing with joined hands in a circle to signal the confirmation of their bonds and a momentary transcendence of bitter conflicts. The bathing party provided great release of tension. I was told that it was a final "washing away of the bad spirits," and with them also the threat of illness, misfortune, or death. But Adolfo described it, like the race to raise the baskets, as "entertaining" for the ancestors.

Once the canoe returned from depositing the ritual remains into the ocean, we returned in sopping, salty clothes and toting buckets of seawater to the temple, now emptied of its sacred objects and its solemnity. The carnival atmosphere continued inside. Participants poured water over each other and danced, sliding their bare feet through the mud on

FIGURE 21. Family bonds are fortified during the dügü; or, at least, fortified family bonds are enacted by a joint plunge into the water at the conclusion of a dügü in Trujillo. Photo by author.

the floor, chanting a playful song of nonsense syllables for half an hour. When the dance ended, many left to change their clothes. The young men were recruited to shoulder sacks of dry sand from the beach to the temple, to make a dry floor.

Last Prayers. Where the earth tablets had rested throughout the events, the buyei dug a hole. As family members returned in dry clothing, they approached the pit one by one to empty drinks into it, offering murmured prayers to the ancestors as they did so. Beer, Coke, and juice were common, but one woman drained a can of V8 into the pit and said, "To take away your hangover, grandfather" *(para quitar-le su goma, abuelo).* After blowing pipe smoke into the pit, Adolfo closed the hole with sand, carefully filling it from the outside toward the center to prevent any liquid from escaping.

Rum Punch. A single small table was placed in the center of the temple. Adolfo mixed furunsu, the beverage that always marks the closing of a dügü. Its main ingredients are beaten eggs, rum, and sugar, though buyeis may add other ingredients to create their own secret brews. Adolfo's furunsu included a dose of hiu, cassava beer. The rum was added last, and the buyei briefly lit the concoction on fire to warm it. Everyone approached the table to receive a cup ladled from the pot, either drinking it or giving it to a friend or relative. As the distribution neared its end, the drummers "stole" the pot and ran off with it, with several women in hot pursuit. Like the "kidnapping" of the woman at the departure of the fishermen, this was a standard and expected comedic break.

Burning the Table. The final act of the dügü proper is that of the buyei's pouring rum on the table, igniting it, and then feeding the flame with liquor as the table is tipped toward each edge in turn. A strong, blue flame cascading from the table to the ground shows evidence that "all sides" of the extended family are satisfied. In this case there was cause for concern, as several of Adolfo's attempts to ignite the rum were unsuccessful. But the flame finally caught and allayed the anxiety, burning a vivid, liquid blue on all sides. Dousing the table with rum to cause a sheet of flame to leap over the table, Adolfo then dramatically slapped the flame down with a wet towel. A deafening cheer erupted, and we rushed to slide our hands into the hot rum on the table and massage it into our heads, necks, and legs. This rum was especially propitious for transferring the ritual's power to one's own person. Friends and family members embraced, and we all congratulated Adolfo on a job well done.

Even so, the work was not completely over. The young ones who had been prepared to receive the ancestors remained in the temple for another three nights, until Monday morning. A year later, as many as could manage it would return to the temple for the *lugusurugayu*, the anniversary of the dügü, a one-day ritual that would fill the building for the last time. After that, the temple would stand empty until it fell into decay or was washed away by waves and storms. As one woman said, "*For now*, it's over." Being "done" is always provisional; there is always another dügü being mounted, always further demands levied on the living by the dead, always a need to renew the relation to the land and to family. But for now, after two weeks of hard work, the families were released from their obligation and were free to scatter.

Interpretation: Healing in the Dügü

There are obviously many levels of "meaning" that an analysis of such a complex ritual could try to distill. Under the weight of such excess, we might feel more than a little sympathy for Frits Staal's infamous essay

"The Meaninglessness of Ritual" (1979), which argued that ritual refers, quite simply, to nothing but itself. Staal noted that most practitioners, when asked about the meaning of rituals, often reply simply, "This is our tradition," and that such responses resist meaning. Yet even that short phrase is complex, implying at least an aspiration for a deep-rooted and long-lasting sense of belonging that points to particular places and kinds of action (*"this* is our tradition") as repositories of essential identity. It also expresses the conviction that such sentiments can be performed and called to mind in those particular places and through those actions. It is not that meaning doesn't exist, but that it doesn't exist in the denotative terms scholars often expect. Meaning seems to be a spatial question of locating and pointing to select events, objects, and actions as intensively compressed representations of the group's being—its memory, history, and continuing existence.

A more tractable problem than what meaning consists of is the question of where it resides. I try to answer the question, How does the dügü "work"?[20] by showing the kind of movements in space, and actions on space, through which the return of the ancestors and healing are signified and conjoined. These objectives are realized by actions of four types: compressing, fusing domains, accenting continuity, and reframing crises. Together these construct a dense ancestral presence. Indeed, this density of presence is the dominant principle in the indigenous or homeland construction of ritual power, as opposed to the principle of extension dominant in diasporic or cosmopolitan ritual.

COMPRESSING

Most obvious in the dügü is the intense compression of the participants with each other and with selected symbols in the confines of the temple—objects, songs, foods, and clothes—for an extended time. The physical contiguity of touching bodies, linked fingers, and synchronized motion effects a sense of social contiguity. Emotional attachment to each other and to the symbols of the ritual—the ancestral tablets, clothing, fishermen, and hammocks—is energized by their physical propinquity. Moreover, this compression increases throughout the ritual, creating centripetal acceleration toward the center and heart of the dügü.

For the dügü to be regarded as successful, both ancestors and distant relatives must travel long distances to the temple. Song lyrics about this travel play on these dual arrivals of ancestors and migrants. Some, especially dügü songs, are sung from the perspective of gubida coming from Sairi, the otherworld, or from St. Vincent. The songs inquire where all of the gubida's descendants are, and who is still to arrive. Other songs are about struggling to return from working abroad, even with the liabilities of a broken paddle and a canoe load of women. The fishermen who depart and then return to set the principal rituals in motion fuse representations of arriving ancestors and arriving migrants. They are both living relatives and spirit beings, deceased ancestors returned. Their stylized return, bedecked as ancestors who pull onto the beach at dawn, forcefully dramatizes the fact that the temple has centripetal power: ancestors, like migrants, are pulled toward it and compelled to return.

The ritual sequence creates multiple frames of graduated arrivals at a "center." At the heart of the dügü lie the earth tablets fashioned from the natal dirt of the ancestor being feted. They are the spatial center of the ritual, as they lie in the middle of the temple and the dances form circles around them. But they are also the center of sacredness, marked by the power accorded them to divine the success of the ritual, by the fact of their constant "guarding" by an elder, and by the prohibitions against approaching or photographing them. The tablets are a maximally concentrated essence of the ancestors.

The walls of the temple containing the tablets form another frame, a perimeter constantly purified—by smoke, incense, and misting with rum—and patrolled to guard against malevolent outside forces. Noteworthy here, especially in comparison with the analysis of a New York ritual, where threats are perceived as coming from outside the ethnic group, is that these malevolent forces are also Garifuna: rival buyeis, envious sorcerers (hechiceros or Obeah-men), intrusive Pentecostal converts, and mischievous local forest spirits.

Beyond the temple walls, the next frame is the ritual area in general, including both the temple and the dibasen, the shaded area where hammocks are strung and cooking is done, and periphery where sacrificial animals are tethered and where well-wishers and curious observers gather. The temple complex is encompassed in turn by the civilized village, outside which lies the uncivilized forest (el monte). These boundaries were accentuated, and consciously contemplated, when the buyei and his entourage marched into the forest to engage and bind the evil spirits at a selected old tree.

From this perspective, the dügü "works" by inscribing progressively sacred zones in participants' conscious experience—from the exogenous world from which the fishermen-ancestors-migrants arrive to the forest confronted by the shaman and his aides at midnight to the familiar village to the sacred temple encircled in white chalk and constantly repurified and finally to the heart of the dügü, the ancestral earth tablets themselves. Each gradation marks an intensification of traditional Garifuna-ness whose intactness—demonstrated by the tablets' wholeness when overturned at the end of the rites—models the ideal of social unity and continuous fidelity to the memory, and place, of the past.

Migrants, travelers, and workers; the family all return, pulled along afferent paths back to the nerve center and heart of memory. They return from the place of disorder to one of (nearly) perfect order. As they come, they mirror the returns of ancestors sojourning from Sairi or St. Vincent. Meaning derives from the progressive spatial compression of the diaspora, as far-flung members of the Garifuna community are sucked into the cultural compactor of the temple and the intense, sweaty proximity. Together they perform "traditional" movements around the tablets that mark the heart of that tradition. Traversing the lines etched by the ritual process itself, those "in diaspora" are rooted again, at least temporarily, in natal soil.

FUSING DOMAINS

Another key feature of the dügü is the re-fusion of domains of experience that are otherwise splintered (Alexander 2004). It re-fuses family members, territory, ancestral memory, and embodied techniques into a single, seamless performance. The dügü compensates for and mitigates the rifts within families caused by migration, evangelical conversions, travails in shipping, tourism, sweatshop labor, or the plain fact that many Garifuna men engender multiple families with complicated affinal relations. It brings into being a vision of cultural integrity—past fused to present, New York and Honduras fused to St. Vincent and Sairi. Normally segregated modes of action are fused in a single frame: traditional foods, clothing, drumming, dance, songs, sacrifice, building materials, canoes, fishing techniques, and language. This integration helps to create an experience of coherence, belonging, and power, defined as the ability to act in concert (Arendt 1970: 41) to solve problems and alter situations, within limits.[21]

But who is the performance of re-fusion for? Distinct from diasporic rituals like the one described in the next chapter, the dügü has no immediate audience other than the participants themselves. Although there is a distant audience—village Pentecostals, other families who have not "taken care of their own" with the appropriate rituals, rival buyeis in other towns who will receive reports about the event, and family members in New York who will watch the videos—the primary audience is the actors themselves.

Because the dügü must intensify the sense of tradition, it foments the performance of certain kinds of actions and suppresses others. Ancestors, like migrants, will only want to return to a familiar place if it feels like home.

ACCENTING CONTINUITY

Most Garifuna men know how to roof a structure with palm branches, butcher a pig, fish with nets, and drum at least some rhythms. Most women know how to extract the toxic juices from a cassava tuber, grate the cassava on a mahogany board with embedded limestone teeth, and cook its dough on an open fire to make flatbread. They know how to dye clothes in achiote and sing at least some of the old songs. True, some traditional skills of the dügü have largely been lost, such as basketry or weaving the fishermen's helmets out of palm fronds, and performing these tasks requires special purchases and travel. But older villagers retain most of the knowledge required to intensify "tradition" in a condensed ritual frame, even though it may not be exercised on a daily basis. The young and the diasporic participants flying in from New York lack these skills, and, for them, witnessing the preparations adds to the dügü's exotic appeal. It is deeply familiar, gorged with the signs of "home," yet also foreign.

Traditional actions take on heightened significance when juxtaposed with modern aspects of village life—concrete block dwellings, recorded music, gas stoves, electric refrigeration, cell phones, and the speaking of Spanish or English. The ritual privileges certain kinds of traditional action, but those actions are not mainly just symbolic, as they are for diasporic practitioners in New York. Fishing from wooden canoes remains a viable, if difficult, livelihood in most villages, and there is no absolute disjuncture between the activities of the ancestors and those of contemporary villagers.

This somewhat unique combination of the everyday scarcity of tradition and its ready availability for special events may account for the dügü's expanding popularity in the last decade. It is both powerful, as distinctive ritual and commemorative action, and plausible, drawing on available habitual practices. The ready presence of these techniques and habit knowledge in the homeland, as opposed to New York, help establish the indigenous authority of local buyeis over their cosmopolitan colleagues. The recognition of such authority helps define the specific quality of diasporic religion: It endows the homeland with special, sacred force, based on perceived exiguities in New York.

The ritualization of ancestors and ancestry in the dügü uses a form of representation whose dominant mode is indexical, to take the Peircean term. The acts and objects used in ritual are not utterly distinct from everyday practices, nor do they represent attempts at the iconic, historical recreation of tradition. They signify, rather, the continuity of certain acts and objects in the present with "what the ancestors did" in the past. The participants invoke the ancestors first and foremost by becoming contiguous with them, beyond the sense implied by spirit possession: dressing like them, fishing like them, building and cooking and singing like them. Objects, acts, and ideologies that communicate continuity with the ancestors (like hammocks, fishing, and collectivism), are foregrounded, while other everyday objects, acts, and ideologies that communicate rupture with the past (like tennis shoes, recorded music, and individualism) are suppressed.

Still, this distinction doesn't occur in any neat way. Some dügüs now use electricity not only for lighting at night, but also for refrigerating food in the buyeis' private altar room. At a recent dügü in Triunfo de la Cruz, at least one buyei carried a cell phone clipped onto her waist sash. Even in the homeland, some modern technologies are legitimized, even within the ritual frame of the dügü, as tradition boosters. Refrigeration facilitates and speeds up the feeding of the ancestors, outboard motors help the fishermen "return" more efficiently, artificial light allows the dancing to go on all night, and cell phones help coordinate the travel of relatives whose attendance is required. In these cases, facilitating tradition overrides possible objections to technological accretions. Yet tradition-boosting technologies must not disrupt the overall sensibility of the encompassing schema, of indexical continuity.

REFRAMING CRISES

The dügü also works by healing the patient whose illness first precipitated the event. It cures by reframing individual malaise as a breach in the relations between living Garifuna and ancestral spirits and repairing that breach. It transfers an affliction that was individual and mysterious to the realm of the collective and predictable. The victim's sudden and surprising symptoms and contortions are revealed to be merely one engagement in an age-old process of exchange with the ancestors, one that can be solved through familiar, and familial, techniques. The most striking aspect of the three dügüs I have taken part in is the degree to which the patient, allegedly the cause of the entire enterprise, disappears from the action. He or she lies in a hammock in the background but is not instrumental, or spatially central, in any of the proceedings.

Yet patients always report relief of symptoms. Of course, once the ancestors confirm the efficacy of the offerings and remove the supposed etiology of the medical crisis, there is enormous social pressure to claim improvement even if physical symptoms persist. I witnessed one case in which a female victim of a stroke had suffered paralysis of one side of her face. In response, she sponsored a chugu. Though her face did not improve, she reported feeling better. The support of her family and community and the recalling of the ancestors offered consolation, if not exactly cure, by resituating the illness in a context and lineage of similar challenges. Her case was somewhat unusual, though: most disturbances that precipitate a dügü carry less-evident physical signs. The most common are psychosomatic issues that can be traced to social, intrafamilial conflict. These are cured by being reframed as social concerns in the ritual grammar of the needs of the gubida and hiyuruha.

There are also, however, crises that do not fit the ritual frame as neatly. In the dügü I have described, there was conflict between brothers: Davíd, the aspiring buyei, and his elder brother Adolfo, the lead buyei. Here was a conflict between territorial authority (locally residing Davíd) and cosmopolitan authority (diasporic Adolfo). Although this conflict could not be expressed directly, it could be enclosed in the ritual frame. The spirit-possessed Davíd sought to lift himself up into the rafters, mimicking the climbing of the pole performed during shamans' initiations, and thereby stake his claim as the buyei sought by the ancestors. But this attempt at elevation was countered, and trumped, by Adolfo's own move. He slung Davíd on his back and carried him into his, Adolfo's, altar space. The vertical bid was neutralized: vertical ascent as a shaman would only come horizontally, through the temple and through the elder brother's authority.

Other mini-crises unfolded, too. Some dancers were regarded as illegitimately possessed, and their performative bids to take center stage as ancestors (and so obtain special treatment and goods, it was alleged) were frustrated. Another impasse arose with the canoe owner from a distant village raising his fare and stalling the ritual at a critical juncture. A funeral procession arriving from down the road produced a momentary threat of death coming too close. Then too, countless local men arrived, allegedly to lend a hand, but in reality to severely deplete the rum supplies. An assistant buyei, stricken by sudden fear, failed to accompany the head shaman on his mission to confront and bind malicious spirits in the forest; thus she risked leaving the edges of the known world insecure. Finally, many families rent by conflict between traditionalists and Pentecostal converts attempted to persuade absent members to come to the temple, often in vain, and were forced to take inventive compensatory measures, such as dancing with extra roosters in hand. They fulfilled the dügü's obligation, but only by sleight of hand, in a ritual invention approved by the head buyei.

In sum, if the earthen tablets of compressed ancestral presence remained serenely intact, around them circled a storm of motion and contest over the nature and meaning of that sign. Garifuna-ness itself remained beyond dispute, even as the specific meanings and responsibilities—of family membership, traditional fidelity, religious hierarchy, and proper observance—were opened to critical inquiry and possible revision. As the dügü revived (or, in some cases, established for the first time) extended family relationships, it also sparked unforeseen conflagrations. Indeed, it was through the very process of surmounting the seemingly endless series of ritual problems that the hoped-for sense of communitas arrived at the end—as attested by the immersion in the sea, the exchanged cups of furunsu, and the joyful embraces following the successful "burning of the table." In every case, the minor crises were rearticulated in terms of spatial boundaries. The constant tiny adjustments required to mount a successful performance of the ritual ideal of the whole family assembled on the most ancestral site were transferred to the idiom, and objects, of graded spatial boundaries marking the return. Traversing those boundaries is the ritual's modus operandi—its ability to work, cure, and convey power.

Given all the practical difficulties of carrying off a dügü—including, today, the difficulty of gathering far-flung relatives together—and all the crises it generates, the reported rise in the number and frequency of performances in the last decade is striking. As Tola Guerreiro remarked: "When I led a dügü in Limón [a Honduran Garifuna village] in 1993, it was something like the first one in fifty years. But now they have them all the time!" This assessment is corroborated by most Garifuna observers. Can it be that the greater the extent of emigration abroad, the greater becomes the need for the authentic "home," presented intensively in the dügü, which is the fusion of memory and territory par excellence?

If the homeland dügü works on intra-Garifuna family relations, the ritual in the New York diaspora community works consciously on the outer frame of Garifuna-ness, the relation of the Garifuna community to the city. I now examine a ritual series in the Bronx, where the dügü, which cannot be performed, is partly replaced by the "return of the ancestors."

CHAPTER 6

Ritual in the Bronx

You followed me to this cold place; now you'll have to make
do with this.

Garifuna shaman in New York, to her spirits

I go home the way other people go abroad, for I have become
the *other* for the people I continue to call my own.

Fatou Diome, The Belly of the Atlantic

With the exception of the dügü, all Garifuna rituals can be, and are,
performed in diaspora. The requirement that the dügü take place on
homeland soil enhances its prestige in the Bronx. It is distinguished as
the return par excellence, a veritable pilgrimage. Yet many Garifuna will
never take part in a dügü. For some, their illegal status in the United
States would render the voyage a one-way journey; others could never
muster the required resources; and others yet are uninterested in such
traditional rites because they are skeptics or Protestant converts. Few,
however, avoid all the rituals of traditional Garifuna religion. In the
Bronx as in homeland villages, less elaborate rituals—the wake immediately following the death of a relative, and the "mass" offered a year or
more later—are events as regular as death itself. More elaborate offerings to the gubida, like the chugu, occur several times a year. In New
York, the individual consultations that consume the largest portion of
the buyei's time proceed very much as in homeland villages, except that
a visit to the buyei, which almost immediately becomes public knowledge in the village, in most cases remains a private affair. This difference

is more consequential than it might appear. In the absence of constant public knowledge of who was or was not present at a ritual, the compulsory, collective quality of ritual is diminished, and its character as personal and elective cultural activity is enhanced.

The closest equivalent to the dügü performed in the Bronx is the "return of the ancestors." The event occurs once a year, on the Saturday night nearest January 15. It commemorates the return of the shamans' spirit helpers (hiyuruha) following their month-long absence during the Christian holiday season. During that time the ancestors are said to return to Sairi, traditionally located in St. Vincent, but now located by many New York Garifuna leaders as "in Africa." The interval is an extension of the traditional period of festivities *(fedu)* between December 24 and January 6 (Epiphany). As the hiyuruha take their ease, so does the buyei, who undertakes no consulting or ritual work.[1] The return of the ancestors marks not only the return of the shamans' tutelary spirits but also the end of the festive season, the return to work, and the rejoining of the everyday struggles that call for the ancestors' intervention.

Despite many similarities, this ritual is not the same as the dügü. Its ritual space and objects are different, and these differences have clear effects on performance. And, whereas the dügü is a crisis-driven intervention performed only sporadically, the return is cyclical, performed annually. What is more, because New York Garifuna cannot presume the ethnic recognition that might guarantee them sites of performance or time dedicated to its observance, the ritual must be carefully orchestrated and planned. Halls must be rented or borrowed and the ritual purpose explained, defended, and rendered explicit. To take the terms of Harvey Whitehouse (2000, 2004), diasporic ritual is pushed toward the "attractor position" of a more doctrinal ritual style and away from the imagistic ritual style more characteristic of the homeland dügü.

Example One:
The Return of the Ancestors, January 2002

For the return ritual of 2002, all Garifuna of New York were invited, from every family, village background, and linguistic group. Those from Corozal attended alongside those from San Juan, Triunfo de la Cruz, and Aguan; Hondurans came along with Belizeans and Guatemalans. Thus the outer frame of the ritual was the ethnic group of the Garifuna as a whole, rather than specific family lineages from given villages.

The public event was held at the community center Vamos a La Peña (Let's Go to the Rock) at 1226 East 144th Street, as it had been many times before.[2] At the time, La Peña was a nonprofit community center in the Bronx, used for everything from musical events and union assemblies to salsa parties, English classes, and help for the hungry and homeless.[3] It was the ideal site not only because it was known by all but also because it could be rented at a reasonable rate, for $250 to $300 a night. The ritual of the return of the ancestors was choreographed by Martina, a respected buyei in the city.

Loaded with supplies, we headed for La Peña. A sign over the entrance declared, "¡Colón viene a descubrir-nos!" (Columbus is coming to discover us!) and depicted two Amerindians laughing. Inside, the walls were covered with art and posters of Che Guevara, Augusto Sandino, and Frida Kahlo. The ritual space was, in a word, thoroughly Latino, leftist, and indigenist in tone—a place of resistance against not only the legacy of Columbus but also the neocolonialism of the twentieth and twenty-first centuries. In the rear office we met the cofounder and day-to-day operator of La Peña, a white Chilean named Don Victor (Victor Toro). The Garifuna women affectionately greeted him as Viejo, "Old Man." On the floor next to his desk was a simple altar consisting of a candle burning before an image of Gabriela Mistral, a Chilean poet and, Don Victor was eager to explain, the first Latin American to win the Nobel Prize for Literature. Don Victor greeted us warmly and brought out a bottle of red wine and some plastic cups. Only he partook, as Garifuna tend to prefer beer and rum. In any case, there was little time for socializing, as we had our own altar to prepare.

To transform the room into a fitting site for a ritual, Martina's helpers built the altar on the floor, preparing its components with smoke, incense, and rum. Beach sand had been gathered the day before from Orchard Beach. There Martina had thrown seven dimes into the sea to ask the permission of Yemaya, the Yoruba and Santería goddess of the sea and maternity. The sand was mixed with sand from Honduras and then spread on the floor, with four limes buried to mark the arms of a cross—the same figure made in the dügü temple by the architecture's four doorways. A central candle was set out for the ancestors and balanced alongside an image of Saint Esquipula. Martina briefly shook her maracas—"to awaken them," as she explained—and then placed them head down in the sand. Next to them, her mureywa, the wand used in divination and to "balance the head" of those possessed by the spirits, was stuck upright in the sand. Statues of Eleggua—the Yoruba

FIGURE 22. Two buyeis in New York consider the next step in assembling the altar during the return of the ancestors ceremony. Photo by author.

and Santería messenger and god of the crossroads—were left to guard each door. A live white dove, with leaves attached to its claws, was tethered over the door frame in homage to Obatala, the Yoruba and Santería deity of the sky and gentle coolness, "for peace." On the walls behind the altar were suspended miniature wooden boats, fishing nets, seashells, and hammocks, all icons of the homeland. By the altar, a table was piled high with food offerings. Because animal sacrifice is difficult in the city ("There's cameras everywhere!" one buyei complained), chickens for use on the altar were purchased freshly killed from a *vivero*—a shop selling live or just-killed poultry. Guests arrived to leave offerings for their own ancestors: brimming plates of rice and beans, cooked chicken, and cassava bread. Others placed liquor bottles, fruit, money, and lit candles before the altar.

With about three hundred people present, all Garifuna, the ceremony proper began around 9 P.M., with men's songs (arumahani). The New York Garifuna community, unlike many homeland villages in Honduras, boasts a group of around a dozen men who are masters of the arumahani and have even recorded them on compact disc "for the reeducation of those lapsed back in Honduras," as their leader told me. Here is another example of the sense in which diasporas *make* religion: the

FIGURE 23. The buyeis' dance at the beginning of the return of the ancestors, at Vamos a la Peña in the Bronx. Photo by author.

tradition is identified as a problem, affixed in rationalized genres, and rendered an explicit, bounded entity suitable for dissemination, even "reeducation." The men linked their little fingers and sang, accompanying their voices with vigorous forward thrusts of the arms. Women's songs (abeimahani) followed. Following these preliminaries, the drums were purified and "heated" for sacred use by being treated inside and out with rum mist, incense, and cigar smoke.

The first dance the drummers played was for the buyeis alone. Each wielded a maraca in each hand, playing fast rhythms in perfect unison between the drumbeats. Confirming her position at the top of the shamans' hierarchy, Martina was the first to enter a state of spirit possession. The senior shamans' spirits must arrive first. Assistants removed her glasses and blew rum on her head to encourage the returning ahari. She was followed quickly by her top protégé, Coqui. Martina embraced her fellows, offering greetings from the returning ancestors. She took long draughts from a bottle of rum, offered counsel to those with questions, and made requests for food and fidelity to the tradition. The trances of her trainees followed, occurring especially during the songs that usually accompany the dügü in the homeland. The gathered shamans, numbering about twenty, played their maracas in magnificent syncopation, at first hunched over to concentrate on the rhythm, and then with arms raised overhead, the furious hissing of their instruments both calling and commemorating the return of their powers.

The "profane" punta dances followed. Most of the shamans left or were roused from their trance states with cold water. Their maracas were set back on the gulei, and the dancers now focused on their personal dance style rather than on staying in time with each other and the drummers. The dance even became a source of ribald jokes for onlookers, as the women "saluted" the drums one at a time. Each one danced up to the drummers with shaking hips and concluding with a pelvic thrust over the center drum, urged on by the laughter of all. Still, one unexpected trance occurred during even the lighthearted punta dance: young Belgium fell backward, her orisha beads swirling around her neck. Watchful elder women kept her on her feet as she bobbed about. After a few minutes, they blew cold water on her head to "cool" the trance—after all, it was not yet time to encourage the full visitation of an ancestor—and Belgium returned to normal consciousness. A freestyle punta dance followed, men and women dancing together. One at a time, individual male partners entered the ring to pursue the women, who also entered one at a time, the man dancing toward the woman even as she remained aloof, never deigning to meet his gaze. After a break for the meal, women's songs were performed again. Finally the ceremony was closed by a reprise of the buyeis' dance, this time marked not by trance but by the shamans' virtuoso playing. It popped and sizzled in flawless time. This mastery, at once technical and rhythmic, is essential to the public display of the shamans' skills, and thus to being a respected shaman.

The event finished at around 3 A.M. Many participants headed for subway stops or vehicles. Others remained to clean up.

The ritual was considered by all the buyeis as a success, especially in view of the inherent limitations of the city space. As one woman commented, "In Honduras the weather is right, the beach is right, and there's no interference. The ancestors like it better. But they have to understand that we can't do everything here, with all this concrete, and that they have to go to Honduras if they need more."

RITUAL CRISIS

Despite its apparently smooth unfolding, the return of the ancestors had begun with a serious problem. On the previous Saturday, the day of Saint Esquipula, the emigrants from Corozal had hosted their yearly party at La Peña.[4] Around midnight, when the dance party was just heating up, the New York police invaded the hall and shut it down, with the allegation of illegal liquor sales. The shamans worried that the return of the ancestors might suffer a similar fate. We had long discussions of hypothetical scenarios. Suppose the police entered when ancestors had already possessed participants, and the ancestors elected to defend their descendants against intruders? Suppose the ancestors were from the period of the eighteenth-century Garifuna wars on St. Vincent and viewed the police as the colonizing British? Violence would surely follow, including possibly deadly consequences if someone were to attack a police officer while in trance. The group considered changing the venue, perhaps to a church, but that choice could lead to conflicts over the nature of the ritual work. How would they explain the event to Protestants, or even to non-Garifuna Catholics, as a necessary affair? The strategy, it was decided, would be to call it a cultural meeting and play down the central role of the ancestors. Still, another venue would almost certainly cost more than La Peña, and in any case switching the site was impossible at this late hour. Instead, we visited the building on the night before the ancestors' return to safeguard the space.

I dropped by Martina's apartment near the Hunt's Point subway stop in the South Bronx so that we could ride together over to La Peña. She had already descended to her aunt's apartment, four floors below. Two Cuban santeros who had been working in the aunt's apartment were just leaving, one wearing a red and white necklace marking him as a child of Shango—the Yoruba and Afro-Cuban god of thunder and the fourth king of the old Yoruba kingdom of Oyo—and the other with a maroon and white necklace designating him as a child of Baba Luaye, the Yoruba and Afro-Cuban god of the earth, pestilence, and healing. They had just completed a "job" invoking the powers of Eleggua—the Yoruba-Santería god of doors and crossroads—to protect the apartment against robberies, which were common in the neighborhood, and against the run of bad luck Martina's aunt had been having. Another Garifuna woman present had just had the same work done. She said, "I was having car accidents all the time, and I couldn't change the locks after separating from my husband. I would wake up at night all the time feeling bad things." The charge for the protection in this apartment was a relatively small $90. For a buyei, vulnerable to much stronger and more frequent spiritual attacks, the fee to secure an apartment was $250.

We protected the big room at La Peña with similar techniques. Martina explained the measures as we proceeded, not only for my benefit but also for that of her apprentice shamans. One woman pulled leaves from a bag and crushed them with garlic cloves and salt. I cut sixteen limes into quarters and squeezed them in a bucket—"eight is for Obatala" (the Yoruba deity associated with the sky, the color white, and peace), "doubled." Sulfur was added, "to heat," along with ammonia and Reckitt's Crown Blue cubes, "to clean the room."[5] Martina asked someone to add holy water, but it had been left at home. We manufactured some by reciting Our Fathers and Santa Marías over water and adding salt. Martina's friend Ana poured rum into the bucket, and each of us blew clouds of rum from our mouths into it as well. Several women breathed cigar smoke over the liquid. Quickly, a separate dry mixture was concocted—corn, beans, and rice, with honey dripped on top—"for abundance"—funneled, by men only, into paper cones—"mano de hombre, for balance," and because "men are more powerful." The paper cones, called "honeycomb like in Africa, or at home" (in Honduras), were then folded closed at top and bottom. Each cone was placed in a plastic bag with a live chicken. Martina painted each of our faces with white eggshell chalk on the forehead and cheeks, "to make us warriors" and because "the Iku spirits [Yoruba spirits of death] don't like it; they have white faces and think you're one of them."

After the door to the outside had been fumigated, we filed out and walked around the block. On each street corner, a woman knelt and wrung the neck of a chicken, leaving the bag behind. We entered La Peña again, stepping over the smoking censer. Shrines to Eleggua, in the form of an inverted cone with eyes and a lit candle next to it, were erected by the two doors. With the perimeter secured, the men now stripped to T-shirts to treat the interior of the building. We mopped the floor with the liquid formula, beginning by pushing the mops in the shape of giant crosses, then mopping the entire floor. The women placed the remaining dry mix in the corners and fumigated the room with cigars and censers. They did the same with rum mist, blowing it from their mouths over the walls, tables, and chairs. Martina completed the mission, moving along the walls and puffing powdered sugar off her open palm, "to sweeten any bitterness," and finished with a spray can of sandalwood scent, "to calm the energies."

The haze hung like a blanket suspended between floor and ceiling. Several women viewed its lingering resilience as a sign of success, and one of them discerned a cross in it. Everyone was happy. Some shuffled a punta and talked of the relief *(alívio)* they felt. Each of us was given three pennies to throw backward over our shoulders at a crossroads later, "to protect our return."[6]

With the preventive medicine in place, the fear of possible police invasion was allayed. I asked one of the buyeis whether she thought of this protective medicine as part of Garifuna tradition. She answered, "No, that was pure Santería." I persisted, "But Garifuna rituals also use the sacrifice of chickens." She said, "Yeah, but in Garifuna ritual we eat them, we don't *leave* them." Martina chimed in, "Even for us Garifuna, this is the year of Yemaya and Shango—Yemaya for cooling things down after 9/11, but with Shango for prosperity."[7] I had expected the juxtaposition of Yoruba and Garifuna religious idioms to cause at least some dissonance, but these responses suggested none. To the contrary, the shamans were proud of having done "pure Santería," a ritual corpus known for its efficacy in securing a place.

The ritual space's perimeter had been fortified against a potentially hostile city by marking the surrounding street corners with offerings that would appease death (Iku), and by acknowledging the power of Eleggua to govern crossroads, entries, and exits. After these "hot" warrior forces were applied to the outer edges of the ritual space, the interior was transformed into a "cool" place, a place "sweetened" by sugar, "calmed" by sandalwood, and ruled by the white dove of Obatala. In another sense, the ritual place was made one of balance, of male and female foods and tasks honeycombed together, "like in Africa"; of three parts "coolness" spiced by one part "heat"—limes, Reckitt's Crown Blue ammonia, and holy water, heated by sulfur. Leaving that guarded place to move outward, we again acknowledged the real dangers of the street. We threw coins over our shoulder at a crossroads to acknowledge deadly power and keep it at bay.

Through these actions, a space with its own prior significations was inscribed with new ones. The actions acknowledged the Bronx streets as a place of potential danger and violence, both from criminals and from the police. But in addition to this recognition of the realities of the city, the ritual gave the space of La Peña additional folds and textures: it was Africanized and, more specifically, Yorubized through the metaphors of cool versus hot, sweet versus bitter, and calm versus agitated to make a secure and propitious haven for ritual. As the Garifuna leaders expected after a job well done, on the next night the ancestors returned without interference from the police.

Example Two:
Departure of the Ancestors, December 14, 2003

The "departure of the ancestors" before the festival season follows a structure similar to that of the return, but on a more private and smaller scale. We met in a ground-floor storage room of an apartment building where one of the New York shamans worked as superintendent. In the early morning, the clouds unfurled a blanket of white, and during the early afternoon heavy snow continued to fall. Despite the weather, people began arriving by 2 P.M. They unfolded card tables and covered them with delicacies for the afternoon banquet for the ancestors: pasta, rice, fried chicken, crayfish soup. They set brimming plates on top of the table, while underneath were set opened bottles of soda and beer, each with a cotton ball stuffed in the neck, "so the spirits can get the essence." One person manned an improvised cash bar. Perched on an overturned milk crate behind a cooler of beer, he raised money for the larger-scale and more costly return of the ancestors, an event that would take place just a month hence. The room was small and freezing cold because of a missing pane in the window. Later, when the room filled with dancers, the cold air would be welcome, but now people donned sweaters and crossed their arms over their chests.

Next to the table the altar was built. As usual, beginning with the most senior buyeis, the shamans placed their maracas head down in the sand alongside lit candles, giving them a quick shake to awaken them. Several buyeis wore the plastic bead collares marking their orisha affiliations: one wore a red and white necklace for Shango, and another wore the pure red beads of La Madama, the spirit of an elderly black female curandera or fortune teller frequently invoked in Puerto Rican Santerismo (a hybrid of Santería and spiritualism that is common in the Bronx). A third shaman admonished them that they shouldn't be wearing their necklaces there because it "mixed spirits," but her reprimand fell on deaf ears. The two in beaded necklaces merely nodded to acknowledge the comment and moved away.

Several of those shivering on wooden benches against the gray concrete wall were freshly arrived from Honduras and eagerly shared news of relatives from home. One fellow among them sold crude, handmade miniature cigars from Honduras in little plastic bags, four for a dollar. Because these sell for a few pennies in Honduras, he stood to make a good profit, and everyone knew it. Nevertheless, several New Yorkers lined up to buy them, noting their reputation for being especially "strong," even causing dizziness. The dizzying cigars seemed metonymic of the homeland itself, raw but exceedingly strong in spiritual force. Whereas in homeland villages the Phillies-brand cigars from the United States are highly valued for ritual work, what was needed here was not the "sweetness" of the refined Phillies but the raw power of the village tobacco.

Meanwhile, a woman recently arrived from Honduras sold plastic bags of Honduran mints, Arke Ice. Several New York Garifuna popped them into their mouths and, rolling the candy on their tongues, exchanged sighs and wistful smiles. Perhaps, like Proust's madeleine, the taste of candy from home was a rope let down from heaven, lifting them from the freezing basement just for a moment and setting them in a fragrant yard of bougainvillea and coconut palms.

The drums began beating in dügü-style rhythm, and the shamans began syncopating their maraca rhythms. As they lifted their maracas in the air, first the leader's and then the others' heads tilted back, eyes closed, and then forward again. They bent over at the hips as their shoulders lightly shook. The spirits had arrived. Seeing this, two Puerto Rican visitors, both santeros, pulled perfume flasks from their pockets and began to massage the contents into their heads and the backs of their necks. They passed a large cigar between them. They'd been invited to the feast by one of the buyeis, and now they fluidly joined in the dance like regulars. Though from a different ritual tradition, the repertoire was also quite familiar: cigar-smoke fumigations, the rubbing of ointments over the head and the back of the neck, and dance leading to trance, the attempt to resist it joined to the pleasure of its pull. When I asked them about their impressions, they described feeling truly welcome and surprisingly at ease.

There followed, however, trances that were less familiar or predictable, not just to the visitors, but to all who were present. One woman was "taken" by a male ancestor, who wanted to dance wanaragua rhythms. In everyday waking consciousness this dance is performed exclusively by males, and the dance was hesitant and uncertain. The dancer tripped and became entangled in the steps, causing doubt as to whether the male ancestor was really present. Another woman performed an hour-long series of gestures that was unfamiliar and disconcerting to many, especially those recently arrived from Honduras. She offered handshake greetings with her arms crossed one over the other and bit into her lit cigar sideways, blowing smoke from both its ends, which then wafted from the extreme corners of her mouth. She snagged a vase of holy water off the altar and drank half of it, dumping the rest over a seated neighbor's head. She poured hot candle wax on her neck and chest—a impressive demonstration of the spirit's power over her body, but not a normal part of Garifuna possession performances. She knocked her forehead against the forehead of those she greeted, simultaneously offering advice and reprimands. Finally, she smashed a glass-encased candle on the floor and, carelessly treading over its shards in bare feet, tried to scale a water pipe mounted against the wall. An embarrassed silence accompanied this failed effort, and she finally slid back to the floor. When another buyei began to pour hot wax on her own skin in apparent imitation of this performance, and to jabber in words that were incomprehensible, there were murmurs of disapproval from those watching and looks of reprimand from the rest of the shamans. They did their best to sustain the ritual in a more familiar fashion.

In conversations during a break between dancing sets, two New York Garifuna told me that they were impressed by the surprising power of the spirits that had recently taken the room, especially in the show of resistance to pain. Others were less welcoming of the strange performance and denounced the two women for bringing Vodou into a Garifuna rite.[8]

Men's songs, women's songs, and punta dances alternated as the ritual returned to its normal cadence. Losing interest after several hours, the Puerto Rican visitors, among others, departed. Finally, Martina's spirit, an ahari named Lulu, focused the attention of the now-intimate crowd of about thirty by delivering a speech through her human carrier. This spirit was the sole public speaker among those possessed; only she had the authority to hush the entire room, though other spirits had given individual consultations earlier in the afternoon. The spirit's public oratory recounted the blessings and challenges of the year past and the auspicious promise of the year to come. Everyone applauded. Some of the food from the table was distributed for a shared meal; the rest was scraped into plastic bags for later disposal in a hole in the ground of a nearby park. The ritual concluded at around 9 P.M.

The productive tension of this ritual derived from the work of adjustment regarding appropriate spirit possession within a context of plural influences. The ritual process moved from the display of dramatically variant possessions to a show of "correct" Garifuna possession. The former were spectacular to a fault, disdained by the buyeis as showy (and foreign) Vodou. Martina, the lead buyei, reoriented the space to a specifically Garifuna sensibility through the controlled, traditional oratory of her distinguished ahari. If the 2002 return of the ancestors emphasized the Africanizing of ritual to adapt to the new space of the Bronx, this ritual of the ancestors' departure showed that that process is channeled in particular ways and is not simply an open-ended creative flux. The influence of the African Diaspora is appropriately manifested in Afro-Cuban and Yoruba models, not putative "Vodou" or other possible versions.

Example Three:
Return of the Ancestors Redux, January 24, 2003

On December 9, 2002, La Peña was evicted from the space it had occupied for twelve years. This left the New York Garifuna shamans with the problem of finding a space for the return of the ancestors in January 2003. Church leaders were approached but, as some Garifuna shamans had feared, even those sympathetic to the buyeis' plight were reluctant to support what they considered a pagan rite. Other community centers proved far too expensive to rent. As luck had it, one of the shamans, by now numbering twenty-nine, had previous experience in local theater. She entreated a local theater company she had worked with to intercede on the group's behalf. By shifting the rubric of the ritual to one of cultural performance and a form of drama, the group was able to secure the use of the gymnasium of a middle school for the evening of Saturday, January 24. Moreover, the theater company agreed to contribute $300 of the $1,000 needed to rent the gym and purchase food. The remaining $700 was made up by contributions of $50 each from the participating buyeis. As compensation, the theater company required only that the event be open to the public.

Though the middle-school gym seemed an ideal resolution to the space problem, it created new challenges for the ritual. For one, the rental secured the gymnasium for only four hours, from 7 P.M. until 11 P.M. The event would need to adhere to the dictates of the clock. Second, laws prohibiting smoking and alcohol use in public schools would preclude the use of tobacco or rum to purify the ritual space. Third, the public nature of this year's ritual demanded that some kind of informational guide be provided in both English and Spanish so that the audience would be able to follow the proceedings. The presence of a non-Garifuna audience also called for expanding the menu of "Garifuna culture" on offer in the planned ritual. The buyei group printed up programs reading "Theater International, Inc. and Halagule Wayunagu present Feast of the Ancestors." Along with a list of the members of the buyei group and a short history of its evolution, this program offered a guide to the ritual proceedings. These were set out in ten distinct "acts," some of which had little or no relation to the ritual itself. Act 7, for example, was a performance of *parranda,* an important genre of Garifuna music but one not usually performed in ritual contexts. Act 8, "Cultural Presentation," showed a variety of dance styles by a girls' performance group called Las Aquellas (roughly, "The Those").

The printed program also labored to specify the meaning of the gathering, instead of leaving it in the more hermeneutically open form of bodily action. It declared: "'Feast of the Ancestors' is a traditional and spiritual Celebration about the arrival of our ancestors. This special occasion takes place once a year around Mid-January. The Feast helps to reunite us [the Garifuna people] to sing, chant and dance with joyful hopes for prosperous year *[sic]* within our community and throughout the world."

In spite of these alterations from years past, the feast of the ancestors fulfilled the shamans' ritual obligations. Better put, it fulfilled both the traditional obligations of the ritual and its new obligations as a cultural performance. Many members of the theater company attended, along with a few dozen outsiders, and were duly impressed by the apparent authenticity of the traditions they witnessed. Still, the novel format was not without drawbacks. As one participant ruefully reported, "The Garifuna people aren't used to coming until nine at least, or to even needing to be on time at all, so lots of people were just coming when we had to leave." The need to purify the space for the ancestors with fumigation was partly solved by persuading the janitor to turn off the smoke alarms for a brief period at the outset. Thereafter, the use of tobacco was proscribed. The blowing of rum, likewise, was reduced to a few short blasts around the entrances at the beginning. Without the use of smoke or misted rum that usually helps to "heat" the heads of those who receive the ancestors in possession trance—or, in more analytical terms, without the material and sensory cues by which mediums learn to expect the visitation of the ancestors—the main event of spirit possession was briefer and much more controlled than usual. What is more, the presence of an audience dampened the desire of some to receive the ancestors in trance. One shaman explained, "Some people [in the audience] don't like that, they don't understand it, and they might feel uncomfortable." Thus many buyeis who usually receive the ancestors did not on this night.

Despite the complications, however, the buyei group viewed the event as a promising solution to the problem of a venue. They plan to continue with the same format, so that the return may become a more permanent form of semipublic cultural performance. And that shift in mode was central to this particular ritual. A set of practices was carefully marked and packaged as a performance of Garifuna culture and given the fixed form of a preannounced program so as to appeal to a diverse public and the demands of finding a public space for ritual performance.

Analysis

These three examples demonstrate three kinds of diasporic adaptations of Garifuna ritual to an urban context. In the first, city space was inscribed with an Africanized, Yoruba texture consisting of a deadly and "hot" perimeter and a contained, "cool" interior auspicious for ritual work. The second illustrated the problematizing of spirit possession, and indeed of the identities of the possessing spirits themselves, in a context of expanded religious pluralism. The third transformed the genre of ritual and the mode of representation into "cultural performance." Here I evaluate these three events in terms of a common sociology of ritual production. In the next chapter, I consider why the Africanizing of Garifuna ritual follows the Afro-Cuban and Yoruba channel and mostly resists other possible influences, like Haitian Vodou.

THE SOCIAL DYNAMICS OF DIASPORIC
RITUAL PRODUCTION

The diasporic rituals involved a division of space different from that of homeland ritual. Each person or family prepared their contribution at home. They dressed, cooked, and made purchases before arriving at the event. The labor required to prepare the ritual produced no fusion of otherwise disparate domains, as in the homeland dügü. Here the effort was atomized in individual apartments and combined in a rented hall just before the event. Attending the ritual became a set-apart act of going out on a weekend, similar to other kinds of urban entertainment. Moreover, attendance was not obligatory but rather an elective ethnic activity, a place in which to "feel Garifuna." Accordingly, intragroup tensions seemed to be replaced by the problem of defining and maintaining the ethnic and spatial boundaries of Garifuna-ness in the city.

The diasporic rituals rely on a more symbolic mode of representation in ritual than the homeland's more indexical style. The objects used in ritual are more detached from any practical or everyday use in the diaspora and therefore bear a heavier symbolic load. This added symbolic weight calls forth a more pronounced articulation and reification of "Garifuna religion" as a whole—with this title emerging as a contested symbol in its own right. In the homeland, the set of ideas and practices on which the ritual is based, because they are indexes of everyday life, are reified as "a religion" to a much lesser degree.

While the homeland ritual is restricted in its explicit semantics—in the cosmology or system of meanings advanced—it is creative in its social applications. Folded into its practice is a long indexical reach that reframes intragroup conflicts as continuities with ancestors. These continuities are both spatial and gestural, incorporating contemporary human practices that are consistent with those of the ancestors: fishing from canoes, sleeping in hammocks, and constructing a temple in the traditional style. In the diasporic venues, by contrast, the crisis of ritual focuses on the group's boundary in relation to other groups and external authorities of the city of New York. Ritual becomes a venue for defining the group in relation to others (Karpathakis 2001: 390), a voluntary act of identification, even a discursive intervention to define and affix the group's social boundary. And whereas memory is implicit in homeland religion, in diasporic ritual it is explicitly reflected on, defined, and given discursive form (Graf and Schachter 1985; Pyysiäinen 2001; Barrett 2004; Whitehouse 2000, 2004). Moreover, it is rearticulated in abstract, symbolic terms that allow analogical links with other religious groups: its dominant value is not density but rather extension. In the third ritual described, for example, the embodied presence of the ancestors was reduced in order to better translate the rite into a performance legible to the public. To the degree that such links are perceived, considered advantageous, and institutionalized, the religion has not only taken a Garifuna diasporic form; it has also joined the African Diaspora and begun to be rethought as an African diasporic religion.

AFRICANIZATION OF THE OUTER FRAME

In the first ritual I observed in the Bronx diaspora, the main crisis centered on the outer frame: the challenge of creating a ritual place in a plural, public space and the fear of and ritual response to police invasion. I expected these concerns to lead to a stultifying "freezing" of the semantics of ritual, as happened to some degree in the theater performance. Instead I found the "freezing" trends—the shift of focus away from internal social dynamics, and the rationalization of Garifuna religion as "cultural performance"—compensated by a fecund melt and irrigation, as diasporic Garifuna made themselves African through an elective syncretizing.

Most dramatic was the incorporation of the symbols and practices of different Caribbean religions: Santería, Santerismo, and also, at least in the assessments of gossip, Vodou.[9] Several dancers wore the beads of orisha affiliation. The dove tied over the door and the altars to Eleggua guarding the corners and doorways are not traditionally Garifuna but rather Santería rites and symbols. Indeed, all the protective work to safeguard La Peña was adapted from Cuban santeros' protective operations on Garifuna apartments. These operations, and the santero Puerto Ricans in attendance at the departure of the ancestors, suggest how such exchanges occur in everyday life, alongside more formal exchanges, such as lectures sponsored by the Garifuna community development center, Jamalali Uagucha, Inc., on Afro-Cuban religion, and reciprocal appearances by Garifuna buyeis at the Yoruba- and Santería-focused Caribbean Cultural Center.[10]

Both forms of diasporic exchange represent a new departure. In the Bronx, Garifuna ritual is institutionally and ideologically solidified in its external frame: it seeks to establish a deep, durable, and consistent identity claim in a plural context. But it is radically detached from homeland meanings, and geographies, of ancestors. Garifuna rituals now signify the reverence not only of family ancestors from Honduras and St. Vincent but also of Africa and African-ness. Of course, the capacity for assimilating and indigenizing "foreign" religious ideas has long been noted as a factor in the resilience of African diasporic religions in the Americas during centuries of threat (Bastide 1978a; Murphy 1988; Walker 1990; Mintz and Price 1992; Sweet 2003). But reasserting African diasporic religious receptivity does not advance our understanding. Certainly the Garifuna are not susceptible to contagion from any and every proximate religious influence, and to imply that they are conveys an image of a promiscuous and capricious superficiality. In this way, the alleged strength of African diasporic religions (resilience through syncretizing) is easily turned back against them. The caricature is as empirically vague as it is ethically dubious. The processes of diasporic syncretizing deserve to be more fully and carefully traced and specified.

Summary

Religious identity is not only accelerated in New York but also dramatically expanded, as an affiliation once seen as "Garifuna" is now reformed as an African Diaspora religion. This change happens through analogic extensions toward other social groups and their religious practices, especially toward the host groups in relation to which the Garifuna are located, namely other Afro-Latin groups like Puerto Ricans, Dominicans, and Cubans. It leads to creative adaptations of other religions' materials and gestures, selectively incorporated to their own practices.

So, for example, New York Garifuna religious leaders begin to describe the wanaragua mask dance that appeared in the dügü as "the same as" the Yoruba *egungun* mask dance. In this analogy, specific religious traditions like Cuban Santería and Garifuna ancestor religion are reframed in a more encompassing schema. Bradd Shore describes the process: "Through analogical schematizing, powerful equivalences (what we usually call 'meanings') can be constructed and reconstructed, formed and reformed" (1996: 364). This process entails abstraction, "the ability to abstract relations from one stimulus set and apply them to another" (352). The abstraction that allows the Garifuna to be read, and to read themselves into, the African Diaspora follows a pattern of "eliminative induction," which entails "deleting differences between analogs while preserving commonalities to make the abstract category that the individual analogs instantiate" (Gick and Holyoak in Shore 1996: 353).

I argue not that the possibility of joining the African Diaspora in New York City occurs *after* the abstraction, rationalization, and discursive articulation of Garifuna religion by a new kind of buyei, which then allows the analogical transfer to transpire, but rather the inverse. The comparisons and analogies between Garifuna religion and other religions arise from a perceptual primary-analogy formation (Shore 1996: 352), the familiarity with a shared set of objects and sources, like the statues of saints obtained in botánicas, and practices, like the visits of ancestors through spirit possession. The primary analogy that is perceived, however, must then be justified and discursively accounted for. It must be justified not to outside observers, but to one's own group—insofar as not all members will have perceived the same primary analogy—and to the practitioners of the other religion, insofar as making common cause or expanding the edges of the shared religion (the boundaries of which are in the process of shifting) is considered desirable.[11] The abstractions that are created as analogical bridges push Bronx Garifuna shamans toward a doctrinal mode, seeking to stabilize definitions of religious meaning and to sediment such meanings in public forums. This stabilization does not yield an expansive "mission religion," as a more completely doctrinal articulation might do, but it does open Garifuna religious practitioners to new religious alliances and generate a shared religious grammar.

To the degree that such primary analogies are selectively matched with those of other groups to become public—or, in Shore's term, "instituted"—cultural models, diasporas can be joined. But the range of analogical matches is constrained by the social context and by the reception by the other group. For example, while one New York Garifuna buyei told me that "Orientals are successful in the United States because of their reverence for their ancestors," drawing attention to the need for the Garifuna to pay more attention to their own ancestors, such analogical extensions are unlikely to take on social force because the Garifuna are not classed in this host society with "Orientals" but rather as black or Afro-Latin. That is, while individual Garifuna may find one or another Asian religion compelling by reason of primary analogy drawn from "reverence for ancestors," a Garifuna-Asian religious *movement* is unlikely because it will be perceived as dissonant, and hence is unlikely to provide the sociopolitical benefits hoped for and badly needed.

The changes in Garifuna ritual in the Bronx that I have described are not open or unconstrained. Certain Afro-Caribbean traditions are regarded as legitimate, even valorized, while others, like Haitian Vodou, are frowned on despite their accepted "Africanness." This distinction does not mean that Vodou influences will never enter the Garifuna repertoire, but it does mean that the New York Garifuna shamans hold marked analogical preferences for Yoruba and Cuban practices. The next chapter investigates the reasons for these preferences.

CHAPTER 7

Finding Africa in New York

> What right do you have to try to change our memory from
> Carib to African?
>
> > Garifuna villager in Honduras to international
> > Garifuna leader in New York

The Authentic Face of Africa:
The Yoruba-Santería Hegemony

When I have asked Garifuna leaders why Santería exerts influence over
other religious groups in the Bronx, I have received many conflicting
responses. One informant asserted simply that "Santería is more encompassing—it's the respect for nature." Others frequently responded that
they were impressed with the dramatic spectacle of oricha like Baba
Luaye (the "king of the earth" and ocha of smallpox, who, when manifested in trance, wears a full-body dress made of raffia grass) or Shango
(the royal oricha of the kingdom of Oyo and of fire, who sometimes carries fire on his head or in his hands). "That's strong stuff, when you see
how intense is their trance," one buyei observed. Moreover, the means
of inciting trance are familiar enough that Garifuna shamans visiting
Santería or Palo Monte ceremonies are susceptible to trance. As another
buyei observed, "I went to their *bembe* [Santería dance ritual] and 'got
hit' *[fue tocado],* and I really needed help. The padrino told me, 'You
landed in the right place.'" Yet another reason expressed was a pragmatic one: "Sometimes during fedu, when our spirits are gone [to Sairi],

you still need some help. Then it's good to have other ones to work with too."

The responses describe adopting the new repertoire to fulfill perceived needs. They do not go very far toward explaining the influence of Santería, however, as the needs are, like their resolutions, created out of the same complex I am seeking to explain. Engaging new religious networks generates new ritual obligations and needs, but it does not tell us why the Garifuna have become engaged that in that network in the first place, or why Santería religion should be seen as "more encompassing" than specifically Garifuna practices.

THE PUERTO RICAN CONNECTION

One obvious reason why the Garifuna are predisposed to engage the Afro-Cuban religious networks is that most of them, the Hondurans and Guatemalans, are Spanish speakers. If the Garifuna spoke French instead, they might gravitate toward Vodou networks. Another reason is that the Honduran Garifuna's main location in the Bronx places them in close contact with Afro-Cuban religious groups, less through direct contact with Cubans than through Puerto Rican communities in which Cuban Santería has been thoroughly digested and indigenized. While the 2000 U.S. Census reported just 8,233 Cubans in the Bronx (among 41,123 in New York City overall), there were 319,240 Puerto Ricans in the Bronx (and 789,172 in New York City overall), a population that is declining but still substantially larger than the next most-numerous groups, Dominicans (133,087 in the Bronx, 406,806 in New York City overall) and Mexicans (34,377 in the Bronx, 186,872 in New York City overall). Although Puerto Ricans were for a long time the dominant and indeed nearly the sole large group of Latinos in New York—in 1960 constituting fully 80 percent of the Latino population—the Cubans were next to arrive en masse, with the revolution of 1959. By now, after two generations of religious exchange, Puerto Ricans have become leaders and purveyors of Santería.

The first santeros on the island of Puerto Rico were initiated in 1954 by Pancho Mora, a Cuban living in New York (Brandon 1993: 106), though the babalawo (divinatory priest) Roberto Bolufer (Ogundé Leni) had already traveled between homes in Havana and Puerto Rico from 1946 to 1959 before settling permanently in Puerto Rico. He opened the first Yoruba temple in Puerto Rico, at least by his own report, and later traveled frequently to perform initiations in Miami as well (David Brown 2003: 93). It was a Puerto Rican priestess, Assunte Seranno, who initiated the first Anglo-American priestess, Judith Gleason, a scholar and practitioner who went on to publish some seven books in English on the Yoruba gods and tradition (Brandon 1993: 107). Others have combined the Cuban tradition with Espiritismo, or Spiritism, to create a new hybrid, Santerismo, especially popular in the Bronx (Brandon 1993: 108–13; Vega 2000; Olmos and Paravisini-Gebert 2003: 171–210).[1] One key figure who emerged from this fusion was Marta Moreno Vega, an Afro–Puerto Rican who, in 1976, founded the Caribbean Culture Center and African Diaspora Institute in Manhattan. The center has been a crucial platform for the Garifuna's entry into the African Diaspora. Arguably, the primacy of Cuban authority over African tradition in New York is maintained mostly through the much larger Puerto Rican networks. Even if, as Joseph Murphy noted, there are four ethnic sides to Santería in the United States—Cuban, Puerto Rican, African, and African American (1988: 53–54)—all act as proxies for the authority of Cuba, and for the Yoruba, through their initiatory genealogies and allegiances.

The Garifuna re-Africanizing process is brokered through the Afro-Cuban religions of Santería and Palo Monte. The dominant Cuban traditions are by now Puerto Rican as well. Hence Africa is reclaimed at least in part through the Puerto Rican Spiritist version of the Cuban version of a Yoruba-centric picture of Africanness. The material evidence for this influence is the appearance of icons like La Madama—a generic black, motherly curandera in Santerismo—and verbal references to the Seven African Powers—the Santerismo reduction of the pantheon of ochas and saints to a limited set with fixed domains of significance—in the material practice and discourse of Garifuna shamans.[2]

AFRICAN AMERICAN YORUBA REVIVALISM

A second stream of influence that constructed the Yoruba-Santería hegemony as the "face" of African diasporic religions in the United States came through the recuperation of Yoruba traditional religion by African American communities in New York. Religion was important in the Black Power Movement of New York, which was influenced by sources as diverse Marcus Garvey, Rastafarianism, Malcolm X, Black Muslims, Stokely Carmichael, and the Moorish Science Temple of the Noble Ali Drew (Curry 2001: 77). In all of these groups, as in black Christian churches, racial authenticity became the standard of liturgy and congregational life (Daniels 2000: 171). The specifically neotradi-tionalist arm of "black religion," however, emerged especially through Cubans and Santería, as the case of Walter Serge King reveals.

The late Walter Serge King (later Oba Ofuntola Oseigema Adelabu Adefumni I, d. February 10, 2005) was born in Detroit. By the age of twenty he was a dancer in the Harlem-based Katherine Dunham Dance Troupe. His voyage with the troupe to Egypt in 1952 awakened his interest in his African roots, a passion that was further quickened by travel to Haiti. An interest in Afro-Cuban dance styles like the rumba led him to a Santería bembe. By 1959, he was initiated alongside his Cuban American friend Chris Oliana in Matanzas, Cuba (Brandon 1993: 114–20; David Brown 2003: 276–78; Clarke 2004: 71–77). On their return, King and Oliana founded Shango Temple (later called Yoruba Temple) on 125th Street in Harlem. They parted ways, however, and their split was metonymic of a larger split between Adefunmi's increas-ingly antisyncretic, proactively black vision of the temple's future and Oliana's Cuban version, in which racial authenticity was downplayed in favor of African cultural forms. For example, King began to refuse to use Catholic saints or Cuban attire for those incarnating the spirits during possession rituals, and he renamed Santería as Orisha-Voodoo—the name showing the influence of his Haitian tours with the Dunham troupe. As King himself recollected, "We had introduced a racism into the religion that didn't exist among the Cubans . . . and . . . they couldn't understand my extremely severe racial attitudes at that time. So that naturally alienated a lot of them" (Palmié in David Brown 2003: 277). Put differently, they had made an explicit ideological cause out of what had previously been unspoken, namely a perceived "whitening" of the Afro-Cuban religion. As Kamari Maxine Clarke has carefully shown, by working out new "narratives of the customary past," they bypassed the Cuban and Cuban-American neo-Yoruba hierarchies through a claim to more direct African and, in part, racially grounded claim of access to protected knowledge (2004: 22, 66).

The new narratives of the customary past led to the attempted pro-duction of "Yoruba space" in the United States. In 1972, King's vision expanded to include the founding of a semiautonomous African state within U.S. territory, the Kingdom of Oyotunji African Village in Sheldon, South Carolina. *Oyotunji* roughly means "Oyo rises again" (Curry in David Brown 2003: 278). The name expresses a return to African roots by allusion to the most powerful historical Yoruba king-dom, whose fall fed the trade in Yoruba slaves in the late eighteenth and early nineteenth centuries. In designing the community, information about reconstructing a traditional Yoruba village was harvested from extent academic literature, including works by Melville Herskovits, William Bascom, N. A. Fadipe, Samuel Johnson, and E. Bolaji Idowu (Hunt 1979). This research provided a territorial locus and, especially after Adefunmi's crowning as *oba*, king, in the ancient capital of Ile-Ife, Nigeria, a material authenticity that attracted African American pilgrims and other tourists to attend ceremonies and admire the "traditional" African society.

What is more, through Oyotunji's institutional and theological wing, the Yoruba Theological Archministry (formerly the African Theological Archministry), its leading intellectuals, like John Mason, added to the circulation of Yoruba studies in the United States. Although academic studies, including many by non-Africans, informed Oyotunji's construction, its own publications, disseminated through the Yoruba Theological Archministry, are those that now reach to the community of Garifuna shamans, especially through venues like the Caribbean Culture Center. But at least one very influential Garifuna leader studied and underwent an orisha initiation at Oyotunji before beginning work as a Garifuna shaman. Moreover, the exodus of Oyotunji residents, from a high of about two hundred in the 1970s to around seventy by the mid-eighties, spread the Yoruba revival movement to urban centers around the country, including New York, as did electronic means of dissemination like the Internet (Clarke 2004: 57–58). While the African American Yoruba movement and the Cuban–Puerto Rican Santería movement in which the Garifuna have become embedded work separately for the most part, Adefunmi and Oyotunji add to the Yoruba's luster as the carriers of authentic Africanness and traditional African diasporic religious orthodoxy.

The Yoruba have become the religious face of Africa in the United States in part as a result of the convergence of Latino and African American identifications worked out in very different ways but in relation to the shared symbol set of the Yoruba gods, the orishas. The religion and its competing authenticities—the Cuban one based on initiatory lineage versus the African American one based on combined African territorial and black racial authenticity—became an arena for the negotiation of race, religious ownership, and membership in the diaspora. In the Yoruba orisha, arrived in the United States especially through Cubans but now circulated far beyond their sphere of influence, multiple layers of race, ethnicity, language and religion converge, allowing for a shared African-American-Caribbean-Latino-Afro-Latino ritual repertoire to take form.

STILL . . . WHY NOT A DIFFERENT AFRICAN ETHNIC GROUP?

The primacy of Yoruba and Afro-Cuban religion was not inevitable. For example, Kongo-based religion could have provided the overarching framework and public face of African Diaspora religions in the United States As a former slave in Cuba, Esteban Montejo, observed in the nineteenth century, slaves' religious lives revolved around "two African religions . . . , the Lucumí [Yoruba] and the Conga. The Conga was the more important . . . because the witches put spells on people. . . . The difference between the Conga and the Lucumí is that the Conga does things, and the Lucumí tells the future" (Barnet 1994 33–35).

As George Reid Andrews puts it:

The Yoruba concurred with the Congo in believing that these spiritual forces exerted direct control over human destiny. But while the Congo located those forces in natural objects, the Yoruba anthropomorphized them into a pantheon of deities, the orishas. The Congo priests worked with their minkisi and prendas (ritual objects) but "the old Lucumís liked to have their figurines, their gods, made of wood," recalled Montejo. "Witchcraft is more common with the Congos than with the Lucumís. The Lucumís are more allied to the Saints and to God." (Andrews 2004: 70–71)

Montejo alludes in his own terms to the ease with which the Yoruba system of anthropomorphic representations was conducive to analogical extensions, or what is often called syncretizing, toward other religions. He offers an implicit argument about religious memory and transmission: it is possible that the Yoruba pantheon was not only transported in the slave trade more recently, and in greater force than religions of other ethnic groups from Africa, but that it was also more easily remembered and attached in the new material and social niches of the New World. This theory seems plausible until we note that the Kongo lineage of Cuban religion is still very much apparent in practice, as Palo Monte, and is also in use among the Garifuna shamans of New York. For the Garifuna as for other users, the Kongo and the Yoruba traditions are distinguished but often woven together in practice. Although Yoruba is the African religious system most widely publicized and spoken about, it is not the only one remembered and transmitted.

Why should Yoruba religion represent the public face of Africa? As Stephen Palmié (2002: 159–201) has eloquently argued, the use of Yoruba-Santería as the "value-space" in relation to which other traditions like Kongo are classified as fast, effective, and dangerous, but not as "pure" or authentic, has layers of history embedded within it. The Kongo tradition, that of the earlier-arriving slave groups to Cuba and Brazil, was sufficiently acculturated to the plantation to come to signify, at least in memory, a kind of slave labor based in relations of coercion. The Yoruba tradition, by contrast, came to represent the stateliness of an advanced, purely African courtly society and civilization. This opposition of brute force and sophistication—such that the ciphers of the Yoruba were made the public articulation of Africanness, black pride, and even Cuban nationalist discourses—was milled by a century-long anthropological grind.

This topic would in itself merit extended study, and indeed that work is now in progress (see, for example, Clarke 2004; Falola and Childs 2004; Matory 2005). Here I simply note that the opposition was forged in part by the efforts of the Yoruba themselves in creating a special status and in exporting their goods, and gods, widely—especially with the rise of the city-state of Ibadan in the nineteenth century (Apter 1992: 36; Matory 1999: 82). Also instrumental in the process were unique figures like Samuel Crowther, who was born in Oyo but ended up becoming an Anglican bishop in England before returning to Africa; he published Yoruba grammar and vocabulary books, thereby establishing Yoruba as an African ethnic entity with a defined culture (Apter 1992: 193–204; Verger 1981: 15; Matory 1999: 15).

The special status of the Yoruba was given the anthropologists' imprimatur when the German art historian Leo Frobenius visited the old capital Ile-Ife in 1910 and photographed brass heads and terra-cotta sculptures that he described as "eloquent of a symmetry, a vitality, a delicacy of form, and practically a reminiscence of the ancient Greeks" (Frobenius in Du Bois 1915: 80). What he saw led Frobenius to the notorious proposal of having discovered the lost Atlantis, nominating the Yoruba deity of the sea, Olokun, as "Atlantic Africa's Poseidon."[3] Frobenius's soaring prose was recapitulated by W. E. B. Du Bois in *The Negro* (1915). Du Bois wrote, "In place of the Yoruban culture, with its city democracy, its elevated religious ideas, its finely organized industry, and its noble art, came Ashanti and Dahomey. What was it that changed the character of the west from this to the orgies of war and blood sacrifice which we read of later in these lands?" (39). His answer, of course, is the slave trade. By his account, the Sudanese cities, and even the famed "high civilizations" of Egypt and Ethiopia, have a mixed character that includes Semitic and Mediterranean elements, even as "the Yoruba cities . . . remained comparatively autonomous organizations down to modern times" (38). Frobenius's descriptions of the pristine purity of Yoruban culture passed into the African American canon through Du Bois, among others.

The Yoruba provided the perfect blend of "high culture" and "pure culture": they had magnificent art and complex religion but little apparent contact with Mediterranean societies that could undermine their position through accusations of borrowing or other influence. By contrast, Kongo religion, at least the official court religion, was already Catholic by the end of the fifteenth century. Similar comparisons between Yoruba purity and West Central African religious mélange were drawn and frequently repeated, not least by Roger Bastide in his monumental *African Religions of Brazil* (1978a: 280–81). Such scholarly accounts fed back into local practice, further exaggerating the initial distinctions and speculations of slaves like Montejo.

THE YORUBA IN GARIFUNA-PRODUCED LITERATURE

The idea of the Yoruba religious tradition as the defining authentic framework for African Diaspora religion in the United States is reproduced in Garifuna literary representations, produced in substantial volume beginning in the 1990s.

The work of Armando Crisanto Meléndez is central, as he has for a generation been the main spokesman for Honduran Garifuna culture in pan-African venues and is regarded as something of a patron saint in both the homeland and diasporic communities. Against the standard interpretation of *Garinagu* as derived from Carib indigenous nomenclature, *Kalinago,* Meléndez (1997) derives *Garinagu* from *Gainagu,* comprising Yoruba roots, *gai* (foods) and *nagu* (prayer or words). This etymology is then reproduced in other Garifuna texts (for example, García 1993: 24). Meléndez reads his own indigenous name, Auyuru Savaranga, as derived from "reyes y deidades africanos" (kings and African deities), especially Shango. If Meléndez locates select Garifuna words in relation to Bantu—*muntu* (Garifuna "person") from Bantu *mutu,* and the dance style *punta* as derived from the Bantu word *bunda* (2002: 83, 91)—he stresses to a much greater degree the Yoruba genealogy of Garifuna religion. Yoruba are the "main origin" of Garifuna culture (2002: 68), including the dügü (55). The main Garifuna ritual, dügü, is not only like Candomblé, Vudu *[sic]*, and Santería (87), it is an integral part *of* Santería (68).

Centeno García, although less Afrocentric in his genealogy, introduces the Garifuna shaman's tutelary spirits as the entities better known as orichas (1996: 99). E. S. Suazo likewise introduces Garifuna traditional religion with references to better-known religions with clear West African origins: "Just as Candomble, Macumba and Vodou are taken by some as 'religion,' and by others as rituals working with sorcery and magic, Garifuna esoteric doctrine also contains unexplored phenomena and secret ceremonies" (2000: 4, 30, 35). Indeed, García (1993) declares that the Garifuna rituals *are* Candomblé, Macumba, and Santería (72), and that all the "strongest" elements come from the Yoruba of Nigeria.

Taken together, the texts—intended for a general Garifuna readership, not for academic audiences—offer no coherent religious conceptions of a specific African provenance, though Yoruba ancestry is strongly privileged. The text by García, *Lamumehan Garífuna: Clamor Garífuna,* offers a plausible reason. He argues that the "Bantus" of the African interior are not "real Negroes"—their skin is too light—while "los negros sudaneses" represent the real *hombre negro,* "without any mixing of blood whatever" (7). Prominent among these pure-blooded Africans are the Yoruba of southern Nigeria. In Meléndez's text, this force and purity are transferred from the body to religion: in Yoruba religion, "the rituals follow fixed patterns *(moldes fijos),* invariable and traditional" (2002: 56). The Yoruba are ciphers of African depth and purity; and since Garifuna religion is Yoruba-descended, it too is authentically *negro* and pure.

This view reproduces a European colonial discourse that has become widespread in the Americas, wherein the "Bantus" or "Kongos" of central Africa stand for mixture, while the coastal Yoruba and Dahomeans (often referred to as Guinea or Nago) stand for purity and authentic Africanness (Dantas 1988; Mintz and Price 1992: 16; Palmié 2002: 159–200; Sansone 2003: 65).

These distinctions are magnified in Garifuna indigenous literature, in the face of the obscurity of the specific ethnic origins of the Garifuna people. "Africa" is an idea and an ideal mediated only through international media, conferences, and institutions within which the Yoruba influence—including the Santería, Santerismo, and Candomblé redactions through which Yoruba religious authenticity is magnified and mediated—predominates. The Garifuna are late-arriving migrants.

When they did begin to arrive en masse, with the precipitous decline of Honduran fruit cartels in the late twentieth century, they sought to establish themselves as cultural players in New York by exploiting the niches that already existed but were saturated by a Dominican, Cuban, and Puerto Rican religious marketplace: botánicas, established benefactors, padrinos de santo, museum displays, bookstores, and so forth. The version of Garifuna religious origins generated in the diaspora has followed that model. Garifuna activists and writers, whose main audience is the Honduran Garifuna community, have also adopted this view and become its purveyors to homeland readers. The market for these accounts of indigenous Garifuna history is skewed toward community leaders and activists, including many shamans. As we have seen, these figures are important because they become local keepers of authentic Garifuna collective memory.

This incipient literature, along with New York shamans' periodic returns to the homeland, is a second means of remittance of the newly minted African diaspora religious identity for the Garifuna. The two channels together form what I earlier called the drive to discourse, the concern to establish firm meanings and origins of ritual events that previously were multivocal and opaque.

All of the relatively immediate causes of the re-Africanization of Garifuna religion unfold against the backdrop of macrohistorical reasons, including the fact that the Yoruba were among the last and largest groups enslaved and brought to the Americas, especially to Cuba and Brazil. Moreover, it is possible that, as Montejo suggested, the specific form of Yoruba religion, the anthropomorphism that rendered it particularly accessible for matching with the Catholic saints, provided propitious niches for attachment and the maintenance of collective memory.

African Diasporic Religions and Racial Shift?

Although the Garifuna were once known to Europeans as the Black Caribs, they have only recently taken up the identity of "black" for their own purposes. Does the reinterpretation of the Garifuna diasporic horizon as African lead to new views on racial identity? What is the relation between the Garifuna adaptation to the neotraditionalist African diaspora religious network and racial identifications? To answer these questions, at least provisionally, I first consider how race and religion

influence one another; I then unhinge "African" from "black" identifications by pointing out the ways they are in tension with each other.
Finally, I consider the ways in which the Garifuna's becoming black
through that partial fusion is different from the typical model of acculturation of Caribbean immigrants in the United States, and how neotraditional African religious practice facilitates that shift.

RELIGION AND RACE

The idea of "binding" is common to both religions and racialism.[4] The
earliest etymology of religion is probably from the Latin *religare*, "to
bind back," as used by Lactantius and Servius. Racialism, similarly,
binds appearance or "blood" to moral and intellectual capacity.
Religion and racialism have additional overlapping domains, like the
interest in affixing ideas of ultimate origins, purity in the realm of transmission—whether of "blood" or of sacred knowledge—and the resulting questions of authenticity and legitimacy. Both religion and racialism
are, in a sense, oracular genres, attempts to read secrets hidden below
the surface, through muffled and muddled understandings of what can
be heard or seen.

Religious and racial beliefs, moreover, are closely linked historically.
The Christian doctrine of universal grace preceded and undergirded
later notions of racial equality, just as the curse of Ham in the book of
Genesis preceded and influenced more ideologically developed forms of
racism (Fredrickson 2002: 11, 44–47). Étienne Balibar (in Balibar and
Wallerstein 1991: 24) writes of race as a type of bodily stigma that is misrecognized as signifying a deep spiritual inheritance. The "danger" of
the invisible Jew, who seems like a Gentile but is in fact intrinsically different, is matched by the danger of "invisible blacks" seeking to "pass"
(Korgen 1998: 40). Here racialism is bound with the idea of a spiritual
inheritance at risk. Thus for example, when the white Virginian Hugh
Davis was whipped in 1630 for having sex with an African woman, the
act was called "a dishonor of God and shame of Christians" (Williamson
in Korgen 1998: 9).

This example shows how the two forms of binding together generate a fearsome kind of rhetorical doubling, what Fredrickson calls
"supernaturalist racism" (2002: 46). The human notion that a certain
physical feature reveals a specific character defect is authorized by the
notion that God (or the gods) made it so. Or, as Frederick Douglass
put it in more pragmatic terms, "Religious slaveholders are the worst"

(in Gilroy 1993: 59). They were "the worst," presumably, insofar as they held views about race that were hypostatized as transcendent truth, just as for Friedrich Nietzsche the "really great haters" were always priests (2003: 16). The dangers that accrue from combining the two kinds of binding is emerging as an important area of study (Prentiss 2003; Goldschmidt and McAlister 2004).

Yet the bundling of religion with racialism has also been also invoked in defense of African Americans. Martin Delany's 1854 essay, "The Political Destiny of the Colored Race on the American Continent," described Africans' inherent religiosity (in Shelby 2005: 39), refuting the colonial accusations of Africans' and Amerindians' utter lack of religion (or memory). And Du Bois wrote that, between races, "the deeper differences are spiritual, psychical differences—undoubtedly based on the physical, but infinitely transcending them" (in Baker 1998: 113). Still, the invocation of an innate African religiosity as a rhetoric of cultural defense leads to unwarranted stereotypes. Variations on the theme of a "natural" African spirituality, borne unconsciously by persons of color, continue in force in the present (Burdick 1998: 105), and continue to burnish the old image of Africans as emotive and creative but irrational—in short, as "primitive." Religion is merely expressive of racial determinations in this view, as in Euclides da Cunha's classic observation in his description of the Brazilian "backlands" at the close of the nineteenth century: "His religion is, like himself, mestizo in character" (1944: 110).

But religion and race can also interact in ways that unbundle earlier fusions. Consider an example of religious "Yorubization" in the United States in a different context. Kamari Maxine Clarke (2004: 231–56) documents how the conversion of black Americans to Yoruba traditional religion does not diminish the meaning of race as a trope so much as shift its position. Divinatory "roots readings" conducted at Oyotunji Village in South Carolina are an important step in an individual's conversion to "authentic" African religion. As the reading discloses the African roots that bestow the prospective convert with an ancient, noble heritage, ideas of race as biological difference are shifted to individual narratives about roots and original territory (256). Divination even reveals the ontological causes of the displacement from that original homeland and the marginality experienced in the United States: inevitably it was caused by the transgressions of an ancestor (nearly always female) that led to enslavement. In these roots readings, the contemporary experience of blackness as marginality itself becomes

contingent and transient. Conversion to neotraditional Yoruba religious practice redeems the ancestral past, even as that recovered, "use-
able past" (235) redeems and redirects the present. In these converts'
narratives, Yoruba culture dethrones race. These shifts happen in and
through religious practice. It is not clear, however, that religious conversion *causes* a shift in racial identification, as some converts report the
opposite, that the experience of racism catalyzed their desire to convert:
"I couldn't live like a good Christian in racist America" (231).[5]

In the Oyotunji example, religious practice is not only affected by
but also has effects on racial subjectivity. How is religious re-
Africanization tied to changes in racial subjectivity for the Garifuna?
Does adopting African diasporic consciousness lead to the diminution
of a racialized identity, or does it lead to "becoming black" (M. Wright
2004)? To answer these questions, I must first uncouple two concepts
typically but mistakenly conflated.

AFRICANNESS AND BLACKNESS

That Africanness and blackness aren't the same seems too obvious to
bear mentioning, yet the two—the first an ethnicity, or cultural marker,
the second a color—are often simply fused, not only in popular vernacular and political exhortation, as critiqued by Shelby (2004: 10), but
also in academic literature, where "the African Diaspora" and "the
Black Atlantic" are liberally substituted for each other. Of course, in
practice, the phrases overlap. Yet race and ethnicity are distinct and vary
independently (Boas 1986 [1928]: 60; cf. Gilroy 1993: 52–53; Rumbaut
and Portes 2001: 4–6; Telles 2004: 106; M. Wright 2004: 2). African
religions, for example, can spread to and take root among whites, as
indeed they have done in Cuba and Brazil. White converts may become
initiated members of the African Diaspora, insofar as diaspora is viewed
as a cultural dispersion (see chapter 1). Ethnic codes and color codes are
not only analytically distinct; they are also distinct in the history of their
deployment. Ethnicity in the United States has often been in tension
with race, marking minority status for immigrant Europeans but at the
same time distinguishing them from blacks after the Great Migration
from the South to northern cities (Winant 1998: 205; Jacobson 2001:
88–90). What is more, ethnicity and race are even often emically distinct identifications. For example, Edmund T. Gordon and Mark
Anderson observed that among Creoles in Bluefields, Nigeria, some
express a black identity closely tied to the cultural styles of Jamaica or the

United States, while some proclaim their African origins, and still others present themselves as thoroughly assimilated into Anglo culture and self-understanding (1999: 283).

To be as precise as possible, I define *Africanness* as referring to identifications with cultures exported from the continent of Africa, including religious cultures. These are sometimes practiced by persons who are not black either by self-identification or by attribution. Cubans or Brazilians of all skin tones take part in African religions—Santería, Palo Monte, Candomblé, Umbanda, and others—and to varying degrees consider themselves, and are viewed by others, as religiously African, though not as black (Pierucci and Prandi 2000; Sansone 2003). *Blackness* refers to social identifications based on color, which may not have any active ethnic reference to African cultures whatsoever and may only partly correspond with actual skin tone (because someone who is black in the United States may be white in Brazil [Telles 2004: 79] or in Central America). This distinction does not mean that there is no black culture in which color and culture are fused. It does mean, however, that black culture is often quite different from overtly Africanist cultural articulations. Black culture is utopian, spread out in space; it tends toward the global, the modern, the hybrid, the routes of transit rather than the roots of territory and tradition (Gilroy 1993; Clifford 1994; Gordon and Anderson 1999; Sansone 2003; M. Wright 2004). Indeed, as Cornel West argues, the distinguishing characteristic of "black religion" is its cultural hybridity (2001: 144–45). It is a form of religiosity whose home cannot be precisely mapped. This imprecision renders it the very opposite of neotraditionalist African religion, whose authenticity is derived from precise ancestral coordinates and exact genealogies of transmission. In the roots readings I discuss above, for example, specific locales in what is now southwest Nigeria are named to authentically plot a person's spiritual inheritance. As a highly schematic gloss of the foregoing discussion, one might say that black culture's dominant spatial mode is utopian, whereas Africanist culture's dominant mode is locative (J. Z. Smith 1978).

Blackness is based on color and on an event-driven temporality and set of narratives about events caused by color-based racism, from the Middle Passage to abolition, citizenship, suffrage, and civil rights (Gilroy 1993: 197), emphasizing the globalization of the U.S. story of race—rather the appeal to places of authentic origins or special ancestral power. Of course, black culture—its music and style—strongly appeals to youths all over the globe. Thus, somewhat paradoxically, black culture is modern, diffused, and global, yet relatively indelible; African culture, by contrast, connotes tradition and locatedness, yet it is far less color-coded, especially the African religious traditions of the Caribbean.

BECOMING BLACK IN THE UNITED STATES

When traditionalist Afro-Caribbean religions are carried to the United States, the lines between African and black articulations of solidarity and continuity become intertwined. The two gears' cogs lock together. Questions of territory, transmission, and authenticity—ethnic questions of Africanness—are now bound to racial questions of biology and blackness, all under systems of religious authority. This is not the place for a history of United States race theory, though, broadly speaking, its idiosyncratic character is based on four factors: the breadth of the category of blackness, which includes a range of people who in Brazil or the Caribbean may or may not view themselves as black; a monopolistic closure on the basis of skin color, to take Max Weber's phrase, whereas in Brazil or the Caribbean blackness is gauged not only by color but also by class, family history, hair texture, facial features, education, status, and so forth; the social stigma and limited socioeconomic mobility strongly associated with blackness in the United States;[6] and the presence of not merely structural racism, which is also built into the colonial legacies and contemporary patterns of Caribbean societies, but also what Mary Waters called "interpersonal racism," the sense that "many whites simply do not see a black person as a human being" (1999: 171). Taken together, these features constitute a "metalanguage of race" (Higginbotham 1992: 255) in the United States that subsumes other sets of social relations into its referential domain of analogic relationships. My particular interest is how the Garifuna, along with other Caribbean groups, react when they migrate into a place where a florid nomenclature of color is reduced to this heavily loaded binary opposition of black and white. When they are painted into a "chiaroscuro of whiteness and darkness" (Orsi 1999: 38), they may undergo nothing less than a conversion of consciousness.

Consider for a moment the example of Piri Thomas's classic autobiography, *Down These Mean Streets* (1997 [1967]). Piri, the child of Puerto Rican immigrants, recalls defining moments of his becoming black after growing up viewing himself as thoroughly Puerto Rican. The transformation occurs through dislocation from his home turf in Spanish Harlem, first in a high-school hallway in Long Island, where he is abruptly and for the first time viewed as Other, then in a tour of the U.S. South, and finally in prison, as the result of a passing Black Muslim affiliation. Piri becomes black, consciously internalizing an imposed monopolistic closure based on what had previously been merely a set of idiosyncratic personal physical features, now made into a "race."[7]

Like Piri, most Caribbean groups of color resist becoming black simply through migration. Haitian immigrants in New York, for example, reinforce their ethnic distinctiveness—most notably as Francophones—in order to resist being simply folded into the category of black American, a category they view as a social liability (Fouron and Schiller 1997; McAlister 1998; Waters 1999; Stepick et al. 2001). Yet despite this "reactive ethnicity," in practice Haitian youths tend toward African American style (Stepick, et al. 2001: 260–61). A similar reactive ethnicity among anglophone West Indian migrants to both New York and London is well documented (Foner 1985; Portes and Stepick 1993; Kurien 1998: 62; McAlister 1998: 119; Waters 1999: 103, 151, 193, 324; Crowder and Tedrow 2001: 112). Resisting racialization into black and white categories is most difficult during adolescence (Korgen 1998; Kasinitz, Battle, and Miyares 2001), with only middle- and upper-class teens successfully maintaining their ethnic difference (Waters 1999: 287). Dominican immigrants arriving in the United States attempt to identify themselves as much as possible with Latino rather than black affiliations, though often without success in the view of white Americans (Levitt 2001: 109). One Dominican who had lived in the United States told Peggy Levitt: "You know, for white people in the U.S., we are just the same as black people. It doesn't matter where you are from. Dark skin is dark skin for the *gringos*" (2001: 111–12). Barnor Hesse described an analogous process of becoming black in Great Britain: "During the twentieth century . . . 'race' occurs three times. The first time as 'coloured colonials'; the second as 'coloured immigrants'; and the third as Black (and Asian) citizens, each dimension marked by descendants who elided, reversed and lateralized this sequence" (1993: 171).

There is, by now, a relatively clear scholarly consensus about the ways Caribbean immigrants of color are "read into" U.S. society in terms of their proximal hosts, often as black or Latino. And strong ethnocultural resistance to this racial reduction is equally well documented.[8] In the typical pattern, immigrants counter inclusion in the category of black with reactive ethnic assertions. Do the Garifuna practitioners of traditional ancestral religion in New York follow this pattern?

Race and the Garifuna in New York

To the Garifuna themselves, they are simply Garifuna or, sometimes, Caribs; no broader classification is required. When color is invoked by Garifuna in Honduras, it is usually in terms of "morenos" (browns), and the village network is referred to as the *morenal* (the area of the browns). While some activists proudly use the term *negro,* in general this term is pejorative and applied by mestizos. Garifuna in Honduras are often subjected to the term *negritos* (the little Negroes) by cab drivers or others they engage in the wider public sphere, often conveying patronizing affection, as in "I love visiting the negrito villages." Nevertheless, homeland Garifuna do not have a rigid racialist view of themselves or other groups, but rather see race as malleable and shifting. This view may be in part due to their history of at least some miscegenation both on St. Vincent and in Honduras. Thomas Young, in 1842, described the St. Vincent islanders as "some being coal black, others again nearly as yellow as saffron" (in Gonzalez 1969: 25). Nancie Gonzalez's fieldwork from the 1950s recorded Garifuna oral traditions of having become darker in color through intermarriage with other Caribbean blacks, especially those from Santo Domingo, since arriving on the Central American coast in 1797 (1969: 26).

Still, Honduran Garifuna were and are aware of being darker than Honduran mestizos. In ritual performance this awareness is apparent in the special attention devoted to, for example, Saint Esquipula, also known as Cristo Negro. Moreover, some have cast their institutional lot with the category of *negro* by founding organizations like La Organización Fraternal Negro Hondureño (OFRANEH) in the 1970s. But, as Sarah England (1999; 2006) incisively shows, black identity in the homeland is balanced against other identifications, depending on the political context. An indigenous Amerindian identification was used, for example, in the 1992 protests against the quincentenary celebrations of Columbus's arrival in the Americas and the attempts thereafter to pressure the Honduran state into signing the International Labor Organization Convention concerning Indigenous and Tribal Peoples in Independent Countries (England 1999: 18–20). That identification has become even more important in the battle over the proposed reform of Article 107 of the Honduran constitution, which would open Honduran beaches to foreign developers and potentially displace Garifuna communities, some of which have been on those sites for more than two hundred years (see note 3 of the introduction).

In the move to the United States, this pattern of generally fluid race identifications punctuated by specific definitions for particular occasions or political situations is both constrained and magnified. It is constrained as the Garifuna are read into categories already bounded by their proximal hosts: they are perceived as blacks (a racial attribution), Hispanics (a linguistic or ethnic attribution), or Afro-Hispanics (a hybrid attribution). And it is magnified through the process of "definitional duress" (Tweed 1997: 95). For example, Maria Elena, a middle-aged Garifuna woman in New York, told me about first learning about the inflexibility of U.S. race categories when she was twelve: "You know how I learned about race in this country? I used to sit in the cafeteria with other foreigners who spoke Spanish or Portuguese. One day, all of a sudden, our table started getting hit with milk cartons! The American black kids were throwing food at us, thinking we weren't speaking English just to distance ourselves from being black. The school had to have an intervention to talk about it." Her story recapitulates a common Caribbean narrative of the shock at "becoming black" on entrance to the United States (cf. Foner 2001: 13; Waters 1999: 53–63).

Privately, New York Garifuna universally acknowledge tensions in their dealings with black Americans. The cofounder of Jamalali Uagucha commented: "They want to run the whole show! They want to pull our census numbers into their category, to get their stuff! But we're not just black, we're Garifuna." Yet in public speeches, the same group proudly proclaims their three thousand years of history stemming from their Yoruba and Ashanti ancestry and emphasizes the "negro fact" of Garifuna ethnicity. In the U.S. context, the claim to authentic roots is staked not via the group's indigenous identification, or through Hispanic or Latino connections, but rather with a strong discourse of African origins. This is also the affinity most often expressed by New York buyeis, both in practice and in their autobiographies.

The American metalanguage of race refracts Garifuna identity in a new way. When Sarah England asked Garifuna immigrants how they identified themselves on official census forms, 41 percent reported that they chose "Afro-American/Black," 38 percent chose "Hispanic," 16 percent chose "Other" and wrote in "Garifuna," and 5 percent chose "Other: Afro-Hispanic" (England 1999: 26). The three most numerous of these identifications present a racial mapping of the three diasporic horizons: Africa, St. Vincent, and Honduras.

Although constrained by U.S. racial codes, for Garifuna in the United States, multiple affiliations are still possible. These are selected depending on context and indicate a process of code switching. Just as Garifuna use religious code switching, from Catholic to traditionalist (and Catholic) to cristiano (evangelical Protestant) (McAlister 1998: 138; Johnson 2002a: 72), they choose among different ethnic identifications. For certain issues, like land claims in Honduras brought to venues like the United Nations or the attempt to claim reparations from Great Britain for the 1797 forced removal from St. Vincent, indigenous identity is the expeditious choice. During the New York mayoral elections of 2001 and 2005, the Garifuna mobilized on behalf of the Bronx borough president, Fernando Ferrer, and here their Hispanic and Afro-Hispanic identifications came to the fore. In the quest for venues, alliances, and support for religious and other cultural events in the city, African diasporic identity is placed front and center.

What is unique in the Garifuna case is that the ethnic reaction to being classified as "black," at least in terms of religion, asserts the distinctively Garifuna tradition through analogues with Afro-Cuban and Puerto Rican Santería, Palo Monte, Santerismo, and the Yoruba pantheon. In other words, the religious reaction to the racial reduction invokes the African Diaspora as much as specifically Garifuna history and practices. This strategy leads to a partial fusion between black and African diasporic identifications. While Sarah England's survey revealed a split in Garifuna census identifications, all the buyeis I interviewed strongly identified as black and Garifuna, rather than, say, Hispanic Garifuna or Honduran Garifuna. This tendency suggests that, rather than resisting racialization in the United States by emphasizing cultural and ethnic affiliations, Garifuna religious culture now leads to stronger racial identifications. Africanness and blackness are fused in religious performances that link Garifuna tradition to the prestige and power of West African origins, and participating in activities perceived as African in the racialist chiaroscuro of U.S. color codes reinforces "black" self-classifications (cf. Telles 2004). Thus I return to the same essentialist fusion between Africanness and blackness that I tried to dismantle earlier in this section. I return to it, however, by showing the processes of its making, and its relation as a particular kind of religious renaissance.

Many Garifuna leaders see this renaissance as a recovery, one that needs to be transmitted to and solidified in homeland villages, and they approach conversion to Africanness with missionary zeal. In October 2004, for example, an important Garifuna leader was returning from an international conference in Senegal to his home in Belize, and he stopped to meet with several New York–based shamans for a strategy session, at which I was present. The expressed objectives of the meeting were to initiate and coordinate a program of black studies in Central America, led by the Garifuna. But in order for the Garifuna to serve as a conduit for this broad regionalist program, it was argued, they themselves would have to be enlightened. Under discussion was how to best re-Africanize the Central American Garifuna communities by constructing new symbols that would draw homeland Garifuna into the pan-African network. The international leader described progress on his plans for the construction of a "Garifuna culture park" in his home country of Belize that would include not only a museum, a study center, and offices but also a series of monuments—beginning with a forty-foot-tall statue of the African continent, engraved with the caption "We are African"—to help implement the new pedagogy. Schoolchildren from Garifuna territory throughout Central America would be bused in to tour the monuments with trained guides and to learn an entirely new history. The purposes of the new African-centered teaching were described as "the analysis of blackness and what it is" and the effort to implement a black curriculum in Garifuna education. But, as one leader reported, there is substantial resistance from the homeland villages. In one example he cited, a villager asked straight out, "What right do you have to try to change our memory from Carib to African?"

Despite such resistance, the group agreed that reeducation is crucial—much as the buyeis' organization faces, and seeks to overcome, homeland resistance to the repositioning of their traditional religion within the African Diaspora. The appeal to territorial Africanness through its monumental force as a statue towering over the Central American landscape here appears as an entryway to the discussion of the condition of blackness. This approach offers a counterpoint to a mestizo version of Central America, in which blackness disappears, along with the Garifuna. Such a discussion is long overdue.

Whether one views this project as an important recovery of origins or a pernicious globalization of U.S. racial definitions (e.g., Bourdieu and Wacquant 1998; Fry 2000), the recovery of the repressed, the return of Africa, does not happen of its own accord. If this expansive African Diaspora culture is in "in the air," it is also a strategic intervention orchestrated by leaders, by which African Diaspora culture serves as a platform for the discussion of blackness and race constructions more generally.

Garifuna cosmopolitans from New York return to Honduras, Belize, and Guatemala carrying a new black self-consciousness. This story is by now familiar in the Caribbean: racializations are internalized by migrants to the United States and then remitted to the homeland. Also instrumental in the process are the global media of film and television, which are overwhelmingly skewed to U.S.-based representations of racial types and tensions. The Garifuna, like other Caribbean groups, are becoming not only a trans-statal society moving between Central America and U.S. cities but also a globalized society deluged with signs that merge Africanness and blackness. England (1999: 8) describes the 1997 bicentennial of the Garinagu landing in Central America, held in La Ceiba, Honduras: "The pervading aesthetic of the Bicentennial was identification with the African Diaspora, as evidenced in the abundance of dreadlocks, cowry shell earrings, Senegalese clothing, and Bob Marley T-shirts. The event was given full coverage by the staff of *Diaspora: A Global Black Magazine* in which the featured report consistently lauded the Garinagu as having 'authentic African culture in its untouched and undiluted form' (John-Sandy 1997: 27)." This globalizing racializing process appears to be narrowing the discrepancy between homeland and hostland articulations of race (McAlister 1998: 135; Waters 1999: 88; Levitt 2001: 60).

But whereas religion and other forms of culture typically serve as means of ethnic resistance to racialization, a means of fortifying sentiments of Haitianness, Cubanness, Puerto-Ricanness, and so on, in the face of the juggernaut of the U.S. racial reduction, Garifuna ancestor religion serves as at once a source of specific ethnic pride and as a gateway to a global black identity. Thus some leaders are even constructing strategies for converting homeland communities to black consciousness.

Summary

Africanness and black identity are analytically, historically, and empirically distinct: the quest for Africanness and becoming black cannot be simply equated. But for traditional Garifuna shamans in New York, the two concepts are mutually reinforcing. Joining the African Diaspora through religion appears also to entail becoming black. If this analysis is correct, the Garifuna case counters the dominant model of Caribbean migration to the United States, in which the assertion of reactive ethnicity is used to avoid being read monolithically as black. By contrast, Garifuna leaders appear to view becoming black not as a reduction but as a political opportunity, both in the United States and in the homeland.

This racial remittance might counter their marginalization from a mestizo national mythology and begin to shape an Afro-Honduran critical mass. Whether the story continues to unfold according to this pattern remains to be seen.

As Dipesh Chakrabarty observed, "The new can be imagined and expressed only through a language made out of the languages already available. Political action is thus loaded with the risk that what was meant to be a break from the past—'something that has never existed'— could end up looking like a return of the dead" (2000: 245). But this risk can be inverted, as Chakrabarty notes, such that the past returns less as a haunting or a retrenchment of traditionalism than as a catalyst for, and a set of resources for, previously unseen futures. The Garifuna's Africanization and their racial shift toward blackness in New York represent creative breaks from the past. These breaks critically alter the horizons of collective memory. But the reexamination of "the past" extends forward and outward, to fresh diasporic alliances and new religious and political possibilities.

Conclusion

"It's a poor sort of memory that only works backwards," the
Queen remarked.

Lewis Carroll, *Through the Looking-Glass*

If ritual is a genre more resistant to innovation than other kinds of
human action—whether because it is kinetically based and buried
beneath conscious critique, or because it has no author and is collectively owned and resistant to individual innovation, or because its very
efficacy depends on the notion of faithful repetition—still, like other
memory forms, it must be constantly renewed with fresh enactments,
or it will die. Even faithful repetitions of homeland rituals change when
performed in new surroundings and in response to new crises.

While diasporic religion sacralizes continuity with a place and people
left behind, in practice it projects and engages new horizons of present
and future affiliations. As we have seen, the contents of a tradition multiply as ritual models are exchanged between homeland and diasporic
contexts. This diversification occurs not only because the materials in
the two sites differ and give religious practice a distinct "feel," although
this is certainly the case. It also occurs because ritual performance in
each site is enfolded within what Lefebvre (1991: 42, 57) called "textures" of space—the contours of representational regimes and signifying practices by which space is made place and filled with meaning.
Here I call attention to three main theoretical issues. The first is the
problem of authenticity that emerges in diaspora; the second is the

divergence in the semiotic logic of ritual performance in diaspora and in the homeland; and the third is the form of community generated by diasporic religion—the ways in which ideas of "being a people" are highlighted and reified, but also by necessity extended to wider social networks.

I attempt to theorize how the work of producing likeness between diasporic ritual events and those of the homeland discloses new horizons of religious identity, and how horizons of pastness are interwoven with horizons of futurity. My conclusions may offer traction for the comparative study of other examples of diasporic religions and the phenomenon of diasporic religion in general.

Back to the Future

As I have shown, diasporas neither simply extend a given set of practices and its practitioners in space nor simply maintain a set of memories about the place left behind through migration, exile, or removal. Rather, they adjust and transform religion as they perform and re-present the left-behind place in new social contexts and places, with different resources. Garifuna ritual actors constitute history as a set of embodied competencies through which the ancestors return; but the question of exactly where they return from—St. Vincent, Honduras, or Africa—is a question that was first opened by Garifuna in New York. In a sense, then, diasporas even construct religion as a discrete entity by problematizing its boundaries and priorities; they shift them from implicit practice to overt debate, and from hegemony to ideological contest.

Diasporic religion calls forth new standards of orthodoxy and orthopraxy and new modes of transmission. On the one hand, Garifuna ritual events are condensed and abstracted as a set of mimetic representations of the homeland shamans and the rites of territorial return they lead. On the other hand, if the versions of ritual in New York are in some ways materially condensed, they are in other ways extended and elaborated by the addition of new objects and practices of the hostland to their repertoire and by becoming systematically articulated and affixed as they jostle for recognition in a culturally pluralist milieu. Moreover, the rituals of the New York diaspora have different social functions. Diasporic ritual performances articulate the external ethnic boundary of the group as a whole rather than delimiting families or other subgroups.

In the dügüs I witnessed in Honduras, by contrast, ethnic identity was self-evident rather than in need of definition and defense.

In sum, diasporic religion is characterized by its more symbolic redaction (a term I explain below), by the formal elaboration of its doctrines, and by a heightened attention to social boundaries. But this shift in performative mode also makes it possible for the religion to be extended to a broader religious community. In New York, an alternative, "cosmopolitan" version of religious authority has emerged. Diasporic practitioners of Garifuna religion, for example, now view their practice as comparable to other religions of the African Diaspora, seeing them all as analogues of a shared metareligion. This possibility is embraced by the religion's actors partly in response to the reductiveness of U.S. racial codes, but also because it presents new niches and spaces of practice and new opportunities for public recognition, as well as a way of reading themselves over and against U.S. racializations. The racial category of blackness is balanced with the ethnic category of Africanness, represented by the ancient and venerable Yoruba gods. By becoming a recognized, authentic African diasporic culture, the group secures recognition, financial support, and spatial niches beneficial to the religion's survival in the city, and a new understanding of itself as a people whose history is interlocked with that of others on a global scale.

When several cultural models for analogically locating or "attaching" a given ritual act are available, code switching becomes possible, perhaps even inevitable (Vertovec 2000: 157; Gargallo 2002: 70–71). That is, the same set of practices can be perceived and articulated as a religion classified as "traditional Garifuna," "indigenous," "African diasporic," "Afro-Latin," or all four. Framing Garifuna-ness may sometimes be an intuitive and mostly unconscious process, but it can also form an explicit response to the perceived discursive needs of a given occasion. A Garifuna youth who cruises the Bronx parks on a Sunday afternoon flying a Jamaican flag on his car, but who also has a Honduran flag and a U.S. flag ready at hand in the backseat, makes choices about his self-presentation in a given neighborhood, though the motivations for each representation may not be conscious or clear even to him. Yet to the degree that such switches become stabilized and exchanged as a recognized means of interaction in a given group, that group's culture is changed. Such informal code switching is initiated by individuals, but to the degree that such individuals are recognized as authoritative memory brokers, their example can be intentionally reproduced and take on normative force. Such has been the influence of the cosmopolitan

Garifuna shamans of New York, who have served as semiotic bridge builders by connecting Garifuna religious meanings to new shores, at first intuitively—by discovering and adopting Yoruba and Afro-Cuban ritual practices in New York—and then strategically, as the informal Africanization of ritual practice has led toward the planned recovery and dissemination of the Garifuna's African past.

This steering process shifts the meaning of Garifuna religion by adding new equivalences and analogical bridges. The bridges then influence the selection of new ideas of origins and new criteria for authentic "returns" across the gaps of time and space that diasporic religious culture seeks to abrogate. In New York, the adoption of the third diasporic horizon of Africa has begun to transform Garifuna religion into a religion consciously and declaratively of the African Diaspora. Of course, the Garifuna are, in part, a people of African descent and are identified as such according to the color and race codes dominant in the United States. In elaborating the construction of that identity, I have not tried to unmask a biohistorical fiction or even to provide an example of the "invention of tradition." Rather, I have tried to show how diasporic memory and its performative returns to the homeland through ritual do not simply happen naturally, but rather take shape as the products of individual human agents and a critical historical funneling. For the Garifuna, for example, the self-conscious recovery and re-presentation of their Africanness is pushed toward specifically Yoruba affiliations despite the rich diversity of their African ethnohistory.

Ethnic and racial identifications are made of selected memories sacralized through the diasporic ritual process. Precisely because of its attention to questions of origins and authentic transmission, diasporic religious culture presents an auspicious semiotic space for the rethinking of historical memory. To return to Lefebvre, with whom this study began, new spaces disclose new versions of the past. Because the diasporic version of the past is instituted and sedimented to a greater degree than the homeland's, moreover, it has the potential to endure and become paradigmatic. Formatted in books and conferences, proposed theme parks, monuments, and routinized orthodoxies of ritual procedure, it can also be disseminated, mission-style, from the new diasporic centers back to the homeland, and beyond. The New York group of shamans, for example, plans soon to send emissaries to Nicaragua, where there are Garifuna communities that have "forgotten the traditions." As one shaman declared: "Just like language teachers have been sent from Belize to reeducate them in our language, we'll send religion teachers." In this way, the homelands too are being called to join the African Diaspora and to thereby revisit their past with fresh perspectives and tools.

Perhaps these findings can be more generally articulated in the following formulation: Diasporic religion sacralizes the idea of continuity with a place and people left behind, even as it in practice opens new horizons of affiliation. It emphasizes the diasporic "idea of the ancestral home" (Lovejoy 1997: 3), even as the place of that home is reconsidered. By elevating the significance of the ancestral land while opening it to excavation, diasporic religious performance mediates between the homeland and the hostland and their temporal coordinates of past and future. It is true that most Garifuna migrants also associate the Honduran homeland with the future, as the site of their planned retirement. But then it is the homeland as the site of an *ancestral* future, that is, as a future constituted of pastness. In the ideal model, one returns to the Honduran village after one's work life is over, as an elder; and one dies there, to become an ancestor. That there are, empirically, modern lives being lived in the homeland does not change the basic (mutually constituting and authorizing) structural positions in Garifuna discourse of New York as the site of modernity and futurity and Honduras as the site of pastness.

When a group extends its imagination in ritual toward the homeland, it does the work of adjustment to appropriate the homeland in a situation of needs and desires in the new land, even as it frames the new environment as "the same." That is the genius of diasporic religion. One of my invisible interlocutors here is Paul Gilroy, who describes Black Atlantic identity as a "changing same" (1993: 101). What is the same is the invocation of authenticity and tradition as responses to destabilizing flux; these invocations increase in volume and frequency with spatial dislocation and social disruption, and so index exactly the opposite of their claims of fidelity to the past (Benjamin 1968: 244; Trilling 1972: 93; Adorno 1973: 9). To be sure, religious performance in general marshals elements of the authoritative past, such as the time of creation, or the founders, ancestors, or elders. Diasporic religion is distinguished by the added challenge of spatial fidelity—the claim that what we do here is faithful in some fashion to what is done there. Once the initial territorial dislocation occurs, such that, say, "Garifuna religion" is marked out as an object, the question of diasporic aperture immediately obtains.[1] On what definition of *then* and *there* should the lens of diasporic ritual be focused? If authenticity is sought in relation to villages in Honduras, why not seek it in relation to earlier and more authoritative ancestors on St. Vincent? Or why not seek it even earlier, in Africa; or among Arawak-speaking Indians on the banks of the Orinoco in South America?

This problem of aperture is why sameness, or at least the appearance of "authentic" transmission (those communications delivered "by a closed chain of witnesses" [Weber 1978: 790]), is such a key part of the diasporic grammar.[2] It is embedded in its own "semiotic ideology" (Keane 2003: 410), a perceived need to mark certain acts as legitimate and others as less so. This marking is itself a transformation misrecognized in diasporic ritual work as a recuperation of the real. Yet this ideology is not merely evoked by the communicative challenges posed by diasporic gaps; it is also called forth by the receiving context of migrants to the United States. There, authenticity matters.

The Authentic, Really

Notions of originality and reality are expressions of spatial power; they found and justify "centers" and "peripheries" (Long 2004: 92), places and events that should be imitated and those taken as derivative. Yet if authentic originality supposes a need for continuity across time and space maintained by reference to singular beings and spatial centers, as a concept it presupposes a rupture, a crisis of continuity overcome only through the labor of memory. *Authenticity* is a noun that only thinly veils a question, or a wish. In the words of the New York Garifuna leader cited earlier, "We did not know who were, or where we came from."

The recognition of a group, and a religion, as representing a discrete and identifiable "culture" is an issue with high stakes attached to it. Immanuel Wallerstein (in Balibar and Wallerstein 1991: 71–85) writes that "identity" is a problem that mainly serves the interests of global capitalism, by dividing groups into legible categories of "core and periphery." and he is right to cast identity as a weapon of economic expansionism. But Garifuna social actors wield this weapon too; they point it at New York City, and even at themselves, when they carry beach sand from Honduran villages for ritual events in the Bronx or play ritual songs on drums transported from the homeland, constructing authenticity with the homeland aura of particular material things (Benjamin 1968: 223–25). Still, material objects are fickle transmitters of authentic identity. Walter Benjamin described how particular objects, detached from their original context, suffer an "auratic decline" and lose their authoritative force even as they gain power through their democratic emancipation, acquiring new meanings and social uses (cf. Sahlins 1981: 69–70). For example, Benjamin writes, an object's temporal authenticity—the question of its continuity in time—is eclipsed by its authorship—the question of its authentic signature and pedigree. It is at such junctures that "the authentic" becomes fetishized as a social and historical need—historical because "historical testimony" suffers when substantive duration, or temporal authenticity, ceases to matter. When historical testimony loses value, the authority of objects (in what Benjamin calls their cult-value) declines as well (Benjamin 1968: 221). The special effect of authenticity is what remains, an aura that guides a sense of history, but now as a present absent, and authenticity from this point must be persuasively performed as a "political" act.[3]

To translate this issue into the terms I used to compare homeland and diaspora ritual performances, the densely compressed ancestral power is "emancipated" in the New York diaspora to include new ancestors and powers. In the diaspora, compression is superseded by extension in the form of an expanded framing of "our people." But this change risks the loss of any homeland link whatsoever: the eclipse of Garifuna religion by the Yoruba gods or by Santería, for example, and the loss of the homeland territorial obligation materially represented by the earth tablets at the heart of the dügü. I understand this territorial risk to be something like Benjamin's "auratic decline." Yet, to pursue the analogy with Benjamin's study of art and its reproducibility, this "decline" is also a reactivation and catharsis, as the object (in this case, ritual performance) is cast into new situations, into contact with new groups of performers and audiences, and new modes of signifying (Benjamin 1968: 220–22). Ritual performance's auratic decline is simultaneously its democratic emancipation, so to speak.

It has been argued that with greater abstraction in representation comes greater potential for dissimulation about the past (Crapanzano 1992: 235; Rappaport 1999: 55–56). I would put the matter less pejoratively: the shift from rituals of ancestral territory itself to rituals of territorial representation allows the critical reexamination of "tradition" in view of present needs, social formations, sources of information, spaces, and material contexts. This is what occurs with Garifuna ritual as it moves between homeland and diasporic articulations. In the move to New York, rituals joined to the homeland in their symbolic repertoire are auratically diminished but democratically emancipated to incorporate new users, open new diasporic horizons, and disclose unseen histories. Yet this expansion can occur only within strict limits. I overheard a Manhattan gallery owner who hired Garifuna drummers to perform one night advise them afterward: "Don't change anything. The Cuban cultural stuff is, you know, already so developed. But this is really primitive, just perfect!" Change must be fitted within the strictures of "the same."

Still, we should not view authenticity as primarily an aesthetic issue. It is a pressing political issue with serious material consequences. Determining "who we are and where we are from" remains crucial in the Garifuna's own collective memory as it is shaped by the politics of identity, with its attendant rights and protections. If power, to crib from Arendt, is "the human ability not just to act but to act in concert" (1970: 41), then making, maintaining, and mobilizing collective identity by locating its authentic origins are fundamental. Yet if articulating authenticity is a compensatory means of finding a voice, and a public face, the need to do so in primitivist formulas ("Don't change anything. . . . This is just perfect") arises only from the posture of a minority group of color in a plural society. Such groups are pressed to perform ceremonies, to "emit signs" (Foucault 1979: 25; cf. Bourdieu 2000: 173).

Listen to Frantz Fanon in *The Wretched of the Earth*: "Because it is a systematic negation of the other person and a furious determination to deny the other person all attributes of humanity, colonialism forces the people it dominates to ask themselves the question constantly: 'In reality, who am I?' " (1963: 203; cf. Mudimbe 1988: 153; Gilroy 1993: 191; Povinelli 2002: 57–60). To be authentic is not just to be pressed to "emit signs," but to emit signs of a particular kind: of deep memory and scenic tribalism. Elizabeth Povinelli writes of the contemporary Australian context: "She [an urban Aborigine] becomes authentically Aboriginal only at the moment she willingly alienates her discourse and identity to the fantastic claim that she is able to transport from the past an ancient practice" (2002: 57). These "timeless" people are forced to act their part in a political theater justifying the nation as the force that brings civilization to the naked primitives, as state nostalgia (Anderson in Ramos 1998: 69; Appadurai 1996). By contrast, those in power are never called on to define themselves; they just *are,* like the omnipresent audience on the subway who ask the New York Garifuna the questions (often well-intentioned) "Where are you from?" and "Who are you?"

Authenticity must be defended convincingly and with the correct tools, especially the correct words. Caliban upbraids Prospero in *The Tempest:*

You taught me language, and my profit on't
Is, I know how to curse. The red plague rid you for learning me your
    language!

And yet, Caliban proceeds:

I must obey. His art is of such pow'r,
It would control my dam's god, Setebos. (*The Tempest,* act 1, scene 2)

Here is the paradox of authenticity: the subaltern must speak in the terms
of abiding, unchanging cultural essences, even though that need is itself
radically transformative: "I am Garifuna. The Garifuna are . . ." Thus the
Garifuna, like many other subgroups contending for limited resources,
have learned the language of ethnic culture. They must find their tongues
to avoid being stirred into a melting pot, whether "Hispanic,"
"Caribbean," or "African American." Ritual leaders in New York, as we
have seen, are writing and systematizing their origins, themselves becoming masters of the special effects of authenticity. Being perceived as an
authentic religious culture is a guarantor of respect and toleration, at
least in places like the United States, where "freedom of religion" is
enshrined both constitutionally and in the mythology of national origins.

This is the texture of the space in which diasporic religion must
dwell. What sort of semiotic logic and forms of community are called
forth in such a place?

The Semiotic Logic of Diasporic Religion

A ritual can mediate between the lived place and the remembered
homeland, or between present and past, in very different ways. The
homeland's "tradition" is itself a sign, a thing represented to consciousness. The sign points in some fashion to the past. But the distinctiveness of homeland memories, or pastness, can be indicated to
consciousness according to quite different modes. Following the model
of Charles Peirce, signs can be divided into symbols, indices, and icons.
I make reference especially to the first two categories to argue that the
performance of memories of the homeland takes on a heightened
symbolic form, whereas homeland ritual performance is more indexical.
This difference matters, and it points us toward the reflections on diasporic forms of community in the next section, because it is through a
process of detachment and abstraction that the "same" rituals come to

signify new authentic horizons and to open religious exchanges with new groups.

THE INDEX AND THE SYMBOL

An index is an existentially motivated sign, "a mode of being of one thing which consists in how a second object is" (Peirce 1955: 76); a relationship of influence or propinquity.[4] Indexicality links the meaning of material things to their situation in space and memory. As Peirce describes it, an index is "a sign, or representation, which refers to its object not so much because of any similarity or analogy with it, or because it is associated with general characters which that object happens to possess, as because it is in dynamical (including *spatial*) connection both with the individual object, on the one hand, and with the sense or *memory* of the person for whom it serves as a sign on the other hand" (quoted in Rappaport 1999: 59; emphasis added).

An index is a representation (of, say, the homeland) that evokes the object in the perceiver's memory. It is contiguous with its object; the sign and that which it signifies "make an organic pair" (1960: §7). Peirce's favorite example of an index is the weathercock, which both points to the wind and is directly affected by it (1960:§5).[5] In my description of the dügü, the earthen tablets occupying the very center of the temple are made, in part, of dirt from the graves of ancestors: thus they represent the ancestors through direct contiguity.

All ritual events signify in layers of overlapping symbolic, indexical, and iconic representations. The question is not one of Honduran village rituals' being only indexical, or of New York rituals' being solely symbolic, but rather of which mode is dominant. My interest in discussing indexicality is to show how the past is signified to participants in contemporary homeland ritual performances. At the outset of the dügü rite, for example, two canoes spend three days at sea fishing and then return to the village, their crew dressed as ancestors and bearing traditional delicacies. In a sense these men represent "ancestral fishing" iconically: their action is similar to that of their forebears. But it is not just a mimetic representation of the past, like Civil War reenactments. Their activity represents the tradition of fishing, but it does so through its actual performance: the ritual fishermen really catch fish. (Civil War reenactors, by contrast, rarely actually shoot each other.) In the village context, fishing signifies the continuity of contemporary village practices with those of the ancestors.

A similar relation obtains for hammocks. They are central to the dügü: when ancestors return in spirit possession, they desire rest. Hammocks link the conceptual domains of rest and ancestry, making ritual performance, despite its frenetic pace, a respite and an oasis set apart from everyday life. Yet hammocks are not merely conventional symbols. Homeland Garifuna ritual actors represent ancestral repose by themselves reposing in hammocks. This action indexes the continuity of contemporary village life with the sleep habits of the ancestors. The memory, in other words, is an embodied performance.

In New York, by contrast, hammocks are never used except as miniature symbols. Because they can represent repose only symbolically, they index the absence and prohibition of continuity with ancestral practices in the diaspora. At the same time as they symbolize ancestral repose, they index the lack of traditional continuity in diasporic rituals. In consequence, the meaning of repose that mediates the past through ritual is changed. In the homeland, repose is performed and enjoyed, in continuity with the ancestors. In the diaspora, by contrast, repose is "repose," the symbol of ancestral rest that is, however, unavailable in New York.

The types of signification, moreover, have practical effects on ritual performance. In the absence of real hammocks, when the spirits of the ancestors return in the Bronx, they must dance without rest, and this constraint radically abbreviates their visits. This suits the constraints of that place: in a rented hall, there is no time for lengthy ancestral repose in any case. What is important is the return of the *type* of "the ancestor," rather than the satisfaction of any specific ancestor. And this, in turn, indexes the Garifuna's own commonsense typology: the homeland is the place of deep ancestral repose, of an abiding and dense yet inert sort of presence. By contrast, the Bronx is the place of little time but decisive action. The homeland is where you begin and end life; in the diaspora is where you make your move.

The dominant mode of representation in diasporic rituals is symbolism. A symbol is a relationship between sign and signified characterized by Peirce as one of futurity, "the mode of being which consists in the fact that future facts . . . will take on a determinant general character" (Peirce 1955: 76). Here the relation between a sign and its object depends on stereotypy and convention. One example is the attempts by New York shamans to define the rules of orthodoxy based on a composite memory of all the shared features of actual rituals participated in. Another is a description of "Garifuna ritual" offered to a curious interviewer, or the printed program for the return of the ancestors. In both cases, the past is rendered present through a set of symbols. "The hammock" is locked in as a signifier of ancestral rest, as a generic ritual term. In Peirce's terms, all the individual instantiations of hammocks are tokens now summarized and abbreviated as a type.[6]

Here is another example: in New York Garifuna ritual performances, uniforms are standardized among participants and carefully prepared, whereas villagers' ritual uniforms in the homeland sometimes appear carelessly matched. "Who are the New Yorkers performing *for?*" one might ask. The answer is that in New York, ritual actors are performing for themselves, representing typical Garifuna-ness with typical traditional costumes. For ritual purposes, it is crucial to dress in *típica* fashion. The reification of a whole domain of objects and actions as típica—as type—its standardization in the diasporic ritual form, and the aesthetically theatrical quality that results, give diasporic ritual a different "feel" of from that of its homeland counterpart, where "tradition" is more fluid and open to interpretation.

In diasporic Garifuna ritual, then, representations of the ancestral past are more mediated by symbolism, stereotypy, and the language of authenticity, of culture and diaspora. Indexical relations of continuity with the territory and practices of the ancestors become, in diasporic performances, symbolic relations to the homeland and the ancestral past. Though new indexical attachments to locality are presented in New York City, they tend to call wider abstractions and analogies into play. Oshun is not merely the goddess of a particular waterfall in Yorubaland or Cuba, but of freshwater in general. Garifuna ritual efficacy requires beach sand from the village of Triunfo, but now the sand of Brighton Beach will work, too, as symbolic "Triunfo sand." This may sound like a romantic lament à la Rousseau ("The Romans were content to practice virtue; all was lost when they began to study it" [1964 (1750): 45]). It isn't. There are great advantages to the diasporic change of giving primacy to the symbolic mode of signification.

One advantage is that, through the emancipation of meaning referred to in the previous section, ritual is at least potentially opened to new participants and new authoritative interpretations when a given sign, like "tradition" or "the spirits," engages expanding communities of discourse (Wuthnow 1989: 3). In the homeland, Garifuna rituals constitute family relations; in the diaspora, they may constitute the collective ethnicity, "Garifuna-ness," and, even more expansively, emplot the Garifuna in the African Diaspora.

THE IMAGISTIC AND THE DOCTRINAL

The social import of the shift in modes of signification becomes clearer when we consider Peirce's nomenclature in relation to the recent contributions on religion, memory and transmission from Harvey Whitehouse (1995, 2000, 2004). Whitehouse presents two modes of religious transmission and collective memory: the imagistic and the doctrinal.[7] The doctrinal mode is characterized by frequent repetition of highly scripted ritual events. Among religions tending toward the doctrinal mode are so-called world religions like Christianity and Islam, which include routinized actions like weekly Bible study or worship meetings, or praying toward the Kaaba in Mecca five times per day. This repetition carves ritual "scripts" into the mind. The kind of memory generated by doctrinal-mode religions is schematic: it contains the broad rules and ritual outline of how the mass is performed, or what is done during the Passover meal. Specific details of who was present or what exactly occurred on a specific ritual occasion, however, are only poorly recalled by participants. Because the sensory scope of ritual is reduced to its abstract form, or "semantic memory," the religion's resources are devoted to discursive elaborations in the form of sermons, exegesis of sacred texts, teaching, and argumentation. To ensure orthodoxy and fidelity in religious reproduction, such transmissions are highly regulated by a religious hierarchy.

The advantages for religious transmission are obvious. Institutional regulation and an emphasis on verbal transmission can bring about a high degree of ideological consensus. Doctrinal religion is, moreover, more easily transmitted than imagistic religions, as the latter are based in painstakingly prepared ritual pageantry and events that generate high emotional arousal. The doctrinal mode allows for the creation of large imagined communities of coreligionists who can easily visualize devotees elsewhere reciting the same texts and repeating similar, standardized ritual acts.

Religions oriented to the imagistic mode are remembered and transmitted through singular or infrequent, spectacular, and often traumatic ritual performances, such as a one-time rite of initiation. With their high level of pageantry and sensory stimulation, they are recalled differently from doctrinal religious transmissions, through what cognitive psychologists call "flashbulb" or "episodic" memory (Tulving 1972; Brown and Kulik 1982). Unlike recipients of doctrinal religious transmissions, those who participate in imagistic ritual events maintain long-term memories of the specific details, including who was present, which objects were used, and the characteristics of the ritual space. Here Whitehouse offers a cognitive reworking of Durkheim's "collective effervescence" (Durkheim 1995: 218–20, 228; Whitehouse 2000: 10): the shock and emotional arousal generated in sensorially intense, elaborate, and infrequent rituals triggers an episodic rather than semantic, or "script," memory.[8]

Whereas rituals evoking episodic memory are effective in forging long-lasting alliances between ritual participants, they cannot be performed for large crowds; nor are they highly transmissible. To the contrary, as ritual events that serve as the cause of the group's cohesion, memory, and experience of power, they are guarded closely, as shared secrets, and their revelation is often proscribed by heavy sanctions.

Whitehouse does not call specific attention to the spatial aspects of religious practice, but the issues are nevertheless abundantly present. For example, his model presents a progression in which a religious movement first evokes intense feelings of cohesion through imagistic rituals, after which those feelings are projected on to a wider number of groups across a more expansive area (2000: 145).[9] Indeed, it was the doctrinal religious mode, with its centralized hierarchy and oratorical, argument-centered style, that helped to provide the conditions for the spatial "great transformation" of the migration to large-scale urban settlements (170).

For diasporic religion, the spatial component of the argument about modes of memory and transmission is inverted. Instead of tracing how the shift in religious mode, from an imagistic one coded in episodic memory to a doctrinal one coded in semantic memory, creates widened imagined communities of coreligionists, here I point to an example of the opposite process: the shift in space has initiated a shift in religious mode. Diasporic Garifuna religion in New York began to adopt the doctrinal mode, even as in the Honduran homeland, the imagistic mode was further developed in response to emigrants' visions from afar of home as a place of special ancestral presence.

HOMELAND AND DIASPORA MODES DEFINE EACH OTHER

This opposition of homeland and diasporic modes is a bit too simple, however. The move to New York has been accompanied by the revitalization of dramatic ritual events in the homeland, endowed with a new patina of authenticity by virtue of their being remembered in, and funded from, the United States. This trend suggests that Garifuna religion combines doctrinal and imagistic modes of performance in a composite form. Even as the diaspora version of "tradition" takes on increasingly doctrinal form—with regular meetings, coordinated uniforms, standardized meanings, and so on—the homeland version of tradition is further elaborated in the imagistic style. The dügü's indexical evocation of the material feel of ancestral memory—through the abundance of food offerings, the size and character of the temple, the synchrony and skill of drummers, the weave of the Carib palm-frond helmets of the fishermen, the depth of knowledge of songs mastered by the women's choir, and the frequency and dignity of possession trances—are key to its perceived healing efficacy. While the two modes are to some degree linked to distinct spaces—the doctrinal with the diasporic New York Garifuna community, and the imagistic with the Honduran homeland Garifuna community—they compose a dialectic of cosmopolitan and indigenous, of values of extension versus density, that play off, constitute, and even stimulate each other. As we have seen, New York Garifuna religious leaders must periodically recharge their cosmopolitan, African diasporic authority by returning to conduct materially and sensorially intense, elaborate rituals in Honduran villages. Meanwhile, homeland village shamans must order Afro-style clothing from distributors in New York to show that they are keeping up with the times.

The two "representational economies" (Keane 2003) are joined. As Keane pointed out, it is a mistake to view them as mere semiotic games with no relation to the lived world; to the contrary, each mode implies, and helps to make, a corresponding form of society.

Forms of Community: Who Are "the People"?

In the New York diaspora, ritual becomes theatrical even beyond the sense in which all ritual is performative (Drewal 1992; Bell 1992). It shifts from being obligatory in the village to becoming an activity voluntarily undertaken as a kind of leisure, one that deliberately exaggerates differences from other forms of social life in order to make identity claims (Appadurai 1996: 39–44). Peggy Levitt (2001: 175–79) records that transnational migrants in diaspora begin to see ritual practice as a self-conscious act rather than as part of the fabric of village life, and that this voluntarist approach is remitted to the homeland to make religious practice there "more formal, instrumental and church-based" (179). In the view of Mette Bovin (1998: 93–112), indigenous groups like the

Wodaabe of North Africa now use ritual as a performative arena to affirm their own identities though "active archaisation" and to speak effectively to outsiders (cf. Mato 2000: 345–48). Ritual is used as a staging ground, as a synecdoche of "the culture," the part strategically highlighted to stand for the whole (Korsch in Eagleton 1991: 95).

The New York context changes the practice of sameness in ritual. As we saw in chapter 3, when the Garifuna shamans' work becomes an object of deliberation and selection within a new network of religions, the symbol-signified relation determining the "meanings" of rituals is opened to revision. Even when the objective is the return to traditions of the homeland, the nature of "return" must be persuasively shown within a context of alternative visions. In short, ritual becomes an ideological forum on the nature of Garifuna-ness and the bounds of its community. Étienne Balibar described the need for social extension among a "people" as the group faces globalization and ideological contest:

> Every "people" . . . is forced today to find its own means of going beyond exclusivism or identitarian ideology in the world of transnational communications and global relations of force. Or rather: every individual is compelled to find in the transformation of the imaginary of "his" or "her" people the means to leave it, in order to communicate with the individuals of other peoples with which he or she shares the same interests and, to some extent, the same future. (Balibar and Wallerstein 1991: 105)

Balibar addresses a crucial question: can community be maintained under radically new conditions? Must older ideas of "peoples" be cast off to find common cause in new urban "tribes"? Garifuna emigrants' experiences respond to the question by pointing to something slightly different from Balibar's admonition. In place of an extension, of leaving their people behind, Garifuna shamans radically expand the definition of "their people" by folding the Garifuna diaspora into the African Diaspora and by ritually hooking Garifuna-ness to the memory of Africa. But even this joining is an ideological process that entails critical decisions about what such a return might mean.

By ideology, I mean the passage of a given issue from being tacit into being the stuff of overt consciousness, contest, and discourse (Bourdieu 1977: 168–69). To take a simple example cited by Catherine Bell, as young Manhattan Jews "return" to orthodoxy, they are aided by new singles programs to help them marry appropriately. In this sense, return is always transformation. Bell comments: "If the choice of a return to orthodoxy is a form of resistance to secularism, it also reinforces some of the more central values of secularism, namely, individual choice and a plurality of options" (1997: 256). The ritual shifts transform social life; and the change is sedimented and rationally "hardened" as a signal and necessary mark of identity (253–68).

These changes in the practice of authentic sameness do not make such rituals any less "religious" or less efficacious at generating relationships between people, or between people and gods, spirits, or ancestors. They do, however, suggest that the pastness of ritual functions differently in the hostland city than it does in homeland villages. It transforms the notion of "the people" by expanding it, embedding the Garifuna within the African Diaspora, and it codifies those transformations by recording them in "hard" technologies of memory.

This basic insight was an important one in the late work of Victor Turner. Other scholars had long noted ritual's apparent capacity to modify time and history in experience (Eliade 1954; Myerhoff 1974; Moore and Myerhoff 1977). By condensing human action into temporary idealized performances that are then applied to everyday circumstances, and by repeating those performances, ritual "overcomes the narrowness of the profane world" (Marx and Engels 1978: 34). Such "meaning" derives from the interpretive possibilities generated by relating the present circumstance to a re-presented past, the changing to "the same."[10] As chapters 5 and 6 show, though, rituals are occasions for airing conflicts as much as for resolving them. It is only in New York that they affirm the group, "the Garifuna" as such, and then only momentarily. It is on just this issue, the brevity and fragility of ritual's supercession of social conflict, that Turner's notion of *communitas* departs from earlier models. Ritual expresses, constructs, and produces solidarity, but only incompletely: every reproduction and new reception contains fissures that may precipitate change, which may or may not be implemented in social revisions.[11] Turner's adjustments of functionalism by and large accept the conservative bias of ritual compared with other kinds of human action, but they read that very conservatism as itself a contingent bid for sociopolitical change (cf. Kertzer 1988: 12; Mach 1993). "Timeless" continuity or authenticity is viewed as itself a choreographed effect. The stress on the "harmonious and cohesive aspect of social relationships" in presentations of ritual, whether by practitioners or analysts, is an "ideological interpretation" (Turner 1967: 33) called forth in and by pluralism, in which the apparently unchanging must in fact be deliberately renewed.

Over time, Turner began to wrestle with the transformation of ritual in urban venues into an ideological form (1969: 131–40: 1974: 169; 1992: 48–60). In the latter, ritual participation takes place within a religious marketplace and is motivated by individual choice rather than corporate ascription (1992: 48). Instead of entailing a potential absorption of the structured self into an experience of the social whole, ritual is inevitably about instating structure, "a signal mark of identity" (1992: 60). Whereas rituals in the village context hold the potential for overarching social integration, in urban contexts social integration occurs only in sub-groups defined in opposition to a network of rivals. Communitas, the experience of the radical leveling of social hierarchy, is not "sponta-neous," as in Turner's earlier formulations, but rather plotted and staged in "rites of intensification" (1985: 159). It is ideological in that it is con-sciously selected action that expresses, and presses, an identity claim. For Turner, there is a downward curve from "spontaneous" communitas to ideological communitas that entails a certain loss (1969: 202).[12]

My research, however, reveals just the opposite: it is only in the urban, diasporic space of New York that the idea of the group as a whole emerges and is celebrated, leveling hierarchy and bestowing the sense of being part of spontaneous communitas. In the homeland villages, individuals, families, and other subgroups use ritual to press particular-ist claims. What Turner calls spontaneous communitas is a deliberate, conscious performance of holism and transcendent meaning, constitut-ing a critique and temporary reaction against the compartmentaliza-tions of modern life (Beyer 1994: 81). In this argument I follow the theoretical lead offered by Harvey Whitehouse: the expansive idea of spontaneous communitas—say, the sentiment of camaraderie based on a shared African Diaspora identity—is not the beginning but rather the end point of a long series of social processes. Sentiments favoring the expansion of the social frame can arise only after imagistic religion has become doctrinal, conceptualized in a schematic form that generates a widened imagined community of anonymous coreligionists. This shift occurs through changes in the transmissive context that make it possi-ble to construe humanity in more abstract, inclusive terms (Whitehouse 2000: 180–85). For the Garifuna, the emigration from rural villages to New York represents such a change par excellence. Only with migration to New York did the harmony of the ethnic group as a whole take on value as part and parcel of authenticity and become normative as cul-tural defense in the theater and representational economy of cultural pluralism. As Whitehouse notes, ideological communitas occurs with the application of that hard-earned conceptual and sentimental unity to a specific cause. This is how Garifuna religion in the homeland became "African Diaspora religion" in New York.

The Changes That Make "the Same"

To the "personal Africas" (Lovejoy 1997: 7) carried in memory by those who were shipwrecked near, fled to, or were captured and brought to St. Vincent during the seventeenth and eighteenth centuries was added a collective memory of being united under the social umbrella of being Carib. The fight against Great Britain and the resulting deportation to Central America in 1797 further defined that ethnogenesis, this time indelibly, as Black Carib. In the twentieth century, *Garifuna* took hold as the ethnonym, for public presentation, of a growing awareness of the group as a people defined especially by their language, religion, and itinerary. And the Garifuna are now expanding their identifications by joining the African Diaspora.

Ritual contexts provide one venue where, in the Bronx, new horizons of authentic origins are delimited. It is not so much that diasporic rituals express the past and the territory left behind, but that they create the past and the homeland through memory and performance (Austin 1962; Firth 1967; Bell 1992; Hollywood 2002). Rituals are themselves platforms for launching new collective memories.

Neither of these venues of ritual performance, the homeland and the diasporic, is more "advanced" or "modern" than the other, but they situate ritual differently in relation to the rest of life. I have tried to demonstrate how the two spaces generate distinct social frames, modes of transmission, and plausible horizons of memory, and thus how one diasporic process—the Garifuna dispersal from Honduras to New York—adopted and was adopted by a second, wider diasporic articulation, the African Diaspora, shifting the principal horizon of memory. But this is a highly schematic view: the reality is more complex. When the Garifuna move to New York and then return home, homeland village rituals are themselves sometimes changed into venues of cosmopolitan performance, even as Garifuna emigrants reindigenize signs detached from the homeland to reattach them in niches of the city. There is constant mutual influence exercised by the two spaces and their respective ritual modes. In fact, each presses the other toward more strident assertions of its particular claims to authority: the indigenous, territorial powers or the diasporic and cosmopolitan ones. The two modes ultimately constitute a single system.

What unites the homeland and diaspora Garifuna within a "changing same" is that both versions share "the same" invocation of ancestors in ritual events led by shamans, while "change" refers to the situated contexts of reception and performance. But even this formulation will not quite do, because what is changing plays back into and transforms what is allegedly the same. Just as the notion of "the people" has expanded, so has the pantheon of spirits invoked by Garifuna. These are now read in relation to a larger family of orishas, muertos, lwa, and other superhuman agents of the African Diaspora. While the ancestors remain central to Garifuna ritual, the content and location of "ancestrality," and thus the ultimate horizon of memory, has moved east, from Honduras and St. Vincent back to Africa. In a sense this process is a recovery of the repressed, but it is a recovery that still had to be, and is even now being, produced through specific interventions. Membership in the African Diaspora turns out to be the end point of ritually reconstituted pasts, rather than their essential origin.

Henri Bergson wrote that memory allows us to "remount the slope of the past." But the ascent is precarious, for the mountain is always slippery and on the verge of escaping us: "Encore le passé où nous remontons ainsi est-il glissant, toujours sur le point de nous échapper" (1896: 79–80).

The past can escape us, but it can also be taken away, or too rigidly imposed. We saw earlier how British authorities writing from St. Vincent Africanized the Black Caribs to justify their conquest of the island, even as the Black Caribs resisted such a reduction and the vulnerability to enslavement that it might produce. Yet if the British won the war of the island and the spoils that fell to the victor, they never won the power to name those who lived there. Whereas the Black Caribs refused Africanization by the British, many Garifuna today, in the wake of a second diaspora to the United States, claim their African heritage through transformed understandings of religious practice. This conversion is carried out in relation to their own needs, as articulated in the space and time of emigration, as a redemptive seizing of the past:

It is not in the form of the spoils that fall to the victor that the latter [spiritual things] make their presence felt. . . . They manifest themselves in this struggle as courage, humor, cunning, and fortitude. They have retroactive force and will constantly call in question every victory, past and present, of the rulers. As flowers turn toward the sun, by dint of a secret heliotropism the past strives to turn toward that sun which is rising in the sky of history. (Benjamin 1968: 254–55)

Appendix

Trajectory of a Moving Object, the Caldero

The work of "worldmaking" . . . tends, when the social world is involved, to construct and impose the principles of division likely to conserve or transform this world by transforming the vision of its divisions.

Pierre Bourdieu, *Pascalian Meditations*

If African Diaspora religious groups indigenize U.S. urban space by hooking ritual to its sites, they also do it by revaluing the meanings of ritual objects. It is not only people who are remade through spatial transit—as in the case of the Garifuna's becoming "black" in the U.S.—but also the materials they exercise in negotiating their relation to new locations, "the things-in-motion that illuminate their human and social context" (Appadurai 1986: 5).

The calderos many Garifuna shamans now include in their altar repertoires have a long history. The Garifuna adopted them from Cuban practitioners of Palo Monte *(paleros)* in New York, but the objects are linked not only to Cuba but also to Kongo Central Africa.[1] Though there are obvious continuities of instrumental reference, such as the manipulations of the object symbol to cure, defend, or attack, each site produced unique versions. For the Bakongo of a century ago, and probably of many centuries earlier, objects called *minkisi* (singular *nkisi*) were collections of organic materials—sticks, plants, bones, cemetery earth, stones, animals, human hair, or fingernail fragments—arranged into bundles or indented enclaves of wooden images. These bundled elements materially composed and located the spirit of a dead person *(nfumbi)*.[2] The materials combined metaphoric and metonymic referents, objects that referenced abstract properties, and objects that forecast specific objectives—what Robert F. Thompson called "spirit-embodying" and "spirit-directing" materials (1984: 118).[3] A dog carcass might connote skill in hunting; seawater, range and movement; bird feathers, the "upper world"; cemetery dirt, the power of the dead; mirrors, the "flash of the spirit"; hair or fingernails, the intended target of healing, protection, seduction, or harm.

In a space dictated by forces beyond one's control, such manufactured objects were available to human control and intervention. They presented the world compacted, a microcosm (Cabrera 1979: 127; Thompson 1984: 119; Olmos and Paravisini-Gebert 2003: 80) of a world whose powers one could contract, pay (by feeding), and direct toward desired ends. In the Kongo context, the objects were initially controlled by collective lineage groups and often bore clan titles as well as being used for personal concerns (MacGaffey 1986: 81, 141). During the colonial period, however, Africans also began perceiving them as having escaped their control and saw this loss of control as the reason for European material dominance, even denominating the storehouses of European factories as minkisi (Palmié 2002: 180).

In Cuban practice, objects were assembled under the broad ethnic canopies of Yoruba and Kongo (David Brown 2003: 116). Here the packets took on the relatively standardized form of "cauldrons" *(calderos)*, also called *ngangas,* whose masters were called *tata nganga.* They continued to exert force as collective symbols of *cabildos de Congos,* Afro-Cuban and (often, as *cofradías,* Catholic) mutual-aid societies (Cabrera in Palmié 2003: 183). But their semantic range shifted with the needs presented by the new space: most strikingly, they became a tool of ritual combat against slavery. The former Cuban slave Esteban Montejo described this kind of ritualized aspiration:

All the powers, the saints, were in that *cazuela* [pot or stew]. . . . With that [cemetery] dirt you made four corners in little mounds to resemble the points of the universe. . . . When the master punished a slave, all the others picked up a little dirt and put it in the pot. With that dirt they vowed to bring about what they wanted to do. And the master fell ill or some harm came to his family because while the dirt was in the pot, the master was prisoner in there, and not even the devil could get him out. That was the Congo people's revenge on the master (Barnet 1994: 27–28).

In addition, the calderos incorporated sticks of specific trees, *palos* (whence the name of the religion, Palo Monte). David Brown suggests that the palos referenced not only trees and "the forest" *(el monte)*, perhaps indexing qualities of rootedness, stoutness, or longevity, but also the stockades of *palenques*, fortresses built by runaway slaves (1989: 373–74). Paleros were remade, at least symbolically, as *palenqueros*, slave warriors and rebels, whose ritual "quarry" became Spanish soldiers (Thompson 1984: 125).

There were further transformations of ritual world-making in the New World. As Stephen Palmié ingeniously observed, the distinct African "nations" were not merely thrust into sudden proximity but mutually constituted each other in Cuba. "Kongo" Palo Monte and "Yoruba" Regla de Ocha, initially based on a set of relatively similar practices of exchange with ancestral spirits, over time congealed into strongly divided semantic chains, each devoted to distinct kinds of power. Palo took on its character as rustic, violent, fast-working, effective, morally ambiguous, "of the forest," and "cosa de muerto," whereas Ocha (oricha practice) was seen as royal, civilized, formal, respectful of hierarchy, and morally pure (Gonzalez-Wippler 1989: 239–40; David Brown 1999: 195; Palmié 2002: 163–64). Further, relationships with the spirits in Palo Monte hardened into the idea of mercenary contracts and captive labor; in Ocha they were based on the idea of a ritual family *(hermanos de santo)* comprised of initiated "children" of the gods *(hijos* and *hijas de santo)*. Capture, enslavement, and command of a Palo spirit were set against the feeding and petitioning of ancestral royalty.[4] These differences extended to appropriation versus procreation, commodity versus gift, and cool femininity versus machismo. Attached social formations differed also: Ocha welcomed a large homosexual population, whereas Palo adopted a homophobic rap. The two sets of practices were associated with racialized markers: of "light" Ocha and "dark" Palo (Palmié 2002: 167–76; Cabrera 1983: 130–31).

In Cuba, therefore, and then in the United States, the caldero object was fitted with an entirely new set of referents. In short, it became "magic," the dark, clientelistic pursuit of fleshly and materialistic aims. But this transformation could be accomplished only through the simultaneous elevation of Ocha to the status of an authentic religion possessing morally upright spiritual goals. Finally, the linking frame between Kongo and Yoruba, Palo and Ocha was provided in Cuba by the arrival of European Spiritism (in the writings of Allan Kardec), which ranged all spirits along a continuum from low to elevated (Palmié 2002: 192; Olmos and Paravisini-Gebert 2003: 171–210; David Brown 2003: 172).

In the United States, after the two waves of Cuban immigration in 1959 and 1980, the caldero was again associated with a new landscape. Ocha and Palo practices maintained by separate and mostly distinct social groups in Cuba began to be freely combined, as spirit families were petitioned to address different needs: this trend led to *cruzada* (crossed) practitioners, who cross-index each oricha with its corresponding nganga.[5] Although ideally the images of the orichas should be kept separate from the Palo muertos, with the Palo caldero kept on the floor or in the ground, in practice city apartments preclude keeping much distance between them.

Here, too, however, the caldero makes a world space within a new world. As one of David Brown's informants reported: "The prenda [caldero] is like the whole world, there is something of everything, wherever you are, you have to put something in it: if I go to New York to establish a point, I have to take something back from there and put it in the prenda. You see, we are like warriors. When an army conquers a country, they leave an occupying army. I live in Union City; if I go to New York to 'work' I will have to leave scouts or guards, build a perimeter, a fortress" (Brown in Palmié 2002: 185). If this report gestures toward ritual interventions evoked during the Ten Years' War in Cuba, from 1868–78 (Palmié 2002: 185), it also suggests the use of the caldero to address a new crisis of territorialization in U.S. cities.

This retracing of the dislocations of a single religious object is, I hope, instructive. The caldero always makes a microcosm of categories and divisions in relation to which its users can work. It contrasts with, but aspires to modify, an encompassing world that is hostile and nearly intractable. But only nearly, as city spaces are mastered—rendered legible, subjected to aspiring action—by applying old objects to new problems, hooking existing symbols to new sites of signification: warfare, gang, ancestors, eating, earth, money, love, transport, the globalized world. At the same time, the object's arrival in a new space presents it to new users. While homeland Garifuna until recently knew nothing about Cubans or their religions, Garifuna in diaspora have adopted the caldero as their own, and in consequence have begun to make their world differently.

Notes

Introduction

1. I use the term *Island Carib* advisedly, to represent the people who lived on St. Vincent in the sixteenth century, prior to the arrival of Europeans. *Carib* was a colonial ethnonym, given on the Columbian voyages, for the peoples of the eastern Caribbean. It served European interests in distinguishing allegedly "good" Arawaks—peaceful and complicit—from their "bad" antagonists, the Caribs—warmongering, resistant, and cannibalistic. This polarization began early in the colonial process. Rivals of the east Antillean islanders described them to Christopher Columbus as fearsome man-eaters: thus variations on *Cariba* and *Caniba* infused representations of the "Caribbean" with long-lasting tropes of the cannibal. Columbus's recopied journals from the voyage of 1492–93 mention not only reports of the fearsome man-eating Caniba, who have "the face of a dog," but also of their dwelling within the dominion of the Great Khan, the Mongol king, signaling to Columbus his presence in the Indies (diary entries of November 26 and December 11, 1492, quoted in Dunn and Kelley 1989: 177, 217). Here, then, the terms *Carib, Caniba,* and *Khan,* and an implied reference to the Latin *canus,* dog-faced, were actively imbricated. From a variant, *Kalinago,* was derived *Garinagu,* now used interchangeably with Garifuna, a variant of *Kalipona.* Kalinago and Kalipona were male and female titles, respectively, for the same group, the so-called Island Caribs.

The bifurcation these terms—*Arawak* and *Carib*—created between "good" and "bad" Indians is especially associated in the scholarly literature with Irving Rouse's formulations in his 1948 *Handbook of South American Indians,* where he canonized the hypothesis that the Caribs had emigrated from the South American mainland into the Lesser Antilles and conquered the previous occupants, killing the men and assimilating the women, thus accounting for the dual dialects of men and women. Rouse later maintained a more considered version of this view, acknowledging that no archaeological evidence has yet confirmed it (1987), and that the categories of Carib and Arawak are clearly distinguished only in scholars' schemes. Most problematically for the Rouse hypothesis, linguists have noted that the "Island Caribs" spoke a language of the Arawakan family rather than of the South American Cariban family. Yet, according to William Young (1971 [1795]: 5), the "Red Charaibs" themselves said that their ancestors came from "the banks of the Oronooko, whence coasting Trinidada, and Tobago, to Grenada, and thence by the Grenadines, they arrived at St. Vincent's, subdued the native inhabitants, called Galibeis, and possessed themselves of the island."

Taino, meanwhile, a term that has been widely used to denote the Amerindian victims of Island Carib aggressions in the Lesser Antilles, and the main indigenous group of the Greater Antilles, was also a scholarly construct. As Rouse himself notes (1987), it derived from a word meaning *good* or *noble*, by which the Western Antilleans distinguished themselves from their Island Carib rivals, and was adopted as the standard ethnonym for the indigenous peoples of the Greater Antilles in the nineteenth century. Scholarly categories therefore played a role in reifying the strategic interests of indigenous rivals.

2. In the early twentieth century, Max Weber (1978) and Franz Boas (1986 [1928]) concluded that ethnicity and race are cultural categories, a contention that has since been widely reinforced. It should follow that the adoption of *cultural* practices, including religion, may variously reify, modify, or transform an individual's ethnicity or race. Yet, as Michael Hanchard points out, it is the nondiscursive, structural parameters of race, that which "goes without saying," that delimit race malleability (1999: 73–74).

3. "Indigenous" articulations of Garifuna culture have been especially crucial in land-rights battles in Honduras. For example, in the months following the October 1998 devastation caused by Hurricane Mitch, President Carlos Flores, along with the incoming president of Congress, Pineda Ponce, and a select group of businessmen, proposed the privatization of coastal territory. This move would have meant striking Article 107 of the constitution, which declares that the coastal zone within forty kilometers of the sea may be owned only by Honduran nationals, or by institutions with a majority constituted by Honduran nationals. The particular motivations for the reform derived in part from the pressure levied on Honduras by international financial lenders like the World Bank to develop a tourism infrastructure. But Article 107 has served as the guardian of Garifuna lands in lieu of more specific legal protections. Although the Garifuna have occupied this territory for two hundred years, they held no official property titles before 1992. Though Honduras's National Agrarian Institute began issuing titles thereafter, progress has been slow and contested. Progress on the acquisition by villages of full communal rights *(dominio pleno)*, under which all individual landholders, Garifuna and outsiders alike, would be subject to Garifuna communal control, has been hotly contested. As the enactment of the reform of Article 107 appeared imminent, Garifuna leaders demanded the legalization of land titles under the auspices of

the International Labor Organization Convention 169, the Indigenous and Tribal Peoples Convention (1989)—especially the articles protecting the unique rights of indigenous peoples to guarantees of respect for the spiritual value of land (Article 13), the recognition of ownership (Article 14), the rights to natural resources on such lands (Article 15), the protection against forced removal (Article 16), the right of return if already relocated (Article 17), the legal protection of the transmission of land rights among members (Article 17), the right to implement sanctions against encroachers (Article 18), and the right to provisions for expansion equal to those provided other groups (Article 19). They also mobilized on Columbus Day 1999 (October 12; in Latin America, el Dia de la Raza), alongside Amerindian Lenca and Tawahka activists in a protest march in the capital, Tegucigalpa. As they marched toward the presidential palace, police blocked their path, firing tear gas and rubber bullets. Twenty marchers were injured. Shortly thereafter, when U.S. Garifuna leaders departed for New York carrying photos and videos of the confrontation to present to the United Nations, President Flores dropped the proposal to reform Article 107.

4. Katherine Verdery's (1994) important intervention proposes the term *trans-ethnonational* to suggest a similar web of emotional and cultural affinities to what I here associate with *diaspora*, and *trans-statal* to designate institutional bonds crossing nation-state territorial boundaries.

5. *Place* is space plus meaning: that is, space that signifies and locates a person within a web of relations. To cite the common example, a house is a space; a home is a place. This signification is suggested even in the etymologies of spatial terms: *site*, from the Latin *situs*, and *place*, from the Greek *plateía* and Latin *platea*, "broad way," suggest local, relational space much more than does *spatium*, with its abstract sense of "interval" or "extent." An excellent summary of approaches to the issue of space versus place is that of Friedland and Boden (1994). Certeau inverts the more common usage: for him, "space is a practiced place" (1984: 117).

6. Tongue firmly in cheek, Brubaker (2005: 14) proposes a slew of additional neologisms: *diasporosity* (to designate the permeability of the boundaries of a diaspora); *diasportfolio* (a new global investment strategy); *diaspersion* (an unkind remark about a diaspora); *diasporapathy* (to characterize putative members of a diaspora who do not respond to the appeals of diasporactivists); *diasperanto* (a project for a common language of the diaspora), and others. I might add additional possibilities: *diasporadic* (the only occasional acknowledgment of being diasporic), *diaspirate* (the breathing of new life into an apparently moribund diaspora), and *diasproliferation* (the cumulative effects of all of the above).

7. Obviously I am writing schematically here. Technically we should think of "indigenous religions," "diasporic religions," and "mission religions" as positions along a continuum of locative versus utopian understandings of power (Jonathan Smith 1987: 94–95); or constructions of power based on distinct principles, on one end the principle of density, on the other the principle of extension (Miller 2005: 27). But these positions are Weberian ideal types in the sense

that no historical religion ever perfectly fits any one analytical model (Johnson 2002b). Thus every religion has some diasporic qualities; and one could argue that a "mission religion" such as Islam is relatively more diasporic than Christianity because of its requirements of the *hajj,* the obligatory return to Mecca, and daily prayers recited while facing toward Mecca, which daily inscribe into one's habitus the sentiment of being separated from a sacred place.

8. See, for example, Bergson 1896; Casey 1987, 1993, 1997; Bachelard 1994; Ricoeur 2004; Halbwachs 1992; Connerton 1989; Whitehouse 2000, 2004; and Shaw 2002.

9. Though Caliban is a clear play on *cannibal,* he is not depicted as literally eating human flesh. His imprisonment by Prospero, however, is attributed to the accusation that he attempted to rape Prospero's daughter, Miranda, in order to populate the island with his own offspring. The portrayal of him as a sexual predator casts him as a metaphorical if not literal cannibal, one who would feast on the flesh of the innocent.

Contra this pervasive idea of the Caribbean's (and the Black Caribs') "mixed" character as the cause of diminished powers, the French doctor Jean-Baptiste Leblond identified the Black Caribs' "croisement des races" as the very basis of their vigor and domination over the Red Caribs (Leblond 2000 [1813]: 109).

10. The lack of memory, or of the possibility of Caribbean history, is a claim still often repeated. Here is V. S. Naipaul (2002 [1962]: 20): "The history of the islands can never satisfactorily be told. Brutality is not the only difficulty. History is built around achievement and creation; and nothing was created in the West Indies."

11. It is difficult to determine at even the basic level, however, which elements of Black Carib were "African" and which "Carib." I suggest that the shamanic paradigm, with its tobacco-aided trances and procedures for extracting illness-causing penetrations, is commonly related to Amerindian, and even earlier North Asian, religious practice. But the former slave Olaudah Equiano, who, as a freeman in England, later wrote his autobiography, described the pipes and tobacco that were always put in graves with corpses in his West African homeland, and noted that the priests or "yearly men" who used such pipes were also "doctors" who expelled poisons (Equiano 2004 [1789]: 17, 177). Equiano's account gives the lie to any attempts to construct strictly bounded culture spheres by the use of lists of features.

12. The Immigration and Nationality Act Amendments of 1965 (the Hart-Celler Act), which abolished the system of national-origin quotas, was part of the civil rights legislation enacted to reduce discrimination in the United States. The act massively increased the number of Black Caribbeans, Latin Americans, and Asians who arrived in the United States. Western Hemisphere immigration was limited, however, to 120,000 per year, and Eastern Hemisphere immigration to 170,000.

13. These influences sometimes had fairly direct effects on life in the village. For example, by the late 1990s, both the villages where I worked boasted adolescent "fashion teams" who traveled to compete against teams from other villages.

The teams modeled categories of couture from "beach" to "evening-wear" to "traditional" *(típica)*. "Tradition" was being ossified and made consumable in relation to the mass media, as "típica" couture was juxtaposed with "modern."

14. I also compared my own notes with other accounts, including those of Conzemius 1928; Taylor 1951; Coelho 1955; Jenkins 1983; Bianchi 1988; Gonzalez 1988; Kerns 1997; and Suazo 2000. Finally, I watched videotapes of dügü rituals that had been mailed from Honduras to the Bronx and took notes on Bronx shamans' knowledgeable commentaries on the proceedings.

Chapter 1. What Is Diasporic Religion?

1. Modern usage begins with Zionist references at the end of the nineteenth century. It was first applied to the African Diaspora in the middle of the twentieth century. The use of the term with reference to Armenian and Greek migrations also predates its application to the African case, but it was not as frequently invoked or discursively dominant (Gilroy 1993: 23, 205–8; R. Cohen 1997).

2. Palmer (1998) notes that the common use of *African Diaspora* today refers to only one in a much longer set of migrations, the first beginning one hundred thousand years ago. He places the second migration stream around 3000 B.C.E., with the mass movement of the Bantu-speaking peoples within Africa and to the Indian Ocean. The third was a trading diaspora initiated around the fifth century B.C.E., as traders, merchants, slaves, and soldiers emigrated to Europe, the Middle East, and Asia. The fourth is the one commonly meant by *African Diaspora* today, caused by the Atlantic trade in enslaved Africans. The fifth stream began during the nineteenth century, with the end of slavery, and has continued to the present. Palmer notes that racial oppression and resistance to it are characteristic only of the last two streams.

3. Tölölyan (1996: 9) reports the related Armenian term *gaghut*.

4. Even Benedict Anderson's (1991) much-misused phrase *imagined community* referred not to notions of belonging produced ex nihilo from individual minds, but rather to subjectivities transformed as a consequence of new institutions and material practices. These included quotidian practices like reading the newspaper, which enabled Europeans in the Americas to perceive themselves as a single, far-flung national community now "reading together" (Anderson 1991; Appadurai 1996).

5. Culture is here understood as a semiotic community, following the framework of Sewell (1999). To speak of a culture in Sewell's sense is not to describe a social collective that uses signs uniformly, but rather a collective in which the meanings of signs overlap enough to produce meaningful social exchange (cf. Wittgenstein 1953; Needham 1972). *Culture* in this broad sense comprises both a symbol system that expresses and communicates social meaning and its implementation in a specific set of practices by a specific group of people. It entails a collection of schemas that exist both as public artifacts and as cognitive constructs within minds, shared among a community (Shore 1996: 46–48).

A conventional approach to building a house is part of a culture, as is a model for celebrating Thanksgiving. Yet there is always a gap between objectivated meanings and their internalization by an individual (P. Berger 1967: 15), such that the Thanksgiving schema need not be followed to the letter in order to be in effect. Culture connotes not the lack of conflict, but rather a model for articulating conflicts which presupposes common terms and processes (Certeau 1984: xvii).

6. Migrations and the urbanism that offers the conditions for diasporas are closely related. In 1910, 80 percent of the population of New York and Chicago were immigrants or children of immigrants (Orsi 1999: 20); in 1997, immigrants and their children constituted 62 percent of the population of Los Angeles, 72 percent of Miami's, and 54 percent of New York's (Rumbaut and Portes 2001: 9).

7. Cross-referencing between diasporic groups is common. The African Diaspora, for instance, took cues from Zionism (Sansone 2003; Frank 1997). Frank argues that Herskovits's attention to the African Diaspora was a form of displaced consciousness of his own Jewishness. As many groups in the United States were informed by the black civil rights movement, Hispanic, Asian-American, and Native American collectives emerged. It follows that diaspora movements should not be viewed as utterly distinct, and one might even argue for a "diasporizing moment" occurring between the 1960s and the present, as pan-ethnic groups formed. The African Diaspora is one such pan-diasporic movement. As Garifuna arrivals in New York begin to socialize, and ritualize, with Cubans, Haitians, Puerto Ricans, and others, they rethink their religious performances and identities.

8. This transformation inverts the status shift previously accomplished by Irish and Jewish immigrants, who became "Caucasians" during the first half of the twentieth century in a process of "antagonistic acculturation" (Devereux and Loeb 1943); they defined themselves in opposition to the new "others," blacks arriving as part of the Great Migration north. These new Caucasians surrendered their particular ethnic affiliations, at least in legal and institutional spheres, for a broader, racialist one (Roediger 1991; Winant 1998; Lipsitz 1998; Jacobson 2001; West 2001). This self-definition reveals the all-consuming force of the racial opposition of black and white in the United States, the minotaur consuming everything in its labyrinth. While contemporary Caribbean immigrants play race down to enhance their social status (thus a Haitian may describe himself not as "black" but rather "French"), European immigrants historically played it up (thus a Dubliner may have identified not as "Irish" but as "white").

9. Several scholars view religion as fundamentally a tool of empire and a discursive artifact, and therefore as not definable, or as infinitely but unproductively definable, and always as an exercise of power (W. Smith 1991; Asad 1993; Masuzawa 1993; McCutcheon 1997). However, there is no reason why a thing constructed even for imperialist purposes should be disqualified from investigation; quite the contrary (Lincoln 2003; Whitehouse 2004). To say that religion is a discursive artifact is true; the question is whether it is a discursive artifact in a way that distinguishes it from all other humanly made forms like art, geography,

race, progress, or medicine, each of which has also helped justify discrimination against putative Others in the construction of "civilizations." In other words, it is not clear why religion bears this load in some unique way. What seems important is not to decide the ultimate objective viability of religion, but rather to specify how one is using the term.

Conflicts over the definition of religion remain based on the tension between broad or functionalist and narrow or content-based framings. In the former view, most famously represented by Émile Durkheim (1995 [1915]), religion is the social arena circumscribed, with positive and negative rules and taboos, as "the sacred." But the specific content of the sacred is shifting: it may be a totem or a flag. Other approaches have focused on the specific content of religions. Exemplary on this side was the perspective of E. B. Tylor (1958), who defined religion quite simply as "belief in gods and spirits." Among the content-based definitions we could include Victor Turner's definition of religion as "an agency-based cosmology for this-worldly purposes" (1962: 190), as well as current cognitivist proposals that define religion as human actions directed toward "moderately counter-intuitive superhuman agents" (Boyer 2001) that optimize a religion's memorability. The first style of definition has the virtue of dynamism, showing religion as ongoing processes of sacralizations and disenchantments, of centering and marginalizing; the latter has the virtues of clarity and of positing a specific category within which comparisons might be drawn.

My own use of *religion* is indebted to the definitional efforts of Bruce Lincoln (2003: 1–7) and Martin Riesebrodt (in press), which bridge the two paths. Lincoln rejects in principle judgments about belief, concern, mood, or feeling, as these are inherently unknowable to the observer. Instead, he defines religion (at least for analytical purposes) as discourse—speech and practice, or what we can call "culture"—of a particular kind. Religion is discourse "whose concerns transcend the human, temporal and contingent, and that claims for itself a similarly transcendent status" (5). This grants his definition a content boundary and a target for investigation. But it also includes the functionalist perspective of the shifting sacred, because it does not limit the objects around which such validity claims can be made. To the degree that anything or anyone is proclaimed as more than human, temporal, and contingent, it becomes an object of religion. As soon as an authority claim is based in scriptures, revelations, or immutable ancestral traditions, which themselves are declared to lie beyond history, they become religious. Religion, then, is processual and a form of framing (6), not a thing in itself.

Objections might be raised against the primacy of discourse in this definition, which practice then operationalizes, as it seems equally plausible, perhaps even likely, that the process is often inverted so that authorizing speech "discursivizes" ambiguous and multivocal practices (see, for example, Staal 1979; Bell 1992; Whitehouse 2000). Riesebrodt's recent contribution addresses this issue by demonstrating religion's existence in its "referential legitimations," the ways in which social actors implicitly recognize a category of something like religion in their historical exchanges, comparisons, borrowings, syncretisms, and legal regulations, quite apart from overt declarations or scholarly definitional debates.

If forced to define *diasporic religion,* I would propose the following:

Diasporic religion is the repertoire of discourses (words, acts, and objects) recognized and exchanged by a given social collectivity that is itself in diaspora—defined by the distance from a homeland, the continued existence of communities in multiple sites, and the conscious salience of, and public expression about, the distance dividing them. This set of practices sacralizes that homeland, the journey from that homeland, or the kinds of superhuman powers perceived as residing or originating in that place, by endowing it with the status of being transcendent, noncontingent, immutable, or beyond human vicissitudes to a greater degree than the hostland, and serves as a basis for organizing communities, ritual practices, and institutionalized formats of transmission around those special places, journeys, and territorialized powers.

Finally, it is worth formally discriminating between two distinct articulations of ideal types: religious diasporas and diasporic religions. *Religious diasporas* I take to denote extensions in space of a group whose most salient reference is religious identity rather than ethnic, racial, linguistic, or any other social bond, and whose process of dispersion is a direct consequence of that affiliation. Here we might consider Weber's invocation of a "Calvinist diaspora" (2002: 7) or the case of Puritans emigrating to North America. The Puritan movement to establish a transatlantic network of settlements was inherently a matter of professed religious affiliation, not of any other distinction from their English and Dutch homeland societies. To take a more recent example, we might consider the "Mormon diaspora" residing in Mexico and elsewhere, whose separateness within their hostland is based on a religious culture anomalous to the mainstream host society (Smith and White 2004).

Conversely, *diasporic religions* are the collected practices of dislocated social groups whose affiliation is not primarily or essentially based on religion but whose acts, locutions, and sentiments toward a distant homeland are mediated by, and articulated through, a religious culture. This second category is by far the larger and more encompassing one. Caribbean and South American emigrants in diaspora, for example, are not religious dissidents as such. Their emigration itself holds no religious meaning, viewed either as a trauma (in the case of enslavement) or as an economic opportunity (in the case of recent labor migrations). Their religious affiliations are companion identifications that take on special salience only in the attempt to give order and meaning to the new space and its relation to the places left behind. This study is especially devoted to the second category, that of diasporic religions. By viewing diasporic religious cultures as consequences of diasporization, not their root cause, we can attend to the creativity of new religious formations articulated in diaspora rather than view diasporic identity as part and parcel of a given religion's origins.

10. To take an example of a "classical" diaspora, Robin Cohen (1997) describes how Judaism became a thoroughly scriptural and rabbinical religion after the destruction of the Second Temple, in 70 C.E., as Jewishness in diaspora

increasingly became a religious identification. But this religious-enhancement hypothesis may be context-dependent. Migrants to the United States rely especially on religion because, as Herberg (1960) argued, religion is an approved and even valorized niche for maintaining distinctiveness in that sociopolitical and legal context. Incorporation in other, more secular host societies, such as Sweden or France, may imply just the opposite: the diminution of overt religious affiliations.

11. It would be a mistake to read Halbwachs as utterly dismissive of individual memory; rather, in his view, group and individual memory are inseparably related. As the individual memory is shaped in accord with "dominant thoughts of the society," group memory is realized and manifested in individual memories (1992: 40, 182). Durkheim, whose legacy Halbwachs inherited and mostly followed, also articulated this view, although it is seldom acknowledged. Durkheim's "collectivity" and "collective representations" are sometimes explicitly described in his work as an "understanding between minds" and a shared product of "individual consciousnesses," even as collective representations "hover above all the minds and individual events" (1995: 441, 443).

12. Judith Butler writes: "We are used to thinking of power as what presses on the subject from the outside, as what subordinates, sets underneath, and relegates to a lower order. This is surely a fair description of part of what power does. But if, following Foucault, we understand power as forming the subject as well, as providing the very condition of its existence and the trajectory of desire, then power is not simply what we oppose but also, in a strong sense, what we depend on for our existence and what we harbor and preserve in the beings that we are" (1997: 2).

13. Appiah (1992) carefully distinguishes *racialist* and *racist*. A racialist regards race as an accurate and salient classifier of groups of human beings, without any necessarily pejorative intent. A racist links such classifications to overtly negative sets of associated characteristics and uses these to reify social hierarchies.

14. See the black nationalist discourses of Martin Delaney, Henry Highland Garnet, Edward Wilmot Blyden, George Padmore, Alexander Crummell, Marcus Garvey, W. E. B. Du Bois, Kwame Nkrumah, and others. However, the various movements assumed very different political objectives, from Garvey's separatism to some Brazilian activists' ideals of national assimilationism (Hanchard 1994). As a more specific identifier, perhaps we should think of the African Diaspora as growing out of a century-long incubation of a sentiment of shared origins, including the moment of Garvey and Du Bois, the Harlem Renaissance, the influence of Melville Herskovits and other anthropologists who insisted on a continuing African legacy, the francophone *négritude* movement of Léopold Senghor and Aimé Césaire, and the U.S. civil rights movement of the 1960s. These layered and accumulating moments collectively established the idea of an African super-"nation" as a political and cultural artifact of the public domain.

15. Ironically, the Jewish (though nonreligious) Herskovits was the primary midcentury advocate of African and New World African continuities, while

E. Franklin Frazier, an African American sociologist trained in the Chicago School, which stressed urban processes of ethnic assimilation, was Herskovits's sparring partner and the primary critic of such cultural continuities (Frank 1997).

16. As Edward Alpers (2005) recounts in detail, the term *African Diaspora* was first employed by George Shepperson in a paper presented at the International Congress of African History held at the University of Dar es Salaam, Tanzania, in 1965 (first published in 1966). To cite an earlier paper by Alpers:

Indeed, when George Shepperson first joined "African" to "diaspora" in 1965, he explicitly did so because of the close parallels he saw between the Jewish diaspora and the dispersal of Africans as a consequence of the slave trade. Shepperson argued that African American and Caribbean intellectuals themselves had for a long time recognized and articulated connections between their own people in exile and that of the Jews. By his application of "diaspora" to the experience of "The African Abroad," as the session at which he presented his paper was entitled and his paper makes plain, he declared as an historian and an outsider that he, too, saw such parallels. Shepperson's achievement here was to recognize the great similarities in the comparative histories of these two great dispersions, especially the role of "slavery and imperialism" in the forced migration of both Jews and Africans, and to name the one by the term used for the other. (2001: 4)

17. The assumption of consciousness as black or a member of a pan-African movement was called a "conversion," as by Marcus Garvey in his speech "Explanation of the Objects of the Universal Negro Improvement Association," recorded in 1921.

18. Moreover, this identification offers no guarantee of being recognized as "African" by those who always identify or are read as black. Although the structures of feeling that constitute black culture originated within communities of African descent, they are no longer the exclusive property of those groups. Hence, in the film *8 Mile* (2002), the white rapper Eminem's grand triumph in the climactic rap showdown is to become culturally blacker than all his (epidermally) black rivals. He achieves this in part by portraying class and rapping skill as superseding skin color as authentications of blackness. Eminem's victorious lyric castigates his phenotypically black opponent as being in fact a bourgeois from a happy family, while his own childhood was one of dysfunctional despair. Yet the conversion of Eminem to authentic blackness is contested, to say the least. Kelefa Sanneh reported in the *New York Times* on a feud in which rival rapper Benzino Scott sings, in his song "Die Another Day": "I'm a king, you a little punk / You the rap David Duke, the rap Hitler / The culture-stealer" (Sanneh 2003).

19. Tölölyan (1996: 32) names the Romani, or Gypsies, as the primary example of a diaspora without even an imagined homeland. If the Romani serve as the ideal type for this kind of floating diaspora, modern blacks may share at least some of its features.

20. For example, Edmund Gordon reports that among Creoles of Bluefield, Nicaragua, some present as "black" and affiliate with signs and symbols of

Jamaica and the U.S. black movement, while others of similar appearance have no interest in Africa and introduce themselves as "Anglo" (Gordon and Anderson 1999: 282–83). Brent Staples recently wrote that Black Seminoles of Oklahoma locate their ancestry, not to mention their claims to civil rights, in their identity as Native American, not African (Staples 2003). Nancy Foner (1985) showed that Jamaican migrants to London and New York adapt differently to the distinct host societies, with those in New York working harder to maintain ethnic Jamaican identifications as a reaction to a more stringently racializing society that would render them simply "black."

21. The 2002 translation by Peter Baehr and Gordon C. Wells of Max Weber's *The Protestant Ethic and the "Spirit" of Capitalism* renders Weber's phrase *stahlhartes Gehäuse* as a "shell as hard as steel," in place of Talcott Parsons's translation, which renders the phrase as "iron cage" (Weber 1992: 121). Their wording is suggestive of the ways social identifications can become a kind of armor against the world, as well as prisons that limit individuals *in* the world. Emigration is often for Caribbeans a dual process of exploitation and expansion.

22. To be sure, all religious rituals are condensations of abstract and complex strings of ideas into manageable scripts and scenarios: "communion with God" is given narrative form in the Last Supper and physically articulated as bread and wine at the altar rail (Leach 1976: 37–38). But condensation has been especially characteristic of African Diaspora religions for reasons of secrecy and restricted space, and not only in the second diaspora: Bastide also invokes the term in discussing the urbanization of Afro-Brazilian religions. Condensation has long been a feature of African Diaspora religions in cities like Rio de Janeiro (Johnson 2002a) and Havana (David Brown 1989, 1999). But the process has been expanded with the second diaspora into cities where such religions are regarded as foreign and where no long-term, organic relation to city development obtains.

23. Defining the *orisha* (Cuban *oricha*, shortened to *ocha*), the deities originally of the Yoruba religion of southwest Nigeria, is a notoriously difficult enterprise, but there is a strong euhemerist strain: the deities of the Yoruba are great ancestors later divinized. One of the first attempts at defining the Yoruba gods came from William Bascom in 1938: "An orisa is a person who lived on earth when it was created, and from whom present day folk are descended. When these orisas disappeared or 'turned to stone,' their children began to sacrifice to them and to continue whatever ceremonies they themselves had performed when they were on earth. This worship was passed on from one generation to the next, and today an individual considers the orisa whom he worships to be an ancestor from whom he descended" (quoted in Apter 1992: 150). In this sense, orishas were patron deities of regional dynasties. They were also forces of various domains of nature and culture. In the New World, the orishas became classifying archetypes of people, including all their faults. For example, the Afro-Cuban thunder god Chango is just, but also a philanderer; the creator of humans, Obatala, is wise, but also aged and fragile; Ochun, the

god of rivers, is beautiful, but evinces a nouveau riche greed; the iron god who clears the paths, Ogun, is brave but also bull-headed.

24. The Petwo deities are those indigenously created in Haiti out of its social and political upheavals since the revolution (1794–1802), though they also appear to derive from Kongo practices. They are "hot," agitated, and violent in comparison with the "cool" West African pantheon (Rada). Stephan Palmié's (2002) notes that in Afro-Cuban practice, Petwo gods are spirit analogues of slave or wage labor, whereas Rada gods are spirit analogues of deep African roots, family lineage, and reciprocal gifts. A similar opposition seems to obtain for Vodou.

25. Eleggua, Ogun, Chango, Oya, Obatala, Ochun, and Yemaya.

Chapter 2. "These Sons of Freedom"

1. The neologism *transculturation* was itself an intellectual product of the Caribbean, first appearing in Fernando Ortiz's *Cuban Counterpoint: Tobacco and Sugar*, originally published in 1940. In part 2, chapter 2, "The Social Phenomenon of Transculturation and Its Importance," Ortiz writes that "the real history of Cuba is the history of its intermeshed transculturations" (1995: 98). The new word is superior to *acculturation*, Ortiz argues, because it does not imply a unidirectional adoption of a new culture. Rather, it suggests the nuances of culture loss or "deracination" as such losses, and the responses to them, continue to inform the immigrants' experience of a new territory. It also connotes the only partial and fragmentary adoption of a new culture, as well as the completely novel creations that are bound to arise through what Ortiz calls neo-culturation (103). More important than this semantic dexterity is the way Ortiz writes about "culture" in the history of Cuba, and by extension in the Caribbean basin in general, as the process of human interaction with, and thinking through, the material resources at hand. Tobacco and sugar, in Ortiz's hands, become a total semiotic system of contrasts through which the world is experienced: for example, whereas tobacco recalls magic (19, 46), and is immutably dark, "the color of its race," sugar connotes not magic but the commodification of a product born brown, then standardized to become white (9). In Ortiz's view, the material products of the island provide the lens through which issues of race and religion are perceived, contemplated, worked, and transformed.

Part 2, chapter 7, "The Transculturation of Tobacco," develops this idea further. It describes the shifting meanings of tobacco, from its ritual uses by the Taíno to its development into a European commodity and secular pleasure, an alkaloid eruption that, together with Chinese tea, Mexican chocolate, and Arabic coffee, fired the imaginative fires of the European Renaissance (207). As Fernando Coronil wrote in his introduction to a recent edition of *Cuban Counterpoint*, Ortiz thereby promotes a perspective that is both counterfetishist—against the view that human agents are utterly constrained by material dictates—and counterhumanist—against the view that human action stands free of the objects and materials of its production (F. Ortiz 1995: xvii–xviii).

If tobacco and sugar can be detached from their status as mere agricultural products and refigured as a symbolic system of meanings applied to every domain of experience, no less are deracinated humans of the Caribbean transcultured through their interactions with each other and with the products through which they know and make themselves. Indeed, Ortiz himself is an example. His early work was written from an evolutionary and racialist posture that disparaged Cuba's impurity and African influence, as in *Los brujos negros* (1906), before he came to view miscegenation as precisely the source of the religious, ethnic, and racial wealth of Cuba in *Cuban Counterpoint.*

One lesson from Ortiz is that religion must be viewed neither as sheer culture loss nor conversion (or "acculturation") but rather as the reading of new conditions through the prism of memory. Another lesson is that religion should be read in and through its materiality—the natural resources that frame and limit it, and the work lives of its enactors in relation to which its meanings are built.

The problems raised by a second term I employ here, *syncretism*, are well known. It at least tacitly marks some religions as "mixed," a term that can only signify in relation to the putative purity of others (Baird 1991). Moreover, the pejorative quality of the allegation of religious mixing—periodically taken up as a weapon in religious turf wars, as during the Reformation (Droogers 1989; Stewart and Shaw 1994; Stewart 1999)—has been imbricated with discourses of purity versus mongrelization in other domains like race and ethnicity, raising further troubling questions. Yet it remains as much circulated as ever, even if usually tempered by scare quotes. It appears, then, to be a term that, though problematic, is indispensable. Instead of inventing a euphemism to sidestep the issue, we should use *syncretism* both more courageously and more cautiously by specifying what it does and does not mean.

First, all religions are confluences or encounters. In the broadest vein, *syncretism* has no classifying power, because it describes all religions (Baird 1991: 146). It has also been cast as a cognitive procedure performed by persons in situations of culture contact, as in Herskovits's classic formulation: "The tendency to identity those elements in the new culture with similar elements in the old one, enabling the persons experiencing the contact to move from one to the other, and back again, with psychological ease" (Herskovits in Apter 1991: 240). Here too the term lacks signifying force, because all cognition works by perceiving and categorizing new phenomena in terms of what is already known. If the term fails both as a description of religion and of human psychology, what possible use can it still have?

For one, though all religions are confluences, the length of the encounter may differ dramatically. Egyptian religious culture was in contact with, and influenced, Greek religious culture over centuries; the encounter of the latter with messianic Judaism helped to spawn Christianity, again over the longue durée. Haitian Vodou was forged over several centuries through the confluence of diverse African religious cultures, Catholicism, Freemasonry, and a particular kind of kin-based tenure of land recognized as the burial grounds of family ancestors. These long fusions can be distinguished from relatively abrupt encounters, or "flash" syncretizing. Garifuna religious culture, as I show, took shape from such flash-syncretizing events, as Africans were abruptly cast onto the shores of the island of St. Vincent, there encountering both indigenous Amerindians and Roman Catholic missionaries, between 1650 and 1700; and again, when the Black Caribs were deported from St. Vincent to Central America in 1797.

Second, even abandoning the distinction between syncretic and nonsyncretic religions, we can retain the verb *syncretize* as a term of historical practice, the process of constructing common ground, memory making through the selection of what to maintain, incorporate or forget, or of mastering skills of code switching between potentially conflicting religious identifications (Apter 1991; Brandon 1993; Johnson 2002a).

Third, the degree to which religious adaptations are openly acknowledged rather than painstakingly hidden in the name of purity suggests a further plausible distinction, between overt and covert syncretizing—between religions that are in their own ideology relatively "open" or "closed" in their indebtedness to other religious traditions, and the issue of purity in discursive constructions of orthodoxy and authenticity (Apter 1991: 256). Charles Stewart calls this discourse "metasyncretic" (1999: 58). For example, in the context of African diaspora religions, many groups use the accusation of "syncretism" to disparage rivals and bolster their own authenticity. Conversely, the Cuban American and Puerto Rican American botánicas that sell the wares used in rituals are brazenly syncretic sites, juxtaposing Spiritist, African, Catholic, and other books and objects within a common framework of spirits and a shared ritual continuum of "cleansing" and pollution (Romberg 1998). Moreover, syncretism's valuation can be inverted to become a nation-building cipher, as has occurred in Brazil, Cuba, and Puerto Rico, places where miscegenation has become the basis of national pride (F. Ortiz 1995; Romberg 1998; Johnson 2002a). The Garifuna take pride in the multiple religious tributaries of their religious culture. They embrace Black Carib, African, and Roman Catholic influences and read themselves in relation to all three, but they code-switch between them depending on the context and the audience.

I offer this short rehabilitation in order to introduce Garifuna religious culture as an ethnogenetic series of syncretizing events. By *syncretizing event* I mean a confrontation and exchange between religious traditions that happened fairly abruptly rather than over centuries, that involved historical practice and choice, that led to dramatic rather than incremental transculturation, and that is acknowledged with pride as multistreamed by the Garifuna themselves. In doing so, I also draw on the original Greek meaning of *syncretism*—"to make two parties join against the third" (Plutarch, *Moralia* 2.490b, as cited in Martin 1983: 136; Stewart 1999: 45) as a temporary alliance between two city-states forged reactively in relation to a common enemy. Garifuna religious culture, that is to say, was made both by the forces it defended the Garifuna against and the groups with which they allied in defense.

2. There is a small but important discrepancy between the original French (in Hennepin's 1704 manuscript) and the English translation provided by Hulme and Whitehead. Where Hulme and Whitehead's version reads "There are a great number of negroes who live with them," the French version in Hennepin reads, "Il y a une quantité de Negres qui vivent *comme eux*" (italics mine). Whether the Africans lived "with them" or "like them," or both, is not entirely clear.

3. By 1764, Sir William Young, Britain's future governor of Dominica and a landholder on St. Vincent, found the Island Caribs completely dominated, "gradually extirpated or reduced to their obedience" (1764: 8). He uses the phrase "Black Charaibs" in writing by 1764 at the latest (W. Young 1971 [1795]: 19).

4. As J. Lorand Matory (1999, 2005) has shown, any panethnic consciousness of Yoruba as a shared ethnicity emerged only out of the colonial processes of the nineteenth century. Before that period it is more accurate to speak of specific city-state identities, such as that of Oyo.

5. Consider the comment of Olaudah Equiano: "Hitherto I had thought only slavery dreadful; but the state of a free negro appeared to me now equally so at least, and in some respects even worse, for they live in constant alarm for their liberty" (2004 [1789]: 117).

6. The Black Carib leaders clearly perceived the imperial intent of Braithwaite's visit. As Bryan Edwards later recounted, the context was as follows: The Duke of Montague in England had obtained the royal rights of possession to both St. Lucia and St. Vincent. But after being driven out of St. Lucia by the French, the British forces turned all their attention on St. Vincent. "Accordingly Capt. Braithwaite was dispatched thither, to try what effect persuasive measures might have in reducing the natives to the British yoke" (Edwards 1799: 105). But this persuasion was not easy. Even as early as 1719, the Black Caribs proved themselves quite capable of repelling a French-sponsored sally of five hundred troops sent from Martinique to dislodge them. Their guarded mien toward Europeans probably also derived from the fact that the rapprochement with the Island Caribs, who had initially tolerated them, long remained precarious; indeed, the increasingly vulnerable Island Caribs were complicit with the French in the 1719 attempt to banish the Black Caribs from St. Vincent (Kerns 1997: 22–23).

7. From 1763, when France ceded St. Vincent to Great Britain, until 1776, the island was administratively subject to the governor of Grenada. In 1776 it gained its own governor, namely Valentine Morris. It again fell to the French (and Black Caribs) in 1777 before reverting again to British dominion in 1783.

8. A small Island Carib enclave, established as a reserve in 1903, exists on the island of Dominica; a small number of Island Carib Amerindians also remain on St. Vincent, though many were killed in the volcanic eruption of Mt. Soufrière in 1902. There are sizable numbers of self-identified Carib Indian descendants in Trinidad and Tobago as well.

9. To balance the British colonial view, especially as represented by William Young II, Hulme recommends reexamining the little-known report of Alexandre Moreau de Jonnès, who as a young man of eighteen fought for France in the wars on and around St. Vincent, but also lived for several months in 1795 in intimate contact with the Caribs. Indeed, Moreau de Jonnès's testimony is surprisingly different from Young's. In his description, although the Red and Black Caribs were distinct and separate groups, the two "tribes" assembled "in important matters"—Moreau de Jonnès's own arrival on St. Vincent apparently being one, understood as related to the shared fight against the British, and the possibility of giving mutual aid during a hurricane being another. Most striking, Moreau de Jonnès describes the Red Caribs as a far larger group than the Black Caribs. Moreover, in describing the deportation from St. Vincent to the island of Roatán, Moreau de Jonnès marks no distinction between the Red and Black ethnic groups: he refers to just "the Caribs" (168).

This is an intriguing revision, and difficult to square with virtually all other reports, including other French ones not necessarily tainted by the "Africanizing" colonial interests that arguably shaded British depictions of the period. Leblond's report from 1767, for example, describes the Black Caribs as clearly a mélange, but much more African than Indian in appearance; and it states that only two families of Red Caribs remained on the island (2000 [1813]: 108, 110). If Moreau de Jonnès appears to inflate Red Carib numbers, Leblond's estimate was surely an exaggeration of Red Carib decimation, as some one thousand were reported on St. Vincent in 1833 (Alexander in Gonzalez 1988:23).

What shall we make of the dramatic contradictions in all of these reports? Hulme's important point about British colonists' self-serving Africanization of the Black Caribs can be expanded. The rhetorical attention to the putative "Africanness," or not, of the Black Caribs as a legitimizing pivot is striking not only because of the British exaggeration of it, but also because of Moreau de Jonnès's denial of it. For he expends as much effort on distancing the Black Caribs from Africanness as William Young II does in homologizing them. In Moreau de Jonnès's description, the Black Caribs are not African at all:

I believed, from the missionaries' tales, that they owed their origin to negro slaves escaped from neighboring colonies. I was much surprised to find them of quite another race. In place of woolly hair, of flat nose, of a gaping mouth set with thick out-turned lips, they possessed the traits of the Abyssinians: smooth hair, long and black, more like a mane, their nose was straight, standing out from the face but slightly curved at the end, and such as you would never see from Cape Bon to the Gulf of Guinea; finally, their mouth was furnished with thin lips in no way like that of a negro, except for the beauty of the teeth. They had, moreover, an air of sovereign pride. (1920 [1858]: 115)

Why this de-Africanizing of the Black Caribs in Moreau de Jonnès's depiction? Perhaps because from his pespective sixty years later (he wrote his memoirs of 1795 in 1858), an indigenous Carib status rendered them more admirable allies and beneficiaries of French protection in this romance than Africans. It is also possible, perhaps even likely, that the Black Caribs appeared more similar to their Amerindian cousins at the end of the eighteenth century than they do today, after two centuries of further métissage with other Caribbeans of African descent. Given this possibility, it seems plausible that all of the Caribs described by Moreau de Jonnès, both "Red" and "Black," might have been classified as Black Caribs by the British, based on their mixed-blood status and their political resistance to the British. The designations of red, yellow, and black were almost certainly applied differently by different colonial groups.

10. George Davidson wrote that the Black Caribs sold their tobacco principally in Martinique, where it was made into *macouba,* named after a district in Martinique where the best tobacco in the West Indies was once grown (1787: 18).

11. Douglas Taylor (1949: 390), who lived much of his life on Dominica, compares many Island Carib terms recorded in the seventeenth century by Breton with mid-twentieth-century Garifuna homologues: *ioulouca* (now *hiuruha*), benign ancestral spirits; *buai* (now *buyei*), shaman; *áhambue* (now *acámbouée*), spirits of the dead; *ufiè* (now *oúpoyem*), ghosts of evil deceased persons; *máfuia (mápoya),* evil bush spirits; *úmeu (oumécou),* spirits of the seashore. Most of these terms remain in use today.

12. The prevalence of saints in homes was noted especially by John Lloyd Stephens (1949 [1841]). Gonzalez (1988: 97) notes that 90 percent of Garifuna consider themselves Catholic, and that this identification is not in any way regarded as contradictory with ancestor rituals. This has been my observation in the communities where I have worked in Honduras as well, although the number of *evangélicos* is higher today than thirteen years ago, and these evangélicos aggressively resist and denounce the ancestor practices.

13. In a letter dated July 1771, the British colonial commissioners wrote: "In our opinion, the most effectual means of reducing them to obedience, will be to carry a road through their country, under protection of a sufficient military force, and after allotting them lands for their ample subsistence, to sell the remainder, which will very fully repay any expenses incurred by the arrangement, and contribute to keep them in order, by mixing white inhabitants amongst them" (W. Young 1971 [1795]: 79). As described in a letter from Valentine Morris on July 26, 1776, the journey from one side of the island to British posts on the other side was sixty miles and took three days; the proposed new road would shorten that distance to just fifteen miles by traversing the island's heights, then plagued by attacks from Black Caribs or runaway slaves (Morris 1787: 6). George Davidson's letter (1787: 20) aptly described the multilayered idea of conversion: "In short, the grand point at present to be aimed at is the civilization of them, and making them industrious, thereby rendering them first human beings before you attempt to make them Christians." The Black Caribs tried to prevent access to their lands from the new roads by posting giant, fierce hounds as gatekeepers (Moreau de Jonnès 1920 [1858]: 142).

14. Hugues, born in France, lived in Saint-Domingue until the beginning of the Haitian Revolution. Sympathetic to French revolutionary ideals, he was appointed commissioner of the French West Indies by the revolutionary council. As a military leader, he retook Guadeloupe from the British in 1794, executed

white French "traitors," armed the slaves, and fomented rebellion in British colonies. He was feared by British estate owners on St. Vincent not only for his aid to the Black Caribs but also because of the threat of his mobilizing their own slaves against them.

15. Forty-four slaves of the Black Carib and 102 Yellow or Red Caribs were also captured, though these were all returned to St. Vincent (Gonzalez 1988: 21).

16. Alexander Anderson's 1798 report attributes the deaths not only to disease but also, bizarrely, to "too much food" (1992: 228).

17. Gullick notes that Chatoyer became a nationalist symbol of St. Vincent during the later twentieth century, most often in the genre of a Black Power symbol (1995: 165).

18. Mondonga is a contemporary region in the interior of the Democratic Republic of Congo, but during and after the slave trade in Central and South America, the label *Mondongo* referred in general terms to the fact that "the man in question came from the interior, roughly to the north and east of the Congo (river) mouth" (Curtin 1969: 188).

19. Hodgson's 1757 report of this event appears in Bard (1965: 338, 357; cf. Thornton 1998: 284). The slave ships in this case were Dutch.

20. Beginning in 1816, the Mosquito King, George Fredrick II, was crowned in Belize, reestablishing the Mosquito Coast's status as a protectorate of Great Britain. Great Britain maintained a semiofficial jurisdiction over that region until 1894, when it was clearly declared as Honduran (as far south as Cape Gracias á Dios) and Nicaraguan (south of the cape).

21. The geographer William V. Davidson (1984a) actually locates this expansion in a series of submovements: the expansion east to Mosquitia from 1803 to 1814, the expansion west to Belize from 1802 to 1832, and the occupation of western Honduras and Guatemala from 1821 to 1836. Ruy Coelho, however, reports the founding of Livingston, Guatemala, by a Garifuna named Marco Díaz in 1804 (1995: 46). In western Honduras, both oral tradition and local histories of La Ceiba place the Garifuna arrival around the mouth of the Río Cangrejal much earlier. According to these accounts, the villages of Perú and Satuye (the latter no longer extant) were founded in 1810, and La Barra—now within the municipal limits of La Ceiba—in 1815 by early Garifuna pioneers like Celestino García and Francisco Nuñez (Canelas Diaz 1999: 41). Garifuna accounts claim founding dates around 1800 for Tela and its surrounding villages as well, though the evidence for these is unclear (García 1994: 26).

22. Swett was a member of a party of Southern gentlemen exploring the possibility of founding a colony in Central America rather than remain in the United States without slavery after the Civil War. Swett recommended against such a move, not only for financial reasons but also for others salient to this book's discussion of diasporic religion and memory: "The sighing of the winds of winter through the lattice, the cheerful fireside, with the domestic scene it is unnecessary to describe, make a picture most of us are familiar with, but is lost, forever lost to the emigrant in Honduras, though it can never be forgotten" (Swett 1868: 123–24).

23. Thomas Young wrote: "The men can hew and plant, hunt and fish, erect a comfortable house, build a good boat, make the sails, &c.; some are capital tailors, and others good carpenters; altogether there cannot be a more useful body of men" (1847: 124). They were mobile and multilingual; many were fluent not only in their own tongue but also in French (and French Creole), Spanish, and English (123). They were a people of "exceptional discipline and incorruptible morals" (Froebel 1859: 184); and "kind, industrious, provident, honest and faithful" (Bard 1965: 324). In short, now that their labor was needed and actual political sovereignty was not at issue, as it had been on St. Vincent, European observers' former lists of the Black Caribs' villainies changed into litanies of fantastic virtue (Kerns 1997: 32).

24. This is in itself a complex history. The Central American rebellions against Spain took shape as Spain capitulated to Napoleon in 1808, Joseph Bonaparte took the throne, and Spain was occupied. After 1814 Spain regained its autonomy under Ferdinand VII, but his reactionary measures and rigorous taxation in the Americas only further alienated the already-drifting colonies.

The contention that the Black Caribs' alliances were based on local loyalties and affinities should not surprise, as no wider imagined community had yet been constructed in Honduras. Even in the mid-nineteenth century, there were virtually no universities or newspapers in Honduras, and politics were disputed on a "localist" basis between the constituencies based in the settlement regions of Comayagua and Tegucigalpa (Barahona 1991: 233). Becerra (in Acker 1988: 34) reports that the first newspaper was founded in 1829, the first book press in 1836, the first bookstore in 1850, and the first public school at the end of the 1850s; these dates serve to reinforce the thrust of Barahona's contention about the lack of a national identity or a public sphere in mid-nineteenth-century Honduras. The Black Caribs' relationship to the incipient nation-states appears to have been capricious at best. My contemporary observations suggest that the relationship to the nation-state is today primarily cultivated through things like national and international soccer, as disseminated by television, and the service of a substantial number of young Garifuna men in the armed services.

25. Born in Spain in 1807, Subirana came to Cuba in 1850 and to the Republic of Honduras in 1856. He worked among the Garifuna on the north coast from 1858 to 1862 (W. Davidson 1984b: 449–51).

26. Swett reported finding six churches in the town of Belize, including two Episcopalian, one Methodist, one Baptist, one Presbyterian, and one Catholic (1868: 78). Additionally, Archibald Gibbs (1883: 151) noted that a Wesleyan community of North Americans was settled just a mile north of the Black Carib village at Punta Gorda.

27. Many Jamaicans arrived in Belizean, Guatemalan, and Honduran port towns like La Ceiba to work for the banana companies beginning in the late 1800s, occupying the so-called Barrio Inglés in that town (Gonzalez 1969: 34; Posas 1993: 16). Similar migration occurred in other Honduran port towns like Tela, Puerto Cortés, La Lima, and Puerto Castillo.

28. One specific catalyst was that, in 1893, the Honduran government began to compel the companies to purchase their bananas on the beach rather than on board ship, with the objective of shifting the costs of fruit spoiled during the transfer to the foreign transport companies' ledgers. This move, in theory, should have aided local producers by saving them money. But it had a quite different effect, motivating the fruit companies to establish their own plantations by buying up the coastal lands (Becerra 1983: 147).

29. Mario Posas (1993: 11) states that the first bananas were shipped out of La Ceiba in 1860 by a company owned by Santo Oteri, with its base in New Orleans.

30. To take just one of many possible examples, the song by Frank Silver and Irving Cohn, "Yes, We Have No Bananas," sold twenty-five thousand copies a day in 1923, and Silver went on the road to play packed houses with his Banana Band. F. Scott Fitzgerald's semiautobiographical novel *Tender Is the Night* describes a 1920s France with resort bands playing the hit tune and one man practicing English by reciting the lyrics (2003 [1933]: 59, 68).

31. As Alison Acker (1988: 59) notes, between 1862 and 1915, concessions were granted to no fewer than 276 mining companies, almost all of them foreign-owned. Virtually all of these were bought out and conjoined into the "New York and Honduras Rosario Mining Company," owned by Washington S. Valentine (whose daughter married the son of the Honduran president, Marco Aurelio Soto [Euraque 1996: 12]). When the world economy dropped the silver standard for currencies in 1900, much of the profitability was lost. The decline of mining set the stage for the fruit companies to become the primary industry in Honduras, accounting for more than 60 percent of all exports by the 1920s (Euraque 1996: 6).

The welcome accorded northern immigrants is described by Swett (1868: 100–06). The potential colony of disgruntled post–Civil War Southerners was offered free land and exemptions from almost all civil responsibilities in Honduras, presumably because they represented immigration of the right type.

32. The power of the fruit companies far exceeded the authority of local government institutions and often actively opposed the very nation-building infrastructures that had provided the incentive for their presence in the first place. In La Ceiba, for example, the Vaccaro brothers' Standard Fruit Company repeatedly shut down the press and, with it, any possibility of dissent from land and policy decisions favorable to their own interests (Canelas Diaz 1999: 40). In 1901, United Fruit took over running the Guatemalan postal service and even collected tariffs from ships arriving at Puerto Barrios, the nation's main port. In the boldest neocolonial incursion of all, in Honduras, General Manuel Bonilla was handpicked, armed, and enthroned as president in 1912 by Samuel Zemurray, the founder of the Cuyamel Fruit Company and the main shareholder of United Fruit. This coup was carried out to repeal threatened export taxes on fruit (Acker 1988: 60–64; Euraque 1996: 7). The U.S. government, under the incoming president Woodrow Wilson, turned a blind eye to such high jinks, perceiving its own national interests and its regional influence to be at stake.

33. Gonzalez (1969: 42) provides rough data on Garifuna dock work with the fruit companies in 1956: United Fruit employed 500 dockworkers and a subsidiary another 650 at Puerto Cortes, and 240 in Tela. In La Ceiba, the Standard Fruit Company employed around 400 people on the docks. Of these, Gonzalez estimates that two-thirds to three-quarters were Garifuna. Although such numbers would supply nowhere near full employment for Garifuna men, they would have been sufficient to provide local employment to a substantial group of men in every village. These numbers include only the positions that were most valued by Garifuna. Many, however, labored in other arenas, such as field work, crating, and crate assembly, or working as foremen, drivers, and bookkeepers (Centeno García 1997: 64).

34. Interview, October 24, 2000, Corozal, Honduras. This interview, like all interviews unless otherwise noted, was conducted in Spanish and translated by me.

35. Interview, October 23, 2000.

36. This is an assessment that scholars are just beginning to consider. As Darío Euraque (2003) recently argued, for example, the recognition of the Garifuna's expanding political power on the Caribbean coast helped to generate an "indigenist" movement in the 1920s and '30s that marginalized blacks, including the Garifuna, and excluded them from the Indo-mestizaje national symbolism of Honduras.

37. Labor solidarity may have been one of the reasons that many Garifuna of the village of San Juan (Garifuna: Durúgubuti), just west of Tela, supported the 1937 armed rebellion against the dictatorship of General Tiburcio Carías Andino (president from 1933 to 1948). The objective of these agents of the Liberal Party against the Nationalist Party was to reinstate the exiled leader Jesús Usmaña after Carías remained in office beyond the constitutionally legitimate period—propped up, like Anastasio Somoza in Nicaragua, Jorge Ubico in Guatamela, and Hernández Martinez in El Salvador, by the fruit companies and U.S. support. The reprisal for this participation was the brutal execution of twenty-two unarmed Garifuna in San Juan (Garcia 1993; Yuscaran 1997; Meléndez 2002: 67).

38. Morales was first elected in 1954 but was initially unable to take office because Julio Lozano Díaz seized power. Though Morales represented a major political advance for the prospects of a civil society and human rights, he was far from perfect and at times imposed civil order with repressive police organs like the new Guarda Civil. Moreover, he was deposed by coup d'état in 1963 by Nationalists who then exacted reprisals against labor unionists, whose names were provided by Standard Fruit (Centeno García 1997: 119–21). My point here is not to portray Morales as a hero but rather to signal the gradually increasing authority of the state with which the transnational fruit companies had to contend. For example, in 1983, when Standard Fruit tried to muscle the Honduran president Suazo Córdova into devaluing the lempira, the Honduran currency, to help cut their losses, Córdova firmly resisted (Posas 1993: 68–69, 76).

39. Candido and Lopez, interviews, village of San Juan, June 15, 2001.

Chapter 3. Shamans at Work in the Villages

1. Santería, or Lukumi, intercedes with a condensed Yoruba pantheon of orichas in terms of petition and exchange. Palo Monte summons the force of the dead, called nkisi, represented in "sticks" *(palos)* kept in iron cauldrons *(calderon, nganga,* or *prenda)*. According to Stephan Palmié (2002), the systems are "calibrated" in relation to each other. The orichas refer to deep African roots and kinship relations; Palo, in contrast, makes reference to mercenary "contracts" and the commodification of humans under enslavement and colonization. The nkisi is not petitioned but rather commanded and even brutalized, and the themes of warfare, military conquest, and the need to "tie" and "bind" enemies and defend one's own territory are central.

2. In some accounts, one reads of distinct levels of powers: for Suazo (2000), following Coelho (1955), the most exalted of departed spirits are gubida, former ancestors who have completed their postmortem sojourn to the land of the dead, Sairi. Below these are hiyuruha, the tutelary spirits who advise entranced shamans (buyeis) during divination and healing procedures. Lower still are the ahari, those recently deceased and perhaps still present in the village. In practice, and in actual discourse, I have found far less clear a hierarchy and far more idiosyncrasies of interpretation among shamans. Even in the scholarly literature there are variations: for example, Marilyn Wells's research in Belize identified the hiyuruha specifically as the spirits of deceased shamans (1982b: 46). Most important is the distinction between helper spirits and afflicting spirits. While both groups are ancestral, helping spirits are in general longer dead, and therefore further removed from earthly life and less needy. In Byron Foster's assessment (1994: 45), the malevolent gubida and beneficial ahari represent stages in a ritual continuum of the effects of spirit possession: the goal of the dügü is to transform harmful, uncontrolled spirit possession, referred to as possession by gubida, into beneficial, controlled spirit possession, referred to as possession by ahari. The ability to control possession is, of course, precisely what differentiates the shaman from the layman. As is common in religions of the African Diaspora like Candomblé, the calling to become a religious leader begins as an uncontrolled affliction or possession. Becoming a shaman is in part a mastery of the affliction, the ability to enter and depart from it at will.

The shamanic work of offering consultations with the spirits is nearly continuous throughout the year; however, from mid-December to mid-January every year, the ahari are said to "return to Sairi," the spirits' otherworld, commonly also understood as St. Vincent (Yurumein). At this time the spirits' and buyeis' services are unavailable.

3. "Family in the big house" refers to the spirits manifested during the dügü, for which a special structure *(dabuyaba)* is constructed (see chapter 5).

4. Dabwi often appears to be not only a spirit with his own separate identity but also Carlos's alter ego. Just as Dabwi is said to be nearing death, so Carlos foretells his own early demise. Just as Dabwi prefers the Toyota 4-Runner, so Carlos longs for such a vehicle. Shamans frequently speak of their most intimate spirit as reflecting their own qualities and desires.

5. In Corozal, I interviewed three devotees of Bahai—Castillo, Brenda, and the late Don Coronil—though, according to them, the total number of Bahais in this particular village ranged from nine to twenty-five. While these individuals support "traditional culture" in general terms, they are also proud of being "modern": they repeatedly called attention to the wastefulness of ancestor rituals and emphasized that such resources could be much more usefully devoted to rational development projects. They also noted specific conflicts: while tradition calls for the wearing of black during a period of mourning *(luto)* following a family member's death, said Brenda, "the prophet said not to wear a sad face or depressing clothes. For me, black is a color for an elegant evening dress." Devotees of Bahai, like Rosicrucians, are mostly private in their religious affiliation; they hold no distinctive rituals, though the Bahais gather periodically for discussions or teaching sessions.

6. For New York Garifuna, hammocks are symbols particularly evocative of the homeland—in part because hanging hammocks from urban apartment buildings is impossible.

7. The medicines dispensed range from the most mundane to arcane herbal formulas. For stomach ailments, Carlitos often gives patients Pepto-Bismol. Mango is recommended for the lungs. In multiple villages I encountered the same non-Garifuna couple from the town of Tela selling their medicines to buyeis out of a suitcase. *Vino de carne* (meat wine, in the form of pills) and *hierro* (iron) capsules were available to remedy impotence. From Peru came the herb *unha de gato* (cat's claws) in capsules for AIDS. "Florida water" was purchased for purifications, and "gluto-phos" for its advertised properties of "cerebral revitalization," along with Chinese soaps and lozenges. One shaman purchased L800 (US$53, a month's wages for a typical worker) worth of medicines all at once from these salespeople. Many other medicines, on the other hand, derive from local herbs. It seems safe to suggest that while some medicines have real curative properties, in other cases the potential cure depends on the charisma of the buyei and the framing of the illness within a ritual system and social context, which changes it from a mysterious individual affliction to a social problem.

8.

Heigüa guringuri lebuga
Agura gubadina
Sefubadina lidagiña idamunia
Sefubaina mowenamuga
Lidan idamuni.

(Translation from Pollito of Corozal)

9.

Gundatina, sal baladina
Gundatina, sal baladina
Gloria, alelulujah, sal baladina
Lidangiñe figo sal baladina.

(Translation from Pollito of Corozal)

Chapter 4. Shamans at Work in New York

1. As a Haitian informant told Elizabeth McAlister, "In New York, it's too closed. It's not open enough. Too much buildings, too much windows. It's not open enough. You need big areas. There's remedies, there's medications it is impossible to find here" (McAlister 1992: 17).

2. I attended a Santería *bembe* with Tola on October 17, 2004, in a school at 106th and Lexington in East Harlem. Judging from her familiarity with people there, it seems fair to call her a regular, and she was clearly a member of the Santería network. On Vodou, she mentioned in particular a party for the lwa Gede at a bar called Tiger's Den after the 2003 Halloween parade in Greenwich Village. Felix Miranda broadened the scope of these interreligious exchanges, citing rituals he attended held by his Trinidadian Indian (South Asian) neighbors, as well as Jamaican Kumina rituals in Brooklyn.

3. President Bush designated the African Burial Ground in Lower Manhattan, where an estimated twenty thousand former slaves and free blacks were interred, as a national monument in February 2006. This designation, however, merely served to open further political disputes as to whether official recognition had diminished the burial ground by underestimating its physical area.

4. Contact with practitioners of Vodou is a recent phenomenon in New York and quite an old one in Central America, perhaps dating back to contact with Haitians already in residence when the Caribs arrived at Trujillo on the Central American mainland in 1797. Cross-influences could derive from even earlier, on St. Vincent, as the Caribs were part of the francophone revolutionary network directed by Victor Hugues.

5. The World Garifuna Organization (WGO) had its seeds in New York in 1994, when representatives from six Garifuna organizations from Honduras, Guatemala, the United States, and Belize met to establish common objectives. As documented in the WGO's literature, the groups were Unification of Garifuna Culture, Libaya Baba Garifuna Students Association, the United Garifuna Association, the Garifuna Guatemalteca-Yurunei Association, the Prometra Society, and the National Garifuna Council of Belize. The organization was formally launched six years later, on April 12, 2000. Its stated objectives include the unification of the Garifuna people, claiming reparations from the British government for historical atrocities committed against Garifuna, and promoting the social, economic and cultural progress of the Garifuna people. The primary organizers behind the group were and continue to be Dr. Theodore Aranda, of Belize, and Felix Igemeri Miranda, of New York. Though the issue is not included in their printed statements, WGO also aspires to the establishment of a Garifuna "culture park," with monuments, exhibits, and a study center in Belize.

The establishment of the WGO as an umbrella organization encompassing all other national and local organizations has failed to achieve unity among these groups. A vociferous battle for resources and allegiances continues, and allegations of self-interested actions taken by leaders are widespread.

6. Following Foucault, I view this as a drive to discourse that always accompanies entry into the public sphere (Johnson 2002a). The transfer from underdetermined ritual meaning to explicit discursive meaning occurs as part of the process of the Garifuna's becoming a known entity in the identity politics characteristic of U.S. society. Practically speaking, this process occurs through representations made in interviews, artistic displays in museums, books, and folkloric presentations in restaurants, festivals, and other venues. Such representations are constrained by several factors, including the competition among various groups for limited semiotic and physical space and the funding required to maintain representations once they come to occupy public space.

Chapter 5. Ritual in the Homeland

1. Common estimates of total costs for the performance of a dügü range from L80,000 ($5,333) to more than L300,000 ($20,000). While the latter figure is probably somewhat inflated, in view of Kerns's (1997: 221) report of an especially lavish dügü in Belize costing $1,300, and most costing much less, my impression is that a dügü does cost drastically more it did than three decades ago. Honduran Garifuna attribute this increase to the growth of a dügü "industry" that thrives on funds from U.S. relatives and on the competition between families and between buyeis, who use the rituals as public demonstrations of wealth and power.

2. A shaman's initiatory process begins in the same way. Becoming a buyei, therefore, is part of the same complex of exchanges between the living and the ancestors. To become a buyei is the ultimate sacrifice, involving a lifetime of serving the spirits. In this exchange the spirits will not merely be satisfied, but will become partners. The discourse of the shaman's sacrifice is no doubt in part self-serving, as there are clear benefits as well as liabilities entailed in the vocation.

3. All monetary conversions are based on an approximate exchange rate of fifteen lempira to one U.S. dollar.

4. Thanks to Paula Chaves for help with translating these song lyrics as well as the comments of the buyei.

5. Foster 1994: 43. He offers a Garifuna transcription as well:

Lirun wawaiyasuni nibari,
Waluahainayanu wabaya gayau.
Wahuyuragubai ganali,
Hadise wenebafa nibari.
Lisemehebeyeri Aurayuna gayaü, raramahayadugu wagiya,
Lisemehebeyeri Aurayuna gayaü, atuluhaina tia gayali.

6. The leaves come from a climbing vine that grows around trees near the village, whose specific name eluded my informants. These are boiled in water. In infusions for use on boats and material structures like walls, disinfectants like ammonia, creolina (a cleaner made of coal tar), and sulfur powder can be added.

7. The dangers of reading symbolic meanings from one place and moment into another were revealed by the following incident: Having learned about the barrier of white powder surrounding the temple, I later saw a shaman spreading a white powder before the door of her home. When I asked whether this space, too, required such special efforts at spiritual protection, she looked up in surprise and said, "This is poison for ants." On another occasion, I witnessed a buyei pouring sand under a young man lying in a hammock in a state of possession. "Does the ancestor want to feel beach sand underfoot?" I asked. She replied, "No, he just threw up."

8. I gave a modest, though in local terms generous, L1,200 ($80) to help resolve the impasse, judging that this amount would help but not in itself alter the course of events. I refused many other requests, such as suggestions that I single-handedly sponsor initiations or lemesi. In such cases I would have been creating ritual events that would not otherwise have taken place.

9. The craft of weaving these baskets of palm fronds is now nearly lost. They must be specially ordered well in advance from a craftsman in the Garifuna town of Limón; in the western villages where my fieldwork was done, no capable artisans remain.

10.

Dibigida niabo guagi
Tidabuyabari Wasana
Au rabuni, amurununi
Wasa narihini Sairi.

Wasana is a female ancestor of the now-anonymous songwriter. I am obliged to Tola Guerreiro for her rough transcription and translation into Spanish. The English translation is my own.

11. The dance is not everywhere standard. A Belizean observed that it was not performed at Belizean Garifuna dügü ceremonies, nor have I seen it at all Honduran Garifuna performances. The dance is often associated with Christmas time, the Day of Kings (Epiphany, January 6), and saints' days. Its inclusion in the dügü may indicate an increase in ritual complexity as the dügüs become more frequent and buyeis compete with each other in demonstrating the most complete traditional knowledge and elaborating the most comprehensive ritualizations.

12. This story is certainly apocryphal. In the Carib Wars of the late eighteenth century, the Black Caribs were notorious for their guerilla warfare, not for direct attacks, whether disguised or not. Moreover, the disguise is not of sufficient verisimilitude to function as a viable battle tactic. The origins of the dance and the white masks are unclear.

13. The English translation is my own, from Meléndez's Spanish version. He also included the Garifuna transcript:

Urruwa irumu naume nadagumein
Luma nasiñumafallerumutina nasiñu,
Gadiliñafuna . . . lugudeme nuni nee
Memenija nanigui da lagumuchun nidane.

14. Jenkins and Jenkins (in Greene 1998: 175–76), working in Belize, report a wide range (four to thirty) in the number of mali that may be performed in any given dügü. In my fieldwork in Honduras, the performance of four mali per day has been standard. This discrepancy may reflect regional variation or an increasing standardization of the dügü during the past two decades.

15. The symbolic importance of cassava and cassava bread has only increased since Hurricane Mitch, in November 1998, when in many villages of Honduras all seedlings were washed away. Moreover, many families now raise pigs, which dig up vulnerable cassava plants. As a result, cassava-bread production, a central communal activity for women, has been suspended in many places.

16. Eastern villages like Limón and even Aguan are reported to have active groups of male singers, and I have also witnessed them in the Bronx. But in Triunfo de la Cruz, San Juan, and Corozal, large western villages close to mestizo cities, few men are actively engaged. Men are at times the objects of ridicule by women, who sometimes used me as their foil: "Look, even the American is trying to learn; what's the matter with you, *pendejo* [coward or idiot; literally 'pubic hair']!"

17. The transcription and translation of this song and the next are from Carlos Castillo of Corozal.

18. The transcriptions and translations into Spanish are by Carlos Castillo and Marcelina Fernandez. The translation into English is my own.

19. Some anxiety was expressed that both boats might arrive in the same village. In that case, different families would be called on to carry out the dügüs.

20. The idea of a ritual's "working," of course, depends on the converse possibility of failure. Such failures, or "misfires," have been addressed, albeit in different ways, by Grimes (1990) and Hollywood (2002), both playing off the linguistics terminology of Austin (1962) and Bell (1992). Examples also appear in Geertz (1973: 122) and Durkheim (1995 [1915]). Bourdieu's description of the horse in a play's script, which interrupts the flow by defecating on stage, provides an analogous example (2002: 2).

21. This definition of power is set against the more standard sociological meaning, the ability to impose one's will on others. World religions, especially Christianity, are often characterized as exerting hegemonic power, while the religions of subaltern groups are often depicted as religions of "resistance." But even among marginal groups, rituals are never simply empowering, never only "resistance": to assert that they are is to repeat a romantic primitivism. Performing a ritual entails submitting one's being to codes and obligations that may be viewed on one occasion and by one actor as empowering and by another as oppressive. The interpretation is often a question of the observer's perspective. Hence Tolstoy: "Philosophic historians at times, when they wish it to be so, when it fits in with their theory, say that power is the result of events; and at times, when they want to prove something else, they say power produces the events" (1931: 1106). At the very least, the dügü entails the forfeiture of economic resources, themselves a form of power, with the hope that the expenditure will be more than compensated in the spirits' aid, which may or may not

take economic form. Ritual should be seen as a wager of resources—time, bodily labor, money, material goods, and social capital—on a hoped-for outcome. It always involves giving up at least one kind of power for a different kind, a superhuman or transcendent version. Whether this exchange is ultimately emancipatory or mystifying remains open to debate in every case.

Chapter 6. Ritual in the Bronx

1. A similar pause obtains in the ritual cycle of the Afro-Brazilian religion of Candomblé, where the *terreiros,* or temples, typically close just before Christmas and reopen just after Easter. For both Garifuna and Candomblé, the breaks suggest the close imbrication with the Catholic ritual calendar. Yet they also suggest a recognition (perhaps implicit) of the separation from Catholic practices. Such breaks confound simplistic assertions of the seamless syncretism between these traditions and Catholicism.

2. I refer here to "the public event" because an additional consequence of ritual performance in the constrained spaces of New York is the segmentation of rituals into parts. A private ceremony for the return of the ancestors was held in a buyei's apartment on the proper day, January 15. The public ceremony, however, needed to be held on a Saturday night to fit work schedules. *Public* in general refers here to being open to all Garifuna, but sometimes it takes on a broader meaning. The return of the ancestors in 1999, for example, was written up and photographed for the *New York Times* (January 31, 1999).

3. The organization Vamos a La Peña was founded in 1987 by Nieves Ayress and Victor Toro, two Chilean activists imprisoned in Chile under Augusto Pinochet. The phrase comes from a poem by the Chilean poet Violeta Parra, referring to a rock where indigenous groups met to plan resistance against the Spanish. Since December 9, 2002, La Peña has itself been exiled and become, in a sense, diasporic. New owners took possession of the building and immediately assumed an adversarial position toward the organization. Despite long legal battles and numerous protests, La Peña's lease was terminated, dealing a blow to groups like the Garifuna and many others for whom the organization's headquarters had provided a welcome shelter. La Peña continues, however, as a multisited movement, El Moviemento la Peña del Bronx. The lack of a spatial center, or "rock" *(peña),* has dissipated, but also disseminated, the movement's work.

4. Bronx Garifuna recall their homeland villages with parties to celebrate the festival of each village's patron saint. Videos of the simultaneous parties in the homeland and in the Bronx are exchanged.

5. Reckitt's Crown Blue is an ammonia-based laundry-whitening product first manufactured in England in the nineteenth century. It remains available today in many botánicas for "baths" or the protective preparation of a room and seems to be associated with the "cooling" and pacifying effects of the color white more generally.

6. The gesture of throwing something backward over the shoulder after engaging in ritual work is not only part of the Afro-Cuban Santería repertoire but is also frequent in Candomblé (Johnson 2002a), suggesting that it has been stabilized as a shared act in African diasporic religions.

7. At the beginning of each year a group of prominent Cuban *babalawos* (diviners, "fathers of secrets") from the Santería religion gather to divine the ruling orishas of the coming year. The results are publicized in the New York Latino press; they are also followed closely by some Garifuna leaders and matched with key events from their own, and the Garifuna homeland, experience. Tola said, "Remember Hurricane Mitch from 1998? That was the year of Oya [the Yoruba-Cuban goddess of the tempest]." In 1999 the orishas were Oshun and Yemoja, and the return of the ancestors photographed for the *New York Times* shows the Garifuna uniforms of that year to be yellow and blue, the colors of Oshun and Yemoja, respectively.

8. The woman who performed these unusual gestures cannot comment on her possible influence by Vodou because protocol mandates that possession priests have no memory of their action or words after the event. The degree of dissociation (to take a psychiatric term) that occurs during trance varies widely, with some dancers in full control of their actions (indeed, fakery is an indigenous as well as an analytical category, and a common accusation in Candomblé as well as Garifuna gubida religion). Regardless of where trance performers fall on this continuum, they almost always report having "no memory."

9. Other Garifuna, especially those residing in Brooklyn, report knowledge of and visits to Jamaican Kumina ceremonies as well.

10. This is the Franklin H. Williams Caribbean Cultural Center/African Diaspora Institute. The statement from the center's website indicates its institutional importance not only in New York but also internationally, as well as its Yoruba focus:

> Since 1976 the Caribbean Cultural Center has remained committed to developing programming that highlights the traditions and cultures of the African Diaspora. . . . [T]he Center has worked to provide our audiences with access to traditional leaders and scholars expert in the African-based traditions which have been transported to and transformed in the Americas.
>
> It is from the Caribbean Cultural Center's 1980 "Expressions International Festival" that the ideas and plans for the implementation of the First International Conference on Orisha Tradition and Culture were developed.
>
> The first conference took place in Ile Ife, Nigeria, in 1981. This historic gathering facilitated the reunion of leaders and devotees of the Yoruba-based traditions from throughout the African diaspora. The meeting of traditional leaders and scholars expert on the religions of Santería (Lukumi), Candomblé, Vodun, Shango and other belief systems maintain the philosophy, traditions, and culture of Africa in the Americas. . . . The three conferences affirmed that communities of African descent throughout the diaspora, have managed to maintain (shared) sacred belief systems that have nurtured the proliferation of common values, ethics, and aesthetic visions that have influenced popular cultures globally. (Caribbean Culture Center 2005)

11. The outside observer, in any case, cannot perceive the primary analogy in the same way as practitioners do, as she or he is biased toward visual models of objects and their relationship. Practitioners' perceptions, based in kinesthetic models, are likely to form classes and relationships differently (Shore 1996: 67). Mitigating this difference, however, is the existence of multiple factions within the same religion, some of who read themselves as cosmopolitans. They not only perform rituals but also videotape them for critical commentary. Because they now also make visual models from their own kinesthetic models, they are on the way toward becoming indigenous ethnographers, and they provide a bridge (as well as a filter) for outsiders' understandings.

Chapter 7. Finding Africa in New York

1. Spiritism arrived in the Caribbean in the late nineteenth century through the teachings of Allan Kardec. Its popularity derived from its healing techniques, enacted through mediums in ways that were as emotionally compelling as they seemed scientific. For Spiritists, mediums became effective healers when possessed by more ancient, enlightened souls. Today, the mediums dress in white or blue medical clothing to offer "passes" *(passos)* over the bodies of their subjects, moving their hands over the skin to attract negative vibrations to their own hands and release them into the air. The healing spirits are from "evolved" civilizations: doctors or healers from Europe, ancient Egypt, or the Aztec empire. Sickness is regarded as "obsession," and the ritual intervention is a "dis-obsession," wherein one medium incorporates the obsessing spirit while other mediums use their evolved entities to advocate for their client's "release." Meetings reflect a high degree of rational, bureaucratic organization.

2. The Seven African Powers include Chango or Santa Barbara, representing sensual pleasure; Eleggua or the Holy Guardian Angel, who represents opportunity; Obatala or Our Lady of Mercy or Las Mercedes, representing peace and harmony among people; Oshun or Our Lady of Caridad del Cobre, for marriage; Oggun or Saint Peter, for war and work for the unemployed; Orunla or Saint Francis of Assisi, who gives power by opening the doors to the past and the future; and Yemaya or Our Virgin of Regla, who represents fertility and maternity (Peréz y Mena 1977: 133).

3. As Wole Soyinka noted in his 1986 Nobel Prize acceptance speech, Frobenius's love of Yoruba art had no bearing on his disgust for the Yoruba people, whom he described as possessing a "degenerate and feeble-minded posterity" unworthy of such beauty.

4. Though this is not the place to recapitulate the history of race theory, it is worth noting, with Appiah (1990: 276), that the binding of biologically heritable characteristics with moral and intellectual qualities is racialist, but not necessarily racist. Racialism can result in positive as well as negative readings of skin color. When Afro-Brazilians "inculture" the Catholic mass by adding drumming

and dance because "that is what black people like," the binding of aesthetic preference to skin color is racialist, though not necessarily insidious (Burdick 2004). Racism occurs when racialist views are taken as negative, evil, contaminating, and warranting action against them.

5. Whiteness has been forged through religion as well. Bennett (2004) argues that Catholic parishes served as the main venue in the transition of New Orleans from a three-race (white, black, and creole) to a two-race society (white and black) between 1890 and 1920. The Brazilian religion of Umbanda has likewise served as a forum for affixing race categories, as it balances European Kardecist, African, and Amerindian influences to varying degrees (R. Ortiz 1978; Diane Brown 1986; Johnson 1998; Hale 2004). John Burdick (1998: 119–48), meanwhile, demonstrated that women evangelical converts in Brazil begin to view being black *(negra* or *preta)* with pride even as their cultural Africanness is diminished by their rejection of the Afro-Brazilian religious options. Among evangelicals, racial or ethnic identifiers are subsumed by the more fundamental, encompassing categories of "saved" and "unsaved" (124). This attitude has led to the accusation that evangelical converts are "whitened." To the contrary, Burdick found, these women express more agency as black women, not only viewing the church as a "haven from racism" (Chestnut 1997: 124) but also engaging in overtly political action to a greater degree than either practitioners of "inculturated Catholicism" or devotees of the African saint Blessed Anastácia.

6. The racializing experience of emigration to the United States is not always simply negative. Maxine Margolis (1994: 234–35) documents that Brazilians arriving in New York (80 percent of whom are "white" by either Brazilian or U.S. standards) find black and white color codes to be more rigidly defined in the United States then in Brazil. Yet they also begin to develop a fuller picture of blacks than is typical in Brazil. In the United States blacks are visible in leadership positions, as members of elites, and as clients in restaurants and stores. In Brazil, though color lines are more fluid, the meaning of color is more rigidly defined: it would be extremely rare to encounter a dark-skinned person dining in a fine restaurant or occupying a position of authority. Afro-Brazilians are always represented on Brazilian television as musicians, soccer players, or domestic servants *(empregadas).*

7. We should note, too, that individuals may be "blackened" or "whitened" against their own will. According to Henry Louis Gates Jr., O. J. Simpson "was famous rather than black; that is, until the African-American community took its lead from the cover of *Time* and, well, blackened him" (1997: 118). Consider, too, the case of Jimi Hendrix, derided as a "white nigger" for playing "minstrel" to largely white audiences (Gilroy 1993: 93).

8. This typical model of Caribbean emigrants isn't monolithic, however. For example, James Clifford (1994) recounts a moment in the 1980s when East Indians in Britain identified as black in an effort to expand their political capital through social and political links to larger and more powerful groups.

Conclusion

1. The aperture metaphor is inspired by Bergson's (1896) description of memory as akin to the focusing of a camera.

2. Authenticity may also describe the degree of conformity between appearance and reality. Lionel Trilling called Wordsworth's protagonist in the poem "Michael" a first exemplar of literary authenticity (1972: 93): as he sits grieving the death of his son, he radiates nothing but grief. There is no dissimulation or distraction, no mask. He is transparent, authentic, truly himself. To raise the question of authenticity is to inquire after the continuity of an object, idea, or person with an original (Benjamin 1968: 220). To be sure, the notion of originality itself is fluid. On that score, Raymond Williams describes the key transition between its denotation of a point in time from which all things arose and its denotation of that which is singular, beginning in the late seventeenth century (Williams 1983: 230).

3. The firm distinction between "cultic" and "political" functions does not consistently hold up even in Benjamin's own examples. Raphael's *Sistine Madonna* was commissioned as a backdrop for the coffin of Pope Sixtus (actually that of Julius II); the "located" meaning therefore suggests the Virgin's coming to fetch the pope to heaven. Surely this sort of posthumous staging is every bit as "political" as Raphael's later museumification.

4. Rappaport (1999: 55) offers a clear example: driving a Rolls-Royce signifies wealth in a way that is different from claiming, "I am rich." The Rolls signifies indexically because it both points to wealth and materially constitutes it.

5. Similarly, the statement "I love you" does not merely point to the abstract existence of love, but is a symptom of a person's condition. It does not merely indicate love: by performing it, it brings love into being (Austin 1962; Crapanzano 1992: 235). A footprint is also an index; it signals a person's current or former presence, and was also caused by that presence. Peirce noted that a footprint in the sand of a deserted island acts as both index and symbol. It is an index of the man whose foot pressed down the sand, and a symbol of "mankind" in general, the abstraction of human presence. Many signs can represent in different modes depending on context. For example, a signature can be either an index or an icon. As index, it signifies a person's authorization through contiguity with that person's actual hand and bodily presence. But it can also become an icon, standing for a person even in her absence, once the signature is authenticated and authorized. On the signature as icon, see Janowitz 2004: 34.

6. Consider again an example adapted from Benjamin's footnotes, Raphael's *Sistine Madonna* (1968: 245–46). It begins its career as a representation of Pope Julius II's imminent death and salvation, and even has the curtains of the funereal nave painted on the canvas. In its second incarnation, the same object has an indexical relation to its context. As the altarpiece of Black Friars' Cathedral at Piacenza, it represents the Christian narrative of the Virgin Birth, even as it helps to constitute the ritual space of the cathedral that situates the sign's users

in the narrative. In its present incarnation, which Benjamin does not discuss, it signifies through what Peirce called Thirdness. It hangs on the wall of a Dresden museum, presumably now as a type of "Renaissance painting" and of Raphael's originality and genius. It refers above all to itself—to the singular genius of its painter, its own aura of authenticity, and its exchange value as art. As viewers approach it, they approach not the salvation of Julius or the Christian salvation narrative so much as "beauty" or "Raphael."

In each chapter of the object's life, its signifying force and range are increasingly freed from context, dislocated, and reconfigured. The social frame to which the painting communicates is, moreover, expanded at each step: from Julius II and his entourage to Catholic visitors at Black Friars' Cathedral to art appreciators in general. To put this in Charles Morris's terms, the syntactic relations between signs are loosened (the painting of the Madonna in relation to the death of Julius II), and the pragmatic relation (the relation between the painting and its viewers) becomes preeminent (Morris in Murray 1977: 197)

We might also say that the painting has moved from the indexical meaning of the token to the symbolic meaning of the type. In Peirce's terms, a token is the specific use of an index; a type is the set of all such specific uses. A token has a specific location in space and time and is context-specific because it has indexical meaning. A type has no such specificity. As token, the painting denoted the Madonna and Child; in connotation, it signified the salvation of Pope Julius II by the Madonna who retrieved his body and guided it to heaven. As type, it is cut free from the indexical meaning of a specific space and time. It connotes the timeless "great art" of the panoptic museum.

7. These function as ideal types, with no actual historical religion operating fully and solely according to one or the other mode. Every doctrinally oriented religion requires periodic, emotionally charged renewals through the imagistic mode, just as every imagistically oriented religion must take on some standardized and discursive doctrinal forms in order to be taught and transmitted at all.

Scott Atran (2002: 155–63) levies a series of criticisms of Whitehouse's theory, including the argument that doctrinal mode religion does not in fact tend toward logically integrated and coherent ideology but rather links judgments and behavioral commitments only discursively (156)—its very incoherence better explaining the need for frequent performance in order to commit the religion to memory in "scripts." He further argues that there are many counterexamples of frequently performed imagistic-mode rituals and seldom-performed doctrinal-mode rituals, and, more important, that research has shown that flashbulb memory often depends on post hoc narrative consolidations (161). I employ Whitehouse's distinction as a heuristic device that is good to think with for considering homeland and diasporic religions' modes of transmission.

8. A simple illustration of the difference between semantic and episodic memory is to ask someone what they did two weeks ago Thursday, and then ask them the circumstances in which they first learned about the attack on the

World Trade Center towers on September 11, 2001. The former memory will likely be recalled according to a script—"I went to work"—which is essentially an abstraction of every day's routine. The latter, insofar as it was extraordinary and shocking, is likely to be recalled in much greater detail, and the person will probably remember the place, time, and company in which the news was heard.

9. Whitehouse's discussion refers to the Paliau movement that began in Papua New Guinea in 1946. The emphasis here seems to have certain echoes not only of Weber but of Robin Horton as well.

10. Such a view is not inconsistent with either Eliadean-style morphology or the structural functionalism most strongly associated with Durkheim (1995 [1915]) and Radcliffe-Brown (1952). Both of these approaches stressed ritual's maintenance of traditional boundaries, whether "religious" or social: the burnishing of temporal authenticity establishes continuity with the past. The point was made most forcefully in Radcliffe-Brown's analogy of social structure with the human body, the continuity of which is maintained as long as it lives, despite the continual sloughing off and renewal of cells (1952: 179–80). Like Durkheim, Radcliffe-Brown located the social force of ritual, and the need for it, in its ability to generate sentiments on which social solidarity depends, paradigmatically in the cult of ancestors (163). As many critics have noted, structural functionalism in its most rigid forms presented a tautology: because societies perdure, everything in society functions to that end; because ritual is part of society, its function must be social maintenance. Yet such critics have exaggerated the degree to which Durkheim and Radcliffe-Brown emphasize ritual's repetitive, formalized force in reproducing structure against history. If a body does not change its overall structure over time, said Radcliffe-Brown, a society does: a pig can become a hippotamus (181) as a "dysnomic" society adapts to change its structural type. And Durkheim noted the final indeterminacy of ritual, the ways the same actions and mental dispositions may be interpreted and applied to very different circumstances (1995 [1915]: 389–90); and, more radically, how collective effervescence may even lead to new political structures, as in the French Revolution (cf. Turner 1992: 139).

Yet the *general* tenor of these and other theories remained functionalist: the need for ritual is accelerated in relation to perceived crises or social "breaches" (Turner 1974). Ritual functions to reestablish solidarity after crises (Malinowski 1922: 48). Even rites of rebellion and misfires of ritual, by throwing conventional structures into relief, reinforce established conventions and social structure, finally rendering what is socially obligatory also individually desirable (see, for example, Durkheim 1995 [1915]: 412; Gluckman 1954; Lévi-Strauss 1966; Turner 1967: 30; Ortner 1984: 4; Mach 1993; Rappaport 1996). Although ritual cannot elide or eliminate social disorder or the shifting of the social frame, so the theory goes, it can thoroughly contain it to mitigate and tame the social risk of abrupt change.

Beginning in the late 1960s, this view of ritual was thrown into question with the so-called processual turn. To be sure, ritual had never been viewed as a closed system. Notably, Arnold Van Gennep's (1960 [1909]) seminal *Rites of*

Passage pointed to ritual as the very catalyst of transformation within a given social system. Yet it was only with Turner's recuperation of Van Gennep that it became commonplace to think of social life as a progression of ritualized movements in space and time that open out to transformations of the social group outside the ritual frame (Turner 1969, 1974, 1982, 1985). The processual turn for the study of ritual began with Max Gluckman's (1954) and Vittorio Lanternari's (1963) rejection of structural functionalism to incorporate the Marxian dialectic into studies of rituals of rebellion, attending to ritual's historicity and capacity for reflexive critique. Even Gluckman saw these inversions as only temporary releases of social tension—which he described with the notorious steam-valve metaphor—that ultimately reinforced the status quo. Still, Gluckman and Lanternari paved the way for more radical revisions to come under the rubric of "practice." Pierre Bourdieu, Victor Turner, Marshall Sahlins, and Clifford Geertz all gave close attention to fissures between structures and agency. Geertz noted the discrepancies between individual experience, social structure, and culture out of which change could emerge (1973: 169), as well as the disjunctures between social ideals presented in ritual and actual practice (cf. Jonathan Smith 1982: 82–95; Bell 1992). Bourdieu (1977: 171) and Sahlins (1981: 69–70; 1985), though in different ways, similarly noted how the same rites, articulated in different contexts, produced different meaning formations, groups, and practical consequences. And Turner, though he began as a follower of Durkheim and a student of Gluckheim, revised his earlier ideas to view the ways communitas—the radical leveling of normal social statuses achieved in the liminal stage of ritual—could be extended from ritual contexts into social life in general. He thus attempted to relate the study of ritual to the social movements of the 1960s (1974, 1985, 1992).

11. The kinds of fissures vary. Peter Berger (2002) has taken pains, for example, to distinguish "locality" from "hybridity" as effects of circulated signs implemented in new contexts. A McDonald's restaurant opened in the Philippines is intended to provide fast food in a clean, efficient space. It is *localized,* however, to become a place where women can gather and linger safely, thus becoming the very opposite of "fast" food. A McDonald's restaurant in Turkey, on the other hand, is *hybridized* by serving falafel instead of only burgers. One can imagine similar processes in ritual: the Catholic saints, or the Yoruba orishas, can be either localized, hybridized, or both.

12. It is hard not to think of the critique of Turner's apparent nostalgia when we read these words of Adorno: "He clings to forms of an immediate togetherness, which are historically irretrievable if in fact they ever existed in any other form. Once capitalism has grown uneasy about theoretical self-assertion, its advocates prefer to use the categories of spontaneous life in order to present what is man-made" (Adorno 1973: 62–63). Geertz demonstrated a similar emphasis to Turner in his comparison of ideology and religion as cultural systems (1973), in his opposition in *Islam Observed* (1968) of "being held by a religion" and "holding a religion," and in his analysis of "ritual failure" caused by pluralism and the disjunction between culture and society.

Appendix

1. *Kongo* here refers to the traditional territory of the Bakongo people. "Traditional Kongo civilization encompasses modern Bas-Zaïre, and neighboring territories in modern Cabinda, Congo-Brazzaville, Gabon, and northern Angola. The Punu people of Gabon, the Teke of Congo-Brazzaville, the Suku and the Yaka of the Kwango River area east of Kongo in Zaïre, and some of the ethnic groups of northern Angola share key cultural and religious concepts with the Bakongo and also suffered, with them, the ordeals of the transatlantic slave trade" (Thompson 1984: 103).

2. These objects became significant in Western intellectual history as well, identified as *feitiços,* "made objects," by seventeenth-century Portuguese sailors plying the coast of Africa, and then appropriated as *fétiches,* the cipher of primitive religion par excellence, by Charles de Brosses in the early 1700s. Later the fetish became a key term in the modern critiques by Marx and Freud, in both cases as a kind of mistaken attribution of value. See especially the series of articles by William Pietz (1985, 1987, 1988) and Tomoko Masuzawa (2000).

3. Analogous objects, called *bocio,* were used by the Fon of Dahomey to bind and capture spiritual force, in part through a "counter-aesthetics" that appropriated and symbolically controlled terror by "cooling" (Blier 1995). In Haiti, such *bocio* and *paquet-kongo* were joined in Vodou aesthetics, especially in the Petwo genre of practice (46–54).

4. In Haitian Vodou a similar duality obtained under the nomenclature of Rada and Petwo rituals and objects; and in Brazil, the Nago or Jeje and the Angolan "nations" of Candomblé coexist, transposed in Rio de Janeiro to "Candomblé" and "Macumba" (Bastide 1978a; Thompson 1984).

5. The process occurred earlier in Cuba (Cabrera 1979: 128–29; Castellanos and Castellanos 1992), but appears to have become further solidified and standardized in the United States. David Brown actually notes four spirit categories employed in the United States—orichas, eguns, muertos, and palos—as well as the Catholic saints. All of these are divided into three religious paths: La Regla de Ocha, La Regla de Congo, and Espiritismo (1999: 182). I maintain the simpler bifurcation of Ocha and Palo, mediated and linked by Spiritism, as most Garifuna users of the religions do not recognize the subtle distinctions between eguns, muertos, and palos, often combining them simply as "muertos," as in "soy muy muertera" ("I'm very attached to working with the spirits of the dead"), as against the orichas and the saints. Indeed, the same icons are often referred to as ngangas, muertos, or orichas depending on the context. This is especially the case for the warrior orichas "of the forest": Eleggua, Ogun, and Ochosi.

Glossary

abeimahani	Women's songs, sung by women forming a line with linked little fingers, and accompanied by rhythmic arm gestures suggestive of shared work.
ahari	Ancestral spirit that aids buyeis; often used interchangeably with *hiyuruha;* usually the spirit of an ancestor in its beneficent mode.
amalahani	Placation songs, sung at climactic intervals during the dügü when roosters (*gayu*) are presented to the gubida.
amuidahani	"Bathing" of the deceased, an intimate family-based ritual held at least six months following a death.
arairaguni	The practice of calling down the spirits during a consultation with a buyei, to divine the nature of a problem and the procedure for its resolution.
arumahani	Men's songs, sung by men forming a line with linked little fingers, and accompanied by rhythmic arm gestures suggestive of shared work.
buyei	Garifuna shaman, healer, and ritual leader.
caldero	Iron pot constituting a contract with a spirit of the dead, in Afro-Cuban Palo Monte, now used by Garifuna buyeis in New York as well.
chugu	Second-largest ritual, performed to feed and fete a dissatisfied ancestor summoned in spirit possession, requiring drummers and a buyei as leader.

curandera	Generic Spanish term for a wide array of folk healers who use herbs and traditional practices to cure illness.
dabuyaba	Temple constructed in traditional palm-thatch style *(manaca)* specifically for a single dügü. Also called *gayunere.*
dibasen	Shelter for sleeping, cooking, and relaxation, contiguous with the dabuyaba.
dügü	The largest ritual event, performed periodically to heal a specific patient or reunite a dispersed family by summoning gubida spirits in spirit possession and placating them over a period of a week.
ereba	Cassava flatbread, the food representing tradition par excellence.
Esquipula	Catholic saint from Guatemala, now also a key Garifuna saint known as Cristo Negro (Black Christ).
furunsu	Rum and egg punch made by the buyei at the conclusion of a chugu or a dügü, just prior to "burning the table."
gayu	Roosters presented to ancestors during the dügü; also the symbol of a buyei's successful initiation.
guagai	Handwoven baskets used during the dügü.
gubida	Spirits of the ancestors that confer benefits on their living descendants, but are also capable of bringing on bad luck and sickness when not appropriately remembered in ritual.
gulei	Shaman's altar; also the room containing the altar during a dügü.
hasandigubida	An illness or other crisis discerned to be caused by a displeased ancestor, a gubida.
hiyuruha	Buyei's spirit helpers and patrons.
idugahatiñu	The start of the dügü proper, marked by the departure and arrival of the traditional fishermen, "the providers."
lemesi	Garifuna "mass" performed for the dead.
lugusurugayu	One-day ritual on the first-year anniversary of a dügü.
mureywa	Baton wielded by buyeis to "balance" spirits when they arrive to take possession of ritual participants' bodies.

ocha	Afro-Cuban term for Yoruba *orisha*, contracted from *oricha*.
orisha	Deity or divinized ancestor in Yoruba religion.
punta	Formerly a funereal dance, now a secularized style of dance and popular music genre. Used for everyday recreation and entertainment, but also as a festive part of rituals for the ancestors.
puro	Cigars used by buyei for ritual work.
Sairi	The otherworld where ancestral spirits reside, sometimes associated with the island of St. Vincent.
sisiri	Maracas used to summon the spirits; a key part of the buyei's toolkit.
toque	Afro-Cuban ceremony involving drumming.
wanaragua	Also called *máscaro;* a mask dance performed almost exclusively by males, in whiteface and gowns.
veluria	All-night wake and vigil held immediately after a community member's death.
Yurumein	Garifuna name for the island Europeans called St. Vincent.

Bibliography

Acker, Alison. 1988. *Honduras: The Making of a Banana Republic*. Boston: South End Press.

Adorno, Theodore W. 1973. *The Jargon of Authenticity*. Translated by Knut Tarnowski and Frederic Will. Evanston, IL: Northwestern University Press.

Alexander, Jeffrey C. 2004. "Cultural Pragmatics: Social Performance between Ritual and Strategy." *Sociological Theory* 22 (4): 527–73.

Alpers, Edward A. 2001. "Defining the African Diaspora." Paper presented to the Center for Comparative Social Analysis Workshop, University of California, Los Angeles, October 25.

———. 2005. *African Diaspora*. New York: Routledge.

Althusser, Louis, and Étienne Balibar. 1975. *Reading Capital*. Translated by Ben Brewster. 2nd ed. London: New Left Books.

Anderson, Alexander. 1992. "Alexander Anderson and the Carib War in St. Vincent (ca. 1798)." In *Wild Majesty: Encounters with Caribs from Columbus to the Present Day,* ed. Peter Hulme and Neil L. Whitehead, 217–30. Oxford: Clarendon Press.

Anderson, Benedict. 1991. *Imagined Communities: Reflections on the Spread of Nationalism*. London: Verso.

Anderson, Mark. 1997. "The Significance of Blackness: Representations of Garifuna in St. Vincent and Central America, 1700–1900." *Transforming Anthropology* 6 (1–2): 22–35.

Andrews, George Reid. 2004. *Afro-Latin America, 1800–2000*. New York: Oxford University Press.

Appadurai, Arjun. 1986. "Introduction: Commodities and the Politics of Value." In *The Social Life of Things: Commodities in Cultural Perspective,* ed. Arjun Appadurai, 3–63. Cambridge: Cambridge University Press.

———. 1995. "The Production of Locality." In *Counterworks: Managing the Diversity of Knowledge,* ed. Richard Fardon. London: Routledge. 204–25.

———. 1996. *Modernity at Large: Dimensions of Globalization.* Minneapolis: University of Minnesota Press.

Appadurai, Arjun, and Carol Breckenridge. 1989. "On Moving Targets." *Public Culture* 2: i–iv.

Appiah, Kwame Anthony. 1990. "Race." In *Critical Terms for Literary Study,* 2nd edition, ed. Frank Lentricchia and Thomas McLaughlin, 274–88. Chicago: University of Chicago Press.

———. 1992. *In My Father's House: Africa in the Philosophy of Culture.* New York: Oxford University Press.

Apter, Andrew. 1991. "Herskovits's Heritage: Rethinking Syncretism in the African Diaspora." *Diaspora* 1 (3): 235–60.

———. 1992. *Black Critics and Kings: The Hermeneutics of Power in Yoruba Society.* Chicago: University of Chicago Press.

Arendt, Hannah. 1970. *On Violence.* New York: Harcourt Brace International.

Asad, Talal. 1993. *Genealogies of Religion: Discipline and Reasons of Power in Christianity and Islam.* Baltimore: Johns Hopkins University Press.

———. 2003. *Formations of the Secular: Christianity, Islam, Modernity.* Stanford, CA: Stanford University Press.

Atran, Scott. 2002. *In Gods We Trust: The Evolutionary Landscape of Religion.* Oxford: Oxford University Press.

Austin, J. L. 1962. *How to Do Things with Words.* Oxford: Oxford University Press.

Axel, Brian Keith. 2004. "The Context of Diaspora." *Cultural Anthropology* 19 (1): 26–60.

Bachelard, Gaston. 1994 [1958]. *The Poetics of Space.* Translated by Maria Jolas. Boston: Beacon Press.

Baird, Robert. 1991. *Category Formation and the History of Religions.* 2nd ed. Berlin: Mouton de Gruyter.

Baker, Lee D. 1998. *From Savage to Negro: Anthropology and the Construction of Race, 1896–1954.* Berkeley: University of California Press.

Baldwin, James. 1977 [1952]. *Go Tell It on the Mountain.* New York: Dell Publishing Co., Inc.

Balibar, Étienne, and Immanuel Wallerstein. 1991. *Race, Nation, Class: Ambiguous Identities.* London: Verso.

Baptista, Marlyse. 2005. "New Directions in Pidgin and Creole Studies." *Annual Review of Anthropology* 34: 33–42.

Barahona, Marvin. 1991. *Evolución histórica de la identidad nacional.* Tegucigalpa, Honduras: Editorial Guaymuras.

Bard, Samuel L. (Ephraim George Squier). 1965. *Waikna: Adventures on the Mosquito Shore.* Gainesville: University of Florida Press.

Barnes, Sandra T. 1997. *Africa's Ogun: Old World and New.* 2nd ed. Bloomington: Indiana University Press.

Barnet, Miguel. 1994. *Biography of a Runaway Slave.* Translated by Nick Hill. Willimantic, CT: Curbstone Press.

Barrett, Justin L. 2004. *Why Would Anyone Believe in God?* Walnut Creek, CA: AltaMira Press.

Barth, Fredrik. 1969. "Introduction." In *Ethnic Groups and Boundaries: The Social Organization of Culture Difference,* ed. Fredrik Barth, 9–38. Oslo: Scandinavian University Press.

Bastide, Roger. 1978a. *The African Religions of Brazil: Toward a Sociology of the Interpenetration of Civilizations.* Translated by Helen Sebba. Baltimore: Johns Hopkins University Press.

———. 1978b. *O Candomblé da Bahia.* Translated by Maria Isaura Pereira de Queiroz. São Paulo: Nacional.

Baumann, Martin. 2000. "Diaspora: Genealogies of Semantics and Transcultural Comparison." *Numen* 47: 313–37.

Beaumont, Monsieur de. 1992 [1705]. "Letter of M. de Beaumont on the Caraïbes and Father Le Breton's Mediation in Grenada, 3 September 1705." In *Wild Majesty: Encounters with Caribs from Columbus to the Present Day,* ed. Peter Hulme and Neil L. Whitehead, 174–77. Oxford: Clarendon Press.

Becerra, Longino. 1983. *Evolución histórica de Honduras.* Tegucigalpa, Honduras: Baktun Editorial.

Behrand, Heike. 2002. "'I Am Like a Movie Star in My Street': Photographic Self-Creation in Postcolonial Kenya." In *Postcolonial Subjectivities in Africa,* ed. Richard Werbner, 44–63. London: Zed Books.

Bell, Catherine. 1992. *Ritual Theory, Ritual Practice.* New York: Oxford University Press.

———. 1997. *Ritual: Perspectives and Dimensions.* New York: Oxford University Press.

Bénitez-Rojo, Antonio. 1996. *The Repeating Island: The Caribbean and the Postmodern Perspective.* Translated by James E. Maraniss. Durham, NC: Duke University Press.

Benjamin, Walter. 1968. *Illuminations: Essays and Reflections.* New York: Schocken Books.

Bennett, James B. 2004. "Catholics, Creoles, and the Redefinition of Race in New Orleans." In *Race, Nation, and Religion in the Americas,* ed. Henry Goldschmidt and Elizabeth McAlister, 183–208. Oxford: Oxford University Press.

Berger, John. 1972. *Ways of Seeing.* London: Penguin.

Berger, Peter L. 1967. *The Sacred Canopy.* New York: Doubleday.

———. 2002. "The Cultural Dynamics of Globalization." In *Many Globalizations: Cultural Diversity in the Contemporary World,* ed. Peter L. Berger and Samuel P. Huntington. Oxford: Oxford University Press. 1–16.

Bergson, Henri. 1896. *Matière et mémoire: Essai sur la relation du corps à l'esprit.* Paris: Félix Alcan.

Berking, Helmuth. 2003. "'Ethnicity Is Everywhere': On Globalization and the Transformation of Cultural Identity." *Current Sociology* 51 (3–4): 248–64.

Beyer, Peter. 1994. *Religion and Globalization.* London: Sage.

Bianchi, Cynthia Chamberlain. 1988. "Gubida Illness and Religious Ritual among the Garifuna of Santa Fe, Honduras: An Ethnopsychiatric Analysis." Ph.D. diss., Ohio State University.

Blier, Suzanne Preston. 1995. *African Vodun: Art, Psychology, and Power.* Chicago: University of Chicago Press.

Boas, Franz. 1986 [1928]. *Anthropology and Modern Life.* New York: Dover Publications, Inc.

Bourdieu, Pierre. 1977. *Outline of a Theory of Practice.* Translated by Richard Nice. Cambridge: Cambridge University Press.

————. 2000. *Pascalian Meditations.* Translated by Richard Nice. Stanford, CA: Stanford University Press.

Bourdieu, Pierre, and Loïc Wacquant. 1998. "Les ruses de la raison impérialiste." *Actes de la recherche en sciences sociales* 121–22 (March): 109–18.

Bovin, Mette. 1998. "Nomadic Performance—Peculiar Culture?: 'Exotic' Ethnic Performances of WoDaaBe Nomads of Niger." In *Recasting Ritual: Performance, Media, Identity,* ed. F. Hughes-Freeland and M. M. Crain, 98–112. London: Routledge.

Boyer, Pascal. 2001. *Religion Explained: The Evolutionary Origins of Religious Thought.* New York: Basic Books.

Braithwaite, John. 1992 [1726]. "Report on the Proceedings at St. Vincent by Cpt. Braithwaite." In *Wild Majesty: Encounters with Caribs from Columbus to the Present Day,* ed. Peter Hulme and Neil L. Whitehead. 177–79. Oxford: Clarendon Press.

Brandon, George. 1993. *Santería from Africa to the New World: The Dead Sell Memories.* Bloomington: Indiana University Press.

Breton, Raymond. 1968 [1665]. *Observations of the Island Carib: A Compilation of Ethnographic Notes.* Translated by Marshall McKusik and Pierre Verin. New Haven, CT: Human Relations Area Files.

————. 1992 [1647]. "Of the Origin, Mores, Religion, and Other Customs of the Caraïbes Commonly Called Savages, Ancient Inhabitants of Guadeloupe." In *Wild Majesty: Encounters with Caribs from Columbus to the Present Day,* ed. Peter Hulme and Neil L. Whitehead, 108–16. Oxford: Clarendon Press.

Brown, David H. 1989. "Garden in the Machine: Afro-Cuban Sacred Art and Performance in New Jersey and New York." Ph.D. diss., Yale University.

————. 1999. "Altared Spaces: Afro-Cuban Religions and the Urban Landscape in Cuba and the United States." In *Gods of the City,* ed. Robert A. Orsi, 155–231. Bloomington: Indiana University Press.

————. 2003. *Santería Enthroned: Art, Ritual, and Innovation in an Afro-Cuban Religion.* Chicago: University of Chicago Press.

Brown, Diane D. 1986. *Umbanda and Politics in Urban Brazil.* Ann Arbor, MI: UMI Research.

Brown, Karen McCarthy. 1991. *Mama Lola: A Vodou Priestess in Brooklyn.* Berkeley: University of California Press.

————. 1999. "Staying Grounded in a High-Rise Building: Ecological Dissonance and Ritual Accommodation in Haitian Vodou." In *Gods of the City,* ed. Robert A. Orsi, 79–103. Bloomington: Indiana University Press.

————. 2003. "Making Wanga: Reality Constructions and the Magical Manipulation of Power." In *Transparency and Conspiracy: Ethnographies of Suspicion in the New World Order*, ed. Harry G. West and Todd Sanders, 233–57. Durham, NC: Duke University Press.

Brown, Peter. 1981. *The Cult of Saints: Its Rise and Function in Latin Christianity*. Chicago: University of Chicago Press.

Brown, Roger, and James Kulik. 1982. "Flashbulb Memories." In *Memory Observed: Remembering in Natural Contexts*, ed. Ulric Neisser, 23–40. San Francisco: W. H. Freeman and Co.

Brubaker, Rogers. 2005. "The 'Diaspora' Diaspora." *Ethnic and Racial Studies* 28 (1): 1–19.

Burdick, John. 1998. *Blessed Anastácia: Women, Race, and Popular Christianity in Brazil*. New York: Routledge.

————. 2004. "The Catholic Afro Mass and the Dance of Eurocentrism in Brazil." In *Race, Nation, and Religion in the Americas*, ed. Henry Goldschmidt and Elizabeth McAlister, 111–32. Oxford: Oxford University Press.

Burkert, Walter. 1996. "The Function and Transformation of Ritual Killing." In *Readings in Ritual Studies*, ed. Ronald L. Grimes, 62–71. Upper Saddle River, NJ: Prentice Hall.

Butler, Judith. 1997. *The Psychic Life of Power: Theories in Subjection*. Stanford, CA: Stanford University Press.

Butler, Kim D. 2001. "Defining Diaspora, Refining a Discourse." *Diaspora* 10 (2): 189–219.

Cabrera, Lydia. 1979. *Reglas de Congo: Palo Monte, Mayombe*. Miami, FL: Ediciones Universal.

————. 1983. *El monte: Igbo-finda, ewe orisha-vititi nfinda; Notes sobre las religiones, la mágia, los superstitiones y el folklore de los negros criollos y el pueblo de Cuba*. Miami, FL: Collección de Chicherekú en el Exilo.

Canelas Diaz, Antonio. 1999. *La Ceiba, sus raices y su historia, 1810–1940*. La Ceiba, Honduras: Tipografía Renacimento.

Caribbean Culture Center. 2005. The Franklin H. Williams Caribbean Cultural Center. www.afrocubaweb.com/caribcultcent.htm. Accessed May 10.

Casanova, Jose. 1994. *Public Religions in the Modern World*. Chicago: University of Chicago Press.

Casey, Edward S. 1987. *Remembering*. Bloomington: Indiana University Press.

————. 1993. *Getting Back into Place: Toward a Renewed Understanding of the Place-World*. Bloomington: Indiana University Press.

————. 1997. *The Fate of Place*. Berkeley: University of California Press.

Cassirer, Ernst. 1955. *The Philosophy of Symbolic Forms*. Vol. 2, *Mythical Thought*. Translated by Ralph Manheim. New Haven, CT: Yale University Press.

Castellanos, Jorge, and Isabel Castellanos. 1992. *Cultura afrocubana*. Vol. 3, *Las religiones y las lenguas*. Miami, FL: Ediciones Universal.

Centeno García, Santos. 1996. *Historia del pueblo negro caribe y su llegada a Hibueras el 12 de abril de 1797*. Tegucigalpa, Honduras: Editorial Universitaria.

————. 1997. *Historia del movimiento negro hondureño*. La Ceiba, Honduras: José Hipólito Centeno García.

Certeau, Michel de. 1984. *The Practice of Everyday Life*. Berkeley: University of California Press.

Césaire, Aimé. 1971. *Cahier d'un retour au pays natal*. Paris: Présence Africaine.

———. 1972. *Discourse on Colonialism*. Translated by Joan Pinkham. New York: Monthly Review Press.

Chakrabarty, Dipesh. 2000. *Provincializing Europe: Postcolonial Thought and Historical Difference*. Princeton, NJ: Princeton University Press.

Chaunu, Huguette, and Pierre Chaunu. 1955–59. *Séville et l'Atlantique (1504–1650)*. 8 vols. Paris: Institut des Hautes Études de l'Amérique Latine.

Cheek, Charles D., and Nancie L. Gonzalez. 1986. "Black Carib Settlement Patterns in Early 19th-Century Honduras: The Search for a Livelihood." *Ethnohistory* 35 (1): 403–29.

Chestnut, R. Andrew. 1994. *Rastafari: Roots and Ideology*. Syracuse, NY: Syracuse University Press.

———. 1997. *Born Again in Brazil: The Pentecostal Boom and the Pathogens of Poverty*. New Brunswick, NJ: Rutgers University Press.

———. 2001. "Jamaican Diasporic Identity: The Metaphor of Yaad." In *Nation Dance: Religion, Identity and Cultural Difference in the Caribbean*, ed. Patrick Taylor, 129–38. Bloomington: Indiana University Press.

Clarke, Kamari Maxine. 2004. *Mapping Yorùbá Networks: Power and Agency in the Making of Transnational Communities*. Durham, NC: Duke University Press.

Clifford, James. 1988. *The Predicament of Culture: Twentieth-Century Ethnography, Literature and Art*. Cambridge, MA: Harvard University Press.

———. 1994. "Diasporas." *Cultural Anthropology* 9: 302–38.

Coelho, Ruy. 1955. "The Black Carib of Honduras: A Study in Acculturation." Ph.D. diss., Northwestern University.

———. 1995. *Los negros caribes de Honduras*. 2nd ed. Tegucigalpa, Honduras: Editorial Guaymuras.

Cohen, Abner. 1969. *Custom and Politics in Urban Africa: A Study of Hausa Migrants in Yoruba Towns*. Berkeley: University of California Press.

Cohen, Milton. 1984. "The Ethnomedicine of the Garifuna (Black Caribs) of Rio Tinto, Honduras." *Anthropological Quarterly* 57 (1): 16–27.

Cohen, Robin. 1997. *Global Diasporas*. Seattle: University of Washington Press.

Coke, Thomas. 1790. *An Address to the Subscribers for their Support of the Missions Carried on by Voluntary Contributions to the Benefit of the Negroes in the British Islands, in the West Indies*. London: n.p.

———. 1808–11. *A History of the West Indies, Containing the Natural, Civil, and Ecclesiastical History of each island. . . .* Liverpool: Nuttall, Fisher, and Dixon.

———. 1992 [1788]. "Thomas Coke's Letter to Wesley." In *Wild Majesty: Encounters with Caribs from Columbus to the Present Day*, ed. Peter Hulme and Neil L. Whitehead, 186–88. Oxford: Clarendon Press.

Comaroff, Jean. 1985. *Body of Power, Spirit of Resistance*. Chicago: University of Chicago Press.

Comaroff, Jean, and John L. Comaroff. 2000. "Millennial Capitalism: First Thoughts on a Second Coming." *Public Culture* 12 (2): 291–343.

Comaroff, John, and Jean Comaroff. 1992. *Ethnography and the Historical Imagination*. Boulder: Westview.

Connerton, Paul. 1989. *How Societies Remember*. Cambridge: Cambridge University Press.

Conzemius, Eduard. 1928. "Ethnographical Notes on the Black Carib (Garif)." *American Anthropologist* 30 (2): 183–205.

Coronil, Fernando. 1995. "Introduction to the Duke University Press Edition: Transculturation and the Politics of Theory: Countering the Center, Cuban Counterpoint." In Fernando Ortiz, *Cuban Counterpoint: Tobacco and Sugar*, x–lvi. Durham, NC: Duke University Press.

Cosminsky, Sheila. 1976. "Carib-Creole Relations in a Belizean Community." In *Frontier Adaptations in Lower Central America*, ed. Mary W. Helms and Franklin O. Loveland, 95–116. Philadelphia: Institute for the Study of Human Issues.

Cosminsky, Sheila, and Emory Whipple. 1984. "Ethnicity and Mating Patterns in Punta Gorda, Belize." In *Black Caribs: A Case Study in Biocultural Adaptation*, ed. Michael H. Crawford, 115–34. New York: Plenum Press.

Crapanzano, Vincent. 1992. *Hermes' Dilemma and Hamlet's Desire: On the Epistemology of Interpretation*. Cambridge, MA: Harvard University Press.

Craton, Michael. 1986. "From Caribs to Black Caribs: The Amerindian Roots of Servile Resistance in the Caribbean." In *In Resistance: Studies in African, Caribbean, and Afro-American History*, ed. Gary Y. Okihiro, 96–117. Amherst: University of Massachusetts Press.

Crawford, Michael H. 1984. "Problems and Hypotheses: An Introduction." In *Black Caribs: A Case Study in Biocultural Adaptation*, ed. Michael H. Crawford, 1–9. New York: Plenum Press.

Crowder, Kyle D., and Lucky M. Tedrow. 2001. "West Indians and the Residential Landscape of New York." In *Islands in the City: West Indian Migration to New York*, ed. Nancy Foner, 81–114. Berkeley: University of California Press.

Curry, Mary Cuthrell. 2001. "The Yoruba Religion in New York." In *New York Glory: Religions in the City*, ed. Tony Carnes and Anna Karpathakis, 74–88. New York: New York University Press.

Curtin, Philip D. 1969. *The Atlantic Slave Trade: A Census*. Madison: University of Wisconsin Press.

da Cunha, Euclides. 1944. *Rebellion in the Backlands*. Translated by Samuel Putnam. Chicago: University of Chicago Press.

Daniels, David D. 2000. "'Ain't Gonna Let Nobody Turn Me 'Round': The Politics of Race and the New Black Middle-Class Religion." In *Public Religion and Urban Transformation: Faith in the City*, ed. Lowell W. Livezey, 133–62. New York: New York University Press.

Dantas, Beatriz Góias. 1988. *Vovó Nagô e Papai Branco: Uso e abuso da Africa no Brasil*. Rio de Janeiro: Graal.

Davidson, George. 1787. *The Case of the Caribbs in St. Vincent's*. London: n.p.

Davidson, William V. 1974. *Historical Geography of the Bay Islands, Honduras*. Birmingham, AL: Southern University Press.

———. 1976. "Black Carib (Garífuna) Habitats in Central America." In *Frontier Adaptations in Lower Central America*, ed. Mary W. Helms and Franklin O. Loveland, 85–94. Philadelphia: Institute for the Study of Human Issues.

———. 1984a. "The Garifuna in Central America: Ethnohistorical and Geographical Foundations." In *Black Caribs: A Case Study in Biocultural Adaptation*, ed. Michael H. Crawford, 13–36. New York: Plenum Press.

———. 1984b. "El Padre Subirana y las tierras concedidas a los indios hondureños en el siglo XIX." *América indígena* 44 (3): 447–59.

Deflem, Mathieu. 1991. "Ritual, Anti-structure, and Religion: A Discussion of Victor Turner's Processsual Symbolic Analysis." *Journal for the Scientific Study of Religion* 30 (1): 1–25.

Demerath, N. J. 2001. *Crossing the Gods: World Religions and Worldly Politics*. New Brunswick, NJ: Rutgers University Press.

Derrida, Jacques. 2002. *Acts of Religion*. Edited by Gil Anidjar. New York: Routledge.

Devereux, George, and Edwin Loeb. 1943. "Antagonistic Acculturation." *American Sociological Review* 8 (2): 133–47.

do Campo, Orlando. 1995. "The Free Exercise Clause and Ritual Bloodletting: *Church of the Lucumí Babalú Ayé v. City of Hialeah*." In *Engimatic Powers: Syncretism with African and Indigenous Peoples*, ed. Anthony M. Stevens-Arroyo and Andrés I. Peréz y Mena, 159–79. New York: Bildner Center for Western Hemisphere Studies.

Drachler, Jacob, ed. 1975. *Black Homeland, Black Diaspora: Cross Currents of the African Relationship*. Port Washington, NY: Kennikat Press.

Drewal, Margaret Thompson. 1992. *Yoruba Ritual: Performers, Play, Agency*. Bloomington: Indiana University Press.

Droogers, André. 1989. "Syncretism: The Problem of Definition, the Definition of the Problem." In *Dialogue and Syncretism: An Interdisciplinary Approach*, ed. Jerald Gort, Hendrik Vroom, Rein Fernhout, and Anton Wessels, 7–25. Grand Rapids, MI: Eerdmans and Rodopi.

Drusine, Helen. 2003. "Cultural Crossroads: The Garífuna." *American Legacy* 9 (3): 15–19.

Du Bois, William Edward Burghardt. 1915. *The Negro*. New York: Henry Holt and Company.

———. 2003 [1903]. *The Souls of Black Folk*. New York: Barnes & Noble Classics.

Dunn, Oliver, and James E. Kelley Jr. 1989. *The Diario of Christopher Columbus's First Voyage to America, 1492–1493*. Norman: University of Oklahoma Press.

Durkheim, Émile. 1995 [1915]. *The Elementary Forms of Religious Life*. Translated by Karen E. Fields. New York: Free Press.

du Tertre, Jean Baptiste. 1992 [1667]. "Jean Baptiste du Tertre and the Noble Savages." In *Wild Majesty: Encounters with Caribs from Columbus to the*

Present Day, ed. Peter Hulme and Neil L. Whitehead, 128–38. Oxford: Clarendon Press.

Eagleton, Terry. 1991. *Ideology: An Introduction.* London: Verso.

Edwards, Brent Hayes. 2001. "The Practice of Diaspora." *Social Text* 66 (19-1): 45–76.

———. 2003. *The Practice of Diaspora: Literature, Translation, and the Rise of Black Internationalism.* Cambridge, MA: Harvard University Press.

Edwards, Bryan. 1794. *The History, Civil and Commercial, of the British Colonies in the West Indies.* London: John Stockdale.

———. 1799. *The History, Civil and Commercial, of the British Colonies in the West Indies.* London.

———. 1801. *An Historical Survey of the Island of Saint Domingo, together with an Account of the Maroon Negroes in the Island of Jamaica.* . . . London: J. Stockdale.

———. 1818–19. *The History, Civil and Commercial, of the British West Indies.* Vol. 4. London: G. and W. B. Whittaker.

Eliade, Mircea. 1954. *The Myth of the Eternal Return.* Translated by Willard R. Trask. New York: Pantheon.

———. 1964. *Shamanism: Archaic Techniques of Ecstasy.* London: Routledge and Kegan Paul.

England, Sarah. 1999. "Negotiating Race and Place in the Garifuna Diaspora: Identity Formation and Transnational Grassroots Politics in New York City and Honduras." *Identities* 6 (1): 5–53.

———. 2006. *Afro–Central Americans in New York City: Garifuna Tales of Transnational Movements in Racialized Space.* Gainesville: University Press of Florida.

Equiano, Olaudah. 2004 [1789]. *The Interesting Narrative of the Life of Alaudah Equiano: or, Gustavus Vassa, the African.* Edited by Shelly Eversley. New York: Modern Library.

Euraque, Darío. 1996. *Reinterpreting the Banana Republic: Region and State in Honduras, 1870–1972.* Chapel Hill: University of North Carolina Press.

———. 2003. "The Threat of Blackness to the Mestizo Nation: Race and Ethnicity in the Honduran Banana Economy, 1920s and 1930s." In *Banana Wars: Power, Production and History in the Americas,* ed. Steve Striffler and Mark Moberg, 229–52. Durham, NC: Duke University Press.

Evans-Pritchard, E. E. 1976. *Witchcraft, Oracles and Magic among the Azande.* Oxford: Oxford University Press.

Falola, Toyin, and Matt D. Childs, eds. 2004. *The Yoruba Diaspora in the Atlantic World.* Bloomington: Indiana University Press.

Fanon, Frantz. 1963. *The Wretched of the Earth.* Translated by Constance Farrington. New York: Grove Press.

Fardon, Richard. 1987. "'African Ethnogenesis': Limits to the Comparability of Ethnic Phenomena." In *Comparative Anthropology,* ed. Ladislav Holy, 168–88. Oxford: Blackwell.

Firth, Raymond. 1967. *Tikopia Ritual and Belief.* Boston: Beacon Press.

Fitzgerald, F. Scott. 2003 [1933]. *Tender Is the Night*. New York: Scribner's.

Flores, Barbara. 2002. "The Garifuna Dugu Ritual in Belize: A Celebration of Relationships." In *Gender, Ethnicity, and Religion*, ed. Rosemary Radford Ruether, 144–70. Minneapolis: Fortress Press.

Foner, Nancy. 1978. *Jamaica Farewell: Jamaican Migrants in London*. Berkeley: University of California Press.

———. 1985. "Race and Color: Jamaican Migrants in London City." *International Migration Review* 19 (4): 708–27.

Foster, Byron. 1994. *Heart Drum: Spirit Possession in the Garifuna Communities of Belize*. 2nd ed. Belize: Cubola Productions.

Foucault, Michel. 1979. *Discipline and Punish: The Birth of the Prison*. Translated by Alan Sheridan. New York: Pantheon.

———. 1980. *The History of Sexuality*. Vol. 1, *An Introduction*. Translated by Robert Hurley. New York: Vintage.

Fouron, Georges E., and Nina Glick Schiller. 1997. "Haitian Identities at the Juncture between Diaspora and Homeland." In *Caribbean Circuits: New Directions in the Study of Caribbean Migration*, ed. Patricia R. Pessar, 127–60. New York: Center for Migration Studies.

Frank, Gelya. 1997. "Jews, Multiculturalism, and Boasian Anthropology." *American Anthropologist* 99 (4): 731–45.

Frazier, E. Franklin. 1974 [1964]. *The Negro Church in America*. New York: Schocken Books.

Fredrickson, George M. 2002. *Racism: A Short History*. Princeton, NJ: Princeton University Press.

Friedland, Roger, and Deirdre Boden. 1994. *NowHere: Space, Time, and Modernity*. Berkeley: University of California Press.

Friedrich, Paul. 1975. "The Lexical Symbol and its Relative Non-arbitrariness." In *Linguistics and Anthropology: In Honor of Carl Vogelin*, ed. M. Dale Kinkaid, 199–247. Lisse, the Netherlands: Peter de Ridder Press.

Froebel, Julius. 1859. *Seven Years' Travel in Central America, Northern Mexico, and the Far West of the United States*. London: Richard Bentley.

Fry, Peter. 2000. "Politics, Nationality and the Meaning of 'Race' in Brazil." *Daedalus* 129 (2): 83–118.

Fustel de Coulanges, Numa Denis. 1979. *The Ancient City*. Gloucester, MA: Peter Smith.

Gadamer, Hans Georg. 1975. *Truth and Method*. New York: Continuum.

García, Victor Virgilio López. 1993. *Lamumehan Garífuna: Clamor Garífuna*. Tornabe, Tela, Atlántida, Honduras: n.p.

Gargallo, Francesca. 2002. *Garífuna, Garínagu, Caribe*. Buenos Aires: Siglo Veintiuno Editores.

Gates, Henry Louis Jr. 1997. *Thirteen Ways of Looking at the Black Man*. New York: Random House.

Geertz, Clifford. 1968. *Islam Observed*. Chicago: University of Chicago Press.

———. 1973. *The Interpretation of Cultures*. New York: Basic Books.

———. 2000. *Available Light: Anthropological Reflections on Philosophical Topics*. Princeton, NJ: Princeton University Press.

Genovese, Eugene D. 1972. *Roll, Jordan, Roll: The World Slaves Made.* New York: Pantheon Books.

———. 1989. *The Political Economy of Slavery.* Middletown, CT: Wesleyan University Press.

Ghidinelli, Azzo, and Pierleone Massajoli. 1984. "Resumen etnográfico de los Caribes Negros (Garifunas) de Honduras." *América indígena* 44 (3): 485–518.

Gibbs, Archibald Robertson. 1883. *British Honduras: An Historical and Descriptive Account of the Colony from Its Settlement, 1670.* London: Sampson Low, Marston, Searle, & Rivington.

Gibbs, Philip. 1786. *Instructions for the Treatment of Negroes, Inscribed to the Society for Propagating the Gospel in Foreign Parts.* London: Shepperson and Reynolds.

Giddens, Anthony. 1990. *The Consequences of Modernity.* Stanford, CA: Stanford University Press.

Gilroy, Paul. 1991. *"There Ain't No Black in the Union Jack": The Cultural Politics of Race and Nation.* Chicago: University of Chicago Press.

———. 1993. *The Black Atlantic: Modernity and Double Consciousness.* Cambridge, MA: Harvard University Press.

———. 2000. *Against Race: Imagining Political Culture beyond the Color Line.* Cambridge, MA: Belknap Press of Harvard University Press.

Glaude, Eddie S. 2000. *Exodus! Religion, Race, and Nation in Early Nineteenth-Century Black America.* Chicago: University of Chicago Press.

Glissant, Édouard. 1989. *Caribbean Discourse.* Charlottesville: University Press of Virginia.

Gluckman, Max. 1954. *Rituals of Rebellion in Southeast Africa.* Manchester, UK: Manchester University Press.

Gmelch, George. 1991. *Double Passage: The Lives of Caribbean Migrants Abroad and Back Home.* Ann Arbor: University of Michigan Press.

Goldschmidt, Henry, and Elizabeth McAlister, eds. 2004. *Race, Nation, and Religion in the Americas.* New York: Oxford.

Gonçalves da Silva, Vagner. 1995. *Orixás da metrópole.* Petrópolis: Editora Vozes.

Gonzalez, Nancie L. 1969. *Black Carib Household Structure: A Study of Migration and Modernization.* Seattle: University of Washington Press.

———. 1984. "Garifuna (Black Carib) Social Organization." In *Black Caribs: A Case Study in Biocultural Adaptation,* ed. Michael H. Crawford, 51–66. New York: Plenum Press.

———. 1988. *Sojourners of the Caribbean: Ethnogenesis and Ethnohistory of the Garifuna.* Urbana: University of Illinois Press.

———. 1992. *Dollar, Dove and Eagle: One Hundred Years of Palestinian Migration to Honduras.* Ann Arbor: University of Michigan Press.

González-Wippler, Migene. 1989. *Santeria, the Religion: A Legacy of Faith, Rites, and Magic.* New York: Harmony Books.

Gordon, Edmund T. 1998. *Disparate Diasporas: Identity Politics in an Afro-Nicaraguan Community.* Austin: University of Texas Press.

Gordon, Edmund T., and Mark Anderson. 1999. "The African Diaspora: Toward an Ethnography of Diasporic Identification." *Journal of American Folklore* 112 (445): 282–96.

Goudreau, Isar P. 2002. "Changing Space, Making Race: Distance, Nostalgia, and the Folklorization of Blackness in Puerto Rico." *Identities* 9 (3): 281–304.

Graf, Peter, and Daniel L. Schachter. 1985. "Implicit and Explicit Memory for New Associations in Normal and Amnesic Subjects." *Journal of Experimental Psychology, Learning, Memory, and Cognition* 11: 501–18.

Great Britain Calendar of State Papers. 1661–68. Colonial Series, America and the West Indies. London: HMS Stationery Office.

Greene, Oliver N. 1998. "The 'Dugu' Ritual of the Garinagu of Belize: Reinforcing Values of Society through Music and Spirit Possession." *Black Music Research Journal* 18 (1–2): 167–81.

Grimes, Ronald L. 1990. *Ritual Criticism: Case Studies in Its Practice, Essays on Its Theory.* Columbia: University of South Carolina Press.

Gross, Jane. 2006. "In Throes of a Diaspora, Two Families Bind." *New York Times,* September 6.

Gullick, C. J. M. R. 1984. "The Changing Vincentian Carib Population." In *Black Caribs: A Case Study in Biocultural Adaptation,* ed. Michael H. Crawford, 37–50. New York: Plenum Press.

———. 1995. "Communicating Caribness." In *Wolves from the Sea: Readings in the Anthropology of the Native Caribbean,* ed. Neil Whitehead, 157–70. Leiden: KITLV Press.

Gupta, Akhil, and James Ferguson. 1997. "Beyond 'Culture': Space, Identity, and the Politics of Difference." In *Culture, Power, Place: Explorations in Critical Anthropology,* ed. Ahkil Gupta and James Ferguson, 33–51. Durham, NC: Duke University Press.

Halbwachs, Maurice. 1992. *On Collective Memory.* Translated by Lewis A. Coser. Chicago: University of Chicago Press.

Hale, Lindsay. 2004. "The House of Saint Benedict, the House of Father John: Umbanda Aesthetics and a Politics of the Senses." In *Race, Nation, and Religion in the Americas,* ed. Henry Goldschmidt and Elizabeth McAlister, 283–304. Oxford: Oxford University Press.

Hall, Edward T. 1990. *The Hidden Dimension.* New York: Anchor Books.

Hall, Stuart. 1996a. "Gramsci's Relevance for the Study of Race and Ethnicity." In *Stuart Hall: Critical Dialogues in Cultural Studies,* ed. David Morley and Kuan-Hsing Chen, 411–41. London: Routledge.

———. 1996b. "New Ethnicities." In *Stuart Hall: Critical Dialogues in Cultural Studies,* ed. David Morley and Kuan-Hsing Chen, 441–50. London: Routledge.

———. 1996c. "What Is This 'Black' in Black Popular Culture?" In *Stuart Hall: Critical Dialogues in Cultural Studies,* ed. David Morley and Kuan-Hsing Chen, 465–76. London: Routledge.

Hanchard, Michael. 1994. *Orpheus and Power: The Movemento Negro of Rio de Janeiro and São Paulo, 1945–1988.* Princeton, NJ: Princeton University Press.

————. 1999. "Race and the Public Sphere in Brazil." In *Racial Politics in Contemporary Brazil*, ed. Michael Hanchard, 59–82. Durham, NC: Duke University Press.

Handler, Jerome S., and Frederick W. Lange. 1978. *Plantation Slavery in Barbados: An Archaeological and Historical Investigation*. Cambridge, MA: Harvard University Press.

Handler, Richard. 1988. *Nationalism and the Politics of Culture in Quebec*. Madison: University of Wisconsin Press.

Harding, Rachel. 2000. *A Refuge in Thunder: Candomblé and Alternative Spaces of Blackness*. Bloomington: Indiana University Press.

Hardt, Michael, and Antonio Negri. 2000. *Empire*. Cambridge, MA: Harvard University Press.

Harris, Joseph E. 1971. *The African Presence in Asia: Consequences of the East African Slave Trade*. Evanston, IL: Northwestern University Press.

Harvey, David. 1989. *The Condition of Postmodernity*. Oxford: Blackwell.

————. 2001. *Spaces of Capital: Towards a Critical Geography*. New York: Routledge.

Hefner, Robert W. 1993. "World Building and the Rationality of Conversion." In *Conversion to Christianity: Historical and Anthropological Perspectives on a Great Transformation*, ed. Robert W. Hefner, 3–46. Berkeley: University of California Press.

Hegel, G. W. F. *The Philosophy of History*. Translated by J. Sibree. Mineola, NY: Dover Publications.

Helms, Mary W. 1981. "Black Carib Domestic Organization in Historical Perspective: Traditional Origins of Contemporary Patterns." *Ethnology* 20 (1): 77–86.

Hepner, Randal L. 1998. "Chanting Down Babylon in the Belly of the Beast: The Rastafarian Movement in the Metropolitan United States." In *Chanting Down Babylon*, ed. Nathaniel Samuel Murrell, William David Spencer, and Adrian Anthony McFarlane, 199–216. Philadelphia: Temple University Press.

Herberg, Will. 1960. *Protestant, Catholic, Jew: An Essay in American Sociology*. Garden City, NY: Anchor Books.

Hernandez, Gilbert H. 1998. *The Garinagu in the Caribbean Basin: Black Caribs*. Dangriga, Belize: F. I. Hernandez Productions.

Herskovits, Melville J. 1990 [1941]. *The Myth of the Negro Past*. Boston: Beacon Press.

Hesse, Barnor. 1993. "Black to Front and Black Again: Racialization through Contested Times and Spaces." In *Place and the Politics of Identity*, ed. Michael Keith and Steve Pile, 162–81. London: Routledge.

Higginbotham, Evelyn Brooks. 1992. "African-American Women's History and the Metalanguage of Race." *Signs* 17 (2): 251–74.

Hobsbawm, Eric. 2002. *Interesting Times: A Twentieth-Century Life*. London: Allen Lane.

Hobsbawm, Eric, and Terence Ranger, eds. 1983. *The Invention of Traditions*. New York: Columbia University Press.

Hollywood, Amy. 2002. "Performativity, Citationality, Ritualization." *History of Religions* 42 (2): 93–115.

Houk, James T. 1995. *Spirits, Blood, and Drums: The Orisha Religion in Trinidad*. Philadelphia: Temple University Press.

Hulme, Peter. 2000a. *Remnants of Conquest: The Island Caribs and Their Visitors, 1877–1998*. New York: Oxford University Press.

———. 2000b. "Travel, Ethnography, and Transculturation: St. Vincent in the 1790s." Paper presented at the University of Miami, September 29–30. Available online at http://privatewww.essex.ac.uk/~phulme/Travel,%20Ethnography,%20Transculturation.htm. Accessed December 1, 2006.

Hulme, Peter, and Neil L. Whitehead, eds. 1992. *Wild Majesty: Encounters with Caribs from Columbus to the Present Day*. Oxford: Clarendon Press.

Hunt, Carl M. 1979. *Oyotunji Village: The Yoruba Movement in America*. Washington, DC: University Press of America.

Hurbon, Laënnec. 1989. "La Iglesia católica en las Antillas francesas durante el siglo XVII." *Cristianismo y sociedad* 102: 61–75.

Irwin, Graham W., ed. 1977. *Africans Abroad: A Documentary History of the Black Diaspora in Asia, Latin America, and the Caribbean during the Age of Slavery*. New York: Columbia University Press.

Jacobson, Matthew Frye. 2001. "Becoming Caucasian: Vicissitudes of Whiteness in American Politics and Culture." *Identities* 8 (1): 83–104.

Jameson, Fredric. 1991. *Postmodernism, or the Cultural Logic of Late Capitalism*. London: Verso.

Janowitz, Naomi. 2004. "Do Jews Make Good Protestants? The Cross-Cultural Study of Ritual." In *Beyond Primitivism: Indigenous Religious Traditions and Modernity*, ed. Jacob K. Olupona, 23–36. New York: Routledge.

Jenkins, Carol L. 1983. "Ritual and Resource Flow: The Garifuna Dugu." *American Ethnologist* 10: 429–42.

John-Sandy, Rene. 1997. "The Garifuna Bicentennial Commemoration, 1797–1997." *Black Diaspora: A Global Black Magazine* 18 (5): 26–28.

Johnson, Paul Christopher. 1998. "Naming and 'African-ness' in Brazilian Umbanda." *Palara: Publication of the Afro-Latin Research Association* 3: 47–64.

———. 2001. "Law, Religion and 'Public Health' in the Republic of Brazil." *Law and Social Inquiry* 26 (1): 9–33.

———. 2002a. *Secrets, Gossip and Gods: The Transformation of Brazilian Candomblé*. New York: Oxford University Press.

———. 2002b. "Migrating Bodies, Circulating Signs: Brazilian Candomblé, the Garífuna of the Caribbean, and the Category of 'Indigenous Religions.'" *History of Religions* 41 (4): 301–28.

———. 2002c. "Models of 'the Body' in the Ethographic Field: Garífuna and Candomblé Case Studies." *Method and Theory in the Study of Religion* 14: 170–95.

———. 2004. "Three Paths to Legitimacy: African Diaspora Religion and the State." *Culture and Religion* 6 (1): 79–105.

———. 2006. "Joining the African Diaspora: Dynamics of Migration and Urban Religion." In *Women and Religion in the African Diaspora,* ed. R. Marie Griffith and Barbara D. Savage, 37–58. Baltimore: Johns Hopkins University Press.

Kant, Immanuel. 1960. *Religion within the Limits of Reason Alone.* Translated by Theodore M. Greene and Hoyt H. Hudson. New York: Harper & Row.

Karpathakis, Anna. 2001. "Conclusion: New York City's Religions; Issues of Race, Class, Gender, and Immigration." In *New York Glory: Religions in the City,* ed. Tony Carnes and Anna Karpathakis, 388–95. New York: New York University Press.

Kasinitz, Philip, Juan Battle, and Inés Miyares. 2001. "Fade to Black? The Children of West Indian Immigrants in Southern Florida." In *Ethnicities: Children of Immigrants in America,* ed. Rubén Rumbaut and Alejandro Portes, 267–301. Berkeley: University of California Press.

Keane, Webb. 2003. "Semiotics and the Social Analysis of Material Things." *Language and Communication* 23: 409–25.

Keenagh, Peter. 1938. *Mosquito Coast: An Account of a Journey through the Jungles of Honduras.* Boston: Houghton Mifflin Company.

Keith, Michael, and Steve Pile. 1993a. "Introduction, Part 1: The Politics of Place." In *Place and the Politics of Identity,* ed. Michael Keith and Steve Pile, 1–21. London: Routledge.

———. 1993b. "Introduction, Part 2: The Place of Politics." In *Place and the Politics of Identity,* ed. Michael Keith and Steve Pile, 22–40. London: Routledge.

Kerns, Virginia. 1984. "Past and Present Evidence of Interethnic Mating." In *Black Caribs: A Case Study in Biocultural Adaptation,* ed. Michael H. Crawford, 95–114. New York: Plenum Press.

———. 1997. *Women and the Ancestors: Black Carib Kinship and Ritual.* 2nd ed. Urbana: University of Illinois Press.

Kertzer, David I. 1988. *Ritual, Politics, and Power.* New Haven, CT: Yale University Press.

Khan, Aisha. 1987. "Migration and Life-Cycle among Garifuna (Black Carib) Street Vendors." *Women's Studies* 13:183–98.

Kilson, Martin L., and Robert I. Rotberg, eds. 1976. *The African Diaspora: Interpretive Essays.* Cambridge, MA: Harvard University Press.

Klein, Herbert S. 1999. *The Atlantic Slave Trade.* Cambridge: Cambridge University Press.

Klimt, Andrea, and Stephen Lubkemann. 2002. "Argument across the Portuguese-Speaking World: A Discursive Approach to Diaspora." *Diaspora* 11 (2): 145–62.

Kolapo, Femi J. 2004. "The Igbo and Their Neighbours during the Era of the Atlantic Slave-Trade." *Slavery and Abolition* 25 (1): 114–33.

Korgen, Kathleen Odell. 1998. *From Black to Biracial: Transforming Racial Identity among Americans.* Westport, CT: Praeger.

Kurien, Prema. 1998. "Becoming American by Becoming Hindu: Indian Americans Take Their Place at the Multicultural Table." In *Gatherings in Diaspora: Religious Communities and the New Immigration,* ed. R. Stephen Warner and Judith G. Wittner, 37–70. Philadelphia: Temple University Press.

Labat, Jean-Baptiste. 1992 [1722]. "A Sojourn on Dominica." In *Wild Majesty: Encounters with Caribs from Columbus to the Present Day,* ed. Peter Hulme and Neil L. Whitehead, 155–68. Oxford: Clarendon Press.

La Borde, Sieur de. 1704. "Avec un Voyage qui contient une relation exacte de l'origine, moeurs, coûtumes, religion, guerres & voyages des Caraibes. . . ." In Louis Hennepin, *Voyage ou Nouvelle decouverte d'un tres-grand pays, dans l'Amerique.* . . . Amsterdam: Chez A. Braakman.

———. 1992 [1674]. "An Account from the Jesuit Missions." In *Wild Majesty: Encounters with Caribs from Columbus to the Present Day,* ed. Peter Hulme and Neil L. Whitehead, 139–54. Oxford: Clarendon Press.

Laclau, Ernesto. 1990. *New Reflections on the Revolution of Our Time.* Translated by Jan Barnes. London: Verso.

Lanternari, Vittorio. 1963. *The Religions of the Oppressed; A Study of Modern Messianic Cults.* Translated by Lisa Sergio. New York: Knopf.

———. 1974. "Nativisitic and Socio-Religious Movements: A Reconsideration." *Comparative Studies in Society and History* 16: 483–503.

Law, Robin, and Paul E. Lovejoy. 1997. "The Changing Dimensions of African History: Reappropriating the Diaspora." In *Rethinking African History,* ed. Simon McGrath, Charles Jedrej, Kenneth King, and Jack Thompson, 181–200. Edinburgh: Centre for African Studies.

Leach, Edmund. 1976. *Culture and Communication.* Cambridge: Cambridge University Press.

Leblond, Jean-Baptiste. 2000 [1813]. *Voyage aux Antilles: D'île en île, de la Martinique à Trinidad (1767–1773).* Paris: Éditions Karthala.

Lefebvre, Henri. 1991 [1974]. *The Production of Space.* Translated by Donald Nicholson-Smith. Oxford: Basil Blackwell.

———. 2003 [1970]. *The Urban Revolution.* Translated by Robert Bononno. Minneapolis: University of Minnesota Press.

Lévi-Strauss, Claude. 1963. *Structural Anthropology.* New York: Basic Books.

———. 1966. *The Savage Mind.* Chicago: University of Chicago Press.

Levitt, Peggy. 2001. *The Transnational Villagers.* Berkeley: University of California Press.

Lewis, I. M. 1989 [1971]. *Ecstatic Religion: A Study of Shamanism and Spirit Possession.* 2nd ed. London: Routledge.

Lincoln, Bruce. 2003. *Holy Terrors: Thinking about Religion after September 11.* Chicago: University of Chicago Press.

Linger, Daniel Touro. 2001. *No One Home: Brazilian Selves Remade in Japan.* Stanford, CA: Stanford University Press.

Lipsitz, George. 1998. *The Possessive Investment in Whiteness: How White People Profit from Identity Politics.* Philadelphia: Temple University Press.

Long, Charles H. 1986. *Significations: Signs, Symbols, and Images in the Interpretation of Religion.* Philadelphia: Fortress.

————. 2004. "A Postcolonial Meaning of Religion: Some Reflections from the Indigenous World." In *Beyond Primitivism: Indigenous Religious Traditions and Modernity*, ed. Jacob K. Olupona, 89–98. New York: Routledge.

Lovejoy, Paul E. 1983. *Transformations in Slavery: A History of Slavery in Africa*. Cambridge: Cambridge University Press.

————. 1997. "The African Diaspora: Revisionist Interpretations of Ethnicity, Culture and Religion under Slavery." *Studies in the World History of Slavery, Abolition and Emancipation* 2: 1–23.

MacCormack, Sabine. 1991. *Religion in the Andes: Vision and Imagination in Early Colonial Peru*. Princeton, NJ: Princeton University Press.

MacGaffey, Wyatt. 1986. *Religion and Society in Central Africa: The BaKongo of Lower Zaire*. Chicago: University of Chicago Press.

Mach, Zdzislaw. 1993. *Symbols, Conflict, and Identity: Essays in Political Anthropology*. Albany: State University of New York Press.

Mahmood, Saba. 2005. *Politics of Piety: The Islamic Revival and the Feminist Subject*. Princeton, NJ: Princeton University Press.

Malinowski, Bronislaw. 1922. *Argonauts of the Western Pacific*. London: G. Routledge.

Malkki, Lisa H. 1997. "National Geographic: The Rooting of Peoples and the Territorialization of National Identity among Scholars and Refugees." In *Culture, Power, Place: Explorations in Critical Anthropology*, ed. Akhil Gupta and James Ferguson, 52–74. Durham, NC: Duke University Press.

Margolis, Maxine L. 1994. *Little Brazil*. Princeton, NJ: Princeton University Press.

Martin, Luther. 1983. "Why Cecropian Minerva? Hellenistic Religious Syncretism as a System." *Numen* 30: 131–45.

Marx, Karl, and Friedrich Engels. 1970. *The German Ideology*. Edited by C. J. Arthur. New York: International Publishers.

————. 1978. *The Marx-Engels Reader*. Edited by Robert C. Tucker. New York: W. W. Norton & Company.

Massey, Doreen. 1993. "Politics and Space/Time." In *Place and the Politics of Identity*, ed. Michael Keith and Steve Pile, 141–61. London: Routledge.

Masuzawa, Tomoko. 1993. *In Search of Dreamtime: The Quest for the Origin of Religion*. Chicago: University of Chicago Press.

————. 2000. "Troubles with Materiality: The Ghost of Fetishism in the Nineteenth Century." *Comparative Studies in Society and History* 42 (2): 242–67.

Mato, Daniel. 2000. "Transnational Networking and the Social Production of Representations of Identities by Indigenous Peoples' Organizations of Latin America." *International Sociology* 15 (2): 343–60.

Matory, J. Lorand. 1999. "The English Professors of Brazil: On the Diasporic Roots of the Yoruba Nation." *Comparative Studies in Society and History* 41 (1): 72–103.

————. 2005. *Black Atlantic Religion: Tradition, Transnationalism, and Matriarchy in the Afro-Brazilian Candomblé*. Princeton, NJ: Princeton University Press.

Mattoso, Katia M. de Queirós. 1989. *To Be a Slave in Brazil, 1550–1888.* 2nd ed. Translated by Arthur Goldhammer. New Brunswick, NJ: Rutgers University Press.

Mauss, Marcel. 1979. *Sociology and Psychology Essays.* London: Routledge & Kegan Paul.

McAlister, Elizabeth. 1992. "Sacred Stories from the Haitian Diaspora: A Collective Biography of Seven Vodou Priestessses in New York City." *Journal of Caribbean Studies* 9 (2): 12–27.

———. 1998. "The Madonna of 115th Street Revisited: Vodou and Haitian Catholicism in the Age of Transnationalism." In *Gatherings in Diaspora: Religious Communities and the New Immigration,* ed. R. Stephen Warner and Judith G. Wittner, 123–60. Philadelphia: Temple University Press.

———. 2002. *Rara! Vodou, Power, and Performance in Haiti and Its Diaspora.* Berkeley: University of California Press.

McCutcheon, Russell T. 1997. *Manufacturing Religion: The Discourse on Sui Generis Religion and the Politics of Nostalgia.* New York: Oxford University Press.

Meléndez, Armando Crisanto. 1991. "Religious Elements of the Garifuna Culture and Their Connotations in the Americas." Translated by Dorothea Lowe Bryce. In *African Creative Expressions of the Divine,* ed. Kortright Davis and Elias Farajaje-Jones, 121–28. Washington, DC: Howard University School of Divinity.

———. 1997. *Adija sisira gererun aguburigu garinagu: El enojo de las sonajas; palabras del ancestor.* Tegucigalpa, Honduras: Graficentro Editores.

———. 2002. *El enojo de las sonajas: Palabras del ancestor.* 2nd ed. Tegucigalpa, Honduras: Editorial Cultura.

Mercer, Kobena. 2000. "A Sociography of Diaspora." In *Without Guarantees: In Honour of Stuart Hall,* ed. Paul Gilroy, Lawrence Grossberg, and Angela McRobbie, 233–45. London: Verso.

Merkin, Daphne. 2006. "What's So Hot about 50? Sex and the Female Boomer Is *Not* Booming." *New York Times Magazine,* February 12, 17–18.

Miller, Daniel. 2005. "Materiality: An Introduction." In *Materiality,* ed. Daniel Miller, 1–50. Durham, NC: Duke University Press.

Miller-Matthei, Linda, and David A. Smith. 1996. "Women, Households, and Transnational Migration Networks: The Garifuna and Global Economic Restructuring." In *Latin America in the World Economy,* ed. Roberto Patricio Korzeniewicz and William C. Smith, 133–68. Westport, CT: Praeger.

———. 1998. "Belizean 'Boyz 'n the 'Hood'? Garifuna Labor Migration and Transnational Identity." In *Transnationalism from Below,* ed. Michael Peter Smith and Luis Eduardo Guarnizo, 270–90. New Brunswick: Transaction Publishers.

Mintz, Sidney W. 1985. *Sweetness and Power: The Place of Sugar in Modern History.* New York: Penguin.

———. 1995. "Slave Life on Caribbean Sugar Plantations: Some Unanswered Questions." In *Slave Cultures and the Cultures of Slavery,* ed. Stephan Palmié. 12–23. Knoxville: University of Tennessee Press.

Mintz, Sidney, and Richard Price. 1992 [1976]. *The Birth of African-American Culture: An Anthropological Perspective*. Boston: Beacon Press.

Mittelberg, David, and Mary C. Waters. 1992. "The Process of Ethnogenesis among Haitian and Israeli Immigrants in the United States." *Ethnic and Racial Studies* 15: 412–35.

Moberg, Mark. 1992. "Continuity under Colonial Rule: The Alcalde System and the Garifuna in Belize, 1858–1969." *Ethnohistory* 39 (1): 1–19.

Moore, Sally F., and Barbara G. Myerhoff, eds. 1977. *Secular Ritual*. Assen, the Netherlands: Van Gorcum.

Moreau de Jonnès, Alexandre. 1920 [1858]. *Adventures in Wars of the Republic and Consulate*. Translated by A. J. Abdy. London: John Murray.

Morris, Valentine. 1787. *A Narrative of the Official Conduct of Valentine Morris, Esq. Late Captain General, Governor in Chief, of the Island of St. Vincent and its Dependencies*. London: J. Walter, Logographic Press.

Mudimbe, V. Y. 1988. *The Invention of Africa: Gnosis, Philosophy, and the Order of Knowledge*. Bloomington: Indiana University Press.

Mufti, Aamir. 2000. "The Aura of Authenticity." *Social Text* 18 (3): 87–103.

Mumford, Lewis. 1961. *The City in History*. New York: Harcourt, Brace & World.

Murphy, Joseph M. 1988. *Santería: An African Religion in America*. Boston: Beacon Press.

———. 1993. *Working the Spirit: Ceremonies of the African Diaspora*. Boston: Beacon Press.

Murray, David W. 1977. "Ritual Communications: Some Considerations Regarding Meaning in Navajo Ceremonials." In *Symbolic Anthropology: A Reader in the Study of Symbols and Meanings,* ed. Janet L. Dolgin, David S. Kemnitzer, and David M. Schneider, 195–220. New York: Columbia University Press.

Myerhoff, Barbara G. 1974. *Peyote Hunt: The Sacred Journey of the Huichol Indians*. Ithaca, NY: Cornell University Press.

Naipaul, V. S. 2002 [1962]. *The Middle Passage: The Caribbean Revisited*. New York: Vintage Books.

Needham, Rodney. 1972. *Belief, Language, and Experience*. Oxford: Basil Blackwell.

Nietzsche, Friedrich. 2003 [1913]. *The Genealogy of Morals*. Translated by Horace B. Samuel. Mineola, NY: Dover Publications, Inc.

Nora, Pierre. 1989. "Between Memory and History: Les Lieux de Mémoire." Translated by Marc Roudebush. *Representations* 26: 7–25.

Olmos, Margarite Fernández, and Lizabeth Paravisini-Gebert. 2003. *Creole Religions of the Caribbean: An Introduction from Vodou and Santería to Obeah and Espiritismo*. New York: New York University Press.

Ong, Aihwa. 1999. *Flexible Citizenship: The Cultural Logics of Transnationality*. Durham, NC: Duke University Press.

Ong, Walter J. 1970. *The Presence of the Word: Some Prolegomena for Cultural and Religious History*. New York: Clarion.

———. 1982. *Orality and Literacy: The Technologizing of the Word*. London: Methuen.

Orsi, Robert Anthony. 1985. *The Madonna of 115th Street: Faith and Community in Italian Harlem, 1880–1950*. New Haven, CT: Yale University Press.

———. 1999. "Introduction: Crossing the City Line." In *Gods of the City*, ed. Robert Orsi. Bloomington: Indiana University Press. 1–79.

Ortiz, Fernando. 1906. *Los negros brujos (apuntes para un estudio de etnología criminal)*. Madrid: Libreria Fernando Fé.

———. 1995. *Cuban Counterpoint: Tobacco and Sugar*. Translated by Harriet de Onís. Durham, NC: Duke University Press.

Ortiz, Renato. 1978. *A morte branca do feitiçeiro negro*. Rio de Janeiro: Editora Vozes.

Ortner, Sherry. 1984. "Theory in Anthropology Since the Sixties." *Comparative Studies in Society and History* 26: 126–66.

Palmer, Colin A. 1998. "Defining and Studying the Modern African Diaspora." *Perspectives* 36 (1): 22–25.

Palmié, Stephan. 1995. "Against Syncretism: 'Africanizing' and 'Cubanizing' Discourses in North American Òrisà Worship." In *Counterworks: Managing the Diversity of Knowledge*, ed. Richard Fardon, 73–104. London: Routledge.

———. 1996. "Which Center, Whose Margin? Notes toward an Archaeology of US Supreme Court Case 91–948, 1993." In *Inside and Outside the Law: Anthropological Studies of Authority and Ambiguity*, ed. Olivia Harris, 184–209. New York: Routledge.

———. 2002. *Wizards and Scientists: Explorations in Afro-Cuban Modernity and Tradition*. Durham, NC: Duke University Press.

Pané, Ramón. 1999. *An Account of the Antiquities of the Indians*. Edited by Jesé Juan Arrom and translated by Susan C. Griswold. Durham, NC: Duke University Press.

Parker, Fred. 1999. "Shakespeare's Argument with Montaigne." *Cambridge Quarterly* 28 (1): 1–18.

Parkin, David. 1991. *Sacred Void: Spatial Images of Work and Ritual among the Giriama of Kenya*. Cambridge: Cambridge University Press.

Peirce, Charles S. 1955. *Philosophical Writings of Peirce*. Edited by Justus Buchler. New York: Dover.

———. 1960. *The Collected Papers of Charles Sanders Peirce*. Vols. 1 and 2. Edited by C. Hartshorne and P. Weiss. Cambridge, MA: Harvard University Press.

Peréz y Mena, Andrés I. 1977. "Spiritualism as an Adaptive Mechanism among Puerto Ricans in the United States." *Cornell Journal of Social Relations* 12: 125–36.

Pierruci, Antônio Flávio, and Reginaldo Prandi. 2000. "Religious Diversity in Brazil: Numbers and Perspectives in a Sociological Evaluation." *International Sociology* 15 (4): 629–41.

Pietz, William. 1985. "The Problem of the Fetish, I." *Res* 9: 5–17.

———. 1987. "The Problem of the Fetish, II." *Res* 13: 23–45.

———. 1988. "The Problem of the Fetish, IIIa." *Res* 16: 105–23.

Pitts, Walter F. 1993. *Old Ship of Zion: The Afro-Baptist Ritual in the African Diaspora*. New York: Oxford University Press.

Pollard, Velma. 1994. *Dread Talk: The Language of Rastafari*. Kingston, Jamaica: Canoe Press University of the West Indies.

Portes, Alejandro, and Alex Stepick. 1993. *City on the Edge: The Transformation of Miami*. Berkeley: University of California Press.

Posas, Mario. 1993. *Breve historia de la ciudad de La Ceiba*. Tegucigalpa, Honduras: Alin Editora, S.A.

Povinelli, Elizabeth A. 2002. *The Cunning of Recognition: Indigenous Alterities and the Making of Australian Multiculturalism*. Durham, NC: Duke University Press.

Prandi, Reginaldo. 1991. *Os Candomblés de São Paulo*. São Paulo: Hucitec/ EDUSP.

Prentiss, Craig, ed. 2003. *Religion and the Creation of Race and Ethnicity: An Introduction*. New York: New York University Press.

Proudfoot, Wayne. 1985. *Religious Experience*. Berkeley: University of California Press.

Proust, Marcel. 1982. *Remembrance of Things Past*. Vol. 1. Translated by C. K. Scott Moncrieff and Terence Kilmartin. New York: Vintage Books.

Pyysiäinen, Ilkka. 2001. *How Religion Works: Towards a New Cognitive Science of Religion*. Leiden, the Netherlands: Brill.

Raboteau, Albert J. 1978. *Slave Religion: The "Invisible Institution" in the Antebellum South*. New York: Oxford University Press.

Radcliffe-Brown, A. R. 1952. *Structure and Function in Primitive Society*. Glencoe, IL: Free Press.

Ramos, Alcida Rita. 1998. *Indigenism: Ethnic Politics in Brazil*. Madison: University of Wisconsin Press.

Rappaport, Roy A. 1996. "The Obvious Aspects of Ritual." In *Readings in Ritual Studies,* ed. Ronald L. Grimes, 427–41. Upper Saddle River, NJ: Prentice Hall.

———. 1999. *Ritual and Religion in the Making of Humanity*. Cambridge: Cambridge University Press.

Raynolds, Laura T. 2003. "The Global Banana Trade." In *Banana Wars: Power, Production and History in the Americas,* ed. Steve Striffler and Mark Moberg, 23–47. Durham, NC: Duke University Press.

Reis, João José. 1993. *Slave Rebellion in Brazil: The Muslim Uprising of 1835 in Bahia*. Translated by Arthur Brakel. Baltimore: Johns Hopkins University Press.

Richman, Karen. 2005. *Migration and Vodou*. Gainesville: University Press of Florida.

Ricoeur, Paul. 2004. *Memory, History, Forgetting*. Translated by Kathleen Blamey and David Pellauer. Chicago: University of Chicago Press.

Riesebrodt, Martin. In press. "Religion: Just Another Modern Western Construction?" In *Rethinking Religion 101,* ed. Bradford Verter and Johannes Wolfart. Cambridge: Cambridge University Press.

Roach, Joseph. 1996. *Cities of the Dead: Circum-Atlantic Performance*. New York: Columbia University Press.

Roberts, Orlando W. 1827. *Narrative of Voyages and Excursions on the East Coast and in the Interior of Central America.* Edinburgh: Constable & Co.; London: Hurst, Chance & Co.

Robertson, Roland. 1992. *Globalization: Social Theory and Global Culture.* London: Sage.

———. 1995. "Glocalization: Time-Space and Homogeneity-Heterogeneity." In *Global Modernities,* ed. Mike Featherstone, Scott Lash, and Roland Robertson, 25–44. London: Sage.

Rochefort, Charles César de. 1992 [1658]. "Relative Values." In *Wild Majesty: Encounters with Caribs from Columbus to the Present Day,* ed. Peter Hulme and Neil L. Whitehead, 118–27. Oxford: Clarendon Press.

Roediger, David. 1991. *The Wages of Whiteness: Race and the Making of the American Working Class.* London: Verso.

Romberg, Raquel. 1998. "Whose Spirits Are They? The Political Economy of Syncretism and Authenticity." *Journal of Folklore Research* 35 (1): 69–82.

Rouse, Irving. 1948a. "The Arawak." In *Handbook of South American Indians.* Vol. 4, ed. Julian H. Steward, 507–46. New York: Cooper Square Publishers, Inc.

———. 1948b. "The Carib." In *Handbook of South American Indians.* Vol. 4, ed. Julian H. Steward, 547–65. New York: Cooper Square Publishers, Inc.

———. 1987. "Whom Did Columbus Discover in the West Indies?" *American Archeology* 6 (2): 85–87.

Rousseau, Jean-Jacques. 1964 [1750]. *The First Discourse.* Edited by Roger Masters and translated by Judith Masters. New York: St. Martin's Press.

Ruhl, J. Mark. 1984. "Agrarian Structure and Political Stability in Honduras." *Journal of Interamerican Studies and World Affairs* 26 (1): 33–68.

Rumbaut, Rubén G., and Alejandro Portes. 2001. "Ethnogenesis: Coming of Age in Immigrant America." In *Ethnicities: Children of Immigrants in America,* ed. Rubén G. Rumbaut and Alejandro Portes, 1–21. Berkeley: University of California Press.

Safran, William. 1991. "Diasporas in Modern Societies: Myths of Homeland and Return." *Diaspora* 1 (1): 83–99.

Sahlins, Marshall. 1976. *Culture and Practical Reason.* Chicago: University of Chicago Press.

———. 1981. *Historical Metaphors and Mythical Realities: Structure in the Early History of the Sandwich Islands.* Ann Arbor: University of Michigan Press.

———. 1985. *Islands of History.* Chicago: University of Chicago Press.

Sanborn, Helen. 1886. *A Winter in Central America and Mexico.* Boston: Lee and Shepard.

Sanford, Margaret. 1974. "Revitalization Movements as Indicators of Completed Acculturation." *Comparative Studies in Society and History* 16: 504–18.

Sanneh, Kelefa. 2003. "Unguarded Lyrics Embarrass Eminem." *New York Times,* November 20.

Sansone, Livio. 2003. *Blackness without Ethnicity: Constructing Race in Brazil.* New York: Palgrave Macmillan.

Sartre, Jean-Paul. 1960. *Critique de la raison dialectique*. Paris: Gallimard.

———. 1963. "Preface." In Frantz Fanon, *The Wretched of the Earth*, 7–34. New York: Grove Press.

Selva Rendón, Ravael Murrilo. 1997. *Loubavagu o "El otro lado lejano."* Tegucigalpa, Honduras: Litografía López.

Sennett, Richard. 1994. *Flesh and Stone: The Body and the City in Western Civilization*. New York: W. W. Norton & Company.

Sewell, William H. Jr. 1999. "The Concept(s) of Culture." In *Beyond the Cultural Turn: New Directions in the Study of Society and Culture*, ed. Victoria E. Bonnell and Lynn Hunt, 35–61. Berkeley: University of California Press.

Shakespeare, William. 1944 [1611]. *The Tempest*. In *The Portable Shakespeare*, 553–624. New York: Penguin Books.

Shaw, Rosalind. 2002. *Memories of the Slave Trade: Ritual and the Historical Imagination in Sierra Leone*. Chicago: University of Chicago Press.

Sheffer, Gabriel. 2003. *Diaspora Politics: At Home Abroad*. Cambridge: Cambridge University Press.

Shelby, Tommie. 2005. *We Who Are Dark: The Philosophical Foundations of Black Solidarity*. Cambridge, MA: Belknap Press of Harvard University Press.

Shepperson, George. 1968. "The African Abroad or the African Diaspora." In *Emerging Themes of African History*, ed. T. O. Ranger, 152–76. London: Heinemann, 1968.

Shore, Bradd. 1996. *Culture in Mind: Cognition, Culture, and the Problem of Meaning*. New York: Oxford University Press.

Simmel, Georg. 1950. *The Sociology of Georg Simmel*. Translated and edited by Kurt H. Wolff. New York: Free Press.

———. 1978. *The Philosophy of Money*. Translated by Tom Bottomore and David Frisby. London: Routledge & Kegan Paul.

Smith, Jeffrey S., and Benjamin N. White. 2004. "Detached from Their Homeland: The Latter-Day Saints of Chihuahua, Mexico." *Journal of Cultural Geography* 21 (2): 57–76.

Smith, Jonathan Z. 1978. *Map Is Not Territory*. Chicago: University of Chicago Press.

———. 1982. *Imagining Religion: From Babylon to Jonestown*. Chicago: University of Chicago Press.

———. 1987. *To Take Place: Toward Theory in Ritual*. Chicago: University of Chicago Press.

Smith, Wilfred Cantwell. 1991. *The Meaning and End of Religion*. Minneapolis: Fortress Press.

Soja, Edward. 1989. *Postmodern Geographies*. London: Verso.

Sollors, Werner. 1990. "Ethnicity." In *Critical Terms for Literary Study*, 2nd edition, ed. Frank Lentricchia and Thomas McLaughlin, 288–306. Chicago: University of Chicago Press.

Soluri, John. 2003. "Banana Cultures: Linking the Production and Consumption of Export Bananas, 1800–1980." In *Banana Wars: Power, Production and*

History in the Americas, ed. Steve Striffler and Mark Moberg, 48–79. Durham, NC: Duke University Press.

Sperber, Dan. 1996. *Explaining Culture: A Naturalistic Approach.* Oxford: Blackwell.

Staal, Frits. 1979. "The Meaninglessness of Ritual." *Numen* 26: 2–22.

Staples, Brent. 2003. "Editorial Observer: The Black Seminoles Keep Fighting for Equality in the American West." *New York Times,* November 17.

Stephens, John Lloyd. 1949 [1841]. *Incidents of Travel in Central America, Chiapas, and Yucatan.* Vol. 1. Edited by Richard L. Predmore. New Brunswick: Rutgers University Press.

Stepick, Alex, Carol Dutton Stepick, Emmanuel Eugene, Deborah Teed, and Yves Labissiere. 2001. "Shifting Identities and Intergenerational Conflict: Growing Up Haitian in Miami." In *Ethnicities: Children of Immigrants in America,* ed. Rubén G. Rumbaut and Alejandro Portes, 229–66. Berkeley: University of California Press; New York: Russell Sage Foundation.

Stewart, Charles. 1999. "Syncretism and Its Synonyms: Reflections on Cultural Mixture." *Diacritics* 29 (3): 40–62.

Stewart, Charles, and Rosalind Shaw, eds. 1994. *Syncretism/Anti-syncretism: The Politics of Religious Synthesis.* London: Routledge.

Suazo, E. Salvador. 2000. *Irufumali: La doctrina esotérica garífuna.* Tegucigalpa, Honduras: Centro de Desarrollo Comunitario.

Sweet, James H. 2003. *Recreating Africa: Culture, Kinship, and Religion in the African-Portuguese World, 1441–1770.* Chapel Hill: University of North Carolina Press.

Swett, Charles. 1868. *A Trip to British Honduras, and to San Pedro, Republic of Honduras.* New Orleans: n.p.

Tambiah, Stanley J. 1979. "A Performative Approach to Ritual." *Proceedings of the British Academy* 65: 113–69.

Taylor, Douglas. 1949. "The Interpretation of Some Documentary Evidence on Carib Culture." *Southwestern Journal of Anthropology* 5: 379–92.

———. 1951. *The Black Carib of British Honduras.* New York: Wenner-Gren Foundation for Anthropological Research.

Telles, Edward E. 2004. *Race in Another America: The Significance of Skin Color in Brazil.* Princeton, NJ: Princeton University Press.

Thomas, Piri. 1997 [1967]. *Down These Mean Streets.* New York: Vintage Books.

Thompson, Robert Farris. 1984. *Flash of the Spirit: African and Afro-American Art and Philosophy.* New York: Random House.

Thornton, John. 1998. *Africa and Africans in the Making of the Atlantic World, 1400–1800.* 2nd ed. Cambridge: Cambridge University Press.

Tölölyan, Khachig. 1994. "A Note from the Editor." *Diaspora* 3(3): 235–41.

——— 1996. "Rethinking Diaspora(s): Stateless Power in the Transnational Moment." *Diaspora* 5 (2): 3–36.

Tolstoy, Leo. 1931. *War and Peace.* Translated by Constance Garnett. New York: Modern Library.

Torres, Arlene, and Norman E. Whitten Jr. 1998. "To Forge the Future in the Fires of the Past: An Interpretive Essay on Racism, Domination, Resistance and Liberation." In *Blackness in Latin America and the Caribbean,* ed. Arlene Torres and Norman E. Whitten Jr., 3–36. Bloomington: Indiana University Press.

Trilling, Lionel. 1972. *Sincerity and Authenticity.* Cambridge, MA: Harvard University Press.

Trouillot, Michel-Rolph. 1995. *Silencing the Past: Power and the Production of History.* Boston: Beacon Press.

Tuan, Y. F. 1976. "Geopiety: A Theme in Man's Attachment to Nature and to Place." In *Geographies of the Mind,* ed. D. Lowenthal and M. Bowden, 44–56. New York: Oxford University Press.

———. 1977. *Space and Place: The Perspectives of Experience.* Minneapolis: University of Minnesota Press.

Tulving, Endel. 1972. "Episodic and Semantic Memory." In *Organization of Memory,* ed. Endel Tulving and Wayne Donaldson, 381–403. New York: Academic Press.

Turner, Victor W. 1962. *Chihamba, the White Spirit.* Manchester, UK: Manchester University Press.

———. 1967. *The Forest of Symbols: Aspects of Ndembu Ritual.* Ithaca, NY: Cornell University Press.

———. 1969. *The Ritual Process.* Chicago: Aldine.

———. 1974. *Dramas, Fields and Metaphors.* Ithaca, NY: Cornell University Press.

———. 1982. *From Ritual to Theater: The Human Seriousness of Play.* New York: PAJ Publications.

———. 1985. *On the Edge of the Bush: Anthropology as Experience.* Edited by Edith L. B. Turner. Tucson: University of Arizona Press.

———. 1986. *The Anthropology of Performance.* New York: PAJ Publications.

———. 1992. *Blazing the Trail: Way Marks in the Exploration of Symbols.* Edited by Edith Turner. Tucson: University of Arizona Press.

Tweed, Thomas A. 1997. *Our Lady of the Exile: Diaspora Religion at a Cuban Catholic Shrine in Miami.* New York: Oxford University Press.

———. 2006. *Crossing and Dwelling: A New Theory of Religion.* Cambridge, MA: Harvard University Press.

Tylor, Edward Burnett. 1958. *Primitive Culture.* New York: Harper & Row.

Uring, Nathaniel. 1726. *A History of the Voyages and Travels of Capt. Nathaniel Uring, with a New Draught of the Bay of Honduras.* London: n.p.

Van Gennep, Arnold. 1960 [1909]. *The Rites of Passage.* Translated by M. B. Vizedom and G. L. Caffee. Chicago: University of Chicago Press.

Van Hear, Nicholas. 1998. *New Diasporas: The Mass Exodus, Dispersal and Regrouping of Migrant Communities.* Seattle: University of Washington Press.

Vásquez, Manuel A., and Marie Friedmann Marquardt. 2003. *Globalizing the Sacred: Religion across the Americas.* New Brunswick: Rutgers University Press.

Vega, Marta Moreno. 2000. *The Altar of My Soul: The Living Traditions of Santería*. New York: Ballantine Publishing Group.

Verdery, Katherine. 1994. "Beyond the Nation in Eastern Europe." *Social Text* 38: 1–19.

Verger, Pierre. 1981. *Orixás: Deuses Iorubás na Africa e no Novo Mundo*. Salvador, Bahia, Brazil: Corrupio.

Vertovec, Steven. 2000. *The Hindu Diaspora: Comparative Patterns*. London: Routledge.

Vickerman, Milton. 1999. *Crosscurrents: West Indian Immigrants and Race*. New York: Oxford University Press.

Warner, R. Stephen. 1993. "Work in Progress toward a New Paradigm for the Sociological Study of Religion in the United States." *American Journal of Sociology* 98: 1044–93.

———. 1998. "Immigration and Religious Communities in the United States." In *Gatherings in Diaspora: Religious Communities and the New Immigration*, edited by R. Stephen Warner and Judith G. Wittner, 3–36. Philadelphia: Temple University Press.

Warner, R. Stephen, and Judith G. Wittner, eds. 1998. *Gatherings in Diaspora: Religious Communities and the New Immigration*. Philadelphia: Temple University Press.

Waters, Mary C. 1999. *Black Identities: West Indian Immigrant Dreams and American Realities*. New York: Russell Sage Foundation; Cambridge, MA: Harvard University Press.

Weber, Max. 1978. *Economy and Society*. Edited by Guenther Roth and Claus Wittich. Berkeley: University of California Press.

———. 1992. *The Protestant Ethic and the Spirit of Capitalism*. Translated by Talcott Parsons. London: Routledge.

———. 2002. *The Protestant Ethic and the "Spirit" of Capitalism*. Translated by Peter Baehr and Gordon C. Wells. New York: Penguin Books.

Weil, Simone. 1947. *La pesanteur et la grâce*. Paris: Librairie Plon.

Wells, Marilyn McKillop. 1982a. "Spirits See Red: The Symbolic Use of Gusueue among the Garif (Black Caribs) of Central America." *Belizean Studies* 10 (3): 10–16.

———. 1982b. "The Symbolic use of Gusueue among the Garif (Black Caribs) of Central America." *Anthropological Quarterly* 55 (1): 44–55.

Werbner, Pnina. 2000. "Introduction: The Materiality of Diaspora—Between Aesthetic and 'Real' Politics." *Diaspora* 9 (1): 5–20.

———. 2002. *Imagined Diasporas among Manchester Muslims*. Oxford: James Currey.

Werbner, Richard. 2002. "Postcolonial Subjectivities: The Personal, the Political and the Moral." In *Postcolonial Subjectivities in Africa*, ed. Richard Werbner, 1–23. London: Zed Books.

West, Cornel. 2001 [1993]. *Race Matters*. New York: Vintage Books.

Westwood, Sallie, and Annie Phizacklea. 2000. *Trans-nationalism and the Politics of Belonging*. New York: Routledge.

Whitehouse, Harvey. 1995. *Inside the Cult: Religious Innovation and Transmission in Papua New Guinea*. Oxford: Oxford University Press.

———. 2000. *Arguments and Icons: Divergent Modes of Religiosity*. Oxford: Oxford University Press.

———. 2004. *Modes of Religiosity: A Cognitive Theory of Religious Transmission*. Walnut Creek, CA: AltaMira Press.

Williams, Raymond. 1983. *Keywords: A Vocabulary of Culture and Society*. New York: Oxford University Press.

Williams, Raymond Brady. 1988. *Religions of Immigrants from India and Pakistan: New Threads in the American Tapestry*. Cambridge: Cambridge University Press.

Winant, Howard. 1994. "Racial Formation and Hegemony: Global and Local Developments." In *Racism, Modernity, and Identity on the Western Front*, ed. Ali Rattansi and Sallie Westwood, 266–89. Cambridge: Polity.

———. 1998. "Contesting the Meaning of Race in the Post–Civil Rights Period." In *New Tribalisms: The Resurgence of Race and Ethnicity*, ed. Michael W. Hughey, 197–211. New York: New York University Press.

Wittgenstein, Ludwig. 1953. *Philosophical Investigations*. New York: Macmillan.

Wright, John K. 1947. "Terrae Incognitae: The Place of the Imagination in Geography." *Annals of the Association of American Geographers* 37 (1): 1–15.

Wright, Michelle M. 2004. *Becoming Black: Creating Identity in the African Diaspora*. Durham, NC: Duke University Press.

Wuthnow, Robert. 1989. *Communities of Discourse: Ideology and Social Structure in the Reformation, the Enlightenment, and European Socialism*. Cambridge, MA: Harvard University Press.

Young, Thomas. 1847. *Narrative of a Residence on the Mosquito Shore*. London: Smith, Elder and Co.

Young, William. 1764. *Some Observations; Which May Contribute to Afford a Just Idea of the Nature, Importance, and Settlement, of Our New West-India Colonies*. London: n.p.

———. 1971 [1795]. *An Account of the Black Charaibs in the Island of St. Vincent's*. London: Frank Cass & Co., Ltd.

Young, William, II. 1992. "William Young's Tour of the Islands." In *Wild Majesty: Encounters with Caribs from Columbus to the Present Day*, ed. Peter Hulme and Neil L. Whitehead, 211–15. Oxford: Clarendon Press.

Yuscaran, Guillermo. 1997. *Cuando Chona cantaba*. Tegucigalpa, Honduras: Litografía Lopez.

Zane, Wallace W. 1999. *Journeys to the Spiritual Lands: The Natural History of a West Indian Religion*. New York: Oxford University Press.

Zerubavel, Eviatar. 1999. *Social Mindscapes: An Invitation to Cognitive Sociology*. Cambridge, MA: Harvard University Press.

Zubrzycki, Geneviève. 2006. *The Crosses of Auschwitz: Nationalism and Religion in Post-Communist Poland*. Chicago: University of Chicago Press.

Zukin, Sharon. 1996. "Whose Culture? Whose City?" In *The City Reader*, ed. Richard T. LeGates and Frederic Stout, 131–42. New York: Routledge.

Index

Numbers in italics indicate figures or maps.

abeimahani. See women's songs
abelaguduni (presenting the "catch"), 164
achiote dye, 108, 155
Acker, Alison, 270n31
additivity, 55
Adefumni I, Oba Ofuntola Oseigema
    Adelabu. *See* King, Walter Serge
Adorno, Theodore W., 285n12
adugurahani. See dügü performance
African Americans: innate religiosity of,
    216; notion of diaspora and, 33, 35,
    38–39; Yoruba revivalism among,
    207–10, 216–17
African Burial Ground (Lower
    Manhattan), 274n3
African Diaspora: analytic features of,
    48–53; Black Carib religion and,
    18–19; Brazilian slaves and, 50; Bronx-
    based shamans and, 128–35, 145; cul-
    ture vs. racial authenticity and, 208,
    209–10, 213; Garifuna consciousness
    and, 18–19, 102, 242–45; Garifuna
    religious conversion and, 6, 22, 46,
    47–48, 229, 230–31; idea of, 259n14;
    institutional networks and, 33; litera-
    ture on, 18, 212–14; migrations of,
    255n2; as nonterritorial, 51–52; origins
    of Garifuna and, 3, 5, 8, 16, 17;
    Oyotunji Village and, 208–9; racial
    identity and, 214–20; spread of
culture of, 224–25; as term, 260n16.
    See also African diasporic religions in
    New York; Yoruba-Santería traditions
African Diaspora and Caribbean Culture
    Center, 48
African diasporic religions in New York,
    53–59; Bronx-based shamans and,
    125–45; comparisons among, 58–59;
    definition of, 53–54; diasporic
    exchange and, 202–3; "return of the
    ancestors" ritual and, 188–89, 191–94;
    ritual return to homeland and, 33;
    spirit geographies and, 135–36;
    Yoruba-Santería religious hegemony
    and, 103, 205–14. *See also* Candomblé
    tradition; Palo Monte; Santería;
    Vodou; Yoruba-Santería traditions
Africanness vs. blackness, 40, 49, 52–53,
    217–19, 225–26; African diasporic cul-
    tures and, 229; definition of terms
    and, 218; Garifuna identity and, 102;
    religious renaissance and, 223–24,
    225; Yoruba-Santería traditions and,
    208, 209–10, 213
Afro-Honduran, as term, 102
ahari (spirits), 272n2
Alpers, Edward, 260n16
Alquiza, Sancho de, 63
altars *(gulei):* African diasporic objects
    and, 113–14, 136–37, *138;* of Bronx
    shamans, 114, 136–37, *138,* 188–89, *189,*
    195; *calderos* and, 247–50;

altars (*gulei*) (*continued*):
homeland *dügü* rituals and, 154; of
homeland shamans, 105, 112–14, *113;*
images of saints on, 110–11
amalahani dance and songs (*mali*), 72,
164–66, 173, 277n14
Amaya, Carlos (Honduran *buyei*), 107–8,
109, 116–17, 123, 135, 272n4, 273n7
Amerindian identity and Garifuna, 3, 5, 8,
221, 254n11
amuidahani ritual (bathing of the
deceased), 94
ancestors, distinctions among, 272n2.
See also ancestor spirits; helping
spirits
ancestor spirits (*gubida*), *172;* Black Carib
religious roots and, 72–73, 84–85;
dances leading to possession by, 18,
149; entertainment of, 160, 175; feeding of, 95–96, 169–70; homeland ritual
and, 93, 95, 148–49, 159, 169–70,
171–73; illness inflicted by, 19, 148;
movements of, 12, 178–79, 228; repose
and, 237–38; role of *buyei* and, 71, 148.
See also helping spirits
Anderson, Alexander, 69, 76
Anderson, Benedict, 255n4
Anderson, Mark, 217–18
Andino, Tiburcio Carías, 271n37
Andrews, George Reid, 210
animal sacrifice: Bronx Garifuna and, 189,
193; homeland ritual and, 96, 161,
166–67; Santería and, 44
Appadurai, Arjun, 100–1
Appiah, K. A., 259n13, 280n4
Aranda, Theodore, 274n5
Arawaks, 232, 251n1
Arce, Manuel José, 81, 82
Arendt, Hannah, 234
arumahani (men's songs). *See* men's songs
assimilation: Bronx Garifuna and, 21, 22;
diasporic religion and, 41; notion of
diaspora and, 33, 34–40
Atran, Scott, 283n7
audience: Bronx rituals and, 198–200,
278n2; homeland *dügü* and, 180–81
"auratic decline," 233–34
authenticity, 282n2; Black Carib rituals
and, 85; diasporic horizons and, 7–8;
diasporic religion and, 40, 45, 227,
231–35; homeland as endowed with,
36; links with homeland and, 45;

232–33; spirit geographies and, 135–36;
"theologization" and, 103

Baba Luaye (Yoruba-Santería deity), 192,
205
Bachelard, Gaston, 13–14
Baha'i (religion), 273n5
Bakongo people. *See* Kongo tradition
Balibar, Étienne, 215, 242
Baliceaux island, 77
banana republic period, 79, 86–93
Barbados, 63, 64–65, 76
Bard, Samuel, 80, 90
Bascom, William, 261n23
baskets of palm sheaves (*guagai*), 151,
159–60, 276n9
Bastide, Roger, 57, 212, 261n22
Baumann, Martin, 35, 42
Baxter, Mr. (Methodist missionary), 74
bead necklaces (*collares*), 136, 195
Beaumont, Monsieur de, 67
Belgium (Bronx Garifuna woman), 136, 191
Belize, 45, 78, 82, 83, 141, 224, 268n20,
272n2, 277n14; *dügü* song from,
152–53; initiation of shaman from,
132–33. *See also* Central American
Caribbean Coast
Bell, Catherine, 242–43
Benjamin, Walter, 45, 233
Bennett, James B., 281n5
Berger, Peter, 285n11
Bergson, Henri, 246
"binding," idea of, 215–17
Black Caribs: African heritage of, 14–15,
64–66, 256; banana republic period
and, 86–93; British Africanization of,
68–69, 266n9; Caribs as term, 3, 5,
102, 251n1; Carib Wars of 1795–96,
76–77, 78; in Central America, 7,
77–86; colonialism and, 5–6, 19,
62–66, 68–70, 74–77, 246; exile from
St. Vincent, 7, 74–77; migration to
U.S., 6–7; origins of, 3, 5, 8, 16–18,
61–70, 245; religion of, 7, 18–19, 61,
70–74, 82–86; soldiering and, 78, 79,
81–82; tensions between Island Caribs
and, 66–69; as term, 3. *See also* Bronx
Garifuna; Garifuna religion;
Honduran villagers
blackness: Africanization of Black Caribs
and, 68–69; diasporic models of, 8; as
Garifuna conversion, 6, 20–21, 40,

221–26; resistance to black identity, 219–20; as term, 218. *See also* Africanness vs. blackness
Black Power Movement of New York, 207–8
Boas, Franz, 252n2
boiyako (buyei). *See* Bronx shamans; Honduran village shamans; shaman
Bolufer, Roberto, 206
Bourdieu, Pierre, 285n10
Bovin, Mette, 241–42
Braithwaite, John, 66–67
Brazil, 50, 281n6
bread making, 157. *See also* cassava bread
Breton, Raymond, 64, 67, 71
Bronx (NY): cityscape of, 54–55; ethnographic research in, 22–23, 24–27. *See also* African diasporic religions in New York; Bronx Garifuna; Bronx ritual performance; Bronx shamans
Bronx Garifuna: African Diaspora and, 47–48, 53, 102–4; assimilation and, 21, 22; code switching and, 38, 40, 141–42, 223, 229–30; ethnogenesis of, 3–7, 18–19, 69–70, 245; Garifuna religious forms and, 21–22; migration to U.S., 6, 19–21; multiple affiliations of, 7–8, 38, 222–23; mutuality with homeland of, 37–38; public recognition and, 25–26, 140–42; race identity and, 221, 222–25; signification of ritual among, 236–38. *See also* Bronx shamans
Bronx ritual performance, 186–204; Africanization of, 128–31, 194, 195–98, 230–31; "departure of the ancestors" ritual, 195–98; forms of community and, 241–45; frequency of, 186–87; mutuality and, 245–46; "return of the ancestors" ritual, 187–94, 198–200; significations in, *138,* 236–38, 240–41
Bronx shamans *(buyei)*: autobiographies of, 126–35; consultations and, 186–87; Kongo traditions and, 210, 247–50; on non-Garifuna influences, 128, 130–31, 205–6; orthodoxy and, 145, 237; public recognition of religion and, 25–26, 140–42; "return of the ancestors" ritual and, 190–91, 192–94; return to Honduras, 142–45
Brown, David, 55, 248–49, 250
Brubaker, Rogers, 10, 253n6

brujas. *See* witches
Brunias, Agostino, *61*
Bulnes, Juan. *See* Walumugu
Bungiu (God), 73, 147–48
Burdick, John, 281n5
"burning the table" ritual, 96, 177
Butler, Judith, 259n12
buyei (shaman). *See* Bronx shamans; Honduran village shamans; shaman

Cabrera, Lydia, 129
calderos (iron pots with objects), 129, *130,* 137, 247–50, 272n1
Caliban (Shakespearean character), 16–18, 234–35
Candomblé tradition, 103, 213, 279n6. *See also* Yoruba-Santería traditions
canoes: Black Carib trade and, 79–81, 86; *dügü* ritual and, 157–58; ritual altars and, 112
Caribbean Culture Center/African Diaspora Institute, 207, 209, 279n10
Caribbean immigrants to U.S.: black identity and, 38, 49, 219–20, 225; diaspora religion and, 45, 47–48; notion of African Diaspora and, 51–52; racial system and, 20–21, 49, 219–20. *See also* Bronx Garifuna
Caribbean Organization of Indigenous Peoples (COIP), 141
Caribbean region and religious modernity, 16–18
Caribs, as term, 3, 5, 102, 251n1. *See also* Black Caribs; Island Caribs
Carib Wars of 1795–96, 76–77, 78, 276n12
cassava bread *(ereba)*: Black Carib trade and, 80; in homeland ritual, 96, 148; Island Carib culture and, 71; production of, 277n15
Castro, Fidel, 92
Catholicism. *See* Roman Catholicism
"cell-phone shamans," 23
Central American Caribbean coast, *4;* Black Carib arrival on, 77, 78–79, 225; Black Carib life on, 79–82; as diasporic horizon, 7–8, 60, 77–86; dispersion of Black Caribs on, 81–82; Garifuna religion and, 45–46, 141–42; migration of Garifuna to U.S. and, 6, 19, 20–21; re-Africanization of Garifuna and, 223–24. *See also* Belize; Honduran villagers

Central American Federation (República Federal de Centroamérica), 81–82
Certeau, Michel de, 54
Césaire, Aimé, 50–51, 52
Chakrabarty, Dipesh, 226
Chatoyer (Black Carib hero), 14, *68*, 69, 75–76, 77
Chaves, Paula, 275n4
Chiquita (brand name), 88
chugu ritual (Bronx), 95–96, 122–24
Church of Our Lady of Mount Carmel (New York City), 44, 47, 56
Clarke, Kamari Maxine, 208, 216
Clifford, James, 281n8
"climbing the pole" ritual *(trepar el palo)*, 108, 173
code switching: diasporic religions and, 58–59; ethnicity and, 40, 223, 229; institutional recognition and, 141; religion and, 141–42, 223, 230
Cohen, Robin, 42, 258n10
Cohn, Irving, 270n30
COIP. *See* Caribbean Organization of Indigenous Peoples
collares. *See* bead necklaces
"collective effervescence," 238
collective memory: banana republic period and, 88–91; diasporic religion and, 46–48; in Honduran homeland, 100, 113; vs. individual memory, 259n11; modes of transmission and, 238–39; notion of diaspora and, 33; St. Vincent in, 100
colonialism: authentic identity and, 234–35; Black Caribs and, 5–6, 19, 62–66, 68–70, 265n6; polarized terms of, 251n1; resistance to, 7–8, 66
Columbus, Christopher, 251n1
commemorative labor, 37–38
communications, in Honduran villages, 23–24
communitas, concept of, 243–44
compression in ritual performances, 178–80, 233
continuity: *cristianos* and, 118–21; homeland *dügü* and, 181–82
conversion, as term, 260n17
Conzemius, Eduard, 84–85, 156
Cornelio, Don (Corozal villager), 89, 164
Corozal (Honduran village): *cristianos* and, 118–21; *dügü* performance in, 24, 96–97, 147–77 (see also *dügü* performance)

cosmopolitan religious performance, 6–7, 22, 241
crises: *dügü* rituals and, 171–73, 182–85; New York rituals and, 191–94
cristianos (Protestant Garifuna), 117–24
Cristo Negro. *See* Esquipula, Saint
Crowther, Samuel, 211
Cuba, history of, 262n1
Cuban traditions: *calderos* and, 247–50; and Garifuna, 206–7
culture, as term, 255n5

dabuyaba. See temple for ritual
da Cunha, Euclides, 216
Davíd (brother of Adolfo), 171–73, 183
Davidson, George, 66, 74, 267nn10,13
Davis, Hugh, 215
death: *dügü* ritual and, 166–67; Iku and, 193, 194; ritualization of, 93–95, 186
"de-diasporization," 33–34
Delany, Martin, 216
"departure of the ancestors" ritual (Bronx), 195–98
"departure of the fishermen" ritual (homeland), 112, 158–61
Derrida, Jacques, 8, 17
"Devil feast," 84
diaspora: analytic features of, 30–40, 48; cross-referencing between diasporic groups, 256n7; defined by relation, 33–35; determination of, 2–3; etymology of, 32; further considerations in meaning of, 35–40; Garifuna migrations and, 3–7; as kind of culture, 35; list-based definition of, 32–33; multiple horizons and, 7–8, 17–18, 45–46, 102–4; notion of, 30–32; relation between religion and, 42–48; and shifting community, 241–46; as term, 9–10, 30–40, 42; urban culture and, 39–40, 256n6. *See also* Bronx Garifuna
diasporic horizons: diasporic religion and, 7–8, 17–18, 45–46, 99–104; for homeland and Bronx Garifuna, 97–98, 99–104, 146–47; memory and, 18–19. *See also* African Diaspora; Honduran villagers; St. Vincent island
diasporic religion: analytic features of, 40–48, 49; code switching and, 58–59; creation of religion by diaspora, 43–46, 228; definition of, 258;

diasporic horizons and, 7–8, 17–18, 45–46, 99–104; dissemination of, 230–31; forms of community and, 228, 241–45; Herberg hypothesis and, 43–44; "homeland" vs. "diasporic" categories and, 99–104; mapping processes and, 55–59; memory making and, 10–15; multiple diasporic horizons and, 7–8, 17–18, 45–46, 102–4; problem of authenticity and, 40, 45, 227, 232–35; profile of, 40–42; religious diasporas and, 258; religious modes and, 6–7, 241; as re-membered, 46–48; ritual and, 42, 45, 46–47, 228, 235–41; semiotic logic of, 228, 232, 235–41; social dynamics of ritual and, 200–1. *See also* African diasporic religions in New York; Garifuna religion
Diaz, Julio Lozano, 271n38
divination. *See* "roots readings"
doctrinal mode of religion, 203–4, 238
Dominican immigrants, 220
doorways, protection of, 137, 179, 192–94
Douglass, Frederick, 215–16
Du Bois, W. E. B., 211–12
dügü performance, 24, 96–97, 147–77; *amalahani* dance, 164–66, 173; ancestors regain their youth ritual, 171–73, *172;* anniversary of *(lugusurugayu),* 177; banquet, 168–71; Black Carib "Devil feasts" and, 84–85; bread making and, 157–58; call for, 147–49; costs of, 148–51, 158, 275n1; dance of the masks *(wanaragua)* in, 161, *163,* 164; departure of the fishermen *(idugahatiñu),* 112, 158–61; facing down the devil and, 167–68; filming and, 155–56, 157; frequency of, 184; healing process in, 177–85; hierarchy among shamans and, 115; last day of, 174–77; making the heart of, 155–57; the mass, 154–55; preparation for, 149–54; presenting the "catch," 164–66; reprising activities and, 173–74; return of the fishermen, 161–68, *162;* revels in the sea and, 175, *176;* signification in, 236–37 *(see also* meaning); Yoruba culture and, 212–13
dügü songs *(amalahani),* 116, 152–53, 155, 179; examples of, 160, 163, 164,

165–66, 170–71. *See also* men's songs; women's songs
Durkheim, Émile, 100, 101, 240, 257, 259n11, 284n10
du Tertre, Jean-Baptiste, 63
Du Vallée (Black Carib), 14, 69

earthen tablets *(mua):* building of, 155–56; as center of *dügü,* 164, 166, 176, 179, 236; meaning of, 156–57, 184; turning of, 157, 175, 180
Edwards, Bryan, 16, 76, 265n6
8 Mile (film), 260n18
Eleggua (Yoruba-Santería deity), 128, 129, 136–37, *138,* 188–89, 192, 193, 194, 280n2, 286n5
England, Sarah, 53, 221, 222, 223, 225
entasy vs. ecstasy, 104–5
episodic memory, 239–40, 283n8
Equiano, Olaudah, 254n11, 265n5
ereba. See cassava bread
Espiritismo (Spiritism). *See* Santerismo
Esquipula, Saint ("Cristo Negro"), 73, 110–11, 188, 191, 221
ethnic communities vs. diasporas, 33–35
ethnic identity: diaspora cultural affiliation and, 38–39, 244–45; Garifuna ritual and, 228–32, 234, 235, 238, 242; race and, 21, 52–53, 217–19; "return of the ancestors" ritual and, 187–88
ethnogenesis of Garifuna, 3–7, 18–19, 69–70, 74, 245
Euraque, Darío, 271n36
evil spirits. *See mafia;* "people of the forest"
Ezili Danto (Vodou spirit), 56

family bonds, 96, 149, *176,* 180–81, 184–85. *See also dügü* performance
Fanon, Franz, 234
Felix (shaman). *See* Miranda, Felix Igemeri
Ferrer, Fernando, 223
fetish objects, 286n2. *See also* altars
fishing rite in *dügü,* 112, 157–68, *162,* 236
Fitzgerald, F. Scott, 270n30
Flores, Carlos (Honduran president), 252n3
Foner, Nancy, 261n20
forest, the *(el monte),* 57, 73, 167–68, 179, 249
Foster, Byron, 152–53, 156, 272n2, 275n5
Foucault, Michel, 259n12

France: Black Caribs and, 70, 74–77, 78;
St. Vincent and, 265n7
Francisco (Bronx Garifuna leader), 134–35
Frank, Gelya, 255n7
Frazier, E. Franklin, 260n15
Frobenius, Leo, 211, 212
Froebel, Julius, 80–81
fruit companies. *See* banana republic period
furunsu (rum punch), 176–77
fusing of domains in *dügü*, 180–81
futurity: *cristianos* and, 121; diaspora and,
8, 32, 144; symbolism and, 237–38

gaps and notion of diaspora, 35–36
García, Centeno, 213
Garifuna culture, 140–42, 198–200; public
recognition and, 25–26, 140–42. *See
also* Bronx Garifuna; ethnic identity;
Honduran villagers
Garifuna religion: African influences and,
72–73, 83–84, 137, 201–3; Catholicism
and, 73–74; as diasporic religion,
40–42, 45–46, 59, 99–104; effects of
migration on, 21–22, 102–4; Garifuna
identity and, 41; in homeland, 93–97;
Island Carib influences and, 70–71;
modes of performance of, 239–41;
positional memory and, 11–12, 13;
public recognition and, 140–42; roots
of, 18–19, 22, 70–74, 213, 246; syncretizing events and, 263n1; "theologization" of, 103, 125–26. *See also*
African diasporic religions in New
York; diasporic religion; Garifuna
rituals
Garifuna rituals, 94–97; adaptations to
urban context, 200–3; history and,
228; mutuality of homeland and diaspora in, 245–46; semiotic logic in,
236–38, 240–41. *See also* Bronx ritual
performance; *dügü* performance;
homeland ritual performance; ritual
performance
Garinagu, as term, 3. *See also* Bronx
Garifuna; Honduran villagers
Garvey, Marcus, 50
Gates, Henry Louis, Jr., 50, 281n7
gayu. See rooster
gayunere. See temple for ritual
Geertz, Clifford, 285n10
George Fredrick II ("Mosquito King"),
268n20

Gilroy, Paul, 231
Glaude, Eddie, 35
Gleason, Judith, 207
Gluckman, Max, 285n10
God. *See* Bungiu (God)
Gonzalez, Nancie, 81, 221, 267n12, 271n33
Gordon, Edmund T., 217–18, 260n20
guagai. See baskets of palm sheaves
gubida. See ancestor spirits
Guerreiro, Bartolome ("Tola"; Bronx
shaman), 25, 276n10; Garifuna culture
and, 129–30, 140; homeland rituals
and, 139, 167–68, 184; initiation of,
126–28; non-Garifuna traditions and,
128–31, 134, 136, 274n2
gulei. See altars

Haitians in New York: black identity and,
220; diaspora as term and, 9; diaspora
religion and, 44, 45, 47, 56, 129. *See also*
Vodou
Halbwachs, Maurice, 12, 46–47
Hall, Stuart, 15
hammocks, 71, 112, 273n6; ancestral repose
and, 237–38; signification of, 237–38
Hanchard, Michael, 252n2
Hart-Celler Act (U.S., 1965), 19, 254n12
healing: *dügü* ritual and, 72, 149–50,
177–85, 241; individual consultations
for, 116–17; nature of shamans' cures
and, 101–2; religious conflict over,
121–24; role of patient in rituals and,
149–50, 182–83
hechiceras. See sorcerers
Helms, Mary, 62
helping spirits (tutelary spirits; *hiyuruha*):
Black Carib religion and, 71, 72–73;
Catholic saints as, 110–11; homeland
Garifuna ritual and, 95, 105, 159, 169;
initiation of *buyei* and, 105–8; spirit
geographies and, 135–36; Yoruba tradition and, 213
Hendrix, Jimi, 281n7
Herberg, Will, 43–44, 259n10
Herskovits, Melville J., 259n15, 263n1
Hesse, Barnor, 220
hiyuruha. See helping spirits
Hobsbawm, Eric, 34
homeland, idealization of: ancestral repose
and, 237–38; Garifuna religion and,
45–46, 231–32; Honduran villages and,
20, 22, 230–32; locus of *dügü* ritual

and, 186; notion of diaspora and, 33. *See also* diasporic horizons

homeland ritual performance: diaspora influences on, 124, 240–41, 245–46; led by Bronx-based shamans, 142–45; portrait of, 93–97; religious conflict and, 121–24; significations in, 236–38, 240–41. See also *dügü* performance; Honduran village shamans

Honduran villagers (homeland Garifuna): African awareness and, 102–3, 214; banana economy and, 88–91; dependence on remittances, 90; dispersal from Trujillo, 79–82; ethnogenesis of, 3–7, 18–19, 69–70, 77–81, 245; ethnographic research with, 22–24; influences from abroad and, 20, 23–24, 37–38, 142–45; land-rights battles and, 252n3; map of villages, *4;* modernity and, 19–21, *21,* 23–24, 26, 221; race identification of, 221; religious conflict and, 121–24; religious culture and, 18–19; ritual as indexical for, 113, 235–38, 241; St. Vincent as homeland for, 99–100. *See also* Corozal; homeland ritual performance; San Juan; Triunfo de la Cruz; Trujillo (Honduran village)

Honduran village shamans *(buyei): cristianos* and, 117–24; diasporic complaints and, 117; *dügü* and, 148–49, 165–66, 167–68; individual consultation and, 116–17; medicines dispensed by, 273n7; return of Bronx-based shamans and, 143–45; rivalries among, 114–16, 150, 153; "shaman" as term and, 104–5; spirit repertoire of, 106, 107, 108, 110–12. *See also* Adolfo; homeland ritual performance

Honduras: banana republic period in, 79, 86–93; battles for independence, 81–82; as idealized "homeland," 20, 22, 45, 139; public sphere in, 269n24; rail system in, 87–88, 91

hooking, 55–56

Hugues, Victor, 76

Hulme, Peter, 68–69

ideology and ritual, 242–45

idugahatiñu. See *dügü* performance, "departure of the fishermen" ritual

Iku (Yoruba spirits), 193, 194

imagined community, 255n4

imagistic religions, 238–39

indexicality, 113, 182, 201, 236–38, 241

indigenismo, 102

"indigenous" and "diasporic" as mutually constitutive, 6–7, 240–41

indigenous religious performance, 6–7

institutional infrastructure: notion of diaspora and, 33, 36–38; ritual sites and, 44–45

International Labor Organization Convention concerning Tribal Peoples in Independent Countries, 221

Irish diaspora, 31, 36–37, 256n8

iron pot with objects *(caldero; nganga; prenda).* See *calderos*

Island Caribs, 16, 18, 155; Africans on St. Vincent and, 62–64; Black Carib religion and, 70–71, 84; tensions with Black Caribs, 66–69, 265n6; as term, 251n1; terms used by, 267n11

Jesús Subirana, Manuel de ("Apóstol de los Caribes"), 83

Judaism: ideology and, 242–43; memory and, 11–12; notion of diaspora and, 31, 32, 42, 258n10

junkunnu. See mask dance

Kant, Immanuel, 11

Kardec, Allan, 280n1

Keane, Webb, 241

Keenagh, Peter, 83

Keith, Minor C., 86, 88

Kerns, Virginia, 275n1

King, Walter Serge (Oba Ofuntola Oseigema Adelabu Adefumni I), 208–9. *See also* Oyotunji African Village

Kongo tradition, 73, 103, 136, 210–11, 212, 247–50, 262n24, 286n1

Labat, Jean-Baptiste, 64–65

La Borde, Sieur de, 61, 63–64, 66, 71, 72

La Ceiba (Honduran town), 87, 88, 91, 92, 269n27, 270n29

La Madama (Santerismo spirit), 137, 195, 207

language: authenticity and, 234–35; Garifuna words and, 211; Honduran Garifuna and, 19–20; sedimentation of Garifuna culture and, 140–41; Yoruba culture and, 211

Lanternari, Vittorio, 285n10

La Peña (Bronx community center), 188–89, *190, 198*, 278n3; protection of, 193–94. *See also* "return of the ancestors" ritual
Leblond, Jean-Baptiste, 69, 254n9
Lefebvre, Henri, 14, 227, 230
lemesi ritual (Bronx), 73, 94–95
Lévi-Strauss, Claude, 100, 101
Levitt, Peggy, 220, 241
Lewis, I. M., 104
Lincoln, Bruce, 257
literature on African Diaspora, 18, 212–14
locality, notion of, 100–1
Los Angeles Garifuna, 19
Lucero (Palo deity), 136. *See also* Eleggua
Lucumí tradition. *See* Santería
lugusurugayu (anniversary of *dügü*), 177

MacCormack, Sabine, 43
mafia (evil spirits): Black Carib religion and, 73, 83–85; *dügü* performance and, 167–68
mainstream society and diaspora groups, 33, 39–40
mali. See *amalahani* dance and songs
maracas *(sisiri):* Bronx *buyei* and, *190, 191,* 195, 196; homeland ritual and, 96; homeland shamans and, 108, 112, *113*
Margolis, Maxine, 281n6
máscaro. *See* mask dance
mask dance *(junkunnu; máscaro; wanaragua),* 72, 161, 163–64, *163,* 203
Mason, John, 209
Masuzawa, Tomoko, 45
material objects: *caldero*, 247–50; diasporic religion and, 46–47, 232–33, 263n1. *See also* altars; Garifuna rituals; ritual performance
Matory, J. Lorand, 265n4
Mattoso, Katia, 50
McAlister, Elizabeth, 47, 129, 274n1
meaning, 276n7; analogical equivalences and, 203–4; of earthen tablets *(mua),* 156–57; hanging of baskets and, 160; healing in the *dügü* and, 177–85; ritual use of tobacco and, 262n1
medicines, 273n7
Meléndez, Armando Crisanto (Auyuru Savaranga), 163, 212–13, 276n13
Meléndez, Beatrice (Corozal singer), 174
memory: Black Caribs and, 16–17; diasporic horizons and, 18–19; diasporic religion

and, 10–15; episodic, and imagistic mode, 239–40, 283n8; notion of diaspora and, 34–35; space and, 1–2, 11–14. *See also* collective memory
men's songs *(arumahani):* homeland *dügü* and, 95, 170–71; New York rituals and, 189–90, 197
Michel, Emeline, 34
migritude, as term, 52
minkisi (altar objects), 247–48
miracle stories, 110–11
Miranda, Felix Igemeri (Bronx shaman), 25, 132–33, 141–42, 274nn2,5
Miskito Indians, 78–79
"mission religions," 12, 253n7
Mistral, Gabriela (Chilean poet), 188
Moco tribe, 64, 65
model sailboats, 113, *114,* 175
modernity: homeland villages and, 19–21, *21,* 23–24, 26, 221; religious, 16–18; return of Bronx Garifuna and, 144–45; temporal gap in diaspora and, 36
Mondongo, as term, 268n18
Montaigne, Michel de, 16
el monte. *See* forest, the
Montejo, Esteban, 210, 214, 248
Morales, Ramón Villeda, 92
Morazán, Francisco, 81
Moreau de Jonnès, Alexandre, 266n9
Moro, Pancho, 206
Morris, Charles, 283n6
Morris, Valentine, 67, 265n7, 267n13
"Mosquito King." *See* George Fredrick II
mua tablets. *See* earthen tablets
muertos (Palo spirits of the dead), 129
mureywa. *See* wand
Murphy, Joseph, 207

Naipaul, V. S., 254n10
National Garifuna Council, 141
Navarette, Luiza de, 63
négritude, 50–51, 52
negro, as Honduran category, 221
New Orleans, 86, 87, 88, 90, 281n5
New York City. *See* African diasporic religions in New York; racial system in U.S.; *entries at* Bronx
nganga. See *calderos*
Nicaragua, 230–31
Nietzsche, Friedrich, 13, 16, 216
Nino, Pastor (Corozal), 118–21, 123

Obatala (Yoruba-Santería deity), 189, 194, 261n23, 280n2
Obeah (religion), 83, 85, 111–12
Ocha (Afro-Cuban religion), 249, 286n5. See also *orishas*; Yoruba-Santería traditions
Ochosi *(oricha)*, 286n5
Ochun (Yoruba deity), 261n23
OFRANEH. *See* La Organización Fraternal Negro Hondureño
Ogun (Yoruba deity), 137, *138*, 262n23, 286n5
Oliana, Chris, 208
Ong, Aihwa, 40
orange-dyed clothing, 155
La Organización Fraternal Negro Hondureño (OFRANEH), 221
orichas (Cuban deities), 261n23, 272n1. *See also* Ocha; *orishas*
orishas (Yoruba pantheon), 56, 129, 137, 209–10; definition of, 261n23
Orisha-Voodoo. *See* Santería
Orsi, Robert, 39, 54
Ortiz, Fernando, 262n1, 263n1
Oshun (Yoruba deity), 238, 280n2
Oyotunji African Village (SC), 208–9, 216

Palmié, Stephen, 211, 249, 262n24, 272n1
Palo Monte (Afro-Cuban religion), 45, 59, 207, 272n1, 286n5; Bronx-based shamans and, 128–29, 131; *calderos* and, 247–50; homeland Garifuna practices and, 103. *See also* Kongo tradition
palos. See sticks
patron saints, 110–11
Peirce, Charles, 235, 236, 237, 282n6
"people of the forest" *(gente del monte; yaguaraguna)*, 111
performatives and notion of diaspora, 36–37
Petwo deities, 129, 262n24
place: defined, 253n5; memory and, 1–2. *See also* space
Ponce, Pineda, 252n3
Povinelli, Elizabeth, 234
prenda. See calderos
Protestant evangelicalism: Black Carib religion and, 85; Garifuna culture and, 20, 267n12; homeland shamans and, 117–24
Proust, Marcel, 1, 12–13

public recognition, 44, 275n6; Bronx Garifuna and, 25–26, 140–42
Puerto Ricans in New York, 196, 206–7, 219–20
punch *(furunsu)*, 96
punta dance, 72, 95, 174, 191, 193
Pupa, Dona (Honduran villager), 152

"quotidian diaspora," 37

race and religion, 215–17
racial identity: African diasporic religions and, 214–20; Yoruba-Santería influences and, 208, 209–10, 213. *See also* Africanness vs. blackness
racialism, 280n4
racial system in U.S.: Caribbean immigrants and, 20–21, 49, 52–53, 219–20; diasporic horizons and, 8; ethnicity and, 21, 52–53, 217–19, 256n8; features of, 219; New York Garifuna and, 221–25
Radcliffe-Brown, A. R., 284n10
Rastafarians, 56
Red Caribs, 155, 266n9
reframing of crises, 101, 182–85
Reis, João José, 50
religion: definition of, 257–58; mapping to new sites, 55–59; modes of transmission and, 238–39; power and, 253n7, 256n9, 277n21; race categories and, 215–17, 281n5; religious modernity, 17–18; syncretism and, 263n1, 278n1
religious diasporas vs. diasporic religions, 258
República Federal de Centroamérica (Central American Federation), 81–82
"return of the ancestors" ritual (Bronx): January 2002 example, 187–94; January 2003 example, 198–200
"return of the fishermen" ritual (homeland), 161–68, *162*
Richman, Karen, 45
Riesebrodt, Martin, 257
ritual performance: authenticity and, 232–35; contested authority and, 143–45; events elsewhere and, 160, 167; forms of community and, 241–45; functionalist approach and, 284n10; future affiliations and, 228–32; materials and, 33, 45–47, 55–59, 129–36; processual turn and, 284n10; religious transmission and, 239–40;

ritual performance *(continued):*
renewal and, 227–28; representations
of homeland in, 146–47; semiotic
logic of, 232, 235–41. *See also* Bronx
ritual performance; Garifuna rituals;
homeland ritual performance
Roatán island (Honduras), 81–82
Roberts, Orlando W., 65, 79
Rochefort, Charles César de, 16
Roman Catholicism, 267n12, 278n1; Black
Carib religion and, 73–74, 82–83, 84,
85; homeland rituals and, 154;
Honduran politics and, 81–82; saints
as helping spirits and, 110–11, 112
Romani (Gypsies), 260n19
rooster *(gayu):* buyei initiation and, 108;
in homeland rituals, 96, 161, 165
"roots readings" (divination), 216–17,
218
Rouse, Irving, 251n1
rum libations: Bronx rituals and, 190, 193;
homeland rituals and, 94, 96, 153,
154, 176–77; homeland shaman and,
113; Vodou practice and, 56

Sahlins, Marshall, 285n10
St. Vincent island (Yurumein), *4;* as
British colony, 69–70, 74–77, 265n7,
267n13; deportation of Black Caribs
from, 7, 74–77; as diasporic horizon,
60, 61–74, 86, 99–100; Garifuna
religous practice and, 7, 70–74, 113,
232; as home of the ancestors, 93, 139,
155; origins of Black Caribs and, 3, 5,
16, 62–64, 245; spirit geography of,
70–71. *See also* Island Caribs
Sairi (ancestral world), 93, 159, 272n2. *See
also* St. Vincent island
Salomon (San Juan village shaman),
106–7, 108–9, 115, 117, 135, 167
"Sambos" (Miskito Africans), 78–79, 83
San Antonio (saint), 111
San Cipriano (saint), 111
San Juan (Honduran village), 23, 24, 89,
111–12, 271n37
San Simon (Guatemalan saint), 111
Santería (Afro-Cuban religion), 272n1;
Bronx-based *buyei* and, 128; as dias-
poric religion, 44–45, 56–57, 58–59;
homeland Garifuna practices and,
103; ruling *orishas* and, 279n7. *See also*
Yoruba-Santería traditions

Santerismo (hybrid diaspora religion),
207, 213. *See also* Spiritism
Santos (Trujillo shaman), 115
scissors, signification of, *138*
Scott, John, 62
"second diaspora" religions, 55
sedimentation, 140–42
semiotic logic, 235–41
Seranno, Assunte (priestess), 207
Seven African Powers, 207, 280n2
Sewell, William H., Jr., 255n5
shaman *(buyei):* characteristics of, 108–10;
death rites and, 94–96; initiation of,
105–10, 126–28, 132–33, 275n2; roots of
Garifuna religion and, 18, 71, 84, 105;
as term, 104–5. *See also* altars; Bronx
shamans; helping spirits; Honduran
village shamans
Shango (Yoruba-Santería deity), 25, 192,
195, 205
Shaw, Rosalind, 12
Shepperson, George, 42
shipwreck narrative, 62–64
Shore, Bradd, 203, 204
Silver, Frank, 270n30
Simpson, O. J., 281n7
sisiri. See maracas
Sistine Madonna (Raphael painting), 282n6
slavery, 50, 62–66, 78
Smith, Jonathan Z., 42
sorcerers *(hechiceras),* 111–12, 117
Soyinka, Wole, 280n3
space: compression of, in *dügü,* 178–80,
233; diasporic religion and, 44–45,
201–2, 230–31, 240; "locality" and,
100–1; material repertoire and production of, 1–2, 13–14, 20–21, 227–50;
memory and, 1–2, 11–14, 236; nonter-
ritoriality of African Diaspora and,
51–52; notion of diaspora and, 35–36;
place and, 253n5; protection of,
192–94; public, and ritual place,
201–2
Spain, rebellions against, 269n24
spirit categories in U.S., 286n5
"spirit gang" (Bronx *caldero* spirits), 129,
137
spirit geographies: for Bronx-based vs.
homeland shamans, 135–36, 144–45;
St. Vincent and, 70–71, 135
Spiritism, 249, 280n1, 286n5. *See also*
Santerismo

spirit possession. *See* trances
spirit possession specialists, 104–5
Squier, E. G., 83
Staal, Frits, 177–78
Standard Fruit and Steamship Company,
    86–88, 90, 91, 92, 270n32, 271n38
Staples, Brent, 261n20
Stapleton, William, 66
Stephens, John Lloyd, 81–82
sticks *(palos)*, 272n1
Suazo, E. S., 213
sugar cultivation, 5, 262n1
"supernaturalist racism," 215–16
Sweet, James, 50
Swett, Charles, 79–80, 85
symbolic representation, *138*, 201, 236–38.
    See also meaning
syncretism, 11, 263n1, 278n1

Taino, 252n1, 262n1
Taylor, Douglas, 80, 267n11
technology and tradition, 182. *See also*
    modernity
Tela (Honduran town), 88, 89, 92
telescoping, 55, 56–57
The Tempest (Shakespeare), 16–18, 234–35
temple for ritual *(dabuyaba; gayunere)*,
    97, 150–52, *151*, 272n3; "cleansing" of,
    154–55, 179; protection of, 155, 179
temporal gap and notion of diaspora, 36
Thomas, Piri, 219
Thompson, Robert F., 248
Thornton, John, 43, 63
típica fashion, 238, 255n13
tobacco, ritual use of, 71; in Bronx, 193, 196;
    in homeland, 96, 112, 154; Honduran
    cigars in Bronx, 195–96; meanings of,
    262n1; shamans' pipes, 112
Tola. *See* Guerreiro, Bartolome
Tölölyan, Khachig, 34, 260n19
Toro, Victor ("Don Victor"), 188
tradition. *See* authenticity; continuity
traditional tales *(úruga)*, 95
trances: audience and, 199–200; contro-
    versy and, 159, 167, 183, 196–97; entasy
    vs. ecstasy and, 104–5; inducement of,
    71; performers' memories of, 279n8;
    young people and, 171–73, 177
transculturation, 262n1; Bronx and, 137;
    Central America and, 78–79; St.
    Vincent and, 61–70
transtemporality, 8

trepar el palo. *See* "climbing the pole"
    ritual
Trilling, Lionel, 282n2
Triunfo de la Cruz (Honduran village),
    23, 24, 111, 115; Tola's narrative and,
    126–27
"Triunfo sand," 238
Trujillo (Honduran village), 23
Trujillo (Spanish Honduras): arrival of
    Black Caribs at, 77–79; banana trade
    and, 88, 92; Black Carib dispersion
    from, 81–82; *buyei* rivalries and, 115.
    See also Honduran villagers
Turner, Victor, 243–44, 257, 285n10
tutelary spirits. *See* helping spirits
Tweed, Thomas, 8, 32
Tylor, E. B., 257

uniforms, 238
United Fruit Company ("the octopus"),
    86–88, 92, 270n32
United States: Garifuna migration to, 6–7,
    19–21; immigration limits in, 254n12.
    See also racial system in U.S.
urban culture: diaspora cultures and,
    39–40, 256n6; need for protection
    and, 103, 129, 194. *See also entries at*
    Bronx
Uring, Nathaniel, 72
úruga. *See* traditional tales

Vaccaro brothers (New Orleans), 86. *See
    also* Standard Fruit and Steamship
    Company
Valadares, Abbé, 74
Valentine, Washington S., 270n31
Van Gennep, Arnold, 33, 284n10
Van Hear, Nicholas, 34
Vega, Marta Moreno, 207
veluria ritual (Bronx), 94
Verdery, Katherine, 253n4
Virgin Mary, 111
Vodou (Afro-Haitian tradition): Bronx
    Garifuna rituals and, 137, 197–98,
    204; cross-influences and, 274n4; as
    diasporic religion, 44, 47, 56, 59;
    homeland shamans and, 111–12

Wallerstein, Immanuel, 54, 232
Walumugu (Juan Bulnes; Black Carib
    leader), 81
wanaragua. *See* mask dance

wand *(mureywa; palos):* in Bronx ritual, 128, 188; in homeland ritual, 96, *113*
Waters, Mary, 38, 219
Weber, Max, 54, 252n2, 261n21
Wells, Marilyn, 272n2
West, Cornel, 218
Whitehouse, Harvey, 43, 187, 239–40, 244
Williams, Raymond, 282n2
Winant, Howard, 8
witches *(brujas),* 111–12
women's songs *(abeimahani):* homeland rituals and, 95, 116, *169,* 170–71; New York rituals and, 190, 197
World Garifuna Organization, 25, 141, 274n5

Yellow Caribs, 155. *See also* Island Caribs
Yemaya (Yoruba-Santería deity), 188
Yoruba-Santería traditions: African Americans and, 207–10; *buyei* views on influence of, 133–35, 205–6; as "face" of African diasporic religions, 205–14; Garifuna literature and, 212–14; other influences on Garifuna and, 210–12; Puerto Ricans in New York and, 206–7; Yoruba studies in U.S. and, 209. *See also* African diasporic religions in New York; Santería; Yoruba tradition; *entries for specific deities*
Yoruba Temple (Harlem), 208
Yoruba tradition: slavery and, 214; Yoruba studies in U.S. and, 209. See also *orishas; entries for specific deities*
Young, Sir William, 62, 64, 74, 75
Young, Thomas, 79, 80, 83, 84–85, 221, 269n23
Young, William, II, 74, 75, 266n9
Yurumein. *See* St. Vincent island

Zemurray, Samuel, 88, 270n32

Text: 10/13 Galliard
Display: Galliard
Compositor: International Typesetting & Composition
Printer and Binder: Maple-Vail Manufacturing Group